The Politics of Ethnic Conflict Regulation

Case Studies of Protracted Ethnic Conflicts

Edited by John McGarry
and Brendan O'Leary

London and New York

First published 1993
by Routledge
11 New Fetter Lane
London EC4P 4EE

Simultaneously published in the USA and Canada
by Routledge
29 West 35th Street, New York, NY 10001

© 1993 John McGarry and Brendan O'Leary

Typeset in 10/12pt Baskerville by Witwell Ltd, Southport

Printed and bound in Great Britain by
TJ Press (Padstow) Ltd, Padstow, Cornwall

British Library Cataloguing in Publication Data
A catalogue reference for this book is available from the
British Library
ISBN 0-415-07522-X
    0-415-09931-5

Library of Congress Cataloging in Publication Data
The politics of ethnic conflict regulation : case studies of
  protracted ethnic conflicts / edited by John McGarry and
Brendan O'Leary.
    p.   cm.
  Includes bibliographical references and index.
  ISBN 0-415-07522-X. — ISBN 0-415-09931-5
  1. Race relations—Case studies.   2. Ethnic relations—
Case studies.   3. Plualism (Social sciences)—Case studies.
  I. McGarry, John.   II. O'Leary, Brendan.
  HT1521.P573   1993
  305.8—dc20   92-45848
                                                     CIP

Contents

Figures

Tables

Contributors

Heribert Adam is Professor in Sociology at Simon Fraser University. He is the author of *Modernizing Racial Domination* (1971) and co-author (with Herman Giliomee) of *Ethnic Power Mobilized: Can South Africa Change?* (1979).

Maureen Covell is Professor in Political Science at Simon Fraser University. She is author of *Madagascar: Politics, Economics and Society* (1978).

Michael Keating is Professor in Political Science at the University of Western Ontario. He is author of *State and Regional Nationalism: Territorial Politics and the European State* (1988) and co-author of *Decentralisation and Change in Contemporary France* (1986).

René Lemarchand is Professor in Politics, School of African Studies, University of Florida. He is the author of *Selective Genocide in Burundi* (1973) and *Rwanda and Burundi* (1970).

Dominic Lieven is Senior Lecturer in Russian Government at the London School of Economics and Political Science. He is the author of *Russia and the Origins of the First World War* (1984) and *Aristocracy in Europe, 1815–1914* (1991).

Diane Mauzy is Associate Professor in Political Science at the University of British Columbia. She is co-author (with Stephen Milne) of *The Government and Politics of Malaysia* (second edition, 1988).

John McGarry is Associate Professor at the Department of History and Political Science, King's College, London, Ontario. He is the co-editor (with Brendan O'Leary) of *The Future of*

Northern Ireland (1990) and co-author (with Brendan O'Leary) of *The Politics of Antagonism: Understanding Northern Ireland* (1992).

Kogila Moodley is director of the Multicultural Program in the Faculty of Education, University of British Columbia. She is the co-author (with Heribert Adam) of *South Africa without Apartheid: Dismantling Racial Domination* (1986).

S. J. R. Noel is Professor in Political Science at the University of Western Ontario. He is the author of *Politics in Newfoundland* (1971) and *Patrons, Clients, Brokers: Ontario Society and Politics, 1791–1896* (1990).

Brendan O'Duffy is writing his doctoral dissertation entitled *Political Violence in Ireland* at the London School of Economics and Political Science.

Brendan O'Leary is Reader in Political Science and Public Administration at the London School of Economics and Political Science. He is the author of *The Asiatic Mode of Production* (1989) and co-author (with Patrick Dunleavy) of *Theories of the State: The Politics of Liberal Democracy* (1987).

Ralph Premdas is Associate Professor in Politics at the University of the West Indies. He is the co-editor of *Secessionist Movements in Comparative Perspective* (1990) and author of articles on Fiji in several journals.

George Schöpflin is Joint Lecturer in East European Political Institutions at the London School of Economics and Political Science and at the School of Slavonic and East European Studies. He is the co-author (with Stephen White and John Gardner) of *Communist Political Systems* (second edition, 1987) and co-editor (with Nancy Wood) of *In Search of Central Europe* (1989).

Gurharpal Singh is Senior Lecturer in Politics at Simon de Montfort University. His doctoral dissertation entitled *Communism in the Punjab up to 1967* was awarded at the London School of Economics and Political Science in 1987.

Acknowledgements

Both editors incurred numerous debts while working on this book. John McGarry would like to thank the Social Science and Humanities Research Council of Canada and King's College Research Grants Committee for funding. He is also indebted to Jim Crimmins, Michael Keating, Margaret Moore and Sid Noel for commenting upon various aspects of the project. Brendan O'Leary would like to thank the LSE Research Committee for assistance, and Brian Barry, Patrick Dunleavy, George Jones, Peter Loizos, Tom Lyne, David Schiff, George Schöpflin and Lorelei Watson for diverse helpful comments on the manuscript. We are grateful to our contributors for agreeing to undertake their tasks and for delivering the finished products in reasonable time. Gordon Smith of Routledge deserves our gratitude for his encouragement and patience. Paul King, our research assistant, was very helpful throughout. Finally we would like to thank our secretaries, Jane Borecky, Sharon Batkins and Vanessa Sulch, for cheerfully carrying out the multiple jobs necessary for the book's completion.

John McGarry, London, Ontario
Brendan O'Leary, London, England

Chapter 1

Introduction

The macro-political regulation of ethnic conflict

John McGarry and Brendan O'Leary

INTRODUCTION

This book began life when ethnic conflict and its regulation were not universally fashionable subjects. Its concerns now have an almost outrageous timeliness. Ethnic conflict is a persistent feature of modernity but the last few years have brought seismic changes in the relations between several ethnic communities around the world. The disintegrations of the Soviet Union and Yugoslavia have burst asunder the borders of these former communist empires. The conventional wisdom had been that the international (for which read the interstate) system had stabilised the borders of the world's states, so that secessions and the redrawing of territorial frontiers through conquest or partitions were phenomena of previous ages (see Mayall 1990). The aftermath of the Second World War and the decolonisation of Europe's empires had, it was said, carved states' borders in stone. Events like the forging of the states of Israel and Bangladesh through war and insurrection, Indonesia's conquests of East Timor and West Irian and India's invasion of Goa were merely exceptions which proved the rule. Today, however, we know the stability of state borders after 1945 (or 1960) owed more to the geo-politics of the cold war than to the triumph of particular norms of 'international order'. It remains to be seen whether the 'new international order' proclaimed over the rubble of the cities of Kuwait and Baghdad presages a new stabilisation of the world's territorial frontiers. Perhaps Saddam Hussein's adventurism was merely the first and least successful of a new round of state- and nation-building projects that will owe more to conquest than consent. At least some Serbians appear to have made this calculation.

The renewed instability of state frontiers is merely one symptom of the global political power of ethnic consciousness and conflict. The last two decades have seen the final collapse of white settler regimes in Africa (in Angola, Guinea-Bissau, Mozambique, Namibia and Zimbabwe). As we go to press the South African system of apartheid, the last bastion of European settler domination in Africa, is on the verge of extinction. However, during the period of apartheid's rise and fall new systems of ethnic domination have been established around the world, in Fiji by native Melanesians, by Morocco in the western Sahara, by Israelis in what was Palestine; and there have been several attempts to establish such regimes that have led to protracted 'civil' wars, notably in Uganda and Sudan. In the post-colonial era, partly because of the fear (or pretext?) that open, multi-party democracies would degenerate into ethnic contests for state power, much of Africa has been under one-party dictatorships or military rule. In the next decade the re-experimentation with democracy under way in large parts of Africa will provide a decisive test of the success of the nation-building efforts of African generals and dictators. Some parts of the world appear to be trapped in deadlock ethnic wars, where no faction is sufficiently powerful completely to control or crush its opponent(s): for instance Burma/Myanmar (Smith 1991), Chad, Peru and the Sudan. In happier zones ethnic communities have been able to negotiate agreed changes to their political systems, notably in Belgium, Canada and Switzerland. Yet other sites of ethnic conflict live in a twilight world between deadlocked war and permanent negotiation: Cyprus, Northern Ireland and Sri Lanka. The Balkans may join them, again. As we went to press, Canada, Cyprus, Israel/Palestine, Northern Ireland and South Africa were the subjects and objects of inter-ethnic negotiations about their political futures. The Indian government and its discontented ethnic subjects have been involved in analogous talks almost from the moment of Indian independence.

The chapters which follow provide a series of case studies from Africa, the Americas, Asia, Europe and Oceania; and from what used to be called the first, second and third worlds. The contributors were asked to focus briefly on the causes of ethnic conflict, but to concentrate on the methods used to manage, control or terminate ethnic conflict in their area of specialist knowledge. The case studies cover examples of relatively benign and amicable relations between ethnic communities, as well as ones where domination is enforced. They cover examples of the normatively desirable as well as the morally appalling. They are not restricted to conflicts which have immediate implications for all of us, like the conflicts in the former Soviet Union, but include examination of places like Fiji and Northern Ireland which add to our theoretical understanding of bi-ethnic conflicts, and a study of Burundi, the locus of two internationally ignored genocides.

Notwithstanding the global comprehensiveness of our sample, readers will immediately think of numerous additional cases which might have been included. However, given the ubiquity of ethnic conflict an exhaustive collection of case studies would have extended to several volumes. In mitigation we plead that this introductory chapter contains some modest discussion of cases not covered by our contributors.

Scientific endeavours, as conventionally understood, are built upon theories and hypotheses, evidence and experiments. The development of a science is often measured by the scale of precision in prediction and postdiction of which it is capable, and by the degree of development of quantified indicators of the phenomena being examined or explained. It cannot be said that the study of ethnic conflict and ethnic conflict management have yet wholly met the aspirations of positivist ideals of social science,[1] and we cannot hope to make good such deficiencies in this introduction. Instead we shall attempt a humbler task, that of classification, the necessary precursor of scientific theory and empirical verification and falsification.

As well as being classificatory, this chapter is both positive and normative. We develop a taxonomy of eight modes of ethnic conflict resolution which maps the empirical forms of macro-political ethnic conflict regulation. Our long-term positivist ambition is to establish whether there are 'laws of motion' which govern the forms of ethnic conflict regulation we are interested in explaining: regularities which enable the 'postdiction' (if not the prediction) of the circumstances under which particular strategies for managing ethnic conflict will be attempted, and successfully implemented. But we also have normative concerns:

to evaluate the merits of the different forms of ethnic conflict regulation, and to establish whether multi-ethnic states can be stabilised in ways which are compatible with liberal democratic values and institutions.

A TAXONOMY OF THE MACRO-POLITICAL FORMS OF ETHNIC CONFLICT REGULATION

Here we confine ourselves to presenting our taxonomy of the macro-political[2] forms of ethnic conflict regulation, and briefly showing its relevance for the case studies elaborated by our contributors, leaving its further development to future research (McGarry and O'Leary, forthcoming). The term 'regulation' is inclusive: it covers both conflict termination and conflict management. Eight distinct macro-methods of ethnic conflict regulation can be distinguished, to wit:

(i) *methods for eliminating differences*
    (a) genocide
    (b) forced mass-population transfers
    (c) partition and/or secession (self-determination)
    (d) integration and/or assimilation
(ii) *methods for managing differences*
    (a) hegemonic control
    (b) arbitration (third-party intervention)
    (c) cantonisation and/or federalisation
    (d) consociationalism or power-sharing.

This is a taxonomy, and not a typology: the classification of entities by logical types. Typologies are heuristics used to codify existing knowledge. Good social science typologies are simple; constructed through the use of logical antonyms rather than empirical observations; and provide a fruitful basis for further theoretical development and empirical investigation. Taxonomy by contrast is the classification of organisms, and originated with the Swedish scientist Linnaeus. Taxonomists aim to place all organisms in a hierarchical classification scheme, in which, to put it very crudely, 'likes' are classified with 'likes'. Taxonomies, unlike typologies, are empirical rather than ideal-typical, *a posteriori* rather than *a priori* categories. Our list of eight modes of ethnic conflict resolution is taxonomic because it was arrived at simply through researching cases of ethnic conflict termination and regulation, and putting together 'likes with likes'.[3]

However, our taxonomy does not suggest Linnaeus-like discreteness or exhaustiveness. Often the eight modes are found in combination and targeted at the same ethnic group(s), or, alternatively, different strategies are aimed at different ethnic groups within the same state. Thus the Nazis practised genocide, mass-population transfers and hegemonic control of Jews. Stalin practised genocide, mass-population transfers and hegemonic control of multiple ethnic groups (see Chapter 3). Yugoslavia under Tito practised elements of control, arbitration and consociation (see Chapter 8). Oliver Cromwell offered Irish Catholics a choice between genocide and forced mass-population transfer. They could go 'To Hell or Connaught!' The USA practised genocide on native Americans, integration of immigrant Europeans and control of black Americans in the deep South. Contemporary Israel practises consociationalism amongst Jews of different ethnic origin but control over Palestinians; it practised mass-population transfers in the past and may do so again. Belgium has practised consociationalism to regulate divisions between its 'spiritual families' and federalism to resolve tensions between its linguistic communities (Chapter 12).

However, it is beneficial to divide our taxonomy through a logical distinction, which creates a typological contrast: some modes of ethnic conflict regulation seek to eliminate or terminate ethnic differences, whereas others seek to manage the consequences of ethnic differences. Thus genocide, mass-population transfers, partition/secession and integration/assimilation are all political strategies which seek to eliminate ethnic differences, at least within a given state. By contrast the strategies which seek to manage the consequences of ethnic differences are those of control, arbitration, federalism/cantonisation and consociationalism.[4]

It is possible, and desirable, to rank the eight methods in the taxonomy normatively, even if it is not possible to construct a simple or lexicographic moral hierarchy. It is not, in our opinion, possible or desirable to say that either difference-eliminating or difference-managing methods are inherently superior. Of the eliminating-differences strategies there are moral justifications for partition/secession (e.g. Barry 1991c; Beran 1987; Buchanan 1991) and arguments for integration (assimilation) which have been advanced by generations of liberals and socialists. However, there is no obvious moral hierarchy which enables people to claim that integration is better than partition (or vice versa), unless there is widespread consent for one option rather than the other, where widespread consent refers to substantial majorities within all the relevant ethnic communities. The merits of partition/secession as against integration/assimilation must be decided by political argument and pragmatic consider- ations, such as feasibility and estimates about long-run efficacy. There is nothing morally weighty to be said in favour of genocide or forced mass-population transfers, the other differ- ence-eliminating strategies, although 'ethical' arguments have usually accompanied the implementation of these gruesome projects.

Of the managing-differences strategies one should be morally unacceptable to liberals, namely hegemonic control (see below). The rest (arbitration, cantonisation/federalism and consociation- alism) are compatible with democratic norms, although there are many liberal critics of the democratic quality of consociational practices (e.g. Barry 1991a, b; Lustick 1979; Glazer 1987). Advo- cacy of the merits of the remaining strategies, namely federalism/ cantonisation, consociation and arbitration, must, however, be tempered by empirical judgements about their feasibility and long-term efficacy.

(i) Eliminating differences

(a) Genocide

The first two extreme and terminal 'solutions' to ethnic conflict are the most abhorrent: genocide and forced mass-population transfers. They often go together. Genocide literally means the killing of a *genos* (a race or kind). There is some controversy as to how the concept should be used, either legally or by social scientists (e.g. Chalk and Jonassohn 1990; Kuper 1981). We think the concept should be confined to cases where the victims share (real or alleged) ascriptive traits, while Harff's useful term *politicide* should be employed for the systematic mass killing of people who may or may not share ascriptive traits (Harff 1992).

Genocide, then, is the systematic mass-killing of an ethnic collectivity (however defined), or the indirect destruction of such a community through the deliberate termination of the conditions which permit its biological and social reproduction. On this definition appalling genocides were perpetrated by the Nazis in the 1930s and 1940s, and within the Communist bloc in Eurasia. The European colonisers in the Americas, and Russians and Turks in the Tsarist and Ottoman empires also perpetrated genocides by this definition. The option of genocide remains available to political actors in the modern world. Despite the infamy won by Hitler and Stalin it is wishful thinking to assume that genocide has become unthinkable.[5] Since 1945 there have been genocides perpetrated in the Soviet Union (of the Chechens, the Ingushi, the Karachai, the Balkars, the Meskhetians and the Crimean Tartars[6]); in Burundi (of Hutu, see Chapter 7); in Iraq (of the Kurds); in Paraguay (of the Ache Indians); in Indonesia (of the Chinese[7] and the indigenous population of East Timor); in Nigeria (of Ibo residents in the north); in Equatorial Guinea (of the Bubi); in Uganda (of the Karamojong, the Acholi, the Lango, Nilotic tribes and the Bagandans); in Pakistan (of the Bengalis in what became Bangladesh); in Burma (of Muslims in border regions); and in Iran (of Kurds and Baha'is). We therefore still live in a world in which genocide is practised; indeed, in absolute terms the twentieth century has been more genocidal than its predecessors. Only confident optimists believe genocide has become outmoded because of the triumph of universal norms in what some sociologists are pleased to call 'late modernity'.

Genocides are usually one-sided – indeed some would say this is one of their defining features (Jonassohn 1992: 19) – and they are intended to terminate ethnic conflict. In the construction of many empires it can be said that genocides 'worked': they secured the relevant territories for imperial rulers. European Jews were the victims of the most atrocious genocide in the Second World War, and the Armenians suffered grievously in the First World War, and in both cases the perpetrators resolved on final solutions, believing it would stabilise their empires. Yet genocides often fail to achieve their objectives and always create explosive and historically entrenched bitterness and fear amongst the descendants of victims. Serb–Croat relations in what was Yugoslavia are inflamed by memories of war-time genocide during the Second World War (Chapter 8). If Russians and indigenous groups in the Baltic states, Ukraine and Kazakhstan are to co-exist peacefully lots of skeletons have to remain buried (Chapter 3). The state of Israel's 'siege mentality' owes its existence to a reaction against the Nazi genocide of Jews.[8] Moreover, one of the consequences in a community which has undergone genocide is a very high birth-rate, which often shifts a political conflict downstream to the next generation.

It is possible to identify circumstances under which genocide is likely to be contemplated. *State genocide* is more likely to occur when:

- an empire is being constructed and maintained (e.g. genocide was used as a deliberate policy of land acquisition and mass terrorisation by European settler-states in the 'new world', Africa and Australasia);
- an ethnic community lacks geo-political resources, such as its own state or a powerful diaspora (like Armenians, European Jews and Gypsies);
- a subordinate ethnic community is left vulnerable within a disintegrating system of control, whether organised by an empire or a party dictatorship, (like Armenians and Bosnian Muslims);
- a given ethnic community (Jews, Ibos, Armenians, overseas Chinese) possesses economic superiority and cultural identifiability in conditions of industrialisation, but lacks military and political power (Gellner 1983: 105);
- the relevant state is not democratic.[9]

Frontier genocide, which by contrast may not be directly implemented by state officials, is likely to occur when settlers, possessed of technologically superior resources, displace natives from their access to land. It is a concomitant of colonisation and conquest.

These conditions are facilitative, not necessary. An obvious necessary condition for genocide appears to be the presence of a racial, ethnic or religious ideology which sanctions a non-universalist conception of the human species, and makes mass-murder easier to accomplish. These belief-systems may be more important than technological capacities for managing mass-killings, as it is the discipline of the killers, rather than their instruments, which may best account for the scale of genocides. The Old Testament God of the Jews (and subsequently of the Christians and Muslims) could be used to sanction the extermination of peoples long before Nazi racism. Some have argued that ideological (as opposed to imperial) genocides are modern: beginning in the religious wars of the Middle Ages they have been carried further by the spread of nationalist and Marxist–Leninist doctrines. We do not agree. For us, the rise and fall of empires is primary in explaining the conditions which facilitate genocide, and genocide is not 'modern', although it occurs in modern times. Moreover, nationalism and racism should be carefully distinguished. Nationalism is not inherently genocidal, though racism may be. Genocides can be instrumental and 'preemptive' as well as being ideological: indigenous peoples were killed by European colonisers on the supposition that their circumstances were those of 'kill or be killed'. The same beliefs seem to have been important in motivating Tutsi genocides of Hutu in Burundi (Chapter 7).

(b) Forced mass-population transfers

Forced mass-population transfers occur where one (or more) ethnic community is physically transplanted from its homeland and compelled to live elsewhere. Some Serbians have coined a chilling expression for forced mass-population transfers, 'ethnic cleansing'. A population (or populations) can also be forcibly 'repatriated' and pushed back towards its alleged 'homeland', as occurred during the high tide of apartheid in South Africa. Forced mass-population transfers must be distinguished from agreed 'population exchanges', i.e. the transfers which accompany agreed secessions or partitions, such as those between Greece and Turkey after the end of the Second World War. The population transfers in Cyprus in 1974/5 were in no sense agreed, by comparison with the Greek–Turk exchanges of the 1920s. They were the result of frightened populations moving under the threat of military coercion. The populations which move after 'agreed exchanges' between states never consider such moves to be voluntary, but their fate must be distinguished from those unilaterally compelled to move.

Forced mass-population transfers may displace but they do not always terminate ethnic conflict. The ethnic turmoil in what was the Soviet Union is partly an outcome of forced mass-population transfers executed by Lenin and Stalin and their successors (Chapter 3). Violence in the contemporary Caucasus is, in part, the result of similar policies pursued by both Tsarist and Ottoman emperors. Palestinians were expelled from Israel during the insurrectionary war which founded the state of Israel, and many Palestinians fear that the settlement of the West Bank by Israeli colonisers is merely the prelude to a further set of expulsions. In turn the creation of a Palestinian diaspora helped precipitate the destabilisation of Jordan, the Lebanon, and even Kuwait. Some presently fear that the Muslims of Bosnia may become the Palestinians of Europe: dispossessed, repressed people living in refugee camps, desperate to recover their former lands. In what soon may be described as the former state of Ethiopia forced resettlement policies exacerbated the civil war and famine-proneness of the country during the mid-1980s. In the last decade the states of Nigeria, Vietnam and Burma have expelled large numbers of residents on plainly ethnic criteria, and India has promised to expel Bengali immigrants (from Bangladesh) from the state of Assam, although this decision has not yet been implemented when going to press.

Forced mass-population transfers, like genocides, are often advocated as integral components of imperial consolidation strategies. They are usually implemented after or during wars and civil wars – consider Oliver Cromwell's 'transplantation' strategies in Ireland, Tsarist and Turkish policies in the Caucasus in the nineteenth century, Stalin's movement of the Volga Germans, Cossacks and others, and Milosevic's 'Greater Serbia' project. Forced mass-population transfers are also likely to be advocated in response to the perceived threat of 'ethnic swamping', as seen in the Assamese demonstrations against illegal Bengali immigration, or in response to economic depressions, when the call for 'repatriation' of 'guest-workers' may be extended to include all those who are not 'sons and daughters of the soil'. 'Ethnic cleansing' by Serbian irregulars in Bosnia demonstrates that forced mass-population transfers can be narrowly instrumental: to establish 'facts' which might make future territorial adjustments 'impossible'.

There are no moral merits to forced mass-population transfers, especially as they facilitate genocidal assaults on vulnerable populations and/or encourage the likelihood that the victims will suffer from famine. Forced mass-population transfers violate minimalist conceptions of human rights and egalitarian politi-cal philosophies. Nevertheless where peoples believe that their homelands have been stolen from them by settler-peoples it becomes thinkable if not justifiable to argue that historic retribution is in order.

(c) Partition and/or secession (self-determination)

Genocide and forced mass-population transfers are obnoxious from the perspective of modern liberalism or modern socialism. By contrast, partitioning territories to permit self-determination or secession can, in principle, respect the rights of ethnic communities. Partition, self-determination and secession are compatible with liberal democratic institutions (universal, periodic and competitive elections, alternations in power, and civic freedoms of expression, assembly and organisation), in that such states can, in principle, permit secessions and preserve democratic institutions. Partition resolves ethnic conflict, if it works, by breaking up multi-ethnic states, or by allowing divorce between those ethnic communities which do not wish to live together in the same state.

Between the years 1948 and 1991 only one new state, Bangladesh, was carved out of an existing state – if we exclude the very numerous cases of decolonisation of European and US-controlled territories in Asia, Africa and Latin America. However, since the collapse of the communist empires of Ethiopia, Yugoslavia and the Soviet Union secession has become a growth-industry, the in-vogue method of ethnic conflict-resolution. Iraq will be next if Iraqi Kurds are allowed to have their way. The secession of Quebec from Canada remains a possibility after Canadians overwhelmingly rejected a proposed constitutional settlement in a referendum in October 1992. There are secessionist or semi-secessionist[10] movements in Europe (e.g. amongst the Basque, Corsican, Northern Irish nationalist, Scottish, Slovak and Welsh peoples); in Africa (e.g. the Polisario movement in the Moroccan-controlled western Sahara, the Dinkas of the southern Sudan and a bewildering variety of communities in the Horn of Africa); in the new republics of the Commonwealth of Independent States (e.g. Nagorno-Karabakh wishes to secede from Azerbaijan, South Ossetia from Georgia, Crimea from the Ukraine, and the 'Dniester Republic' from Moravia); and in central and southern Asia (e.g. the Khalistan movement for a Sikh homeland, the Kashmiri independence movement, Tibetans in Communist China, and the multiple ethnic secessionists of Burma).

The normative idea behind principled partitions and secessions is the principle of self-determination.[11] The key problem with the principle of self-determination as a means of eliminating ethnic conflict is that it begs four questions:

- Who are the people?
- What is the relevant territorial unit in which they should exercise self-determination?
- What constitutes a majority?
- Does secession produce a domino effect in which ethnic minorities within seceding territories seek self-determination for themselves?

In what were Yugoslavia and the Soviet Union these questions are hardly academic. As Lieven and McGarry and Schöpflin show here they have given rise to multiple civil wars. There are many other hard cases in seeking to apply the doctrine of self-determination. In Transylvania there are two major populations (Hungarians and Romanians) mixed together in the same region along with other smaller communities. In Northern Ireland each ethnic community claims that it is part of another nation, and wishes the putative boundaries of that nation to be the relevant jurisdiction for decision-making (Chapter 6).[12] In Quebec, native Canadians, who occupy a huge proportion of the province's land-mass, are unwilling to secede from Canada with the Francophone majority (Chapter 2). In the Punjab (Chapter 4) and Kashmir, Hindus vehemently oppose the very idea of secession. In Slovakia, the Hungarian minority fears that the secession of the Slovaks from Czechoslovakia will be detrimental to their interests.

The constitution of a majority for self-determination begs the question of a majority in what region? In moderately complex cases the principle of self-determination seems indeterminate. As Ivor Jennings remarked:

On the surface [the principle of self-determination] seem[s] reasonable: let the people decide. It [i]s in fact ridiculous because the people cannot decide until somebody decides who are the people.

(Jennings 1956: 56)

Exercising the principle of self-determination is only straightforward where there is no large or disgruntled ethnic minority within the relevant region affected by the proposed secession *and* when the seceding area includes the great majority of those who wish to leave. Unfortunately it is difficult to think of instances where these optimum conditions have applied. Norway's secession from Sweden was an exemplary case. So was the case of Swiss Jura. Here, in an 'internal secession', plebiscites were held commune by commune to produce a result that split the new canton into two, along religious lines (Protestants voted to stay with Berne canton). By contrast the partitions of Ireland and India left significant minorities behind in Northern Ireland and Kashmir. Even when secessions seem straightforward, and the seceding areas appear reasonably homogeneous, new conflicts can emerge fairly rapidly. The Ukraine is a possible future example. Most commentators have focused on the dangers posed by the sizeable Russian minority, but less attention has been paid to the deep historical, cultural and geographical divisions between Catholic westerners (who were annexed by Stalin) and the Orthodox (who have been linked to Russia for some three centuries). After the glow of national liberation fades, so might Ukrainian national unity.

There have been some ingenious proposals about how to construct a normative liberal theory of secession (e.g. Beran 1984; 1987), which can answer Jennings's question: 'Who decides who are the people?' Beran advances the argument that every (self-defined) area within a liberal democratic state should be given the right to secede, provided the same right is extended to every sub-area within the proposed secessionist territory. This argument answers the serious accusation that self-determination creates a dangerous domino effect by saying two different things:

- there is nothing wrong with allowing a state to fragment on the principle of self-determination; and
- the fact that the seceding units themselves should grant the right of self-determination within their boundaries should put a prudential check on the aspiration to seek self-determination in territorially problematic zones.

Adam and Moodley accept the thesis that people should be entitled to secede from democratic states. They think that it is important to reduce the fears of the Zulu-based Inkatha and white extremists that a democratic South Africa will become a vehicle of ANC/non-Zulu black power (Chapter 10). They think that the inclusion of a secession clause in the new South African constitution will create incentives to accommodate ethnic minorities (for a contrary argument see Buchanan 1991: 159–61).

However, the right of secession seems unlikely to be entrenched in many modern liberal democratic constitutions,[13] and secession is likely to continue to have a bad press amongst liberals and socialists. But with the collapse of the global cold war, there is now much greater room for successful secession and the alteration of borders artificially frozen by the strategic interests of the superpowers – as the reunification of Germany suggests. The cold war had elevated the stability of boundaries into a necessity: rather than face nuclear confrontation each superpower respected the boundaries of the other's client-states, at least in Europe. 'Globalisation' and the increasing power of supra-state organisations may also make some international boundaries less inviolate.

Secession remains an option very likely to produce violence, and problems (initially) as bad as the ones it is intended to solve. Partitions can lead to population movements, often involuntary ones, and populations on the move are highly vulnerable to massacre, as happened during and after the partition of the Indian subcontinent (Khoshla 1950). Whether implementing secession is straightforward, on Beran's lines or not, the proposal of any community to secede from any state is likely to encourage key elites in the affected states to behave in chauvinistic and war-like ways. Normally secessionist movements provoke elites satisfied with the existing state into mobilising 'Unionist' movements against traitors. It was ironic to watch American commentators warning the Soviet Union during 1990–1 to allow its republics the right to self-determination. As Gorbachev observed, Lincoln's heirs have short memories.

What can be said of a general nature about the circumstances under which secession/partitions are likely to be carried out? Three external phenomena matter most and need to be studied closely: the nature of the inter-state system (is it permissive or restrictive?); the aftermath of wars (which often lead to territorial transfers/partitions, often without any considerations of consent) and the disintegration of empires (although this observation is almost tautological).

People seek full self-determination, in the form of independent statehood, for a variety of reasons. The urge for self-government may be motivated by a reaction against ethnic discrimination and humiliation, by the pragmatic expectation that the new nation-state will have greater economic and political freedom, by the wish to have a state in which different public policies will be pursued, by the desire for power and prestige amongst nationalist elites, or to protect a given ethnic culture from extinction. Not much of a very general nature can be successfully sustained about the economic circumstances or motivations of full-scale ethnic secessionist movements (Connor 1973). One observer notes that secessions are demanded both by economically advanced groups (e.g. Basques, Catalans, Ibos, Lombards, Sikhs, Tamils) and by economically backward communities (East Bengalis, Karens, Kurds, Slovaks); and that the secessionist communities can be located in either backward or advanced regional economies (Horowitz 1985: 229ff).

Most importantly enthusiasm for the principle of self-determination flows from the democratisation of the world. Democratisation means that the people are to rule. The statist declares that the people are all those who are resident in a given state or political unit's boundaries (the civic nationalist); the nationalist that they are the nation (the ethnic nationalist). In a few happy cases - Iceland - these two answers approximately coincide. However, in most cases the two definitions of the people do not coincide. In the general case the definition and championing of the people are up for grabs, and the possibility of partition/secession enters into the fabric of any state where the ethnic and civic nationalisms may point to different definitions of the nation.

Once democratisation poses the issue of the definition of the people a clustered set of issues automatically follows: the most important of which are the definition of citizenship, the possession of the franchise, the state's boundaries and the organisational structure of the state. These issues create incentives for political entrepreneurs to make party-building efforts out of ethnic cleavages, whether at the foundation of the state or afterwards. Politicians in multi-ethnic states have multiple incentives to play the ethnic card: whether it be Randolph Churchill playing the Orange card in the UK in the 1880s or Jean-Marie Le Pen playing the Algerian card in France in the

1980s. It is not possible to immunise the democratic process to exclude potentially explosive civic and ethnic issues. They are always there for mobilisation by the oppressed or the opportunist or both. Those who lose out politically under existing state arrangements and policies, whoever they may be, may always choose to redefine the rules of the game by playing the ethnic card in the arena of party politics.

A final reason why ethnic questions are potentially explosive, and raise the possibility that some people(s) will be tempted to exercise self-determination through secession is simple. Ethnic questions raise relatively non-tradable issues. Nationality, language, territorial homelands and culture are not easily bargained over. They create zero-sum conflicts, and therefore provide ideal materials for political entrepreneurs interested in creating or dividing political constituencies.

Having suggested reasons why democratisation increases the likelihood that political actors will seek self-determination for their community and thereby destabilise existing multi-ethnic states we must make two qualifications. First, destabilisation is likely to be contained if the relevant state or region exists in a milieu of other liberal democratic states. Thus far, in the twentieth century, liberal democracies have never gone to war against one another. Second, there are some circumstances under which the destabilising effects of democratisation upon multi-ethnic states can be muted, and inhibit the impetus to consider secession. These factors include:

- internal territorial segregation which permits self-government ('good fences make good neighbours');
- demographic dominance (where the large group is sufficiently secure not to fear the minority (or minorities) and behaves in a generous way);
- demographic stability (where one or more groups are not outgrowing or 'outfalling' one another); and
- a history of pre-democratic co-operation amongst ethnic political elites which gives the post-authoritarian state a reasonable chance of promoting accommodation.

(d) Integration and/or assimilation

A fourth method of macro-political ethnic conflict regulation is built upon the idea of trying to eliminate differences within the state by seeking to integrate or assimilate the relevant ethnic communities into a new transcendent identity. Whereas civic integration has the more modest object of creating a common civic, national or patriotic identity,[14] ethnic assimilation aims to create a common ethnic identity through the merging of differences (the melting pot).

Integration/assimilation has been the official aspiration of civil rights leaders in the USA, the African National Congress in South Africa, unionist integrationists and the integrated education lobby in Northern Ireland (Chapter 6), and the democratic left in those European countries striving to cope with immigrant influxes. Though inconceivable a few years ago, integration/assimilation has been embraced by pragmatists in South Africa's National Party who believe that the economic status quo can be secured and improved under liberal integration better than under apartheid (Chapter 10).

Usually people who advocate integration policies favour reducing the differences between ethnic communities, ensuring that the children of the (potentially rival) ethnic communities go to the same schools, socialising them in the same language and conventions, encouraging public and private housing policies which prevent ethnic segregation, and ensuring that the workplace is ethnically integrated through outlawing discrimination. Liberal integrationists promote bills of rights with equal rights for individuals, rather than communities. Assimilation policies go further. They favour the merging of ethnic identities, either into one already established identity (e.g. a French identity) or into a new one (e.g. a Soviet or Yugoslav identity). The ultimate proof of successful assimilation is large-scale intermarriage across the former ethnic boundaries which leads first to their blurring and then to their eradication. Integrationists and assimilationists also support 'catch-all' political parties, arguing against ethnic political parties, and aim to shun all policies which might show up differences between communities.[15]

This strategy of ethnic conflict management is driven by both high-minded and instrumental motives. Liberals and socialists, with the best of intentions, associate ethnic pluralism with sectarianism, parochialism, narrow-mindedness and chauvinist bigotry. They maintain that those opposed to integration either want or risk societal disintegration. Canadian integrationists demanded a Charter of Rights after 1945 to prevent a repeat of the war-time internment of ethnic minorities (Japanese, Italians and Ukrainians). White liberals in the USA funded court cases promoting black integration. Other liberals in North America sincerely advocate the assimilation of aboriginal minorities as the best way to end the atrocious conditions on reservations (e.g. Gibson 1992). Likewise the European left generally espouses the integration of immigrants because it abhors racism and discrimination. However, sometimes integrationism is not so high-minded: in Northern Ireland those who advocate integration of all as either British or Irish citizens are often merely interested in scoring ethnic points; while in South Africa some of those who advocate integration are either interested in preserving their economic privileges (whites) or see it as a way of establishing majority control (blacks). Sometimes integrationism is not even accompanied by formal generosity – consider white Canadians or white Britons who rail against Sikhs being allowed to wear their turbans where others would not be permitted to do so.

The targets of integration/assimilation policies respond in various ways – partly as a function of their perceptions of the motives lying behind the policies. Integration/assimilation policies are often targeted at migrants in liberal democratic states. These policies are more overtly liberal than the form of quasi-control associated with *metic* or guest-worker policies. In Canada, immigrant communities have acquired a Canadian civic identity on top of their original ethnic identity. The United States has proved a 'melting pot' in which some ethnic assimilation has taken place, although it would be better to say that white Protestants have assimilated (Swedes, Norwegians and Germans), and that white Catholics (Irish, Italians and Poles) have gradually assimilated. After 1945, both Canada and the USA have had some success in integrating Asian immigrants. Similarly, 'New Australians' have emerged in the wake of post-war continental European migrations. But these cases of moderately successful integration/assimilation involved migrations to a 'new' country, where the migrants, in principle, were willing to adapt their cultures to their new host country and accept a new civic identity.

Qualitatively different integration/assimilationist projects are those aimed at uniting (moderately) different communities against a common foe. The Anglican ascendancy in eighteenth-

and nineteenth-century Ireland promoted pan-Protestant unity against an insurgent native/Catholic threat. The South African government has ensured that all whites (English, Greeks, Italians, European Jews) and not just Afrikaners have benefited from apartheid, to create pan-white unity against blacks. Israeli governments have sought to downplay Sephardic–Ashkenazi differences in the interest of presenting a united front against Palestinians. During the nineteenth century the dominant English minority in Quebec welcomed Irish and other English-speaking immigrants as allies against French-Canadians. Contemporary *Québécois*, troubled by the low birth-rate amongst Francophones, have recently turned to non-white but French-speaking immigrants (from Haiti, Senegal and former French colonies) to bolster their linguistic community.

Mutually agreed integration/assimilation projects have reasonable prospects of success. However, where ethnic communities seek more than civic equality or equal opportunity and insist on autonomy or self-government (or where no external threat can compel pan-community unity) integration/assimilation policies fall on stonier ground. Ethnic communities living in their ancestral territories, for example, are often less willing than individual migrants to shed their culture or accept some new overarching identity. In the USA and Canada native Americans resist assimilation and hold out for varying degrees of self-government (or what we call cantonisation below). They call themselves 'first nations' to stress the moral superiority of their claims to cultural protection.[16]

Assimilation in contested homelands, however high-minded, cannot work where it involves assimilation on one community's terms: if one community's language, culture, religion and national myths are given precedence then we are not talking of assimilation or integration but of annexation; in such cases people complain of *ethnocide*, the destruction of a people's culture as opposed to physical liquidation of its members. This complaint is the standard one raised by the indigenous peoples of the world. Some forms of integration and assimilation appear to require coercion: compulsory educational homogenisation and the imposition of standard cultural codes as preconditions of full industrial and welfare-state citizenship. Making peasants into French people in the nineteenth century, the schooling of black South Africans in Afrikaans, the 'Russification' practised by the

Tsars and the Communist Party of the Soviet Union (CPSU), the periodic attempts at Anglicisation of French Canada in the eighteenth and nineteenth centuries, and the 'Romanisation' implemented by Ceaucescu in Transylvania, are policies cut from the same cloth. But even arguably more neutral strategies of integration/assimilation encounter significant resistance: as with Nehruvian secularism in India (Chapter 4), or Yugoslav (Chapter 8) and Soviet communism (Chapter 3). These efforts to establish transcending or pan-ethnic identities are often seen by minorities as disguised forms of cultural annexation, although the same policies may be rejected by the relevant dominant communities who see transcendent or pan-ethnic identities as detrimental to their (Hindu, Serbian or Russian) cultures.

Those who regard assimilation/integration strategies as benign forms of ethnic conflict regulation in contested homelands underestimate the difficulties involved. Optimistic observers of South Africa need to be counselled that it will be some time before representative Afrikaners and blacks embrace the ANC and the National Party respectively. The Hutu in Burundi, as Lemarchand suggests, are unlikely to abandon their distinct identity or their ethnic organisations just because such actions would fit the agenda of the Tutsi-dominated government (Chapter 7). In the foreseeable future, Northern Ireland Catholics, Basques and Croats are unlikely to be integrated or assimilated with their ethnic enemies. In fact, resistance to unwanted assimilation or integration projects is likely to be very high,[17] and can provoke ethnic revivals and secessionism in response, as has occurred in Burma, Ghana, Iraq, Sudan and Uganda (Horowitz 1985: 567–8). It is axiomatic that modern ethnic identities can only be significantly sustained through educational and neighbourhood segregation of some kind, because these conditions are necessary to preserve a cultural critical mass in the relevant communities. Some go further and claim that such communities require broadcasting media and control over access to land to sustain their identities. Such arguments explain why policies designed to compel people to be schooled together and to be neighbours are provocative, and possibly productive of violence. In short, unless assimilation/integration projects are targeted at people willing to acquire a new civic identity (like voluntary migrants) and to modify their ethnic identity, they produce rather than provoke conflict (Nordlinger 1972: 36–9).

For these reasons, amongst others, many liberal democracies which are managing large-scale immigrations, or multiple recently established ethnic communities, have realised that multi-cultural policies make greater sense than straightforward integration or assimilation strategies. They are abandoning the spirit of classical liberalism to manage immigrants. In England and France, at least in previous generations, liberals had a general bias towards integration/assimilation as macro-political forms of ethnic conflict resolution – at least within the metropolitan cores of their empires. However, this strategy seeks to resolve ethnic conflict by eliminating ethnic differences when the relevant problem is the desire of members of ethnic communities to maintain differences: which liberals committed to the right of individuals to choose their own conceptions of the good find it hard to argue against. This difficulty leads to a normative division of opinion between liberal integrationists (who are accused of intolerance) and liberal multi-culturalists (who are accused of surrendering liberalism to a form of relativism which tolerates illiberalism, e.g. in the form of Muslim schools). Liberal multi-culturalists are on their way to considering the merits of macro-political ways of resolving ethnic conflict which rely on managing differences rather than eliminating them (e.g. Kymlicka 1991).

Political engineers seeking to resolve ethnic conflict also frequently recommend the development of catch-all political parties to break down the salience of ethnic cleavages, i.e. they advocate electoral integration. For example, the absence of Great Britain's political parties in Northern Ireland before 1989 led one enthusiast for electoral integration to argue that the British party boycott was 'the fundamental reason' for continuing conflict in the region (Roberts 1990: 132). Those persuaded of the merits of engineering electoral integration include the military framers of Nigeria's second constitution, which forced political parties to develop some support in all regions of the state.

Such electoral integrationist projects may be well-intentioned ways of regulating ethnic conflict, but they are mostly based on wishful thinking. If there are parties which already mobilise across ethnic divisions then political stability is likely to be greater, and that is all to the good, but the belief that one can generate parties with such effects through heroic acts of will or engineering is fundamentally utopian, especially if the relevant ethnic communities have already been mobilised behind different conceptions of nationalism. As one astute observer generalises:

> It is sometimes possible to maintain a system of party align-
> ments cutting across a communal cleavage. It is usually
> possible to shift from this to a system where parties articulate
> the communal cleavage. But it is extremely difficult if not
> impossible to move in the reverse direction, because of the
> primitive psychological strength of communal identification
> and the effects of social reinforcement on maintaining the
> political salience of communal identification.
>
> (Barry 1991b: 146)

In addition to the agreed and coercive forms of integration/ assimilation we have discussed there are also cases where the dominated community (or communities) has sought assimilation/integration, but has been denied it. America's 'melting pot' has not successfully extended (if it was ever so intended) to blacks or Afro-Americans. Until the 1950s the local white majorities in the deep South worked a system of control, and sought to prevent any kind of integration, let alone assimilation. While blacks, with some exceptions,[18] support integration, and won formal victories to establish this goal in public policy in the 1950s and 1960s, American cities and schools remain segregated and racial life-chances are still dramatically unequal.[19] In Northern Ireland, the unionist government and party blocked the integrationist ambitions of at least some Catholics in the 1960s, precipitating the current long wave of political violence. If, as at least one academic anticipates, the Palestinians switch their demands from separate nationhood to demanding civil rights within the Israeli state, we might expect a similar pattern there (Nusseibeh 1990).

While some liberal and bourgeois elites within dominant ethnic communities might favour integration/assimilation of the dominated, as a way of broadening the legitimacy of their regimes, they may find that such ambitions provoke a furious backlash from their co-ethnics in less privileged positions. In Northern Ireland in the late 1960s moderate integrationist unionists lost all influence over their 'followers'. The current South African government is gambling that it can integrate blacks before it has to face the white electorate again: if it fails it may go the way of all flesh.

(ii) Managing differences

(a) Hegemonic control

The most common system of managing as opposed to eliminating ethnic conflict practised in multi- or bi-ethnic states is that of 'hegemonic control', a concept first developed by Ian Lustick (1979; 1987) although we use the term slightly differently (O'Leary and Arthur 1990; O'Leary and McGarry 1992: chs 3 and 4). Hegemonic control has been the most common mode through which multi-ethnic societies have been stabilised in world history. Imperial or authoritarian regimes controlled multiple cultures within their territories through coercive domination and elite co-option.[20] They suppressed latent divisions between ethnic communities which might otherwise have been manifested, especially in conditions of economic modernisation. The control was 'hegemonic' if it made an overtly violent ethnic contest for state power either 'unthinkable' or 'unworkable' on the part of the subordinated communities: ethnically-based slave-systems were exemplary cases of authoritarian hegemonic control. Hegemonic control in imperial or authoritarian regimes need not have rested, although it often did, on the support of the largest or most powerful ethnic community. What was necessary was control of the relevant coercive apparatuses: thus ethnic minorities in Burundi, Fiji (after 1987), Liberia (before 1980) and South Africa (until 1990–1) were able to sustain hegemonic control because of their control over security and policing systems. In Burundi the Tutsi govern through a form of control which Lemarchand calls 'authoritarian containment' (Chapter 7).

Hegemonic control is therefore coercive and/or co-optive rule which successfully manages to make unworkable an ethnic challenge to the state order. However, there is a key difference in coercive regimes which practise hegemonic control. In authoritarian empires there was usually no grand objective pursued to eliminate ethnic difference – although one might argue that the world religions propagated transcendent identities. By contrast, in communist hegemonic systems, a new transcendent identity was consistently proclaimed: one which would eventually eliminate ethnic differences as irrelevant to people's civic identities as citizens. However, after initial post-revolutionary fervour it was rare for this vision to be articulated as one which would utterly eradicate ethnic difference, and the policies of communist parties primarily focused on suppressing the politicisation of ethnic differences (Chapters 3 and 8).

In liberal democracies hegemonic control appears less feasible than in authoritarian regimes. Liberal democracies with statist conceptions of citizenship permit, indeed facilitate, ethnic organisation and mobilisation; and ethnic contests for state power become eminently 'thinkable' and 'workable' within liberal democratic or open institutions. Think of how Irish nationalism was facilitated by the democratisation of the United Kingdom, or of how ethnic nationalism was encouraged by glasnost in the Soviet Union. Similarly the breakdown of the Franco regime after 1975 facilitated ethnic challenges to the Spanish state (Chapter 9), although of a less severe variety. The liberal optimist might therefore conclude that democratisation spells doom to systems of hegemonic control.

However, systems of hegemonic control, or ethnic domination, can be constructed in formally liberal democratic states. The most obvious method is when formally liberal democratic institutions are monopolised by a minority of the state's population. Thus white South Africans and Rhodesians established forms of settler-control over other ethnic communities, while preserving liberal democratic rules for their own community. Citizenship and representative government were confined to the *Herrenvolk*. Minority control within a given region is very common: consider Serbian domination of Albanians in Kosovo, or the treatment of the majority Bengalis in what was East Pakistan. In Fiji, the native minority, frightened by electoral returns which threatened their participation in government, supported a coup in 1987 which shifted towards a system of minority hegemonic control (Chapter 11).

But hegemonic control can occur in states in which the majority or entirety of the relevant state's adult population have formal access to citizenship. Democracy in its most primitive meaning is understood as 'majority rule'. Where political 'majorities' constantly fluctuate, as people change their minds on the key policy or political issues of the day, then majority rule is a sensible decision rule, infinitely preferable to the kind of minority rule practised by emperors, military dictators or one-party regimes. However, where there are two or more deeply established ethnic communities, and where the members of these communities do not agree on the basic institutions and policies the regime should pursue, or where the relevant ethnic communities are not internally fragmented on key policy preferences in ways which cross-cut each other, then 'majority rule' can become an instrument of hegemonic control. Northern Ireland (1920–72), and the deep South of the USA (c. 1870–c. 1964), are examples of regions within liberal democratic states where formal majoritarianism co-existed with hegemonic control over the relevant minority. The relevant majority monopolised the police and judicial systems, manipulated the franchise to consolidate their domination, practised economic discrimination in employment and the allocation of public housing, and institutional discrimination against the minority's cultural and educational system(s), and ruthlessly repressed minority discontent. As Noel shows, the Canadian state practised control over aboriginal groups (Chapter 2). Natives were policed through the white judicial system, denied certain privileges if they left reservations and denied the (federal) franchise if they remained on them (until 1961).[21] In India, the demands of Sikhs for an autonomous Punjab partly arose from their fear that Nehruvian tolerance had increasingly given way to Hindu chauvinism, presaging a move towards control as the preferred Hindu method of governing India (Chapter 4). Since 1969 Malaysia has been moving away from consociationalism towards control: prompting Mauzy to describe the present arrangements with the label 'coercive consociationalism' (Chapter 5).

The normative lesson is obvious: a majoritarian system of liberal democratic government, designed to create strong powers for the governing party, is no guarantee of liberty for ethnic minorities. A 'winner takes all' system in the presence of ethnic parties ensures that ethnic competition will be regarded as a zero-sum conflict. Where two or more ethnic communities wish to belong to different external nation-states the potential instability of majoritarian liberal democracy is even more obvious, and the temptations to establish a system of control by the majority are correspondingly greater.

Some maintain that systems of hegemonic control can be normatively defensible. Lustick maintains that control is often the only alternative to continuous war – he had in mind the Lebanon after 1976 (Lustick 1979). However, this quasi-Hobbesian reasoning (any state is better than none) is suspect.

Consider first the consequences of universalising Lustick's argument. It would lead one to maintain, as some do, that the dictatorial CPSU and the Yugoslav League of Communists were morally justified precisely because they suppressed ethnic conflict in the Soviet Union and Yugoslavia, that one-party states in Africa and Asia are similarly defensible, and that the re-imposition of Ba'athist control over the Kurds is preferable to continuous civil war in Iraq.

There are at least five further difficulties with universalising Lustick's limited defence of hegemonic control. First, the options in any given ethnic conflict are rarely simply between those of control and continuous ethnic war – although there will be plenty of political entrepreneurs seeking to advance precisely this argument. Second, some of the options (federalism/cantonisation, arbitration and consociationalism) have some record of success in stabilising deeply divided societies in ways compatible with liberal democratic norms, whereas any system of control is easily convertible into a system for the execution of genocide, ethnocide, forced mass-population transfers and other violations of human rights. Third, partitionist or secessionist options are almost invariably more desirable than the imposition of control. If the relevant partition or secession is even moderately well executed it should ensure that more people can enjoy legitimate self-government than would be the case under a system of control. Fourth, under systems of control the subordinated minority will always seek to 'internationalise' their plight under the relevant hegemonic group or party/dictator, and thereby threaten the stability of the relevant regime as well as the international order. Therefore one can use stability arguments which are the converse of Lustick's. Fifth, if a system of control eventually breaks down, its practices will have added to the accumulated stock of ethnic grievances. Repression sidelines moderates, bolsters extremists and obstructs prospects for future accommodation, as Singh and O'Duffy demonstrate has been true in both the Punjab and Northern Ireland (Chapters 4 and 6, respectively). The same story is true of the West Bank and Gaza Strip. One might also argue in a realist fashion, although the evidence would need careful appraisal, that wars may sort matters out more successfully than exercising hegemonic control, and even create incentives for post-war co-operative behaviour.

(b) Arbitration (third-party intervention)

Arbitration of bi-ethnic or multi-ethnic states is the least recognised mode in the literature on ethnic conflict regulation, except perhaps in international relations and peace studies (Hoffman 1992). The main classification problems with the concept of arbitration are deciding whether or not it includes:

- both internal and external arbitration;
- what one of us elsewhere has called 'co-operative internationalisation' (O'Leary 1989); and
- forceful intervention by a self-appointed umpire concerned to establish stability in a given region.

These three classification problems share one feature. One must decide whether to classify any conflict-regulating activity which is the outcome of third-party intervention as arbitration, or to confine the term arbitration to cases where the relevant third-party intervention is characterised by procedural neutrality of some kind. Our preference is for the latter more exclusive usage.[22] Many third-party interventions, as we shall see, are indistinguishable from efforts to establish control of a given region. However, we believe that arbitration can be internal or external and includes 'co-operative internationalisation'.

Arbitration on our construal entails the intervention of a 'neutral', bi-partisan or multi-partisan authority. It differs from other methods used to stabilise antagonistic societies because it involves conflict regulation by agents other than the directly contending parties. Integral to the concept of arbitration is that the disinterestedness of the arbiter makes it possible for this person (or institution, or state) to win the acquiescence if not the enthusiastic support of the contending ethnic segments; and thereby dampen the violence which would otherwise occur. An arbiter provides governmental effectiveness where war or anarchy might otherwise prevail. Arbitration is distinguishable from *mediation* because the arbiter makes the relevant decisions, whereas mediators merely facilitate them. Thus from 1991 until we went to press, the EC had been mediating rather than arbitrating in what was 'Yugoslavia'.

In a system of arbitration the role of the arbiter is portrayed like that of a conciliator presiding over a family quarrel. The arbiter pursues the common interests of the rival segments in the relevant society as he or she perceives them; regulates the political exchanges between the segments as an umpire (to prevent a further and more dramatic breakdown in state order); and presides over ethnic elites who have varying incentives to engage in responsible and co-operative behaviour. Arbitration, in principle, can establish the conditions for longer-term democratic conflict resolution: secessions, partitions, power-sharing or even the peaceful integration or assimilation of the rival communities. But third-party interventionists can play the role of self-appointed arbiters and act to reconstruct the old system of ethnic control – as, for example, occurred when a Russian Tsar handed back Hungary to Habsburg control in 1849, or when the British empire handed Northern Ireland to the Ulster Unionist Party. Alternatively, self-appointed arbiters can presage the creation of a new system of control by handing power to a different ethnic segment(s), as some maintain Syria will eventually do in the Lebanon.

The prerequisite for agreed arbitration is that the arbiter's claim to neutrality be broadly accepted by the major contending ethnic segments. Not all professed arbiters pass this test. Since 'neutrality' is rhetorically superior to 'partisanship' and useful for domestic and international consumption, the self-present-ations of arbiters must be treated with scepticism: few observers credited Syria's intervention in Lebanon or Soviet federal intervention in Nagorno-Karabakh with impartiality, and the disinterestedness of US arbitration in the Middle East is widely questioned. Irish nationalists in Northern Ireland did not regard the British government as a neutral arbiter after 1972 (Chapter 6, and see O'Leary and McGarry 1992: ch. 5). The British govern-ment appeared to acknowledge this fact when it signed the Anglo-Irish Agreement in 1985, providing a role for the Irish government as guardian of the nationalist minority in the region (O'Leary and McGarry 1992: ch. 6).

Arbitration of ethnic conflicts is of two broad types, the internal and the external, each of which can be performed by different kinds of agent. *Internal arbitration* can be executed by an individual who is not a member of the main antagonistic ethnic communities: for example, Julius Nyerere in post-independence Tanzania. It can be fulfilled by statesmen with the moral authority to transcend their ethnic origins: for example, Mahatma Gandhi in the Indian subcontinent, or President Tito in Yugoslavia. It can also be managed by someone who can claim a connection with all the major ethnic groups: for example, Siaka Stevens in Sierra Leone. Internal arbitration can also be performed by institutions as opposed to individual agents. The monarchy in pre-1965 Burundi played an arbitration role over Tutsi and Hutu (Chapter 7). The US Supreme Court, under the leadership of Chief Justice Warren, arbitrated conflicts between blacks and whites in the 1950s and 1960s. Federal governments, like supreme courts, can arbitrate ethnic conflict within the constituent units of their federation, as occurs regularly in Canada, where the Ottawa government has constitutional responsibility for indigenous minorities in the provinces. While few US blacks or Canadian natives regarded the relevant federal governments as their institutions, they clearly thought them more impartial than state or provincial governments.[23] Finally, internal arbitration can be performed by a political party. One-party states claim to absorb key members of rival ethnic communities and regulate their rival aspirations. This argument was advanced by Nkrumah in Ghana in the 1960s, Nimeiri in Sudan in the 1970s, and Mugabe in Zimbabwe in the 1980s. However, it is empirically difficult to distinguish this (alleged) form of arbitration from hegemonic control. In a competitive political system, by contrast, internal arbitration can be performed by a pivotal political party, one judged to be sufficiently disinterested by the other contending factions to be able to chair a cross-ethnic coalition. The Alliance Party has long sought to perform this function, without success, in Northern Ireland; and the Indian Congress Party has long claimed to be a reasonable arbiter of ethnic conflicts in India's regions, a claim which has become steadily more threadbare in the years since Nehru's death.

External arbitration by contrast suggests that ethnic conflict cannot be successfully managed within the relevant political system. It is a potentially useful conflict-regulating device during processes of decolonisation, where an external force still possesses authority, but less effective when the conflict zone is a strong sovereign state. External arbitration can be performed by a single external agent or state, a bi-partisan authority, or a multi-partisan force. Multi-partisan arbitration or co-operative internationalisation, as originally envisaged for United Nations' peacekeeping (and peacemaking) forces, has been performed with intermittent success in Cyprus, and parts of the Middle East and Africa, for example in Namibia. However, this kind of arbitration is usually a sign that the relevant ethnic conflict is seen as insoluble and as a dangerous threat to the security of an entire set of states. There is truth in the cynical observation that 'when the UN come, you know that your problems are with you for ever'. However, adjudication of international law by the International Court of Justice shows that we do have instruments for multi-partisan arbitration of ethnic conflicts, should we choose to develop them.

Bi-partisan arbitration in its fullest form involves two states sharing sovereignty over a disputed territory[24] – in the form of a condominium – but it can also involve an agreement by a state which maintains sovereignty over the relevant region to consult with another interested state over how that region's government is conducted, and to grant the external government a role as guardian of an ethnic minority within the relevant region. One example is the Anglo-Irish Agreement between the British and Irish governments, signed in 1985 (Chapter 6; O'Leary and McGarry 1992: ch. 6). The Italian and Austrian governments in 1946 came to an agreement over South Tyrol, ensuring the German-speaking community 'complete equality of rights with the Italian-speaking inhabitants within the framework of special provisions to safeguard the ethnic character and the cultural and economic development of the German-speaking element' (see Alcock 1970; Hannum 1990: 432–40). The Finnish and Swedish governments reached a similar agreement over the Åland islands – although this agreement in effect set up a Swedish canton within Finland, a canton with the right to prevent Finnish citizens from settling on the islands (see Ålands landsting 1988). Other bilateral agreements between states over contested regions and national minorities existed in inter-war Europe (see Hannum 1990: ch. 17).

(c) Cantonisation and/or federalization

There are two territorial principles of macro-political ethnic conflict regulation, cantonisation and federalisation, both of which can be used to manage ethnic differences in ways which are fully compatible with liberal democratic norms.

Cantonisation might more accurately be designated as 'communisation' after the communes which operate beneath the cantons in Switzerland. It might also be considered synonymous with devolution organised on an ethno-territorial basis. However, we prefer the term cantonisation because unlike communisation or devolution it is a term distinctively associated with the regional management of ethnic differences. Under cantonisation the relevant multi-ethnic state is subjected to a micropartition in which political power is devolved to (conceivably very small) political units, each of which enjoys minisovereignty. Although it is usual to discuss cantonisation in the context of federalism – as the Swiss paradigm might suggest – the principle of cantonisation is separable, in principle, from formally federal forms of government. Cantonisation must be distinguished from mere administrative decentralisation, common in unitary states: it is built upon the recognition of ethnic difference and allows for asymmetrical relations between different cantons and the central government. The democratic Spanish state, erected after the fall of Franco, which is, formally speaking, an asymmetrical form of decentralised unitary state, can be considered an example of relatively successful cantonisation, with the notable exception of the protracted conflict in the Basque Country (Chapter 9).

Cantonisation is really an application of the fashionable (Catholic) idea of subsidiarity to ethnic relations: decision-making power is managed at the lowest appropriate level of a political hierarchy. Cantons are usually designed to create ethnically homogeneous units where majority rule is practically coterminous with the self-government of all the relevant community.[25] Where ethnic conflict is high then the partitioning of existing governmental units to create ethnic homogeneity is the operating administrative principle, as happened in the case of the Bernese Jura. Cantonisation decomposes the arena of ethnic conflict and competition into smaller more manageable units: it involves a negotiable form of 'internal secession'. Under 'rolling cantonisation' policing and judicial powers can be gradually devolved to those areas where the population expressed a wish to exercise such powers, and where it is judged that the experiment had some prospects of success. In the newly independent state of Bosnia a carefully designed form of cantonisation may have made a great deal of sense and prevented the possibility of extensive blood-letting between Serbs, Croats and Muslims.

However, cantonisation is fraught with potential difficulties, notably the drawing and policing of appropriate units of government, winning consent for them, and the ever-present threat that the cantonisation of policing and judicial powers might be used by paramilitary organisations to seize control of parts of the relevant territories, and treat them as 'liberated zones'. This might explain why the Bosnian government would not consider cantonisation, especially the botched version suggested by the European Community's officials.[26] Yet cantonisation is often as realistic as pushing full-blooded nationalist positions, whether these be integrationist, secessionist or irredentist. Cantonisation is more gradualist in its implications than drastic partition of state-boundaries because it permits governments the freedom to reverse any experimental initiatives which go badly wrong. The Canadian government seems to be moving in the direction of cantonisation after its recent recognition of the 'inherent right' of native peoples to self-government 'within the Canadian federation' (Chapter 2).

'Pseudo-cantonisation' is also a possible political strategy, where territorial decentralisation of ethnic conflict is used to facilitate or disguise control, and merits the condemnation of liberals and socialists. For example, the South African government established a number of barren 'homelands' for blacks in an unsuccessful attempt to de-legitimise their demands for power at the centre, and successive Likud governments in Israel (1977–92) refused to partition 'Eretz Israel', instead offering Palestinians a form of autonomy which no representative Palestinian could embrace.

Overlapping cantonisation and federalism there exists a grey area of territorial management of ethnic differences which is often found in conjunction with external arbitration. International agreements between states can entrench the territorial autonomy of certain ethnic communities, even though the 'host state' does not generally organise itself along either cantonist or federalist principles: for example the agreement between Italy and Austria guaranteeing the autonomy of South Tyrol, or the agreement between Finland and Sweden guaranteeing the autonomy of the Åland islands.

Federalism is similar but not coterminous with cantonisation as a device for regulating multi-ethnic states: the states, provinces or *Länder* are usually much larger than cantons.[27] By federalism we do not mean the kind of pseudo-federalism which used to characterise the Soviet Union. In a genuine federation the central government and the provincial governments both enjoy separate domains of power, although they may also have concurrent powers. Constitutional amendments require the consent of both levels of government. Federations automatically imply codified and written constitutions, and bicameral legislatures. In the federal as opposed to the popular chamber the smallest component units are usually disproportionally represented, i.e. over-represented.

Federalists maintain that if the boundaries between the components of the federation match the boundaries between the relevant ethnic, religious or linguistic communities, i.e. if there is a 'federal society' (Stein 1968), then federalism can be an effective conflict-regulating device. In the cases of Belgium, Canada and Switzerland the success of federalism in conflict regulation, such as it is, is based upon the historic accident that the relevant ethnic communities are reasonably geographically segregated (Chapter 12). Federalism is less desirable for communities which cannot control federal units, because of their geographical dispersion or paucity of numbers – as with Quebec Anglophones, Francophones outside Quebec, Flemish-speakers in Wallonia, Francophones in Flanders, blacks in the USA and indigenous peoples in Australia and North America. One reason why federalism proved totally insufficient as a conflict-regulating device in Yugoslavia was because there was insufficient geographical clustering of the relevant ethnic communities.

Geographically clustered ethnic communities chose multi-ethnic federations for a variety of reasons. First, federations have often evolved out of multi-ethnic colonies, where secession might have provoked conflict with those who wanted to keep the polity unified. Second, even if a history of common colonial government did not promote any overarching cultural loyalties – for example through what Anderson (1983: ch. 4) calls 'administrative pilgrimages' – it usually creates elites (soldiers, bureaucrats and capitalists) with an interest in sustaining the existing regime's territory. Third, large federal states can often be sold economically – they promise a larger single market, a single currency, economies of scale, reductions in transactions' costs and fiscal equalisation. Fourth, large federal states can be marketed as geo-politically wise, offering greater security and protection than small states. Finally, the personal philosophies and dispositions of federation-builders matter: the Macdonald-Cartier alliance in Canada (Chapter 2) and Nehru's leadership in India were critical in establishing and sustaining their federations.

Unfortunately federalism has a poor track-record as a conflict-regulating device in multi-ethnic states, even where it allows a degree of minority self-government. Democratic federations have broken down throughout Asia and Africa, with the possible exception of India – whose survival is partly accounted for by the degree of central control possible in its quasi-federal system. Federal failures primarily occur because minorities continue to be outnumbered at the federal level of government. The resulting frustrations, combined with an already defined boundary and the significant institutional resources flowing from control of their own province/state, provide considerable incentives to attempt secession, which in turn can invite harsh responses from the rest of the federation: the disintegration of the Nigerian and American federations were halted only through millions of deaths. As the ingenious federal engineering of the Nigerian second republic went down before a military coup the jury must remain out on the success or otherwise of democratic federalism in resolving Nigeria's ethnic dilemmas. India, the most successful post-colonial federation, faces secessionist movements in Kashmir and Punjab, and Canada is perennially threatened with the secession of Quebec (although this, like Godot, never comes). As Lieven and McGarry and Schöpflin demonstrate, even the sham federations of the Soviet Union and Yugoslavia provided various ethnic movements with the resources to launch successful secessions during 1991-2 (Chapters 3 and 8, respectively). The threat of secession in multi-ethnic federations is such that Nordlinger actually excludes federalism from his list of normatively defensible conflict-regulating practices (1972: 32). Integrationist nation-builders in Africa have distrusted federalism precisely for this reason. Federations have been especially fragile in bi-ethnic societies. The Slovaks moved rapidly to snap the hyphen in the redemocratised Czecho-Slovakia. With the possible exception of Belgium (Chapter 12) there is not a single case of successful federalism based upon dyadic or two-unit structures (Vile 1982). Even the Belgian federation technically has four sub units, even if it is built around a dualist ethnic division, and the EC has helped sustain the unity of Belgium. Even relatively successful multi-ethnic federations appear to be in permanent constitutional crises. Not only do the division of powers need to be constantly renegotiated as a result of technological advances, economic transformations and judicial interventions, but to maintain stability supplemental consociational practices are often required at the federal and subcentral levels of government (see Chapter 12).

However, despite the difficulties associated with it, genuine democratic federalism is clearly an attractive way to regulate ethnic conflict, with obvious moral advantages over pure control. The argument that it should be condemned because it gives rise to secession and civil war can be sustained only under two circumstances. First, if in the absence of federalism, there would be no secessionist bid *and* if it can be shown that ethnic conflict cannot be justly managed by alternative democratic means. Second, if the secessionist unit would be likely to exercise hegemonic control (or worse) over its indigenous minorities: as some maintain will be the fate of the Hungarian minority in an independent Slovakia.

(d) Consociation or power-sharing

Political relationships can be organised between ethnic communities to prevent conflict according to *power-sharing* or *consociational* principles. These principles can operate at the level of an entire state, or within a region of a state characterised by ethnic conflict: they are relevant to both central and local governments. Consociational principles were invented or re-invented by Dutch politicians in 1917 through till the 1960s, and by Lebanese politicians between 1943 and 1975. Malaysian politicians experimented with consociationalism between 1955 and 1969, Fijians on and off between 1970 and 1987, and Northern Irish politicians for a brief spell in 1974.

Consociational democracies usually have four features (Lijphart 1977a):

- *A grand coalition government* which incorporates the political parties representing the main segments of the divided society;
- *Proportional representation, employment and expenditure rules* apply throughout the public sector;

- *Community autonomy* norms operate under which ethnic communities have self-government over those matters of most profound concern to them; and
- *Constitutional vetoes* for minorities.

Consociational principles are based upon the acceptance of ethnic pluralism. They aim to secure the rights, identities, freedoms and opportunities of all ethnic communities, and to create political and other social institutions which enable them to enjoy the benefits of equality without forced assimilation. In some zones of ethnic conflict around the world the relevant populations effectively have a simple choice: between creating consociational democratic institutions or having no meaningful democratic institutions at all. A case in point is the Lebanon whose delicate consociational compromise was destabilised by Israel and Syria in 1975/6 and by the impact of the Palestinian diaspora. By no means have all consociational experiments proven successful – as the cases of Cyprus, Lebanon and Northern Ireland indicate – but some of them have. The best normative case for consociational arrangements is that they involve the self-government of the relevant communities, and they are better than the alternatives: majority domination, bloody partition, secessionist warfare and the unthinkable options of forced population transfers and genocide.[28]

However, the consociational model of ethnic conflict regulation is easily destabilised because it is most likely to exist in a multi-ethnic or bi-ethnic region in which no one ethnic community can easily dominate the others. To work consociational systems requires at least three fundamental conditions to be present. First, the rival ethnic segments must not be unreservedly committed to immediate or medium-term integration or assimilation of others into 'their' nation or to the creation of their own nation-state. Nationality conflicts appear to have an irreducibly zero-sum character. Preventing ethnic communities from developing full-scale and exclusive national consciousness requires political elites either to downplay the state's national identity in a world in which the pressures to do the opposite are very powerful, or to develop an artificial and transcendent national identity, which may prove very difficult. Second, successive generations of political leaders must have the right motivations to engage in conflict regulation and sustain the consociational system. The leaders of the rival ethnic communities must fear the consequences of ethnic war, and desire to preserve the economic and political stability of their regions. They must, for example, believe they are incapable of governing on their own (or establishing hegemonic control). Their motivations may be self-interested or high-minded, but without them there is no prospect of producing a consociational arrangement. The moment rival elites believe that the benefits of war exceed the costs of peace a consociational system is doomed. Third, the political leaders of the relevant ethnic communities must enjoy some political autonomy themselves, so that they can make compromises without being accused of treachery. If they lack confidence – for example because they are outbid by external irredentists or by rival leaders in the capital city – they will not be prepared to engage in hard bargaining. This condition not only requires restraint on the part of external elites outside the affected area but also within the relevant ethnic communities. This condition is most exacting as the dangerous phenomenon of outflanking, of Sharon outflanking Shamir, of Ian Paisley's Democratic Unionist Party outflanking the Ulster Unionist Party, of Butadroka outflanking Mara, is latent in all proportional representation consociational systems.

These are demanding requirements. If these conditions are not present, as in the Lebanon, Northern Ireland, Malaysia, Cyprus and Fiji, then consociational experiments break down. An even more depressing conclusion is also possible. Consociational practices may work to calm ideological, religious, linguistic or ethnic conflicts, but only if these conflicts have not become the bases of separate national identities. Consociationalism may only be practicable in moderately rather than deeply divided societies (Horowitz 1985: 571-2). This conclusion is not appetising for enthusiasts of consociationalism in Burundi, Fiji, Northern Ireland, Malaysia, Lebanon and South Africa.

CONCLUSION

In the chapters which follow our contributors examine ethnic conflict regulation in a variety of hotspots and cooler locations. We hope our framework allows readers to classify the mode or modes of conflict regulation used in each case study, and to judge their morality, feasibility and consequences. The comparative evaluation of ethnic conflict regulations matters because we are all ethnics of one kind or another, even when we want not to be, and because our community relations are too important to be left to ethnic partisans. Political scientists have few more important duties than to contribute to hard-headed but ethical analyses of ways of resolving ethnic conflict.

NOTES

1 Pioneering and exemplary trailblazing works have been carried out by Walker Connor (1973), Donald Horowitz (1985) and Arend Lijphart (e.g. 1968, 1977a, 1984).
2 Micropolitical forms of ethnic conflict regulation are smaller scale, and include *inter alia* rigorous discrimination and segregation, equal opportunities policies, affirmative action programmes, community relations and cultural encounter groups, specific forms of electoral representation, etc.
3 Although the eight methods were arrived at taxonomically two of them are *typologically* related, namely consociationalism and control (Lustick 1979), and arbitration (or third-party intervention) can be typologically contrasted with them (McGarry and O'Leary, forthcoming).
4 Eliminating and managing differences are mutually exclusive strategies from the perspective of the target ethnic community. However, there is no reason why a state may not seek to eliminate differences between some ethnic communities while seeking to manage differences with others.
5 For a contrary view, see McNeill (1986: 71).
6 Some believe that these were cases of forced transfers rather than genocide because Stalin's express intention was to remove these peoples from militarily sensitive areas, and not to kill them. However, by the 'indirect destruction' element in our definition they count as genocides.
7 The Chinese were (conveniently) treated as coterminous with Communists: so it is difficult to distinguish genocide from politicide in Indonesia. Estimates of the number of victims in 1965–6 range from 500,000 to 1,000,000.
8 In response to the Israeli-organised Palestinian catastrophe some Palestinians wish to execute full-scale retribution, by driving Israelis 'into the sea'.
9 However, frontier-genocides occurred in all the parliamentary colonies of the British empire which became the 'white dominions'.
10 We use the term semi-secessionist movements to cover those seeking to leave one state to unite or re-unite with another. Strict secessionists seek to create an independent state, and are often wrongly called irredentist. It is states which seek to expand to complete their nation-stateness which are properly irredentist. Naturally irredentist states

and semi-secessionist movements often go together (e.g. the Republic of Ireland and Irish nationalists in Northern Ireland).

11 Self-determination can in principle be exercised to agree to integration, assimilation or cantonisation (autonomy). However, full self-determination is often understood as isomorphic with secession.

12 However, Northern Ireland unionists are ambiguous about whether they believe the boundaries of the UK or of Northern Ireland should be the ultimate jurisdiction for constitutional decision-making.

13 The one liberal democracy to have granted the right of secession is the United Kingdom. In 1949 it granted the right of secession to the Northern Ireland parliament, and in 1985 it granted the right of the people of Northern Ireland to become part of the Republic of Ireland. However, this right, as Irish nationalist critics point out, was not one which the local majority of unionists were ever likely to choose.

14 Horowitz calls civic integration 'inter-ethnic nationalism' (1985: 567). Civic integration (which involves equal citizenship without ethnic assimilation) may seem like a strategy for managing rather than eliminating differences. However, as it is aimed at barring ethnicity from the public arena, we consider it an elimination strategy.

15 Integrationists/assimilationists are especially sceptical about consociational arrangements which they believe entrench ethnic divisions and reward divisive political leaders.

16 There are, however, some examples of assimilation within and across historic homelands, as George Schöpflin has reminded us. Substantial numbers of Slavs were assimilated as Germans and Austrians (see Vienna's telephone directory). Likewise, Germans and Slavs were assimilated by Hungarians; Ukrainians and Germans were assimilated by Poles; and some Poles were assimilated by Russians. Where urbanisation is occurring, and the assimilating group is relatively open and prestigious, the assimilands may not care to preserve their ethnic identity.

17 A Canadian native chief described the policy of the Trudeau government in the late 1960s as one of 'peacetime genocide'. The policy aimed at removing some historic rights which had been conferred on natives.

18 Some blacks (e.g. Malcolm X and Louis Farakhan) have rejected the American way, preaching separatism, black consciousness, self-reliance and, on occasions, secession.

19 The undeclared goal of American public policy in major conurbations appears to be that of controlling rather than integrating blacks. The Reagan and Bush administrations have effectively quarantined blacks and controlled them through increased spending on police and prisons: leading to more young blacks being in prison than in higher education by the end of the 1980s. While control works reasonably well, from the perspective of whites, it can lead to sudden breakdowns – as we saw in Los Angeles in April 1992.

20 Co-opting elites as a technique for monopolising power should be distinguished from offering to share power – the former is characteristic

of control, the latter of consociationalism. Some leaders of the ANC believe that the South African government is offering them the former under the guise of offering them the latter.

21 South Africa's government was fond of reminding the US and Canadian governments that their treatment of aboriginals is like apartheid – and many native and left-wing intellectuals agreed.

22 In legal literature adjudication is the term usually used to refer to neutral third-party intervention (coupled with an imposed decision), while arbitration can often involve non-neutral third parties (e.g. commercial arbitrations) pushing the parties towards compromise (our thanks to David Schiff).

23 US blacks welcomed the intervention of federal troops to replace Arkansas state-troopers at Little Rock in 1957, just as native Canadians welcomed the intervention of federal troops to replace Quebec provincial police at Oka in 1990. Northern Irish Catholics welcomed the intervention of British troops in Northern Ireland in 1969. They were preferable to the local Royal Ulster Constabulary and the 'B Specials'.

24 We have argued elsewhere for the merits of this way of regulating ethnic conflict in Northern Ireland (O'Leary and McGarry 1992: ch. 8).

25 Cantons could be designed to achieve a very local form of power-sharing government between the rival ethnic communities, especially where communities are so intermingled as to prevent neat partitioning: however, the logic of this system is really that of local consociationalism.

26 Address by Bosnian foreign minister at the London School of Economics, March 1992.

27 Indeed the constituent units of federations can be subdivided into cantons to manage ethnic conflict, as the Canadian government proposes to do in the North-West Territories.

28 Discussions of the circumstances under which consociationalism is likely to succeed can be found in Barry (1991), Lijphart (1977a, 1985), McGarry (1990), McGarry and Noel (1989) and O'Leary (1989).

Chapter 2

Canadian responses to ethnic conflict

Consociationalism, federalism and control

S. J. R. Noel

INTRODUCTION

The management of ethnic conflict has long been, and remains, a
fundamental prerequisite for the maintenance of Canada as an
effective political entity. For more than two centuries, under a
variety of constitutional regimes, successive governments have
sought to overcome deep divisions of language, religion and race
that pose an ever-present threat to social peace and stability. The
means employed in pursuit of that often elusive goal have varied
widely across a broad spectrum of responses. Depending on the
period, the location, and the specific parties to the conflict,
virtually every possible response has been tried in one circum-
stance or another. My aim in this chapter is not to explore the
entire spectrum but rather to identify the three most important
types of conflict management responses that have been (and the
two that are) employed in the Canadian state. These, I shall
argue, broadly conform to the well-known theoretical models of
consociationalism, federalism and control.

CONSOCIATIONALISM

The great ethno-linguistic cleavage that runs through the very
heart of Canada is generally portrayed as that which separates the
English-speaking majority from the French-speaking minority.
This simple characterisation, however, is misleading in several
important respects. Not only are there other important cleavages
of region and ethnicity that must be taken into account, but the
cleavage between the two 'founding peoples' (as the French and
English like to call themselves, to the annoyance of others) is in

fact exceedingly complex, and so too are the political bridging mechanisms that have evolved in response to it. Of the latter, the most effective and durable have been either essentially consociational or, more commonly, have incorporated consociational features into their design – often in cases where the original intent was quite the opposite. Consociationalism, indeed, has rarely if ever been a preferred option in Canada; rather, it has generally been resorted to reluctantly and grudgingly as a second choice after other options have failed, or adopted as a default position when no agreement could be reached on any alternative. But for this to be understood it is essential to look briefly at the underlying facts of demography and history, which tend to be variously interpreted but which are never far beneath the surface of Canadian constitutional and political arrangements.

The uneven geographical distribution of the two main linguistic groups, combined with Canada's federal system of government, ensures that both groups constitute minorities within significant political jurisdictions: thus the French are a minority (25.1 per cent) in Canada as a whole and the English are a minority (11.5 per cent) in Quebec. Municipal boundaries and regional concentrations further complicate the pattern: the city of Westmount, for example, is a separate English-speaking municipality entirely within the boundaries of the predominantly French-speaking city of Montreal, and elsewhere in Quebec there are English-speaking enclaves; in New Brunswick (67.7 per cent English) the French-speaking Acadians are a minority in the province as a whole but constitute a majority in its northern region; in Ontario (84.2 per cent English) there are predominantly French communities, containing English-speaking minorities, in the regions contiguous to Quebec; and in other English-speaking provinces there are French-speaking enclaves of varying number and size.

In consequence, both French and English tend to share at least one common approach to issues of language. That is, both are prone to assert their right to linguistic dominance, as a majority, in some places or circumstances, and their right to special protection, as a linguistic minority, in others. Hence, the premier of Alberta (a province where the French constitute 1.2 per cent of the population) rails against 'enforced bilingualism', a generic linguistic grievance that covers everything from the composition of the federal civil service to the labelling of breakfast cereal boxes; in Sault Ste Marie, Ontario, local councillors (led by a mayor of Italian origin) redundantly declare their predominantly English-speaking municipality to be 'English only'; a member of the Franco-Manitoban minority, having received a traffic ticket printed in English only, takes his case all the way to the Supreme Court of Canada and wins, forcing Manitoba (2.8 per cent French) to undertake the costly task of translating more than a century of statutory regulations into French; while in Quebec officials of that province's *Commission de protection de la langue français* (reviled by the English minority as Orwellian language police) go about enforcing a unique 'inside/outside' language law which prohibits the commercial use of English on the outside but permits it on the inside of stores in displays where the use of French is 'markedly predominant'. Such rumblings are the raw material of ethnic conflict. They are rooted in interests that are not easily reconciled within any system of democracy that relies simply on the principle of majority rule.

It is also important to recognise that from the conquest of Quebec by Britain in 1759 until well into the nineteenth century the French constituted a clear majority of the Canadian population. The British conquerors, moreover, in spite of their general preference for the anglicisation of colonies, came early to the realisation that in the case of Canada the cost of anglicising a resentful and potentially rebellious French majority by force would be inordinate, and sensibly opted to allow them to continue their way of life relatively undisturbed. This conciliatory approach was eventually codified in the Quebec Act of 1774, a British imperial statute which became the Magna Carta of French-Canada. Under its far-reaching provisions the French were guaranteed official recognition and protection of the distinctive features of their society, including their Roman Catholic religion, language, customs, seigneurial system of land tenure and civil law. In effect, notwithstanding the conquest, because they were a majority of the population of Quebec the Act guaranteed the French a special status within both Canada and the British empire. It did not confer upon them the right to political representation, since no provision was made for an elected legislature; it did imply, however, that under the new regime there would be at least some degree of power-sharing, which in practice meant patronage-sharing. Accordingly, members of the traditional French elite were soon appointed by the governor to a substantial share of offices in the legislative council, judiciary, militia and local administration.

In the Quebec Act, and in the practical accommodations and arrangements that followed from it, there may thus be seen the first cultivation in Canada of the plant of consociationalism. But it was a stunted domestic variant that had to be liberally fertilised with patronage. And the French were never to forget that it was their position as a majority that had originally secured for them the benefits they derived from it.

Despite this unpromising beginning, by the 1840s, now cross-seeded with representative democracy, consociationalism had been transformed into a vigorous new hybrid that dominated the Canadian political landscape. Again, it was not the first choice of either the English or the French – but it was the second choice of both.

The seminal event that inspired this development was the creation of the Union of the Canadas in 1841. Ironically, the intent of that Union had been not to foster consociationalism but to eradicate it, and to ensure that it would never take root again. This abrupt reversal of British policy was based on the analysis of Lord Durham, who in his 1839 report on political unrest in Canada wrote that he had found 'a struggle, not of principles, but of races; and I perceived that it would be idle to attempt any amelioration of laws or institutions until we could first succeed in terminating the deadly animosity . . . of French and English'. His remedy was a new constitution designed specifically to deprive the French of any share of political power, and so force them at last to abandon their 'vain hope of nationality' and acquiesce in their cultural assimilation. The new legislative union of the provinces of Upper Canada (Ontario) and Lower Canada (Quebec) was accordingly arranged in such a way that the French, who constituted an overwhelming majority in Lower Canada, would be reduced to a permanent minority. Though the total population of Lower Canada was at the time substantially greater than that of Upper Canada, both provinces were allocated an equal number of seats in the new legislature; hence, the combined total of Upper Canadian seats and seats controlled by Lower Canada's English minority would ensure overall English dominance. Calculations of this kind, however, were soon rendered irrelevant by other calculations. Political opinion in Upper Canada was not in fact divided along ethno-linguistic lines but along conservative-reform lines, particularly over the issue of democracy, as expressed in reform demands for 'responsible government' (i.e., control of the executive by the legislature). And it was not long before an astute reform elite correctly calculated that a coalition of reformers and French moderates could also control the legislature – and that this would serve their mutual interests better than any alternative. The architects of the Union thought that they had designed a structure for the domination of an ethno-linguistic minority; but what they had actually designed, unwittingly, was a hothouse for the growth of consociationalism.

Development thereafter was rapid. Faced with a constitution that could easily have ignited a civil war, and recognising the peril for both their peoples, English and French elites negotiated their own power-sharing agreement: in essence, they agreed to form a coalition ministry, share the rewards of office, power and patronage on a pragmatic but roughly proportional basis, and respect one another's rights to internal autonomy in matters of local concern. Despite initial British resistance, and some strong domestic electoral challenges, within a decade English–French coalition government had become the Union's most distinctive feature, the *sine qua non* of political success, accepted as the norm even by extreme conservatives who had once opposed it.

The organisation of the machinery of government under the Union reflected its dual nature. Each ministry was effectively headed by co-premiers, one English and one French, who were the leaders of their respective parties in the governing coalition. (Hence the unique convention of identifying ministries or 'administrations' by hyphenating the names of their co-premiers: e.g., 'the LaFontaine–Baldwin administration'). Most major cabinet portfolios were similarly shared, with a corresponding bifurcation in the bureaucracy that typically extended from top to bottom in government departments (a structure that also facilitated the sharing of patronage). But there were also exceptions for reasons of economy or practicality, and always a high premium was placed on the art of political brokerage. In actual practice, therefore, the working arrangements of the system were often flexible, tailored to local circumstances, and settled through negotiation and compromise. The principle of duality served as a useful guideline, but it was rarely invoked as a doctrine. Even the location of the capital was settled in a pragmatic – yet consociational – fashion: it was agreed to rotate it, biannually, between Quebec City and Toronto. This curious arrangement worked surprisingly well until Ottawa was selected as the site for the construction of a permanent capital in 1866.

Viewed as a whole, the political system of the Union operated unmistakably, if not perfectly, in conformity with the theoretical model now commonly identified as consociational: the two provinces that made up the Union were functionally separate political subsystems, joined only at the top through a form of overarching accommodation between the members of their respective governing elites; proportionality was practised in the distribution of offices and the allocation of government benefits; and at least an informal mutual veto existed through the convention of requiring concurrent majorities in both sections of the legislature to sustain a government in power. Indeed, in view of the Union's broad electoral franchise, its early acquisition of responsible government, and the fact that its first French–English coalition ministry (reform-bleu, LaFontaine–Baldwin) took office in 1842 – six years before the creation of the Swiss federation – it was arguably the very first consociational democracy.

FEDERALISM

The antithesis of a system of democracy built around the principles and practices of accommodation and power-sharing is a system of unqualified majority rule. In English-Canada, once the demographic balance had tipped clearly and irreversibly in its favour, a powerful populist movement arose whose members – known as 'Clear Grits' – demanded precisely that. The reasons for their rise, apart from the obvious appeal (to a majority) of the idea of representation by population, were several: anti-French and anti-Catholic prejudice; the nearby example of the United States; a large influx of British immigrants (who naturally tended to find the Union's tradition of accommodation unacceptably alien and un-British); and, among both agrarian and commercial interests who wanted unhindered expansion into the west, a fear that the preservation of duality would mean sharing that vast new territory with the French. Many English-Canadians were repelled by such notions, continued to regard the Union as a proud achievement, and continued to support a moderate pro-Union elite. But by 1864 the Clear Grit anti-accommodationists had gained sufficient electoral support to disrupt the normal process of French–English coalition-building, resulting in frequent legislative deadlocks and unstable ministries, and pushing the Union to the brink of disintegration.

Hence, when the Canadian federation was formed in 1867 one of the major aims of an influential group of English-Canadian federalists was to roll back the process of power-sharing that had become entrenched in the Union of the Canadas. Some of their number even believed that in the new constitution – which established a Parliament based on the principle of representation by population – they had ensured its total obliteration: 'Is it not wonderful?', the Grit leader George Brown exulted, 'French-Canadianism entirely extinguished at last!' To Brown's chagrin, however, the first federal ministry bore a disturbing resemblance to the type of ministry it was supposed to replace: it was a coalition headed by Prime Minister John A. Macdonald, a moderate conservative schooled in the consociational politics of the Union; it included George-Etienne Cartier, the leading French-Canadian politician of his time; and once again it rested on a basis of accommodation across segmental lines.

Nevertheless, though partially disguised by these signs of continuity, the context had changed fundamentally. In the larger federation (now composed of Ontario, Quebec, New Brunswick and Nova Scotia) the French constituted only about a third of the population, and thus were reduced to about a third of the seats in Parliament; the principle of duality was therefore no longer sustainable. In effect, the French were forced to give up the wide range of powers they had shared in the Union and settle for territorial autonomy in Quebec over a narrow range of powers, primarily those affecting civil law, religion, local institutions and culture, that were deemed essential to preserve the distinct character of their society. The long-term result was to discourage French hopes of expansion into western Canada and encourage an enclave-building mentality in Quebec. Federalism, then, represented a significant shift away from dualism and con-sociationalism as responses to ethnic conflict and towards territorial segregation and hegemonic inter-ethnic relations.

The precise extent to which Canada shifted away from con-sociationalism after 1867 is open to question, with the answer depending on the interpretation that is placed on French-

Canadian participation in the federal government. There can be no doubt that after 1867 the constitution and the formal structure of the national government became overwhelmingly majoritarian in character: a prime minister, rather than co-premiers, headed the executive; the House of Commons was a replica of Westminster, with all members elected from single-member constituencies by simple plurality; elections were fought between national parties on a winner-take-all basis; equal regional representation was entrusted to an ineffectual appointed Senate, useful mainly as a source of party patronage; apart from minimal French and English language guarantees and a few provisions relating mainly to denominational education, there was no constitutional recognition of group rights; and, in general, there was no provision of the institutional sites for inter-elite bargaining that are normally present in consociational systems.

In Canada, however, constitutions seldom work as intended, and the 1867 constitution was no exception. To understand the Canadian system, and particularly its conduct of inter-ethnic relations, it is essential therefore to look beyond the formal machinery to the informal processes and operational norms that prevailed in the day-to-day practice of politics. These were complex, variable, and frequently disputed – but they also contained a substantial element of consociationalism.

Above all, consociationalism came to reside within the national political parties. For it was there that politicians from both subcultures made the bargains and accommodations they believed necessary to maintain the federal system (and also, it might be added, to have any hope of attaining the constitution's modest ideal of 'peace, order and good government'). Both recognised the perils of fragmentation inherent in a winner-take-all system, and devised arrangements to mitigate the worst effects. In practice, this produced a form of party competition that tended to be relentlessly distributive, oriented to the proportional sharing of material benefits, and patronage driven. Writing in 1906, the French political scientist André Sigfried observed of Canadian elections:

> Whoever may be the winner, everyone knows that the country will be administered in the same way, or almost the same . . . [but] let a question of race or religion be raised, and you will immediately see most of the sordid preoccupations of patro-

nage or connection disappear below the surface. The elections will become struggles of political principle, sincere and passionate. Now this is exactly what is feared by the prudent and far-sighted men who have been given the responsibility of maintaining the national equilibrium. Aware of the sharpness of certain rivalries, they know that if these are let loose . . . the unity of the Dominion may be endangered. That is why they persistently apply themselves to prevent the formation of homogeneous parties . . . a French party, for instance, or a Catholic party. . . . The clarity of political life suffers from this, but perhaps the existence of the federation can be preserved only at this price.

The great Canadian political invention of the nineteenth century, the historian Frank Underhill concluded, was not the constitution but 'the composite bi-racial, bi-cultural party, uniting both French and English voters'.

Because French-Canadians tended to be more cohesive in their voting behaviour than other Canadians (who were inclined to subdivide along regional, religious and economic lines) their support became the key to national political power. The dominant national party thus became the one that could best appeal across segmental lines, and particularly to Quebec. Electoral success depended on the acceptance of power-sharing conventions that made the winning party, in effect, a grand coalition in which the French were proportionately represented. This was not always possible, but it was the ideal, and any major deviation from it was always perceived as a weakness. As a result, first under the Conservatives and then under the Liberals, Quebec members occupied roughly the same proportion of federal cabinet posts (30 per cent) as Quebec's proportion of the population. By 1887 the Liberal Party was led by a French-Canadian (Wilfrid Laurier, Prime Minister 1896–1911), and since then the Liberal leadership has rotated between French and English (King–St Laurent–Pearson–Trudeau–Turner–Chretien). Usually, when an English-Canadian is prime minister, a senior cabinet minister from Quebec will be recognised as the 'Quebec lieutenant', with special responsibilities and powers over all federal projects affecting his own province.

Moreover, since party rule took hold early in Canada, it naturally imparted a certain consociational colouring to the

evolving *modus operandi* of various components of the government. The prevalence of party patronage after 1867 ensured a
roughly proportional sharing of federal public service appointments (eroded by reforms in 1918 but restored after 1966 by
federal bilingualism policies); the tradition developed of
appointing English–French 'co-chairs' of Royal Commissions
(commonly used in Canada to recommend national policies or
defuse contentious national issues). Proportionality gradually
came to be the rule in many national offices, from the Supreme
Court to the boards of Crown Corporations and regulatory
agencies; and rotation became the norm in the holding of
symbolically important offices, including those of Governor-
General, Speaker of the House of Commons, and Chief Justice of
the Supreme Court. In addition, the elevation of the First
Ministers' Conference (a meeting of the federal prime minister
and the ten provincial premiers) into a role of major significance,
a key locus of inter-elite bargaining, became a further important
manifestation of consociationalism in practice.

   While these developments have characterised the normal operation of the Canadian federal system, it must also be observed
that at times of crisis that system has exhibited a pronounced
tendency to lurch in the direction of majority rule. In Quebec,
where the French-speaking population constitutes a distinct
society with its own powerful provincial government to represent
its interests, majority rule inevitably produces 'Quebec versus the
rest of Canada' conflicts that Quebec can only lose. There have
not been many of these, but in each – over the suppression of the
Metis rebellions in the west and the execution of the Metis leader,
Louis Riel, in 1885; over the use of French as a language of
instruction in the schools of Manitoba in the 1890s; over the
imposition of conscription in two world wars; and over the
amendment of the constitution in 1982 – the result has been the
same: the isolation of Quebec, in spite of the presence of Quebec
ministers in the federal cabinet, and a serious strain on the fabric
of national unity.

CONTROL

One interpretation of these events is to treat them as evidence of
an essentially hegemonic relationship between English-Canada
and Quebec; as showing, in other words, that inside the

Canadian federal state's velvet glove of consociational democracy lies the iron hand of English-Canadian domination. Arguing thus, Gordon E. Cannon maintains that although 'the minority French sub-culture has had a constant representation in the national cabinet . . . this representation has been more symbolic than substantive' (Cannon 1982). After 1867, he concludes, 'consociational practices disappeared', and did not reappear until the 1960s, when Canada reverted to a 'semi-consociational' condition. During the intervening century, he seeks to show, the analytical concept which best explains Canadian inter-ethnic relations is not consociationalism but rather the 'control model' as defined by Ian Lustick (1979).

The control model offers an alternative explanation of the existence of stability in deeply divided societies, only in the cases considered stability is maintained not through power-sharing but through domination: specifically, through the 'sustained manipulation of subordinate segment(s) by a superordinate segment'. Some of the examples cited are South Africa under apartheid, Jews and Arabs in Israel, Mestizos and Indians in Bolivia, and Arabs and Kurds in Iraq.

Lustick enumerates seven variables which fundamentally define the model and differentiate it from consociationalism:

1 Resources are allocated according to the dominant group's interest 'as perceived and articulated by its elite' rather than through inter-elite accommodation.
2 Linkage between the groups is 'penetrative': the dominant group 'extracts what it needs . . . and delivers what it sees fit'.
3 There is an absence of the 'hard bargaining' between subcultural elites that characterises consociational systems.
4 The 'official regime', or state apparatus, is not a neutral umpire in ethnic conflict but instead acts as 'the administrative instrument of the superordinate segment or group'.
5 The existing political order is legitimated by the ideology of the dominant group, rather than by reference to the 'common welfare'.
6 Relations between elites are 'asymmetric' and the major concern of the dominant group's elite 'is to devise cost-effective techniques for manipulating the subordinate group'.
7 The 'visual metaphor' is a puppet on a string rather than a balanced scale.

Cannon applies each of these variables to English–French relations in Canada and finds that each supports his control hypoth-
esis. The value of such an exercise is that it calls attention to
certain economic and socio-psychological dimensions of inter-
ethnic relations that are too often overlooked in applications of
the consociational model, which tend to be primarily political in
focus. To that extent the control model provides a fresh and
illuminating perspective on some important aspects of English–
French relations. But, as an interpretation of the operation of the
Canadian federal system between 1867 and 1960 it is deficient and
unconvincing.

What it fails to take into account is that Canada – in sharp
contrast to the control regimes identified by Lustick – was a fully
functioning parliamentary democracy in which the French-
Canadian minority enjoyed equal political rights. Their
Members of Parliament therefore possessed the same democratic
legitimacy – conferred upon them by their success in free
elections – as their English counterparts; and they were proportionately represented in the executive not at the discretion of
the majority, or as part of some elaborate scheme of manipulation, but because effective governance, indeed even the very
survival of the federation, was not possible without them – as
every brief departure from that norm so clearly demonstrates.
The maintenance and gradual expansion of consociational
practices such as rotation in office, proportionality and co-
chairing were likewise matters of *realpolitik*, pursued, usually
with no great enthusiasm, because there was no practical
alternative to power-sharing. Federalism, moreover, ensured the
French-Canadians of a secure territorial base in Quebec, where
they constituted the politically dominant majority. The difference between their political status and that of subordinate ethnic
groups in South Africa, for example, or Israel, is thus so extreme
as to invalidate their inclusion in the same regime category. To
do so is to contemplate not the past but only some imaginary
future: of the National Party in Pretoria rotating its leadership
between white and black South Africans, or Arabs being proportionately represented in every Israeli cabinet.

Where the control model does apply in the Canadian case,
however, is as an explanation of relations between non-aboriginal
Canadians (French *and* English) and the aboriginal peoples.
While the latter were not party to the original Confederation

agreement of 1867 – in which the only mention of them is a brief statement placing 'Indians and Lands reserved for the Indians' under federal jurisdiction – soon thereafter a system of inter-ethnic domination and manipulation was erected which, point by point, is brilliantly illuminated by Lustick's model.

An extended application is beyond the scope of this chapter. The following brief outline, with references to Lustick's seven variables, is intended only to indicate the closeness of the empirical fit.

1 The Canadian federal government (in which aboriginals played no part) assumed responsibility for the allocation of resources whose control was contested, including the greatest resource of all, the land itself, and unquestionably acted purely in the interests of the dominant white majority. Native leaders were coerced or manipulated into signing vaguely worded treaties which were then deemed to constitute the complete surrender of territorial rights over vast areas (and which have since become the subject of interminable litigation). The result was the progressive marginalisation of the aboriginal people onto 'reserves' where they were treated, legally and for all practical purposes, as wards of the federal state.

2 Linkages between the dominant English and French groups and the aboriginal peoples were grossly unequal, 'penetrative in character', and starkly extractive.

3 No genuine hard bargaining took place between non-aboriginal and aboriginal elites, and any attempt by the latter to engage in such bargaining was taken to 'signal the breakdown of control' and suppressed.

4 Representatives of the official regime (for example, the Department of Indian Affairs, the Royal Canadian Mounted Police, the courts, the military and reserve administrators) were enforcers rather than umpires, their offices 'staffed overwhelmingly by personnel from the superordinate segment'.

5 The dominant group's 'well-articulated group-specific ideology' was a self-serving blend of Christian religiosity and possessive liberal individualism which equated 'progress' with the conversion of 'savages' and the material advancement of 'white civilisation'.

6 The main legal instrument used to put into place 'cost-effective techniques for manipulating the subordinate group'

was a comprehensive Indian Act which, in effect, gave control of aboriginal affairs to federal bureaucrats, undercut traditional aboriginal methods of government, and substituted a system of clientage.

7 The visual metaphor, at best, was that of 'a puppeteer manipulating his stringed puppet'; at worst it was of an endangered species whose forest habitat was being clear-cut by loggers.

This was the system that prevailed for approximately a century, but it prevails no more. It began to unravel in the 1960s, and since 1982 – a year which in this as in so many other respects marks a Canadian constitutional and political watershed – it has all but collapsed. As in 1867, the aboriginal peoples were not participants in the negotiations leading up to the 1982 Constitution Act; this time, however, their exclusion roused them to mount a furious protest. At the time it seemed to have failed: their interests were ignored in the new Charter of Rights and Freedoms (apart from a brief statement 'affirming' the existence of their rights but not defining them), and some of the tactics they adopted (such as appealing to the Queen and the British Parliament) seemed self-defeating and naive. But their efforts nevertheless turned out to have far-reaching consequences. International as well as national attention was attracted to the aboriginal cause, which gained the support of environmental movements and others concerned with the world-wide treatment of aboriginal peoples. Most important of all, it galvanised the hundreds of aboriginal groups in Canada – whose political efforts in the past had always been hampered by their geographical separation and their many differences of language, culture and economic interest – into an unprecedented level of cohesion and support for national aboriginal organisations. These in turn gave rise to a new highly educated and politically sophisticated aboriginal elite who are better equipped than their predecessors to deal on equal terms with their French and English counterparts. As one of their number, Chief Ovide Mercredi, leader of the Assembly of First Nations, explains: 'We are a product of your educational system. We have studied Greek and Roman philosophy. We have studied Western civilization; we have memorized in your schools the historical events of your people. We know you exceedingly well.' They also know the intricacies of the

Canadian constitutional process exceedingly well. Mercredi in particular has few equals in his mastery of the techniques of television politics. Articulate, moderate, well-briefed – and, like other leading national politicians, French or English, supported by an entourage of professional policy advisers, speech-writers, image consultants, and organisers – he has become a key figure at the constitutional bargaining table, *de facto* the equivalent of a provincial premier.

The aboriginal peoples have thus terminally disrupted the long consociational minuet that Canada's English and French elites have so exclusively and obsessively danced with one another. Included in the understanding between those two partners, central to their shared conceit as 'founding peoples', was a belief in their mutual right to exert a regime of control over the original inhabitants of the land. But that understanding has collapsed, and so has the regime it once sustained. In the bargaining for a new inter-ethnic accommodation all of the moral high ground and much of the constitutional initiative has been seized by the aboriginal elite, who have become the hardest bargainers of all. Though they represent less than 5 per cent of the population, it is unlikely that any new accommodation can be reached unless it explicitly includes them and has their support – which means it will have to include aboriginal segmental autonomy (which they demand as their 'inherent right to self-government'), a broad land-claims settlement, and constitutional guarantees that recognise their special status as a 'distinct society'.

TWO CONCEPTS OF DEMOCRACY

Today the unresolved tension in Canadian federalism is not between consociationalism and control, democratic and non-democratic alternatives, but between two equally legitimate and historically rooted conceptions of democracy. One, widely but not passionately held, has at its core the idea of democracy as power-sharing. The other, also widely held and articulated with growing vehemence, has at its core the idea of majority rule.

The idea of democracy as power-sharing is present with distinctive variations in the political cultures of French and English Canada, and also in the political cultures of the aboriginal peoples. It rests on a set of assumptions about the nature of civil society that is essentially conservative. It accepts the primacy of ethno-linguistic identities; it believes that a large measure of autonomy in the conduct of local affairs is the surest guarantee of individual liberty; it understands federalism as a 'community of communities' in which each province or community is entitled to 'special status' in matters of particular concern to it, in which anomalies are tolerated, and group rights protected; it sees government as best serving its citizens in a distributive rather than a visionary capacity; it believes in a politics of security, where there are only incremental gains and losses; it believes in government through accommodation and compromise, and in leaving democratically elected leaders the room to bargain in good faith. It is, in short, essentially consociational.

The idea of democracy as majority rule arises out of the Anglo-American tradition of liberal individualism, and while it is perhaps most widely held in western Canada, it is present everywhere, even among a minority of aboriginal Canadians, and has many adherents in Quebec. It views citizenship as the only legitimate basis of political identity; it believes in equal legal rights for all citizens, guaranteed in the constitution and uncompromised by the protection of minority-group interests; it believes in the primacy of national goals (whether of Canada or, in the case of Quebec nationalists, of Quebec) over local particularisms; it either sees federalism as a replica of the United States, giving all provinces exactly the same legal powers and equal representation in a popularly elected Senate, or (in the case of Quebec nationalists) rejects it altogether; it sees the federal government (or, in the case of Quebec nationalists, the Quebec government) as the main bearer of the national vision; it believes in a politics of principle, a contest of opposing ideas where compromise is tantamount to the surrender of integrity; it believes in the use of referendums, and in political leaders who derive their authority from a popular mandate. It is, in short, populist and majoritarian.

The periodic crises and sudden lurches away from a consociational norm that I have suggested characterise Canadian national politics, (and which present students of comparative politics with so much difficulty in categorising the degree to which Canada is consociational), should be understood also as lurches toward a competing conception of democracy. That conception too pre-dates confederation, its modern exponents echoing with uncanny if generally unconscious fidelity the rhetoric of the Clear Grits of the mid-nineteenth century. They appeal to the same majoritarian impulse, the same suspicions about a system that operates so differently from the ideal of American democracy, and the same impatience with the time-consuming rituals of accommodative politics.

Their periodic success is not hard to explain. Power-sharing is always a labour-intensive political activity, producing outcomes that have to be patiently crafted; it often appears impossibly slow and inefficient; and neither its processes nor its outcomes are easy to justify by appeals to simple, well-understood legal or political principles. It is not surprising that Canadians occasionally become frustrated with it. But when the majoritarian impulse is not resisted and majoritarian solutions are imposed the results are invariably the same: first, a breakdown of inter-ethnic relations that threatens the very existence of the federation; and second, a long and painful effort to find a new consociational balance that will repair the breach of trust between the affected communities.

THE PROSPECTS FOR A NEW ACCOMMODATION

The immediate cause of the current breakdown is the controversial 1982 Constitution Act that was forced through over the strenuous objections of the aboriginal peoples and, in breach of a long-standing convention, without the consent of the Quebec government. Ironically, at the time the leader of the Liberal Party and prime minister was a French-Canadian, Pierre Trudeau, and Quebec was as usual proportionately represented in the federal cabinet. Trudeau's position was that he and the other Quebec ministers were entitled to speak for Quebec, and that the Quebec government (then controlled by the separatist Parti Québécois) would obstruct any federal attempt to change the constitution. In particular, the Quebec government could hardly be expected to support the entrenchment of a Charter of Rights which included minority language and education rights, since these might be used by the English minority in Quebec to challenge that province's French-only laws. Originally seven of the other nine provincial governments had sided with Quebec, but, faced with Trudeau's threat to by-pass them and hold a national referendum on the issue, they reached a compromise with the federal government and switched sides. The effect was the political isolation of Quebec, creating a sense of betrayal among Quebec's French majority and awakening old fears of English domination, some no doubt genuine, some no doubt fanned by the Parti Québécois. In 1984 the federal Liberal Party (now led by John Turner) was swept out of office, losing virtually all of its Quebec seats.

The new Conservative government's remedy, which it hailed as a measure of 'national reconciliation,' was the 1987 Meech Lake Accord – a package of proposed constitutional amendments, supported by all ten provincial premiers in office at the time, that was designed to entrench English–French power-sharing (hitherto mainly a political convention) more firmly in the constitution. It also sought to make power-sharing more difficult to abrogate by restoring the principle of minority veto and explicitly recognising Quebec as a 'distinct society'. But the Accord was widely opposed, especially outside Quebec, and expired in 1990 when it failed to obtain unanimous provincial ratification. In retaliation, the Quebec government boycotted further constitutional negotiations and threatened to hold a referendum on sovereignty if no acceptable offer was forthcoming from English Canada.

After a seemingly endless procession of federal and provincial commissions, public forums and parliamentary committees – their hearings televised, their reports voluminous, their proposals mutually contradictory – a new federal proposal was presented which the Quebec premier deemed acceptable as a basis for renewed negotiations. As a result of those negotiations a new agreement, known as the Charlottetown Accord, was reached in 1992. This document was substantially broader in scope than the Meech Lake Accord in that it included, in addition to the recognition of Quebec as a 'distinct society', a number of provisions designed to meet the demands of 'non-Quebec' ethnic and regional interests. These provisions included a formal recognition of the native peoples' 'inherent right to self-government' and (mainly as a concession to the Western provinces) a new American-style elected Senate in which all provinces would be equally represented. In spite of the endorsement of the Quebec government, public opinion in Quebec was overwhelmingly opposed on the grounds that the new Accord offered Quebec too little; while in English Canada, predictably, it was opposed on the grounds that it offered Quebec too much. Also, like the Meech Lake Accord, it provoked the hostility of a diverse coalition of individuals and interest groups who refuse to accept any compromise that gives constitutional recognition to ethnic or linguistic differences, holding instead to an ideal of 'equal citizenship' – their commonly used code for majority rule. When submitted to the people in simultaneous referendums held on 26 October 1992, the Charlottetown Accord was resoundingly defeated in both Quebec and English Canada.

The result is a constitutional and political vacuum that is unlikely to remain unfilled for long. It also seems increasingly clear that if any future accommodation is to succeed it will have to transcend (as the Charlottetown Accord attempted but failed to do) both the majoritarian morass of 1982 and the consociational exclusivity of the Meech Lake Accord. It will have to satisfy the government and people of Quebec that their national interests will continue to be best served by their partnership in the federation – and satisfy the governments and peoples of the other nine provinces that whatever is agreed upon is not a sell-out to Quebec; it will have to broaden the base of power-sharing to include an aboriginal 'third order of government'; and it will have to reassure the many Canadians who are of neither English nor French origin that it is not a scheme to preserve the power of an English–French elite cartel. There are a number of reasons why a broad power-sharing accord of this kind will be difficult to reach.

First, in Quebec ethno-nationalism mixed with majoritarian democracy has produced a potent ideological force that is totally inimical to power-sharing. Its main vehicle is the separatist Parti Québécois (the major opposition party in the Quebec National Assembly) whose leader, Jacques Parizeau, argues the case against federalism and consociationalism with lucidity and frankness: both Quebec and Canada would benefit, he maintains, if each were subject only to the wishes of its own majority, free of the illogic and contradictions of divided sovereignty and the immobilising entanglements of linguistic duality. There can be no doubt that popular support for this position has been strengthened by the failure of the Meech Lake and Charlottetown Accords.

Second, the failure of those Accords demonstrates that majoritarian sentiments are also extremely strong in English-Canada, perhaps especially in the west but elsewhere as well. One factor reinforcing majoritarian sentiments is the extraordinary popular success of the Charter of Rights and Freedoms. With its ideal of a common citizenship based on equal individual rights, it has become (at least for many in English-Canada) the single most cherished symbol of national political life. Constantly cited, pervasively influential, it signifies the change of an era: it is now common, for example, to refer to 'pre-Charter' or 'post-Charter' politics. Another factor is the critical role played by a group of provincial premiers who preside over provinces with no significant French-speaking minorities (but which otherwise are as disparate as Alberta and Newfoundland). They themselves epitomise their own bailiwicks: unilingual, without experience of the bilingual, bicultural milieu of national institutions, dogmatically attached to a rights-based, quintessentially American view of federalism. They are nevertheless able exponents of the position that Quebec is a province like the rest, entitled to no additional or different legal powers, no special status, no recognition as a 'distinct society' unless the phrase is empty of meaning – subject, in other words, to the will of the majority.

Third, the ethnic composition of Canada has changed dramatically in the past quarter-century through continuing large-scale immigration, particularly from Asia, southern Europe, the Caribbean and Latin America. These new immigrants choose to settle disproportionately in English-Canada, particularly Ontario and British Columbia, and this, combined with a low birth-rate in Quebec, has steadily eroded Quebec's share of the Canadian population. It thus becomes increasingly difficult to justify special French language and education rights or the provision of bilingual government services in provinces where the French minority is outnumbered by other ethnic groups. Moreover, those groups have become increasingly well-established, well-organised and politically active. They like to see themselves as 'Charter Canadians', whose rights to equality of opportunity and protection against racial or ethnic discrimination in employment, housing and social services are at least as important as French–English issues. They also tend to be deeply suspicious of French–English power-sharing – to regard it, in effect, as a cosy deal between two privileged elites to exclude all others from equal participation.

On the other side, in spite of the rejection of both the Meech Lake and Charlottetown Accords, there is also substantial popular support for a constitutional settlement. Many Canadians simply do not want their country to split apart. And if they cannot be politically unified under a single overriding national identity, like their American neighbours, or ethnically homogeneous, they are prepared to accept their diversities, share power equitably, and maintain the overarching accommodations necessary to make the federation work. It is supremely ironic that it is the aboriginal peoples, who were so long left out of the consociational bargain, who have become the essential catalyst in restoring the legitimacy of and energising support for this point of view – perhaps because they, more than any other ethnic group in Canada, have experienced at first hand the consequences of unrestrained majority rule. They are also the inheritors of a long tradition of power-sharing through tribal confederacies, and whenever they have been given the opportunity in modern Canada to practise self-government they have unhesitatingly adopted it. They alone embrace consociationalism as a preferred first choice, an inherently fair and flexible system of democratic government. In the process they have reawakened a general Canadian awareness that the likely alternatives are worse – and that in politics, after all, getting one's second choice is not necessarily a bad outcome.

Chapter 3

Ethnic conflict in the Soviet Union and its successor states

Dominic Lieven and John McGarry

INTRODUCTION

The Bolsheviks came to power in 1917 ill-equipped to govern a multi-ethnic state. Marx had seriously underestimated the strength and durability of nationalist feeling in the modern world and most Russian Marxists expected economic development to bring with it the growth of class consciousness and the decline of any sense of ethnic solidarity. Moreover, unlike their Austrian counterparts, Russian Marxists were not forced to temper their theoretical assumptions about nationalism through practical experience of competing with nationalist currents and movements in a more-or-less open political system. Of the two wings of Russian Marxism, the Bolsheviks, more centralist, more authoritarian and, as regards their cadres, more Russian than their Menshevik rivals, seemed the less likely to show any sensitivity or flexibility in governing the various ethnic minorities of the former Russian empire.

Nevertheless, if Marx's theories provided few guidelines for the practical problems of governing the multi-ethnic Soviet State, they did help to legitimise Soviet control over Moscow's far-flung empire. Nineteenth-century empires were in general dominated by a single nation proclaiming its right to a leading and civilising mission because of its material power, its superior culture and the benefits these would bring to the other ethnic groups within the empire's frontiers. By the mid-twentieth century such arguments could no longer justify the rule of one nation over others. For the rulers of the USSR the existence of a supra- and anti-nationalist ideology justifying the rule of a multi-ethnic party was an important factor in the survival in an anti-imperialist age of what was, territorially, the old Russian empire virtually unchanged.[1] The ability of Marxist–Leninist ideology to combat and compete with nationalist doctrines for the hearts and minds of the Soviet population has always been, and remained until the end of the Soviet regime, very important for the rulers of the USSR. Correspondingly, the discrediting of Marxism–Leninism and the unleashing of democratic forces which took place in the 1987–91 period was bound to have far-reaching centrifugal effects.

Although in 1917 the Bolsheviks paid lip-service to the principle of national self-determination, they reserved this right only to a nation's working class and stressed that the Communist Party, the class's vanguard, alone could speak on the workers' behalf. In fact, force decided which areas of the former Russian empire would come under Bolshevik sway and which would remain independent. Poland fought off a Soviet assault; Menshevik Georgia failed to do so. In the Baltic provinces and Finland, foreign intervention helped to secure victory for Bolshevism's conservative and nationalist enemies, even though Communism had widespread support in these areas, especially in Latvia. Finally, in the mid-1920s, large-scale Islamic resistance to the Soviet regime in central Asia was also crushed, partly through a crafty policy of cultivating the support of local radicals but above all by military means. If a supra-national ideology was one pillar of the Soviet multi-ethnic state, coercion – or control – was from the start a still more important one. None of the Soviet peoples were given, until 1991, any choice as regards membership of the USSR, and force was used ruthlessly against any national group seeking independence. Consciousness that Moscow possessed both the means and the will to repress would-be secessionists was a vital factor in Soviet political stability.

Yet Moscow's policy towards the non-Russians in the 1920s was by no means merely crude and coercive. For this Lenin must take much of the credit. Though deep-dyed in his orthodox Marxist contempt for nationalism, he was no Russian chauvinist and bore no ill-will towards the cultures of the USSR's national minorities. He was genuinely appalled to see arrogant, centralising intolerance developing in the Communist Party officials who made up the new imperial elite and was determined to show both Soviet non-Russians and the colonial subjects of the European empires that the USSR was not Tsarism in new clothes but an association of equal peoples of varying cultures, races and colours. The need for this demonstration was all the more clear because of the failure of socialist revolution in Europe, the USSR's isolation, and Lenin's desire that the Soviet Union mobilise what was later called the 'third world' to overthrow imperialism's headquarters in Europe and North America.

In theory the Union of Soviet Socialist Republics, formed in 1922, was a voluntary association of equal sovereign states which retained the right to subsequent secession. The non-Russian republics were all to be on the USSR's borders, so that secession would not entail chaotic internal boundary changes and population shifts. Each Soviet Socialist Republic (SSR) had its own flag, national anthem, legislature (Soviet) and government. The upper house in the Union's Supreme Soviet in Moscow was made up of representatives of the republics. Under the constitution, the Union government dominated some fields of policy, notably foreign affairs and defence, but certain others were largely reserved to the republics. Although the names, number and boundaries of the republics changed slightly over time, the basic federal constitutional system survived intact for seven decades.

COMMUNIST PARTY CONTROL AND FEDERALISM

From the start much of this federalism was a fraud. The Union was not voluntary and claiming the right of secession was a certain path to a labour camp, if not worse. The Soviets, in theory elected by the local population, were in fact rubber-stamp bodies whose members were nominated by Communist Party officials. Key institutions, such as the army and security police, were tightly centralised. The division of rights and spheres between the centre and the republics was couched in vague legal terms whose meaning was determined by the central authorities. No effective judicial review existed, the courts being totally under the Union Party leadership's control. A federation built on these foundations would have been dominated by the centre in any circumstances: given the fact that the Russian republic was larger in population and resources than all the others put together, Moscow's control was certain.

Probably the most important fact about the Soviet Union's constitution was that whereas the state apparatus was, at least in theory, federated, the Communist Party was not. The Bolshevik leaders made no bones about the fact that the Soviet Union's ruling party was a monolithic, centralised organisation, governed by the rules of 'democratic centralism' which required absolute obedience to Moscow's commands from its members in the republics and regions. Even in Lenin's lifetime it was the party not the state which had ultimate sovereign power in Soviet Russia, and this was embodied in the supreme authority of the party's Politburo and Central Committee over all other institutions. In the 1920s, particularly after Lenin's death, the party's republican, regional and local committees grew rapidly in power, dominating other government agencies at these levels and providing the institutional base for the rise of Stalin, as party general secretary, to supreme power, a process which further undermined the position of the republican governments.

Yet, except during the oppressive period of Communist control under Stalin, federalism was never a complete fraud. The republics, admittedly to somewhat varying degrees, became focuses for local patriotism and loyalty. This was true even to some extent in central Asia, where 'nations' such as Uzbekistan, Tadzhikistan and Turkmenistan were initially largely the product of Soviet administrators' efforts to impose workable territorial boundaries on often nomadic societies of clans and tribes all united in allegiance to Islam. From the outset Moscow was determined to recruit local Communists to fill the ranks of the republican parties and to administer their territories. Especially in the 1920s, but even in the post-Stalin era, Moscow's attitude towards local languages, cultures and schools was considerably less repressive than had usually been the case in the last decades of the Romanov empire.

For a non-Russian ethnic group, having one's own SSR did matter. In 1914, for instance, the Volga Tatars were, economically and culturally, the standard-bearers of Islam in the Russian empire; central Asian peoples, the Uzbeks for example, were well behind them in every way. The reversal of this situation by the 1980s reflected in some measure the fact that Uzbeks possessed their own SSR while Muslim citizens in the Russian Soviet Federative Socialist Republic (RSFSR), like the Volga Tatars, did not. Equally, when the inhabitants of Nagorno-Karabakh demanded the right to return to the Armenian SSR, this demand was fuelled not only by nationalist sentiment or fear of Azeri pogroms but also by the justified belief that membership of their own SSR would provide much better protection for their culture, language and heritage. And, in the wake of democratisation and the abortive coup of August 1991, the SSRs provided the institutional platforms from which various ethnic groups staked and won their claims to self-determination.

STALINIST CONTROL

In the period of the New Economic Policy (NEP) Moscow's respect for local languages and cultures was greater than in any other period of Soviet history but the onset of Stalin's dictatorship dramatically worsened the position of non-Russians. Though the whole Soviet rural population suffered severely under collectivisation, the area worst hit was the largely Russian region north of the Caucasus, together with the Ukraine and Kazakhstan. Five million Ukrainian peasants died in the famine of 1932–3. If possible the plight of the Kazakhs, a semi-nomadic people suddenly coerced into joining miserably equipped and poorly administered collective farms, was even worse; between 1929 and 1936 the number of Kazakh households declined from 1.2 million to 565,000. Hesitation by some local cadres in executing Moscow's murderous policies led to purges. Stalin's sense that he did not totally control the party-state machine was one cause of the 'Great Terror' in the late 1930s, during which most of the USSR's political and cultural elite was exterminated. If terror declined on the eve of the war, between 1941 and 1945 a number of nationalities, including the Crimean Tatars and Volga Germans, were deported *en masse* to Soviet Asia at horrific cost in lives and suffering. After 1945 terror continued, bearing down particularly hard on the middle classes and other suspect groups in the annexed territories of the Baltic republics and the western Ukraine.

Terror was not the only element in Stalin's repression of the non-Russians. The Five-year Plans destroyed the considerable element of local economic autonomy that had existed under the NEP. Centralisation, which inevitably meant Russianisation, was imposed in the cultural and linguistic spheres, while non-Russians were forced to learn crudely distorted versions of their peoples' histories and were in some cases cut off from direct access to their cultural heritages and pushed into the Russian cultural orbit by the imposition of the Cyrillic alphabets. Stalin aimed to create an inward-looking and monolithic society and to root his regime in a crude and xenophobic mass culture, homogeneous in its values and instincts. Anything that was cosmopolitan, independent-minded or that derived its culture from sources other than the Soviet classroom was to be rooted out. The assault on non-Russian elites, on ethnic religions and traditions, on the old Russian intelligentsia, especially its influential Old Bolshevik cohort, on the Jewish population – all these derived ultimately from the same source.

The relationship between the nationalities problem and telling the truth about Stalin that emerged under glasnost was one consequence of these policies. For much of the Russian intelligentsia 'coming clean' about Stalin was virtually the most important touchstone of Gorbachev's good faith. But telling the truth – or even three-quarter truths – about Stalin was bound to have different effects in the Ukraine and Kazakhstan than it did in Moscow. Powerful nationalist movements have been fuelled by memories more distant and less awful than the Ukrainian famine or collectivisation and terror in Kazakhstan.

LIMITED LET-UP

Under Stalin's successors, Khrushchev and Brezhnev, pressure on Russians and non-Russians alike was considerably reduced. The end of arbitrary mass terror and the 'thaw' brought much greater freedom of expression, the rehabilitation of parts of national cultures and a less completely twisted interpretation of history than had existed under Stalin. Indigenisation of cadres got under way again, though a solid convention was established that certain key officials in the republics, the most important being the Party Second Secretaries, should generally be Russian, watchdogs over the activities of the 'native' administrations. Ruling through the medium of local elites made it likely that Moscow would have a more sensitive grasp of local needs and feelings, and that its regime would be less offensive to native pride. A sharp look-out was kept, however, for nationalist tendencies among the republican leaderships: the Latvian First Secretary was, for instance, dismissed for this crime in 1959 and the Ukrainian one in 1972. Repression of even potentially nationalist tendencies among the population remained ruthless, the Brezhnev regime destroying the Ukrainian dissident movement with particular ferocity. The highly centralised Stalinist economic system, tampered with by Khrushchev, was preserved almost untouched under Brezhnev, under whom central planners and all-Union ministries continued to ride roughshod over local needs and sentiment. It was Khrushchev's treatment of the Kazakhs which best illustrated just how ruthlessly the central leadership was prepared to trample on an ethnic minority when it felt that overall Soviet interests so required. The massive Slav immigration into Kazakhstan which resulted from Khrushchev's Virgin Lands scheme turned the Kazakhs into a minority in their own republic. To achieve this, Khrushchev overrode the objections of the Kazakh Party leadership, sacking their republic's bosses and replacing them with Slavs.

There were distinctions between the nationalities policies pursued by Khrushchev and Brezhnev. The former still held to some of the naive vigour and idealism of the revolutionary era. His 1961 party programme proclaimed the old faith that economic development would lead to the rapid erosion of an ethnic sense of identity and to the creation of a truly homogeneous Soviet people. Brezhnev, more conservative and more inclined to listen to those who knew something about ethnic and national realities, confined himself to claiming that an overall Soviet patriotism, as well as culture and values, had come into being and was living harmoniously alongside the pride that ethnic groups legitimately possessed in their own cultures, languages and histories. Brezhnev's overall strategy, which amounted to the satisfaction of the major vested interests and 'trust' in bureaucratic cadres, had an important impact on his treatment of the non-Russian elites. In practice, these elites were given considerable leeway to run their own republics so long as nationalism was kept under control and the local economy's performance was not too disastrous. Liberated from Stalinist purges or Khrushchev's continual shuffling of cadres, free too of a Western-style independent press, judiciary, legislature or public opinion, bureaucrats ruled in an often thoroughly lethargic, corrupt and nepotistic style; and nowhere did corruption, nepotism or the 'sabotage' of the state's economic policy go further than in central Asia.

This was, moreover, not the only worrying development in the non-Russian republics in the Brezhnev era. If stability and inertia ruled triumphant, beneath the surface anti-Soviet feeling remained very strong in the Baltic and western Ukraine, as did the sense of national identity (though not overtly of a specifically anti-Soviet variety) of the Transcaucasian peoples. In central Asia the main long-term concern of the Soviet authorities was that the still overwhelmingly rural, indigenous population was little touched by Soviet culture or values. Demographic trends reinforced this problem. Between 1897 and 1959 the Russian population had steadily increased in relation to other Soviet ethnic groups. Between 1959 and 1979 this tendency was dramatically reversed, at least where Russians were compared with the Soviet Muslim population. By 1979 Muslim birth-rates were over four times those of Russians: indeed, in the 1970s more Muslims than Russians were born in the USSR. Predictions as to future demographic trends are always uncertain but it was reasonable to expect that by the year 2000 roughly 35 per cent of Soviet males of conscript age would be Muslims. The precise long-term political consequences of this demographic trend were impossible to predict but the Soviet leadership under Brezhnev undoubtedly saw the 'yellowing' of the population as a major potential problem for their successors. If the Brezhnev regime had no answer to this problem (or, indeed, to other potential nationalist threats) save increased stress on the nationalities' need to learn Russian, it can at least be said in Brezhnev's defence that his government viewed inter-ethnic tensions more realistically than had any of his predecessors.

GORBACHEV AND THE LOSS OF CONTROL

When Mikhail Gorbachev succeeded Konstantin Chernenko in March 1985 the nationalities issue was far from being at the top of his agenda.[2] Gorbachev is Russian, and his whole career had been passed within the Russian republic, which may help to explain the insensitivity to the minorities' feelings evident in the early period of his rule. The fact that, to a degree not seen for decades, Gorbachev's Politburo was almost exclusively Slav and overwhelmingly Russian may also in part have reflected the

General Secretary's lack of long-established friends and clients in the republican party machines.

Gorbachev was also to some extent a Russian nationalist, if of course one remembers that in the spheres in which he moved the terms Russian and Soviet were often confused. Among the party elite, the Russian patriot was expected to be loyal to the party and to its definition of socialism, though a key element in the latter's appeal was that it represented the 'Russian way' in politics, economics and social values. Gorbachev's programme was in many ways a nationalist one. Until the 1970s Soviet leaders could still imagine that their country, though no doubt behind the West in many respects, was catching up. Since then Moscow had become aware, however, that the gap was rapidly widening again. Gorbachev's main aim was to reverse this trend. Failure to do so would have offended the leadership's self-esteem and self-confidence, its patriotism, and its faith in the Soviet system. The ability to remain a military superpower on a par with the United States would have been undermined. The price of empire would have become too great to bear, first at the periphery in the form of new advances in Africa or subsidising clients such as the Cubans and Vietnamese, then nearer home as the cost of maintaining political stability in Eastern Europe through subsidy, and where necessary invasion, became prohibitive. Domestic tranquillity would also have suffered as battles to divide a shrinking cake between institutions and regions increased and the desires of the Soviet consumer became further frustrated. Public morale and faith in the Soviet regime would have dropped still further, as would non-Russians' sense that they had anything to gain, either materially or in terms of pride, from membership of the USSR.

After Gorbachev's accession, relations between the centre and the republics revolved around a number of questions. In most republics the language issue, linked inevitably to questions of culture and education, loomed large; so, too, did concern over the environment; history, partly the study of the nations' past as a whole but, and more pressingly, searching for truth about the Stalin era, was also an area of conflict. Looming behind the historical issues discussed with increasing degrees of openness was the still taboo question of the original Russian or Soviet annexation and with it of the whole legitimacy of Soviet power.

Above all, however, what united the Soviet minorities under Gorbachev was the effects of his reform programme itself. To a great extent the key to stable nationality relations before Gorbachev came to power was inertia. Plenty of potential grievances existed in most republics but their articulation was not only made very difficult through censorship and repression but also seemingly hopeless, given the regime's intransigence on most points. But a Soviet regime which weakened the censorship and held back its policemen; announced an era of openness and public discussion; denounced both Stalin and Brezhnev; issued ringing calls for legality and democracy; and subsequently permitted democratic elections in the Republics: this regime was bound to awaken non-Russian elements critical of many aspects of Soviet rule. For those interested in maintaining control over the nationalities, perestroika and glasnost came to represent a nightmare.

With openness and subsequent democratisation after the republican elections of March 1990, republican governmental and even party institutions became mouthpieces of local nationalist demands. They exposed a key weakness in the Soviet political system. Up to then federalism had undoubtedly contributed to Soviet political stability through its use of national symbols, its co-option of local elites and its concessions in certain fields such as cultural affairs. The price paid in terms of duplication of administrative institutions and ethnic elites' quiet sabotage of some central policies had been well worthwhile. The republics were, however, nations in embryo, with complete institutions of government, national symbols, a legitimate standing in Soviet law and even a right to secession written into the constitution. As the leaders of some of these republics became spokesmen for nationalist movements, the problems of governing the USSR worsened considerably. Early signs of this occurred in Armenia and Azerbaijan in 1988, although in this case ethnic antagonisms were inter-republican rather than initially directed against Moscow. This was not the case in the Baltic republics which began their campaign against Soviet power around the same time. With the centre becoming increasingly discredited as a result of economic collapse, Gorbachev's failure to strengthen his position through election, and ultimately the disastrous coup of August 1991, republican elites were well positioned to preside over the disintegration of the Soviet Union and the transfer of power to their own power-bases.

THE REGIONAL RESPONSE

As vast differences exist between republics, one approach to the minorities issue under and after Gorbachev is to look at each republic, or at least region, separately.

The Baltic republics[3]

Latvians and Estonians are traditionally Protestant, their histories and cultures strongly marked by German and Scandinavian influences. These former republics are richer, more industrialised and more urbanised than any others. Within their homelands, however, both Latvians (now roughly half the population of Latvia) and Estonians were threatened by low birth-rates and Russian immigration. Both Latvia and Estonia are historically small, well-defined areas which their indigenous population, like the Lithuanian, has dominated demographically since time immemorial. All three republics enjoyed independent statehood between the wars.

Once glasnost was proclaimed and the issue of Stalin put on the agenda, the position of the Soviet authorities in the Baltic was bound to become difficult. The Ribbentrop–Molotov pact, by means of which the USSR acquired Lithuania, Latvia and Estonia, was a piece of diplomatic realpolitik unrivalled in its ruthlessness and, as it turned out, its folly. Nothing that happened in the Baltic republics after annexation reconciled their people to Soviet rule, indeed quite the opposite. Moreover, the people, particularly of the two northern republics, tended to look on themselves as aspirant Scandinavians and to see Soviet rule as having robbed them of a high standard of living. To a greater extent than almost anywhere else in the USSR, Russians were generally not only disliked but also despised.

It is not surprising that the Baltic republics regained their independence first. Both morally and in international law there was no question of their right to this independence. In some ways, however, their fate has been similar to that of the ex-European colonies in the Pacific and the latter's recent history teaches useful lessons. It is true that the Fijians (see Chapter 11) were not first granted independence and then twenty years later – like the Balts – re-annexed by the colonial power as a result of a deal with Hitler. Nor was a large proportion of the Fijian population murdered, deported or forced into emigration. But under colonial rule Europeans acquired large estates in Fiji and imported a huge Indian population to work them, turning native Fijians into a minority in their own country. Upon independence it was natural that native Fijians should seek control over their only ancestral homeland, arguing that the Indians were immigrants whose culture's survival was in any case secured by the existence of a vast Indian motherland to which they could if necessary return. But the slogan of 'Indians go home' in Fiji is no more realistic, or democratic, than the corresponding cry for Ulstermen to return to Scotland, or for Russians to get out of Latvia and Estonia. If the experience of other ethnically divided communities is a guide, stability in the Baltic may in the end require a form of power-sharing with guaranteed control over its own affairs devolved to the Russian community. It will be difficult, however, to sell this idea to Latvians and Estonians just recovering control over their homelands after decades of colonial persecution. But in some ways the most frightening aspect of the ethnic conflict in the former Baltic republics is that it is small beer in comparison to some of the inter-communal explosions which could occur in the bigger republics.

Central Asian republics

The contrast between the history of the Baltic and central Asian republics is almost total. In central Asia republican boundaries have almost no historical legitimacy, loyalty traditionally going to clan and Islam. No modern tradition of statehood exists in these areas and the native population, overwhelmingly rural, is far less skilled, educated or interested in national politics than in the Baltic. It is also much poorer and dispersed over a far greater area. The demographic situation is the precise opposite to that in the Baltic republics, with Muslim birth-rates soaring and Russians actually emigrating from the region in large numbers.

When Gorbachev held his referendum on preserving the union in March of 1991, there was an enormous central Asian vote in favour, and the secession of these republics towards the end of 1991 was reluctant, a result of Russian withdrawal more than a desire for independence. Yet it is unlikely that there will be any going back. Central Asian Muslims are in culture, values and history totally different from Russians. Most of them only came under Russian rule between the 1850s and 1880s, in other words well after Algeria was acquired by France and just before the 'scramble for Africa'. Central Asia's history under Soviet rule has not been happy and plenty of skeletons are buried very shallowly.[4] Already politics in some of these republics, such as Uzbekistan and Tadzhikistan is strongly influenced by Islamic parties. The Muslim territories of the ex-USSR are returning to their traditional place in the Islamic Middle East. As in the successor states to the Ottomans, the collapse of empire and its supra-national ideology will leave a great vacuum. States exist but genuine nations possessing historical legitimacy and ethnic homogeneity do not. The rulers of these states are likely to emulate the ruthless attempts made by the leaders of independent countries in the Middle East to create genuine nations out of disparate clans, regions and ethnic groups whose only overarching loyalty is to Islam. Battles over frontiers and minorities are certain, and larger republics will cast a greedy eye on the oil, gas, gold and other riches of their smaller neighbours. The most that one can hope for is that, as in post-colonial Africa, rulers will decide that the bad frontiers created by imperial powers are better than the anarchy that no recognised frontiers would ensure.

Potentially the most dangerous dispute in the region is between the Kazakhs and the Russians. In Kazakhstan the two communities are almost evenly balanced.[5] The Russians predominate in northern and western Kazakhstan where most of the republic's oil, gas and gold deposits lie. The existing demographic balance between the two communities is, however, fragile since the Kazakh birth-rate is four times the Russian one. Not much love is lost between the two races. Twenty years before Khrushchev flooded Kazakhstan with Slav immigrants, Stalin killed more than a quarter of the Kazakh population in his eighteen-month collectivisation drive. Sixteen years before that the imperial army massacred scores of thousands of Kazakhs in the wake of the 1916 rebellion. If democratic politics develop in Kazakhstan these memories will provide powerful ammunition for demagogues. In northern Kazakhstan violence has thus far been avoided between Cossack revivalism on the Russian side and, on the other, the Kazakh Azat movement, which is dedicated to the republic's territorial integrity and indigenous culture. President Nazarbaev presides intelligently over this bubbling volcano, preaching to all the message that Kazakhstan is a potentially rich country whose economic development depends crucially on inter-ethnic peace. If Kazakhs are inspired to hold back from conflict in the knowledge that the demographic future belongs to them; if Russians can be convinced that their economic lot is better in Kazakhstan than in Russia; then maybe Kazakhstan's peace and unity can be preserved. The odds are certainly against this. A pessimist might compare Russo-Kazakh relations with those between the English and Irish, or indeed to what the latter might be had Cromwell and the famine occurred within living memory.

Ukraine[6]

The situation of the Ukraine and Belorussia is different again, in that these Slav and largely Orthodox republics, whose languages are close to Russian, were viewed traditionally in Moscow both as possible allies and as potentially the easiest targets for assimilation. These hopes strongly coloured the CPSU's policies on cadres, dissent, religion and language, especially in the Ukraine. Matters were, however, complicated by the fact that whereas the bulk of the Ukraine has been ruled by Russia since the seventeenth century, western Ukraine is not only Catholic but was also annexed at the end of the Second World War in the face of bitter local resistance. Of all the evil legacies bequeathed to the Soviet leadership by Stalin, his annexation of the heartland of nationalism in the western Ukraine was one of the most unnecessary and most dangerous. The existence of this alienated national population, linguistic grievances over increasing russification, environmental disasters (Chernobyl) and, above all, the discrediting of the centre and communism in the wake of economic collapse and the abortive coup of August 1991, led to the Ukrainian ex-communist elites also jumping aboard the secessionist bandwagon, to be joined by Belorussia. A referendum in December 1991 recorded massive support for this move.

It was Ukrainian independence which rang the death-knell of the Soviet Union. With the Ukraine gone, a rump Soviet Union became unthinkable except in the short run. Within the rump Russians would not only have been overwhelmingly dominant, they would also have been left virtually alone with the central Asians, something neither side would have relished. Ukraine's secession therefore catapulted a number of other republics towards an independence for which they were unprepared and which they would probably not have chosen of their own volition.

The newly independent Ukraine contains 11 million Russians. It includes the Crimea, a region which has a Russian ethnic majority and the main base of the Black Sea fleet. This region was never Ukrainian before Khrushchev handed it over as an anniversary present in 1954 to celebrate 300 years of Russo-Ukrainian union. At present, except in the Crimea, the Russian community in the Ukraine is relatively quiet, in part because it thinks it will be better fed outside Russia. Eventually, however, there might be pressure from Kiev to create not merely a Ukrainian state but also a Ukrainian national–cultural identity. There certainly will be the need for Kiev to 'rationalise' (i.e., close) many of the inefficient all-union factories and mines which employ the Russian minority. It is not hard to anticipate the fanning of popular resentment both by former Communist officials in the Ukraine and by some politicians in Russia. Meanwhile Russian military leaders, in 1985 still naively confident of superpower status, will within a decade be contemplating the loss of most of their Baltic and Black Sea bases, the division of the armed forces and the collapse of their country. This scenario promises trouble. It is very difficult to predict the lines along which Russo-Ukrainian relations will develop after independence. There is relatively little historical hatred between Russians and Ukrainians (at least central and eastern Ukrainians) on which demagogues could play but plentiful room exists for mutual resentment and misunderstanding in the process of separation. It is conceivable that the Crimea could become the Kashmir of Russo-Ukrainian relations, a prospect which is all the more alarming in that in this case it would be the more powerful country which would be opposed to the territorial status quo. In this situation the logic which has driven Pakistan towards the creation of a nuclear deterrent to preserve its territorial integrity might impel the Ukraine to hold on to the weapons it already possesses. At which point there exists the probability of a wasteful arms race and even the dreadful possibility of all-out war.

Relations with Russia aside, the independent Ukraine faces other difficulties. It will have to integrate diverse provinces with three warring Christian churches and two imperial traditions – one Austrian, the other Russian – which have left very distinct and different marks on contemporary western and central-eastern Ukraine respectively. Chernobyl and the Donbas region are ecological disasters. The government in Kiev will also have to cope with Europe's greatest swathe of rust-belt mines and industries. Donbas miners are half as productive as their equivalents in the Siberian Kuzbas and the Ukrainian coal industry is massively subsidised. Everywhere in Eastern Europe the closure of rust-belt mines and factories presents great political problems, which are exacerbated when it is a government dominated by one ethnic group which is attempting to put workers from minorities out of a job.

The Transcaucasus

The Georgians and Armenians are, like the Belorussians and (most) Ukrainians, Orthodox Christians but similarities more or less stop there. The Georgian and Armenian languages are totally different from Russian; moreover by the standards of the Baltic, Ukraine or central Asia there are very few Russian colonists in the Transcaucasus. Birth-rates are relatively high and no Georgian, Armenian or Azeri had any reason to fear the extinction of his national culture or to struggle against Russians for jobs in the local party or state apparatus. Historically, relations between the Georgians and Armenians on the one hand and the Russians on the other have been relatively good. There was a considerable degree of local consent to the original union with Russia, and the Armenians in particular have good reason to feel that it was their Russian cousins who saved them from extermination at the hands of the Turks.

The main ethnic conflicts in the Transcaucasus do not involve the Russians directly. For Armenians, it is their conflict with Azerbaijan over Nagorno-Karabakh which holds their attention. This region in 1979 contained 162,181 people, three-quarters of whom were Armenian. Nagorno-Karabakh is in Azerbaijan and is wholly surrounded by Azerbaijani territory, though parts of it are close to the Armenian frontier. Initially assigned to Armenia in 1920, the area has been under Azerbaijani rule since 1923, which has been the cause of a number of muted protests from the Armenian population in Nagorno-Karabakh over the last quarter-century.

The onset of Gorbachev persuaded some Armenians that long-held grievances might now be remedied but a monster petition from Nagorno-Karabakh, calling for incorporation into Armenia, was rejected by Moscow in February 1988. For the Politburo, there was no easy solution to this problem. To have refused Armenian demands would have been to poison relations with a traditional friend and to face lasting problems of public order. To have acceded to Armenia's request to annex the region would have infuriated the Azeris and would have invited a spate of demands for similar treatment from other groups equally discontented with the territorial status quo. Arbitrarily to have raised Nagorno-Karabakh's status to that of an autonomous republic or to have subordinated it directly to the RSFSR, also unconstitutional actions if opposed by the Azerbaijani SSR, would have been to risk the impression of bowing to demonstrators' pressure while very probably satisfying none of the parties to the dispute. Moscow responded traditionally by refusing concessions on the territorial issue but directing extra funds to meet the demands of the Armenian population in Nagorno-Karabakh in the fields of education, culture and access to the Armenian media. Not surprisingly, these attempts at Russian 'arbitration' did not satisfy the Armenians and violence escalated, exposing in a humiliating manner the hollowness of claims to have created a 'Soviet people'.

Predictably, after the collapse of the USSR, the dispute between Azerbaijan and Armenia became the first conflict between former Soviet republics to turn into all-out war. The Armenians won the first round in this struggle by driving the Azeris out of Nagorno-Karabakh and conquering a corridor of land between the disputed region and Armenia. No Azerbaijani leadership could, however, accept this result and survive. Baku is therefore counter-attacking in order to regain Nagorno-Karabakh and itself drive a corridor through Armenia to the isolated Azeri province of Nakhichevan. As in some other inter-ethnic conflicts in the former USSR the risk exists that outside powers will become involved. Turkey not only sympathises with the Azeris, a Turkic people, but also has rights recognised by international treaties to uphold the territorial integrity of Azerbaijan. Meanwhile Muslim Iran, nervous at the prospect of instability and even secession in its Azeri-dominated northern provinces, secretly tilts towards Christian Armenia.

Moldavia (Moldova)

In Moldavia outside intervention is even likelier than in the Caucasus. The province was annexed from Romania by Stalin in 1940. To secure Moscow's hold, Stalin added to Moldavia a strip of land on the left bank of the River Dniester, most of whose population were Ukrainian or Russian. As Moldavia moved towards independence in 1990–1, the self-proclaimed Trans-Dniester region began to assert its right first to autonomy and ultimately, in 1992, reunion with Russia. As is often the case, an initial conflict over language and historical symbols moved into 'small-scale' inter-communal rioting and murder, and by 1992, into outright war between Romanian-speaking Moldavians and the Slavs of the Trans-Dniester region. Solutions to this conflict are complicated by the fact that 40 per cent of the Trans-Dniester population are Romanian-speakers and more than half of the Russian population lives outside the Trans-Dniester area. 'Ethnic cleansing' is therefore already under way. Both Moldavian-Romanian and Trans-Dniester forces are well supplied from former Soviet arsenals. Neither the Russian nor Romanian governments can afford for domestic political reasons to turn a blind eye to the fate of their co-nationals in Moldavia. The Ukrainian government is as directly though more equivocally involved, unable to ignore the claims of Moldavia's Ukrainian minority but terrified that any assertion of Moscow's power in favour of Russians outside the Russian republic could set awful precedents for the Crimea and eastern Ukraine. The threat of all-out war in the cause of 'frontier rectification' from Romania all the way to the Russo-Ukrainian border is a distinct possibility.

Russia

The disintegration of the Soviet empire did not follow primarily from the strength of peripheral secessionist movements. In a rather unusual turn of events, the Russian heartland also opted out of the system in 1990–1, and the victorious section of its elite led by Yeltsin was not interested in maintaining empire by force. Whereas the English nationalist identifies wholeheartedly with the Union Jack and gloried in the British empire, the Russian was always more equivocal in his support for the Tsarist and Soviet empire. In part this is for the simple reason that life under the imperial state, Tsarist and Soviet, has been thoroughly unpleasant for most Russians, who, unlike the English, had never either chosen or controlled the state's rulers. Moreover, unlike most English, the majority of Russians had good reason to believe that they were, in economic terms, losers rather than gainers from empire.

There was also, however, a deeper feeling that the state and its rulers were culturally alien to Russia. The nineteenth-century Slavophiles, on whose ideas so much of later conservative thinking has been based, saw Petersburg's cosmopolitan court and aristocracy, the capital city's western architecture, and the soulless, impersonal rationalism of the imperial bureaucratic machine as deeply un-Russian. When after the revolution there was created a Marxist state which proceeded to destroy the Russian church, village and even language (i.e. Sovspeak) such sentiments grew in force. Represented most famously today by Alexander Solzhenitsyn, they were a powerful factor in the collapse of the USSR. They competed with a more imperial, statist Russian nationalism which gloried in the Soviet Union's superpower status and the size of its dominions.

These two strands of Russian nationalism, mutually exclusive at their extremes, in watered-down form can be found together in individuals, in political parties and in Yeltsin's government. Burdened with the terrible political costs of, first, financial stabilisation and then economic restructuring, both the Yeltsin government and Russia's democratic parties also risk being torn asunder by the question of what support, if any, should be given to the Russian minorities outside the Russian republic. No Russian government can turn a blind eye to the fate of the 25 million Russians who live outside its borders.[7] If, on the one hand, the need for political stability and Western support to achieve economic recovery deters Moscow from extremist nationalism, on the other hand the blows to Russian national pride and self-confidence could in time prove unendurable. The fact that Yeltsin personally and the whole Russian democratic movement can be blamed for undermining the Soviet regime, destroying the Russian empire, and thereby dooming millions of Russians to alien rule is a major extra handicap burdening those who are struggling to create lasting democracy in Russia. The fate of northern Eurasia at least will depend in large part on how Russian nationalism develops in the 1990s.

Russia itself is a vast country of different peoples, and it is possible that it too will fragment along ethnic lines. Already, Chechen-Ingush and Tatarstan have made efforts to ensure that the disintegration of the Soviet empire does not stop at Russia's borders. Indeed it is just conceivable that even the Russian-majority areas of the Russian republic will fragment, as the Spanish community of South America did in the early nineteenth century and the English-speaking Americans almost did in the 1860s. The odds, however, are against this. Fragmentation would run against the whole grain of Russian history. Moreover, feeling threatened and humiliated by non-Russian neighbours, the Russians are more likely to stick closer together than to risk separation. With Moscow in confusion, local autonomy is often not only desired but also a necessity for effective solutions to local problems. It remains a far cry from this to permanent division of the Russian land. In 1942, for instance, Australia and New Zealand discovered that Britain could no longer defend them and found an alternative protector in the USA. That was the end effectively of Britain's Pacific empire. But it is difficult to imagine Russia's Pacific provinces seeking an alternative protector to Moscow and hard to think where they might find one.

The aftermath of the Ottoman empire's collapse presents worrying possible parallels with events in the former USSR. With the empire gone and its imperial Ottoman ideology discredited, Ataturk reconstituted the Turkish rump-state on a national basis. Turkish nationalism, derided and controlled by the Ottomans, was given free rein. The Kurdish minority, unwilling and unable to assimilate into the Turkish nation, was harshly treated. The empire's collapse ushered in a ferocious struggle for the borderlands and it was Ataturk's victory in this war which won him the charisma that underpinned his republican regime. It is conceivable that amidst the ruins of empire somewhat similar developments could occur in Russia.

It is true that the ex-Soviet officer corps lacks the prestige, political experience and maturity of its twentieth-century Ottoman equivalent. The latter had lived through 150 years of decline before 1914 and, through the Young Turk movement, a decade of intensive political activity and education in the years immediately before imperial collapse. By contrast, Soviet generals, like their Tsarist counterparts, were narrow military specialists with little political wisdom or experience. The last few years in Russia have, however, forced the army into politics and have begun to teach its leaders the political art. If the initial White generals in 1918 were political children, by 1920 Wrangel was a much more sophisticated politician from a younger generation that had begun to learn the lessons of the revolutionary years. By the time Wrangel came to lead the White movement victory was beyond the generals' grasp. Lenin had seized his opportunity and ruthlessly consolidated the Bolshevik's grasp on power. This time around there are no Lenins. The time for a Russian Ataturk may well come in the 1990s.

Countering this pessimistic scenario is an increasing awareness in late twentieth-century developed societies that empires do not pay. Germany and Japan, defeated in war and deprived of their colonies, learned the lesson that it is the skills and the work ethic of the metropolitan population, not the possession of empire, which is the key to power and prosperity in the modern world. The responsibilities and burdens of empire and great-power military status are more often a liability than an asset. Intelligent young Russian generals may understand this.

CONCLUSION

On the one hand, obvious benefits could flow from the demise of Communist control in the Soviet Union. The Soviet neo-Stalinist regime was a brutal and incompetent tyranny which criminally mismanaged the country's human and natural resources. In the long term, its demise should allow this vast area of the globe not only to live better itself but also to make the contribution to the world's economic prosperity that the region's vast resources and its peoples' relatively good education warrants. However, it is also clear that the end of the empire has ushered in a period of great instability in relations among the former Soviet peoples. It will require statesmanship of the highest order and a considerable amount of good fortune if any major part of this region is to have a democratic and peaceful future.

NOTES

1 On the transition from Russian to Soviet empire, see R. Pipes, *The Formation of the Soviet Union*, Cambridge, Mass., 1964.
2 R. Karklins, *Ethnic Relations in the USSR*, Winchester, Mass., 1986, is an excellent study of the nationalities issue on the eve of Gorbachev's reforms.
3 For background on the Baltic republics, see R. Misiunas and R. Taagapera, *The Baltic States, Years of Dependence, 1940–1980*, London, 1980.
4 For more details on Islam in the former Soviet Union, see A. Bennigsen and M. Broxup, *The Islamic Threat to the Soviet State*, London, 1983.
5 For background on Kazakhstan, see M. Olcott, *The Kazakhs*, Stanford, 1987.
6 For a good review of pre-Gorbachev politics in the Ukraine, see B. Krawchenko, *Social Change and National Consciousness in Twentieth-century Ukraine*, London, 1985.
7 Here potentially is fertile ground to be exploited by chauvinist politicians in Moscow. The role of just 1.5 million Pieds Noirs in Algeria or 900,000 Ulster Protestants is a warning of just how significant these 25 million Russians could be.

Chapter 4

Ethnic conflict in India
A case study of Punjab

Gurharpal Singh

INTRODUCTION

The assassination of Rajiv Gandhi on 21 May 1991 dramatically highlighted the increasing levels of ethnic violence in India. Twice within seven years a member of the Gandhi 'dynasty' had fallen victim to assassins aggrieved at the Indian state's ethnic policies. Paradoxically, Rajiv Gandhi's death and the sympathy vote it generated for the successful Congress-I party in the national elections (June 1991) helped to disarticulate, for the time being at least, an even greater ethnic threat to the Indian political system: that posed by the Bharatiya Janata Party (BJP), the Hindu revivalist party and its commitment to create a Hindu state. Violent ethnic conflicts which once occupied a peripheral space in Indian politics (Kashmir, Punjab, Assam, Nagaland) have increasingly become embedded in its core. In the short and medium term the future of Indian democracy seems to be largely contingent on its ability to resolve these conflicts.

This chapter examines the prospects for the Indian state to arrive at such a conclusion by undertaking a detailed evaluation of its ethnic conflict management policies in the north-western state of Punjab. Along with Kashmir, the Punjab represents one of the most pressing problems confronting the Indian state. The last seven years have seen a formidable array of initiatives in an attempt to solve the Punjab question. Consequently a case study of Punjab provides valuable lessons for ethnic conflict management in south Asia. The rest of this chapter is divided into five sections: section one outlines the framework within which ethnic conflict has been regulated by the Indian state since 1947; section two examines the causes of ethnic conflict in Punjab; section three evaluates the post-1984 political initiatives that have been attempted to solve the Punjab question; section four reflects on the immediate short-term implications of these initiative failures; and finally, in light of the previous sections, the conclusion advances new proposals that might provide the basis for a constructive re-evaluation of the Punjab question.

THE INDIAN STATE AND ETHNIC CONFLICT MANAGEMENT SINCE 1947

India is the most ethnically diverse society in the world. The complex stratification of caste unique to it is also overlaid with equally complex identities of language, religion and regionalism that straddle imprecise geographical boundaries (Phadnis 1990). Yet comparatively, the intensity of ethnic conflict since 1947 has been relatively low. More remarkably, this diversity has co-existed with the model of a third world democracy. Explanations of this achievement in the main fall into two schools of thought: the instrumentalist and the primordialist (Taylor and Yapp 1979).

Instrumentalists maintain that ethnic identities in India are not immutable but have been shaped and reshaped on a regular basis. In his seminal work on nationality formation in north India, Brass (1974) identified the critical role of ethnic elites in influencing the nature of ethnic identities. The relative autonomy of ethnic elites – as opposed to simply manipulative tendencies – Brass argued, was further enhanced by the character of the Indian state established after independence. Shaped in the image of the Indian National Congress (INC) the new state embodied two key principles: a commitment to secularism and democracy. Whereas the former was viewed as symbolic of India's modernism and indicative of its determination to reject religiously based separatism, the latter introduced corrosive political participation which, it was hoped in time, would undermine solidified ethnic opposition. Indeed, soon after 1947 four guidelines were established for regulating ethnic conflict. First, no secessionist movements were to be tolerated; where necessary they would be suppressed by force. Second, given the commitment to secularism 'no demand for political recognition of a religious group would be considered'. Third, no 'capricious concessions would be made to the political demands of any linguistic, regional or other culturally defined group'. Finally, 'no political concessions to cultural groups in conflict would be made unless they had demonstrable support from both sides' (Brass 1987).

These guidelines were firmly followed by the INC under Nehru's premiership (1947–64), during which he created the 'Congress System' – a dominant one-party system in which the INC combined the function of political development with political competition by espousing a centrist ideology, adopting secularist leadership and allowing considerable autonomy at the state level. Naturally the 'Congress System' incorporated elements of both 'domination' and 'dissent' and in some ethnically plural states like Punjab the INC often resembled an intra-consociational coalition, vertically organising and accommodating hostile ethnic groups. Thus when in the early 1950s the demand for the linguistic reorganisation of Indian states became vocal, despite Nehru's reservations, it was conceded as a fulfilment of the INC pre-independence pledge to reorganise Indian states on a 'modern' basis. In contrast, the campaign for a Punjabi-speaking state led by the main Sikh political party, the Akali Dal, was firmly resisted on the grounds that it was a movement for a political recognition of a religious demand. Only after the Akali Dal reframed its proposal in *linguistic* rather than *religious* terms was the *Punjab Suba* (Punjabi-speaking state) conceded in 1966.

With the election of Mrs Indira Gandhi to the INC leadership, the 'Congress System' and the above guidelines were soon undermined. Mrs Gandhi, in her quest for absolute control of the INC, destroyed the 'Congress System' and, after 1971, power became increasingly centralised in New Delhi, reflected above all by the imposition of the Emergency (1975–7) and the reconstruction of the INC as Congress-I (Indira). Following Mrs Gandhi's return to office (1980), the process of centralisation was accelerated. Power within Congress-I flowed from the centre and the personality of Mrs Gandhi and not from the provinces or the party machine. Opposition state governments were regularly destabilised through the arbitrary use of President's Rule.[1] Congress-I state chief ministers held their posts as a matter of loyalty to Mrs Gandhi; and recalcitrant chief ministers were circumvented by the frequent promotion of dissident Congress-I factions. Within this new framework, the principled management of regional and ethnic conflicts was almost abandoned. In fact by flirting with Hindu communalism as a new hegemonising ideology for the Congress-I, Mrs Gandhi first inflamed religious passion among the Sikhs and then, in a dramatic act in June 1984, put them to the sword. In short, argue instrumentalists, explanations for the rise of ethnic conflict in contemporary India are to be found in the policies and the personality of Mrs Gandhi who systematically dismantled the elaborate framework for ethnic conflict management established by her father, Nehru (Brass 1987).

For primordialists, who maintain that ethnic identities are given and follow inexorably from cultural identities, 1947 resulted in the creation of two ethnic states: Muslim Pakistan and Hindu India (Robinson 1974). At the time a fortuitous conjunction between INC secular elites and the social pluralism of Hindu society negated the need for an explicitly confessional Hindu state. The peculiar version of Indian secularism *Sarva Dharma Sambhava* (equal treatment of all religions) implicitly recognised the hegemonic position of the Hindu community (83 per cent) (Vanaik 1990). Consequently, in usurping the secular discourse, the INC leadership was able to institutionalise Hindu ethnic sentiment through the 'Congress System' and effectively marginalised minority ethnic discourses as 'religious', 'communal' and 'obscurantist'. Moreover, such a coalescence was made possible by the long-term logic of Indian nation-building which required a basic ethnic common denominator. Thus, while the rhetoric of principled secularism officially proclaimed India as a multi-cultural society, its actual implementation was compromised, especially in the case of non-Hindu minorities, with a uniform, homogenising cultural policy (Rudolph and Rudolph 1989). Furthermore, at an executive level this implementation was enforced by a highly centralised Westminster-style political system which was at best 'quasi-federal' and gave the centre considerable residual powers, including the right to impose political closure at state level through President's Rule. Only since the mid-1960s – coinciding with the demise of the 'Congress System' – has the disjunction between the INC's professed aims and actual practice become apparent. This development, insist primordialists, has been reflected most dramatically in the rise of the BJP which eschews Congress's 'pseudo-secularism' for a confessional Hindu state (Malik and Vajpeyi 1989).

The divide between instrumentalists and primordialists is not as sharp as the above account may appear to suggest. For example, whereas the primordialists concede that ethnic identities can be materially affected by the process of modernisation, the instrumentalists on the other hand recognise the ethnic constraints on elite autonomy. Perhaps the key area which remains problematic for the study of ethnic conflict in India is how the developmental role of the Indian state – patterned as it has been on the Soviet model of economic development – has materially affected ethnic identities. In the case under consideration the compulsions towards cultural integration at an all-India level have been strongly resisted by a self-conscious ethnic minority in the Punjab which has experienced rapid economic development following the onset of the Green Revolution.

CAUSES OF ETHNIC CONFLICT IN PUNJAB

On 4 June 1984 the Indian Army, in a meticulously co-ordinated Operation Blue Star, invaded the Sikhs' holiest shrine, the Golden Temple. The objective was to eliminate organised secessionist violence that had plagued the state of Punjab since the early 1980s. Its consequences were the deaths of about 1,000 security personnel and Sikh militants, followed four months later by the assassination of Mrs Indira Gandhi and pogroms against Sikhs in Delhi in which approximately 3,000 people died. Since 1984 almost 17,000 people have died in ethnic-related violence in Punjab. Explanations of the causes of this conflict fall into three categories: (i) regional; (ii) national; and (iii) exogenous (Singh 1987).

Regional: Sikh ethno-nationalism

In the age of 'ethnic revival' it is tempting to explain the conflict in Punjab as a consequence of Sikh ethno-nationalism. Brass (1974) has observed that 'of all the ethnic groups and peoples of north India, the Sikhs come closest to satisfying the definition of a nationality or a nation'. The achievement of a 'cohesive Sikh identity', he adds, has at times the 'appearance of an invincible, solidary, national force'. But these drives towards nationhood, particularly after 1947, were contained by the parameters of linguistic regionalism set by the INC and its alliance with secular

Sikh political elites who successfully divided the community and supported the formation of a *Punjabi Suba*. By the early 1980s, it is argued, the conditions for such an instrumentalist pattern of rule no longer prevailed. Whether by default or design the Akali Dal agitation (1981–4) reopened the Sikh national question, and in the process became a 'freedom movement', a Sikh revolution in the making. Seen in this light, Blue Star was not a security operation, but the clash of two nations, the first 'war for Khalistan' (a separate Sikh state) (Akbar 1985).

The Sikh ethnic revival, it is suggested, is both reactive and modern. It is reactive to four types of discrimination perceived by the Sikh community in India since 1947: constitutional, economic, religious and cultural (Singh 1987). It is modern in the sense that though much of its inspiration derives from historical achievements, its objective is essentially to recreate a unit in which the Sikh community is an effective unit of political power. Since the late 1970s this revival has focused on the Anandpur Sahib Resolution (ASR) that calls for the self-determination of Sikhs in a genuine federal union of Indian states in which the centre's powers are limited to foreign relations, defence, currency and general communications. In addition it is also underpinned by the alleged discrimination against Punjab in the 'unprincipled' linguistic reorganisation of the state in 1966 which led to the exclusion of the state's capital (Chandigarh) and many Punjabi-speaking areas, and the loss of important hydro-electric and river-water resources (Bhullar *et al.* 1985).

Regional: modernisation

A large body of literature which recognises the importance of the ethnic cleavage between Sikhs and Hindus nevertheless isolates the modernising impact of the Green Revolution in Punjab as the critical variable in the rise of ethnic conflict in the state (Singh 1987). The Green Revolution, it is argued, accelerated the emergence of mass society through urbanisation, consumerism, mass literacy, modern communications and the disintegration of face-to-face village communities. Rapid social change outpaced familiar political practices and the ability of institutions to regulate it. In consequence ethnic identities became firmer emblems of social and political competition. For example, Sikh capitalist farmers, who had been the main beneficiaries of the

Green Revolution, challenged the traditional ascendancy of Hindu mercantile capital in the state by articulating their interests through the ASR which was posited as a new developmental order based on decentralisation, ethnic and religious pluralism and the use of ethical incentives to promote development – in contrast to Congress-I's rigid regime of quasi-monopoly party government, industrial domination of agriculture and a socialist distributionist philosophy (Leaf 1985). In short, this perspective maintains that the 'Punjab crisis has not, fundamentally, been a clash between Sikhs and Hindus, nor between Sikhs and Indira Gandhi. . . . It has been a clash between two visions of the future of India's proper political and social constitution' (Leaf 1985).

National: Congress-I

A third set of explanations is provided by the instrumentalist school which emphasises the primacy of Congress-I's role in creating the Punjab conflict. As outlined above, the essential argument is that Congress-I under Mrs Gandhi reversed the guidelines for ethnic conflict management established by Nehru so that by the late 1970s the Congress had negated its political development role and pursued political competition without restraint. When out of office (1977–80), Congress-I actively encouraged Sikh militants in order to destabilise the moderate Akali Dal government. Subsequently, upon return to national power (1980), Mrs Gandhi arbitrarily imposed President's Rule and dismissed the Akali Dal ministry. Further, she persisted with clandestine support for Sikh militants to check moderate Akalis (organised under the Akali Dal but highly factionalised) and the ruling faction within the new Congress-I state government (elected after six months of President's Rule). When in response to these manoeuvres the Akali Dal launched an agitational campaign that gradually assumed the guise of 'Sikh revolution' around the ASR and economic and territorial demands, Mrs Gandhi held several discussions with moderate Akali leaders (1981–3) but made no serious effort to differentiate between their principled and non-principled demands. Ironically, the demands which Mrs Gandhi was prepared to concede were *religious* rather than economic or territorial. In short, according to this perspective, 1984 was not an isolated event but the culmination of ideological and organisational decay that had begun in the Congress with the assumption of leadership by Mrs Gandhi (Brass 1987).

National: modernisation

A fourth set of explanations veer towards a primordialist interpretation by applying the modernisation thesis to India. The Punjab crisis, it maintains, cannot be attributed simply to either Mrs Gandhi or Congress-I but is a reflection of contemporary India, its 'new self', revealing more clearly the contradictions which underlay the consociational 'Congress System', between the INC secular elites and their communal, albeit highly pluralised, Hindu constituency (Vanaik 1990). The modernising process, far from being restricted to Punjab, is evident in wider Indian society through equivalent indicators of urbanisation, mass communications and the disintegration of local communities. This development, it is suggested, has triggered the delayed emergence of a vibrant Hindu ethnicity that has eroded Congress's management of a traditional (religious) following and modern (secular) leadership. Consequently, though Mrs Gandhi and her party made a special contribution to the enfeeblement of the Indian state, their options were limited by the compulsions of competitive politics, especially the politics of opposition parties who were equally unwilling to concede Sikh demands either for reasons of religious sentiment or pragmatic politics. And if the Punjab question ultimately led to disaster, it was because Mrs Gandhi and her party followed the same rules of the game as those pursued by their principal political rivals (Singh 1987).

Exogenous

Finally, there are exogenous explanations which look outside Punjab and India. Although they are often associated with the extreme fringes of Indian politics, the *White Paper on the Punjab Agitation*, published after Operation Blue Star, also drew attention to the 'influence of external forces with a deep-rooted interest in the disintegration of India' (GOI 1984). Implicitly it alleged the involvement of Pakistan; explicitly it listed Sikh militant organisations based in Europe and North America.

Today over a million Sikhs reside outside India, in particular in Europe and North America. The Sikh diaspora has been at the forefront of the ethnic agitation, providing both material and intellectual support for militant groups waging an armed campaign for Khalistan (Barrier and Dusenbery 1989). Arguably, though the latter's interests intersect with those of Pakistan in extending ethnic wars/terrorism in India's peripheral states, this conjunction has often been exaggerated in order to deflect criticism from actual policy failures.

POLITICAL INITIATIVES SINCE 1984

Since June 1984 the Punjab has become a graveyard for political initiatives. The most recent of these was dramatically thwarted by the postponement of Punjab Legislative Assembly (PLA) elections on the eve of polling (21 June 1991). This section examines why the various initiatives have failed to provide a critical breakthrough. A related issue is whether the experience of the last seven years suggests that the Indian state is reverting to the Nehruvian guidelines or following Mrs Gandhi's policy, or developing a third perspective.

Even by the normal turbulent standards of Punjab politics, the years since 1984 have been quite exceptional: they have witnessed quasi-militarisation, endemic terrorism, and an ill-fated attempt to restore the democratic process. A systematic evaluation of these developments remains outside the scope of this chapter. Instead we shall review the political initiatives undertaken to resolve the Punjab question and the responses they have generated among the Sikh community. In the main these fall into four chronological phases: (i) following Operation Blue Star the attempt at a 'Political Solution' associated with the Rajiv–Longowal Accord and the Akali Dal government of Barnala (September 1985 to May 1987); (ii) the ruthless 'Anti-terrorist Solution' identified with the policies of state governor S. S. Ray and the Punjab police chief Julio Rebeiro (May 1987 to November 1989); (iii) the search for a 'Principled Solution' associated with the minority National Front government at the centre of V. P. Singh (December 1989 to October 1990); and (iv), the 'Unprincipled Solution' attempted by the successor to the latter, the minority Janata Dal (S) government (October 1990 to June 1991).

Political solution: the Rajiv–Longowal Accord and the Barnala ministry

Mrs Gandhi's assassination, the election of Rajiv Gandhi as Congress-I leader, and the latter's landslide victory in the December 1984 national elections, were accompanied by a widespread expectation that the new leadership would mark a fundamental breach with the Indira era by re-establishing Nehruvian values. Initially Rajiv Gandhi did not disappoint. He moved decisively to usher in a new regional policy of 'rule by accord' (Nugent 1990). In Punjab the territorial, economic and religious demands that had fuelled the Sikh agitation before 1984, and were held to be non-negotiable by Mrs Gandhi, were recognised in the Rajiv–Longowal Accord. For the moderate Akali Dal (Longowal) (AD(L)) the accord provided a return to democratic politics. For Rajiv it represented a dynamic breakthrough, a befitting start to his 'clean' premiership. Although the accord was open to potentially conflicting interpretations, and suffered an immediate setback with the assassination of Longowal in August 1985, at this juncture there was sufficient commitment among both parties to pursue a political solution.

Longowal was succeeded by Barnala whose ability to transform the 'Political Solution' into an enduring settlement depended upon marginalising Sikh militants by delivering on the accord. In the initial stages he had a promising start by winning overwhelming support for his stance in the PLA elections (September 1985) in which the AD(L) obtained 80 per cent of all Sikhs polled and secured seventy-three seats in the 117-seat assembly. With militants marginalised and a majority Sikh government, most informed observers felt that a rapid implementation of the accord would lead to the return of normalcy in state politics without the regular central intervention that had become the hallmark of Mrs Gandhi's administrations.

However, within five months the 'Political Solution' was in ruins. By early 1986 Rajiv's reforming zeal came to a strategic halt as the Congress-I government at the centre reverted to interference in the AD(L) government for short-term political gains (Nugent 1990). Whereas the centre increasingly viewed the AD(L) administration in terms of *containing* militant terrorism, its *capacity* to do so was undermined by the reluctance of the centre to implement provisions of the accord. The transfer of Chandigarh, scheduled for 26 January 1986, was first delayed, then postponed, and eventually suspended for an indefinite period. Other provisions in the accord (see Table 4.1) were either nullified or produced outcomes hostile to Sikh interests. The ultimate reversal of policy was marked by the appointment of a highly partisan Congress-I state governor and the imposition of President's Rule in Punjab in May 1987. Officially this step was justified on the grounds of prevailing 'chaos and anarchy' in Punjab. According to opposition parties, however, the measure was taken to improve Congress-I's weak position in the impending Legislative assembly elections in the adjoining state of Harayana which was directly affected by the provisions of the accord (Singh 1991).

ANTI-TERRORIST SOLUTION

President's Rule signalled a distinct change in the centre's policy. Henceforth, political solutions were to take second place to executive measures to re-establish law and order. First, the new administration which was directly accountable to New Delhi, was instructed to pursue a ruthless anti-terrorist policy with the aim of eradicating terrorism. Second, the security apparatus in the state was reorganised. In addition to the central reserve police force, the border security force and the regular use of the army, the Punjab police force was strengthened with the creation of new senior posts and mass recruitment at constable level. Third, anti-terrorist legislation – National Security Act (1980), Punjab Disturbed Areas Ordinance (1983), Terrorist Affected Areas (Special Courts) Act (1984), and Terrorist and Disruptive Activities (Prevention) Act (1985) – was rigorously enforced with official approval for police encounters ('shoot to kill') where known terrorists were apprehended. Fourth, counter-insurgency was given a high priority with employment of irregular hit squads intended to infiltrate and liquidate terrorist groups. The new mood of determination was aptly summarised by Rebeiro himself: to give a befitting reply to 'bullets with bullets'.

However, instead of containing terrorism, vigorous anti-terrorism exacerbated the Punjab crisis. The terrorist and state-terrorist killing rate rose sharply from 1,246 (1986) to 3,074 (1988). Police encounters, moreover, politically disarmed the

Table 4.1 Rajiv-Longowal Accord (1985)

Issue	Agreement	Implementation up to 1988
Anandpur Sahib Resolution (ASR)	Referred to Sarkaria Commission	October 1987: Commission report rejects ASR approach to centre–state relations
Transfer of Chandigarh	To be transferred to Punjab by January 1986. Punjab to compensate Haryana with equivalent territory for a new capital. Other territorial disputes to be settled by a commission	Three commissions (Matthew, Venkatar Amiah and Desai) fail to provide an agreement. Strong opposition in Haryana July 1986: Union government suspends the transfer for an indefinite period
Sharing of Ravi-Beas waters	A tribunal headed by a Supreme Court judge to adjudicate. July 1985: consumption as baseline	May 1987: Eradi tribunal reduces Punjab's July 1985 level while doubling Haryana's share
November 1984 Anti-Sikh Delhi riots	Referred to Mishra Commission	February 1987: absolves Congress-I of responsibility; places guilt on Delhi police
Army deserters	To be rehabilitated and given gainful employment	August 1985: of 2,606 deserters, 900 had been rehabilitated
Political detainees	Release of political detainees and withdrawal of special powers	Limited releases: May 1988, 59th constitutional amendment – provision for emergency powers
Religious autonomy	Enactment of an all-India Sikh Gurdwaras Act	Not enacted; May 1988: Religious Institutions (Prevention of Misuse) Ordinance

policy as frequent deaths of innocent individuals touched a raw nerve in the violent culture of rural Punjab. Increasingly the anti-terrorist machinery resembled a non-accountable police state whose regular pronouncements that the end of terrorism was imminent were treated with incredulity by professional observers. In the event even Rebeiro confessed failure. Terrorism in Punjab, he admitted, could not be eliminated by anti-terrorism. Above all, it required a 'political solution'.

More seriously the anti-terrorist solution had a profound impact on the course of Sikh politics. In a short space of two years the moderates in the AD(L) were sidelined by the emergence of a more radical leadership under Akali Dal (Mann) (AD(M)) which forged close links with armed militant groups. Rejecting the Rajiv–Longowal Accord and exploiting the mass sentiment against the anti-terrorist policy, the AD(M) quickly established control over the institutions and structures of Sikh politics. The centre's deliberate actions to disarm this development by dividing Sikh militants spectacularly backfired, culminating in another security operation (Black Thunder) on the Golden Temple (May 1988). Bereft of policy the centre adopted the 59th Constitutional Amendment which extended the period of President's Rule for three years and included a provision for the declaration of a state of emergency in Punjab (Singh 1991).

Seeking a 'principled solution': the National Front government

Rajiv Gandhi's decision to hold national parliamentary elections in November 1989 was accompanied by an announcement that elections would also be held in the thirteen constituencies in Punjab. This event was the first test of public opinion since September 1985, and the result transformed the Punjab problem. Armed militant groups who had boycotted the 1985 poll now participated under AD(M). The result produced a landslide victory for AD(M) which won eight seats, and two of its (non-party)-supported candidates were also successful. In contrast, the Congress-I obtained two seats while the Janata Dal could secure only one. The magnitude of AD(M)'s victory was reflected in the total rout of Sikh moderates of the AD(L) (and associated factions) who between them polled only 6.1 per cent of the total vote (Singh 1991).

AD(M)'s victory presented several difficulties for the new National Front minority government at the centre. First, the latter was now confronted with increased ethnic consolidation among Sikhs reinforced by the 'anti-terrorist' policy and articulated by the AD(M) in terms of the ASR as its minimalist demand. Second, the National Front government, because of its minority status – it depended on the BJP and Communist parties to survive in the central parliament – was unable to promise even the implementation of the Rajiv–Longowal Accord. Third, the capacity of the new government to impose a unilateral solution was limited by the lack of political support for its coalition partners in Punjab and the determination of Congress-I to use the Punjab issue to undermine the National Front itself. In this context the search for a 'principled solution' was largely reduced to symbolic actions – prime ministerial visits to the Golden Temple, replacement of administrative personnel, repeal of the notorious 59th Amendment, a new inquiry into the Delhi riots and moral pressure on the AD(M) leadership to de-escalate its demands. When the latter, however, refused to compromise, the centre faced with the Punjab legislative assembly elections (10 May 1990, following the repeal of the 59th Amendment), responded by extending President's Rule by six months. The official explanation for this decision was that free and fair elections could not be held until peace was restored; the unofficial, that the AD(M) and militants would have won and created a 'Latvian scenario'.

After the extension of President's Rule, the National Front government followed a three-fold strategy with the aim of holding PLA elections in November 1990. First, a new anti-terrorist 'action plan' was implemented on the assumption there were only 173 'hardcore' terrorists operating in the state. Second, efforts were made to placate popular discontent about the security forces by another change of state governor. Third, a renewed attempt was made to establish an anti-AD(M)/militant coalition by encouraging other parties and Sikh moderates (AD(L)) and Akali Dal (Badal) (AD(B)) to form a united front. But once again these measures failed to provide the critical breakthrough. In fact the militants became more emboldened within the AD(M) and launched an assassination campaign against AD(L) and AD(B) members. By September the centre's strategy was in disarray. In that month alone about 600 people died in terrorist and anti-terrorist violence, bringing the total for the year to about 3,500. Politically, the anti-AD(M)/militant bloc remained weak with the prospect of AD(M) victory at the polls even more certain than in May. Confronted with the repeat of earlier events, the centre once more extended President's Rule by six months. Exuding a sense of failure, V. P. Singh acknowledged that the centre's policy could have been ill-founded. 'One thing I will regret all my life', he said on the eve of the constitutional bill to extend President's Rule, 'is not holding elections [for the PLA] within six months of the government taking office' (*Financial Times*, 2 October 1990).

'Unprincipled solution': Janata Dal (Secular) government

With the resignation of the National Front government over the temple/mosque controversy and the formation of a breakaway Janata Dal (S) minority government supported by Congress-I, the Punjab problem was put on the 'back burner'. In the ensuing impasse the militants intensified their activities in a series of atrocities which led to widespread concern that the 'centre's writ did not run in Punjab'. The new government reacted to these developments by sending troops of the 9th division of the Indian army to the border districts of the state and replacing the governor with a former chief of army staff. At the same time the new prime minister, Chandra Shekhar, offered to discuss the Punjab question with Sikh leaders, including militants.

In the first round of discussions between the new government and AD(M), the latter presented a memorandum that emphasised the need for Sikhs to have 'the right of self-determination in order to preserve their religious, political and cultural identity'. Indeed, the circumspect language of the Rajiv–Longowal Accord was forsaken for a wholesale denial of Sikh integration into the Indian union. The relationship between Sikhs and the Indian union, the memorandum maintained, could only be determined after elections to the PLA under United Nations supervision (*The Tribune*, 2 January 1991).

Perhaps recognising the incompatibility of this demand with what his minority government (of sixty MPs) was able to deliver, in early 1991 Shekhar authorised clandestine negotiations with minor militant groups who were prepared to pursue regional power through PLA elections. Against the backdrop of the collapse of the Janata Dal (S) government, another extension of President's Rule in Punjab and the calling of national elections (March and April 1991), a new deal was brokered in which Shekhar as the outgoing prime minister authorised elections in Punjab in return for guarantees that the minor militant groups ('democratic militants') would desist from using the elections as a referendum on Khalistan. Publicly, this understanding was legitimised as a way of bringing the militants into the national mainstream and preventing an 'open revolt in Punjab'. Privately, however, there was an unspoken agreement that the success of 'democratic militants' might outmanoeuvre the 'armed militants' and the seemingly intransigent AD(M) leadership as well as enabling the beleaguered Janata Dal (S) to secure a few additional parliamentary seats from Punjab.

The notification for PLA and parliamentary elections certainly had the desired effect. Factional and strategic differences between 'democratic militants' and 'armed militants', between factions in the AD(M), and between the latter and the traditional moderates in AD(L) and AD(B), were openly exposed. Congress-I's decision to boycott the poll (with a threat to revoke it if elected at the centre) further heightened these divisions as the election became a contest *between* Sikh political groups. While the campaign progressed the 'armed militants', who opposed the poll, intensified their activities, killing twenty-four state and parliamentary candidates. Yet despite escalating violence the state administration and the Election Commission insisted that elections be held. But as the results of the national election became available, with a clear indication that Congress-I would form the next government at the centre, the Chief Election Commissioner, after talks with the new Congress-I leadership, postponed the Punjab elections (until 25 September 1991) on the eve of polling. Formally, he justified his action by insisting that the increasing level of violence had impelled him to make this unprecedented decision; informally, it was generally assumed that 'the Chief Election Commissioner had bent backwards to please his new masters' (*Indian Express*, 23 June 1991).

To conclude this section we need to note some general points on the character of centre-led initiatives. Evidently the optimistic assessments of the ability of Rajiv Gandhi to restore the Nehruvian guidelines were misplaced. His failure to reform Congress-I led to a rapid U-turn in early 1986 in which he reverted to the policies of his mother – of increasing centralisation of power in New Delhi, open accommodation of Hindu sentiment, and a frequent resort to force. Instead of treating the Punjab problem as *sui generis*, it was intimately connected in Congress-I calculations with the maintenance of political power in north-west and north India, the 'Hindi Belt', which provides 42 per cent of all parliamentary seats. Thus the imposition of President's Rule (May 1987) for political gain in the predominantly Hindu state of Haryana fatally disarmed the moderate Sikh leadership and emboldened the AD(M) and militants to launch a strategic movement for the capture of Sikh political institutions. Subsequently, in the absence of an effective political solution, the security apparatus provided the main instrument for suppressing ethnic strife.

Nor did the election of a National Front government at the centre lead to a radically new departure. Constrained by its coalition partners and external supporters, especially the BJP, the relationship between the government's regional policy and accommodation of the dominant ethnic sentiment was clear in its handling of Punjab and Kashmir. In Punjab, the National Front was willing to bargain regional *political power* with Sikh moderates (AD(L) and AD(B)) and their allies – in a united front against AD(M) and militants – for a de-escalation of *ethnic demands* implicit in the ASR and the Rajiv–Longowal Accord. The Janata Dal (S) government pursued the same formula but with 'democratic militants' as the key player.

Hyper-instrumentalism from the centre has failed to generate a parallel legitimising instrumentalism among the contemporary Sikh political leadership. Its most overt exercise has driven all leading Sikh political groups into the ethnic shell of primordialism. Although they are now fractured – into 'democratic' and 'armed militants', a highly factionalised AD(M), and marginalised moderates (AD(L) and AD(B)) – nonetheless they are increasingly entrapped in the rhetoric of Sikh self-determination which has now emerged as a minimalist goal. Thus, whereas the experience of the last seven years has led even the moderates to insist that the 'Sikh struggle' has gone beyond the framework established by the Rajiv–Longowal Accord, the 'democratic militants' justify their actions in terms of the 'AK47 and the ballot box'. It was in recognition of this growing ethnic consolidation that Shekhar proposed PLA elections with a view to accentuating the disjunction between *political power* and *ethnic demands*. Paradoxically, the postponement of elections in June is likely to reinforce the latter.

Overall, perhaps the key lesson of the various initiatives is that the Punjab crisis has not been accompanied by a radical innovation in the process of ethnic conflict management by the Indian state. Rather, the half-hearted attempt by Rajiv Gandhi to emulate his grandfather soon collapsed into the familiar policies of his mother. Where there has been a change is in the new form of overt instrumentalism practised by the two non-Congress governments at the centre after 1989, the willingness to offer political power at the regional level for compromised ethnic demands. In this respect the change follows the pattern established in other south Asian states beset by intractable ethnic conflicts, in particular Sri Lanka and its handling of the Tamil question. It reflects also the new situation where the official policy of multi-culturalism and multi-ethnicity is readily compromised in deference to the claims of Hindu ethnic sentiment that is forcefully articulated by the BJP. As the record of Congress-I and the National Front governments of Punjab has illustrated, the pursuit of power at the centre is intimately connected with the position that minority ethnic demands be delegitimised. Ironically, in this context, the one Nehruvian guideline on which all national parties concur, and indeed now emphasise, is that secessionist movements, especially led by minority ethnic groups in India's peripheral states, should be suppressed by force whatever the consequences.

CONCLUSION: ALTERNATIVE POLICY INITIATIVES AND THE PUNJAB PROBLEM

Reviewing the Indian state's policy on Punjab since 1984, the above account appears to suggest that this conflict is increasingly irresolvable. The traditional transactional role of the Indian state seems to be frustrated by the rise of primordialist ethnic demands, both in Punjab and the rest of India. While this analysis seems to be valid, it tends to overlooks the limited opportunities for a realistic solution that still exist. V. P. Singh was the first to admit that during his tenure as prime minister that the centre's policy was badly counselled, in particular by the CPI(M) leadership and its jaundiced position on Punjab. Likewise, the demand for Sikh self-determination has within it many shades of grey and, as Longowal demonstrated in 1985, the ASR is quite malleable depending on the political conjecture. Anyway, endemic factionalism among the latter will always erode political cohesion (Pettigrew 1975). There is, therefore, some room for manoeuvre but any new initiative needs to be realistic and framed with a short implementation period.

Unrealistic initiatives, on the other hand, abound. A partition of Punjab, however much desired by Sikhs or Hindus, is unlikely to be peaceful or 'civilised' (*Economic and Political Weekly*, 15 September 1990). Similarly, expectations that Congress-I can re-create a new party machine in the form of a new 'congress-system', are largely misplaced. Rather the demise of the 'con-gress-system' and the search by its consociational 'pillars' for autonomy may produce new national and regional consocia-tional orders but only after efforts at hegemonic assertion through communal or secular ideologies have been exhausted. Equally, though the movement towards a new federalism in the Indian union has gained strength – and is supported by some national parties – it is unlikely to accommodate the ASR's demand for Sikh self-determination which has as its essence a claim for hegemonic control. An accommodation of this kind can only be possible if a new, largely Sikh, state is created (which would require further reduction of existing territorial boundaries and/or transfer of the Hindu population), or if the Hindu minority in Punjab (which has a relatively higher demographic growth rate) is willing to accept hegemonic control. The latter prospect is extremely unlikely because the Punjabi Hindu politi-cal leadership, whether in the INC/Congress-I or BJP, has, since 1947, argued for cultural and religious integration of Sikhs into 'mainstream' Hindu society. In fact, it was a reluctant convert to a *Punjabi Suba* after having campaigned for two decades that the demand be denied by the simple procedure of Punjabi Hindus declaring Hindi – not Punjabi – as their mother-tongue during the decennial census. The option of Sikh hegemonic control is unlikely to be accepted because of the inherently second-class status implicit in it for the minority community (O'Leary 1989), especially as Punjabi Hindus see themselves as the frontier 'sword arm' of India and have been historically adept at drawing on a powerful pan-Hindu constituency.

In contrast, realistic solutions should not only extend the narrow limits of contemporary Indian statecraft in managing ethnic conflict but also draw valuable lessons from the failed initiatives. Essential among these ought to be four consider-ations.

First, there is a need to build an India-wide consensus on

Punjab so that the issue can be delinked from the pursuit of power at the centre and treated as *sui generis*. On past performance the Congress-I and the BJP will be reluctant to relinquish the 'ethnic card'. This obstinancy, however, might waver in the face of rising disaffection, the difficulties of coalition building in New Delhi, and growing vocal opposition of the Indian army to the job of doing the politicians' dirty work in Punjab (*India Today*, 30 April 1991). In the absence of a national consensus any partisan solution will ultimately invite a partisan response.

Second, a new solution if it is to endure must address the 'psychic humiliation' of Sikhs since 1984, the question of self-determination, and include a rapidly enforceable package of concessions along the lines of the Rajiv–Longowal Accord. A new accord is likely to be favourably received if it includes the territorial, economic and religious demands. Symbolic measures, for example, a formal resolution in the national parliament recanting the 1984 army action, would also be appropriate. Above all, it needs to reverse the post-1947 pattern of agreement–non-implementation–negation that has characterised the centre's dealing with the Sikh political leadership. This could be achieved by constitutional guarantees that would give it the seal of a 'historic' settlement. Formulated in these terms, such a package is likely to prove attractive to most Sikh political groups (with the exception of 'armed militants') who might, as a *quid pro quo*, redefine self-determination more equivocally. As for Hindu minority fears of hegemonic control, these could be assuaged by political realism that highlights the difficulties of sustaining majoritarian Sikh rule, the relatively favourable experience since 1966, the logic of such an action for Sikhs outside Punjab, and the ultimate ability of the centre to employ its residual powers.

Third, a realistic solution would also need systematically to dismantle the powerful security–judicial apparatus that has come into being since 1984. Not only has this apparatus failed to contain ethnic conflict in the absence of an effective political policy, it has contributed significantly to its intensification (*Economic and Political Weekly*, 6 January 1991). The leadership of the security personnel has actively opposed political initiatives, often citing the possibility of a backlash from any future Sikh state government. Although this fear could be assuaged by a general amnesty for political offenders that might be traded for any victimisation against the security personnel, the repeal of anti-terrorist legislation ('black laws') will prove difficult, especially as some of these measures have all-India implications. Regionally specific legislation, on the other hand, (e.g. special courts) could be quickly repealed while the enforcement of more general legislation could be more closely supervised with the possibility of greater accountability of the security and judicial machinery.

Finally, in dealing with Sikhs the centre needs to overcome a major unspoken assumption that has guided its policy since 1947: namely, that underlying all Sikh demands is a primordialist drive towards a Sikh state. This orientation is essentially ahistorical, overlooks the reactive character of modern Sikh ethno-nationalism, and overestimates the potential for state-building in the unpromising plain of Punjab (Pettigrew 1991). Paradoxically, this bias in policy formation has engendered Sikh primordialism instead of undermining it. The partition of Punjab in 1947 was opposed most strongly by the Sikh community. Equally, a separate Sikh state today will have the most negative consequences for Sikhs themselves. But if the movement towards such a state becomes irreversible, it will be because the framework of the Indian union established in 1947 has failed to provide the political, cultural and religious guarantees promised to the Sikhs at independence by the INC's leadership rather than as a historical realisation of an inevitable process.

POSTSCRIPT

The return of a minority Congress-I government at the centre under the leadership of the septuagenarian Rao raised high expectations that his neo-Nehruvian 'consensus politics' would provide a principled reappraisal of the Punjab problem. Instead his rhetorical mist has disguised a familiar policy of hyper-instrumentalism. The Punjab legislative assembly elections (scheduled for September 1991) were first delayed and then postponed until February 1992. In the event they were held despite a unanimous boycott by leading Sikh (moderate and militant) organisations and required a security umbrella of 250,000 military and paramilitary personnel. Although the result produced a landslide for Congress-I, the turnout was only 24 per cent (Singh 1992). The restoration of the 'democratic' process under these conditions almost precipitated a total breakdown of law and order in March and April. Since then the main function of the new administration has been to provide legitimacy for the ruthless anti-terrorist activities of the security forces. Surprisingly, the latter did achieve some degree of success but the alienation of most Sikh political groups from the state's political process continues.

NOTE

1 Article 356 of the Indian constitution empowers the centre to take over the administration of a state and declare President's Rule (direct rule from New Delhi). Currently, the length of President's Rule is limited to a period of one year (two successive terms of six months) after which any subsequent extensions require a constitutional amendment. Although envisaged as a residual power of last resort, Article 356 had been used sixty-five times by March 1982. The frequency with which this article has been applied in undermining state governments is often determined less by constitutional considerations than the political calculations of the party in power at the centre.

Chapter 5

Malaysia

Malay political hegemony and 'coercive consociationalism'

Diane Mauzy

INTRODUCTION

In most cases of deeply divided societies where consociational arrangements have been utilised, consociationalism has only served as a transitional and short-term solution. Therefore, *what happens to post-consociational states* is of considerable interest. The record appears to be mixed. In some cases, like Austria, the arrangement has proven so effective that over time the salient divisions dissolve and the state finds it can tolerate competitive politics and electoral winners and losers without engendering an explosion of violence and instability. In other cases, however, such as Lebanon, consociational arrangements have broken down and widespread ethnic violence and political instability have become endemic. Malaysia, falling in between, represents yet another possible outcome. The deep ethnic divisions have not been overcome, yet despite a sharp – but not complete – decline in accommodative practices, an increase in coercion and authoritarian responses to political challenges, and the unambiguous assertion of political hegemony on the part of the dominant ethnic group, serious ethnic violence has not occurred and the country is relatively stable. Conflict is managed through practices which I have called 'coercive consociationalism'.

THE EVOLUTION OF ETHNIC DIVISIONS AND THE POLITICAL INITIATIVES TO MANAGE CONFLICT TO MAY 1969

Until the watershed of May 1969 (ethnic riots and state of emergency), Malaysia was a country where the techniques and practices of consociational democracy were used effectively to maintain ethnic peace and political stability (Lijphart 1977a: 153). Malaysia had a system of governance that involved, beyond the trappings of parliament and elections, an independent judiciary, a reasonable tolerance of opposition, and a considerable, if not perfect, respect for the principles of the rule of law. The real problem for democracy has always been the protection of the rights and interests of minorities. Malaysia handled this problem consociationally through genuine consultation, bargaining and compromise among ethnic elites in a broad ruling coalition.

Malaysia represents a very difficult case for the successful management of ethnic conflict. At independence in 1957 there were two main groups – the Malays and the non-Malays (Chinese, Indians and others) – which were nearly equal in numbers and which were primarily non-territorially based but, even where adjacent, were living side by side but in separate groups (Furnivall 1948: 304). These groups were divided by the coinciding cleavages of race, language, religion, customs, areas of residence and, to a large extent, by type of occupation. Predictably, they lined up on the same opposing sides on virtually every politically relevant issue.

The Malays, along with some aboriginals and, since the formation of Malaysia in 1963, the natives of Sabah and Sarawak, are the indigenous people. Collectively they are known as the *Bumiputra*. The Malays, who are Muslims, are the pre-eminent ethnic group in Malaysia by virtue of their numbers and political power (they control the government, civil service and military). Despite this, the Malays and other *Bumiputra* remain less urbanised, less educated and heavily engaged in traditional occupations (such as rice farming and fishing). More *Bumiputra* fall below the poverty line than non-*Bumiputra*.

At independence, the non-*Bumiputra* – or to use the more common term, the non-Malay – percentage of the population was composed of 37 per cent Chinese, 11 per cent Indians and 2 per cent others. The non-Malays are mostly non-Muslim, primarily urban, with significant numbers engaged in retail trade or in the professions. Although segments of the non-Malays are among the poorest in the country, as an aggregate they are economically better off than the Malays. Furthermore, the widespread perception has been that the Chinese have dominated the economy and, through various means, have inhibited Malay participation. This perception is not completely accurate (and is becoming even less accurate), but in ethnically divided states perceptions and myths are as important as the objective truth.

The non-Malays were brought to the country as 'birds of passage' ('guest workers') by British colonial authorities from the 1870s to the outbreak of the Second World War. To 'protect' the Malays from being swamped by the more aggressive immigrants, the British, who ruled in collaboration with the Malay aristocracy, gave the Malays certain 'special rights' involving government employment, education and land reserves (Means 1972: 29–61). The preferential policies were also paternalistic, encouraging the Malay peasantry to maintain their traditional way of life. Hence, a dual economy developed: a European and non-Malay (and sometimes Malay aristocracy) modern urban economic sector, and a traditional rural Malay economy centring around rice production and fishing.

In the early 1950s, with the prospect of independence on the horizon, the British instituted local and municipal elections in Malaya and let it be known that independence would not be granted until it was clear that the various races of Malaya could live together peacefully. During the important Kuala Lumpur Municipal Election in 1952, an *ad hoc* alliance was struck between the United Malays National Organisation (UMNO) and the Malayan Chinese Association (MCA). As a team they registered a conclusive electoral victory against a Malay-led purportedly multi-ethnic party. This same pattern of *ad hoc* alliance victories followed in other local and municipal elections, until the national leadership of the two parties decided to link the organisations nationally and on a permanent basis. The Malayan Indian Congress (MIC) joined the Alliance the next year.

Following the overwhelming Alliance victory in the 1955 Federal Legislative Council Elections, the Alliance leaders met to work out a memorandum to the Constitutional Commission. The basis of these proposals was an ethnic *quid pro quo* package deal, often called the 'Bargain' (Milne and Mauzy 1980: 36–42). These proposals were subsequently incorporated into the 1957 Federation of Malaya Constitution. Specifically, the elite compromises gave the non-Malays revisions in citizenship regulations and, most important, the granting of *jus soli* after independence. In return, the non-Malays accepted Malay 'special rights'

(Article 153), Islam as the state religion (but freedom of religion guaranteed), Malay as the sole official language from 1967 (unless parliament decided otherwise), and the continuance of the functions assigned to the Malay Rulers. The 'Bargain' consisted of another, unwritten but acknowledged, level as well. At the elite level, the non-Malays recognised that the Malays should, by virtue of their indigenousness, be politically supreme (which would be achieved by UMNO controlling the highest offices of government, by the official symbols of a Malay state – Islam and the Rulers, and by having, eventually, Malay as the sole official language). In return the Malay elites recognised the right of the immigrant races to make Malaya their home and primary source of national loyalty, and (less explicitly) agreed that the non-Malays should not be unduly subject to restrictions disadvantageous to their economic activities, although they were to give assistance to the Malays to help them catch up economically.

Consociationalism requires overarching elite co-operation in order to be instituted and stable non-elite support to be maintained. Until its non-elite support eroded, Malaya/Malaysia represented, according to Arend Lijphart, 'a reasonably successful consociational democracy' (Lijphart 1977a: 150). Overarching elite co-operation characterised the operation of the political system. Inter-ethnic bargaining, compromises and 'package deals' by the elites were the *modus operandi*, rather than the practice of majoritarianism. Institutionally, consociation was practised through the sharing of governmental power in an inter-ethnic cabinet and a grand coalition of parties representing the major ethnic divisions. There was rough proportionality between the partners, although the Malays were recognised as being *primus inter pares* in the political system and thus held, as if by right, the posts of prime minister and deputy prime minister.

THE MAY 1969 RIOTS: A WATERSHED

The May 1969 elections followed five years of escalating ethnic militancy, largely because of the federal conflict with Singapore and its expulsion from the federation in 1965, and the issues raised by the Singapore leaders who challenged the 'Alliance concept' of governance, and because of the Language Act of 1967 which made Malay (Bahasa Malaysia) the sole official language. In an atmosphere of mounting ethnic tensions, the elections were more closely contested than previously, but still left the Alliance with a clear parliamentary majority and in control of most of the state governments. The opposition viewed their gains as a victory of sorts, while the Alliance considered the results as a setback and a threat to the survival of the Alliance system of rule.

In this highly inflammatory setting, the primarily non-Malay opposition held a provocative 'victory' parade in Kuala Lumpur. This was followed the next day by a Malay counter-rally, which had been preceded by the arrival into Kuala Lumpur of truckloads of armed Malays. The outcome was predictable: ethnic riots, arson, hundreds of gruesome deaths and thousands of injuries, temporary chaos, a state of emergency declared and order restored by the Royal Malay Regiment of the army.

During the twenty months of emergency rule, when the state was basically run by a civilian–military National Operations Council (NOC), Deputy Prime Minister Tun Razak, head of the NOC, called for a 'new realism' in the country. What this translated into was a reformulation of the terms of consociation (Mauzy 1983).

On the one hand, the Alliance was replaced by the Barisan Nasional – a considerably expanded grand coalition (from three to nine, then to eleven parties) – that brought into the fold the major Malay opposition (for several years only, as it transpired), although not the main non-Malay opposition party. Accompanying the expanded coalition was the Constitution (Amendment) Act, 1971, and revisions to the Sedition Act meant to depoliticise the system as far as possible by 'entrenching' ethnically sensitive issues (citizenship, the national language, Islam, Malay special rights, the Rulers) in the Constitution and prohibiting the questioning, even in Parliament, of these issues.

Inter-ethnic agreement on amendments to the Constitution, as well as on the principles of and guidelines for the New Economic Policy (NEP) and a national ideology (*Rukunegara*), was worked out by the National Consultative Council (NCC) in 1970. The NCC was a politically high-powered and widely representative body, including top ministers and representatives from many non-governmental organisations, meeting behind closed doors to 'establish positive and practical guidelines for inter-racial co-operation and social integration'. Since Tun Razak wanted to avoid a 'divided council', all agreements required unanimity. The fact that these discussions took place while the country was under emergency rule, and with the prospects for a return to parliamentary rule uncertain and subject to agreement being reached, helped promote attitudes conducive to reaching consensus.

These moves, to strengthen the coalition and to limit the ability of ethnic outbidders to use emotional ethnic issues for political purposes, moves ratified by the NCC, could be seen as enhancing consociationalism (although democracy became more tentative as a result, since order and stability were deemed more important to the general good than certain individual rights common to full democracies).

On the other hand, the 'new realism' meant accommodation on essentially Malay terms (Milne and Mauzy 1986: 41-7). Tun Razak stated on several occasions that UMNO could rule alone, but in the interests of national unity preferred to 'share' power. But the fiction of a government of nearly equal ethnic partners was no longer maintained. It could be clearly seen that the Malays were the hegemonic power, and intended to remain so at any cost for the foreseeable future. There was still to be consultation and some bargaining at the elite level, but some Malay positions and policies were now deemed 'non-negotiable'.

In the Cabinet, after parliamentary rule was re-established in 1971, proportionality in a qualitative sense became less meaningful: the Chinese lost the Commerce and Industry portfolio, and then, in 1974, they lost Finance. The Malays now held all key portfolios. Numerically, the power sharing seemed genuine: the proportion of Malays in the Cabinet declined slightly (to about 62 per cent) because of the inclusion of representatives from the new coalition parties, but the proportion of Chinese and Indians did not increase.

More important was the fact that the 'Bargain' was terminated. The top UMNO leaders had concluded that the underlying cause of the May riots was Malay economic dissatisfaction. To correct ethnic economic imbalances and the identification of race with economic function, a New Economic Policy (NEP) based on preferential ethnic policies would be instituted.[1] The rationale and guidelines for this policy, formulated in detail by bureaucrats and some foreign advisers in the Department of

National Unity under the direction of a Malay minister, were agreed to by the NCC.

The justifications for the NEP were two-fold. First, the new nationalist Malay political elite, brought into positions of political prominence by Tun Razak, strongly believed that the non-Malays had never lived up to a condition of the 'Bargain', that they were actively to help uplift the Malays economically. Second, the imperative of national unity required a more equitable ethnic distribution of wealth. However, the Malays would not confiscate the wealth of non-Malays, and a key feature of the NEP would be that preferences would be instituted only in an expanding economy, so that while the Malays would be 'catching up' proportionately, all groups would experience growth absolutely, and hence no group would be deprived. Nevertheless, if and where necessary to meet preferential goals, some growth would be sacrificed.

As well as correcting ethnic economic imbalances, the NEP also had another goal, which involved class-based and hence 'colour-blind' preferences: reducing and eradicating poverty irrespective of race. This was largely a reaffirmation of a programme to combat rural, and mainly *Bumiputra*, poverty. This prong was less elaborate and less controversial.

Under the twenty-year NEP, a number of socio-economic targets were proposed for the *Bumiputra* (but in reality primarily for the Malays). The most widely quoted goal was for the *Bumiputra* to manage and own at least 30 per cent of the total corporate commercial and industrial activities in all categories and scales of operation by 1991.

In addition to a battery of rules, regulations and quotas, the government would actively intervene to help the *Bumiputra* achieve these targets. As a key strategy, the state would actively acquire (by voluntary transactions) the assets of existing businesses, which it would hold 'in trust' for the *Bumiputra* until such time that these assets could be turned over to *Bumiputra* individuals. Institutions were set up to help the Malays get business training and advice, secure loans and accumulate capital, and buy shares of businesses. Through regulations, the government would force all but small business operations to restructure their ownership to meet ethnic guidelines and quotas for management and ownership shares; institute ethnic quotas for entry into tertiary institutions – although targets were vague and never publicly stated, at one point the percentage reserved for Malays reached about 75 per cent; require non-Malay businesses to offer shares for sale (often below market value) to *Bumiputra*, as a way of stimulating the creation of a Malay capitalist class. Further, the government would virtually reserve certain occupations and categories of businesses for small *Bumiputra* businessmen through the issuance of licences and, finally, the government would support new *Bumiputra* businesses by awarding its substantial contracts on an ethnic basis. As it turned out, a major responsibility of the government would also be to bail out or absorb the losses from failed Malay business ventures.

The 13 May conflagration galvanised the Malays into action to change the basis of the politico-economic system. However, the violence tended to paralyse many non-Malays, who could not help but note the high percentage of non-Malay victims of the riots, and had to wonder if they had any future in the country. In this rather shattered state, the non-Malay political and economic elite were relieved that their wealth and businesses had not been confiscated, and that they had successfully negotiated their targeted share of corporate wealth from 30 to 40 per cent (at the expense of the foreign sector, which was reduced to 30 per cent). They were glad to have ethnic representatives in the governing coalition and what they hoped would be a share of power, albeit small. In the NCC, they agreed with the Malay political elite on the need for – indeed, the justice of – a 'new social contract' that would give socio-economic preferences to the Malays for twenty years through the NEP.

COERCIVE CONSOCIATIONALISM IN AN AUTHORITARIAN STATE

Since the early 1980s and the accession of Dr Mahathir Mohamad as prime minister, the state has become more repressive, accommodation has been marginalised, and ethnic relations have deteriorated, although there have been no serious ethnic clashes.

The *Bumiputra* have been winning the numbers game: they now have an absolute majority of the population (nearing 60 per cent), and thirty-year projections have their percentage climbing to nearly 80 per cent. For the Malays, a psychological barrier has been surmounted: the non-Malays are no longer looked upon as being capable of challenging for ultimate power; therefore the

Malays no longer fear losing control of their native soil. Now, the non-Malays are viewed mainly as a 'minority' problem which could adversely affect political stability and hence foreign investment. Indeed, one Malay economist confidently (and optimistically) stated that there was no point seeking long-term ethnic solutions because there would soon be no ethnic problems to worry about.[2]

Coupled with unchallengeable political hegemony, the NEP has produced a veritable socio-economic revolution in Malaysia that has elevated the Malays to near economic parity with the non-Malays. Further, the faces of cities and towns, university campuses, banks and financial institutions, and corporate boardrooms have radically changed in twenty years from a situation where not many Malays or Islamic symbols were visible to one where there are mostly Malays and Islamic symbols.

In the past, the Malays have quickly united in the face of a threat to 'race, land or religion'. Now, predictably perhaps, Malay political hegemony has created an ethnic confidence that allowed for something that in the past would have been unthinkable: a split in the ruling party, UMNO. This was the result of the dominating style and personality of Dr Mahathir, and his decision after being challenged in UMNO party elections to reject reconciliation and instead conduct a massive purge that extended down the UMNO organisational ladder. This 'winner-take-all' attitude solidified the rift and led to a petition by a group of ousted dissenters to the high court to nullify the party elections because of illegalities.

A key consideration in the UMNO rift and eventual split was the effect of UMNO disunity on ethnic relations. What it amounted to was that all of the top Malay leaders, feeling insecure and defensive, were constrained in their ability to make ethnic compromises because of the fear of being labelled as 'soft' conciliators and not as sufficiently 'tough' 'Malay protectors'. The easiest way to secure support from the rural Malays in intra-ethnic competition was still to appeal to Malay nationalist emotions by invoking anti-Chinese rhetoric. Since ethnic polarisation and acrimony had been on the rise in the period under Dr Mahathir's leadership, it was not difficult for political mobilisers to fuel volatile ethnic emotions. Ironically, a number of observers believed that this tension and conflict over political issues formed a sharp contrast with a climate of general ethnic cordiality that had been slowly building since 1969 – a feeling that the ethnic groups, although they hold stereotypical images of the other groups and do not mix easily, do not automatically harbour ill-will for the others.

In October 1987, the beleaguered prime minister, battered by internal challenges and mounting criticism of his rule generally, struck back. From all appearances, the government dangerously allowed an escalation of ethnic tensions so that it could order a clampdown and hence silence a whole range of critics (Mauzy 1988: 213–22).

The crisis started when the Ministry of Education assigned non-Mandarin-speaking Chinese to administrative posts in some Chinese-language primary schools. To supporters of Chinese education and language, this appeared to be a plot to undermine the position of Chinese primary education, always an emotional issue. The situation was allowed to fester for weeks, until some Chinese groups, including leaders from the parties in the ruling coalition, held protest rallies, and some Chinese schoolchildren boycotted classes. UMNO Youth then countered with a large rally to defend the education ministry and especially its minister – Mahathir-loyalist, UMNO vice-president and strong future contender for the prime ministership, Datuk Anwar Ibrahim – against perceived Chinese 'insults'. By the time the speakers had finished, the Malays had been worked up into a state of rage and it was only because of careful police work that an ethnic confrontation was avoided as the crowds were dispersed.

More worrisome was an UMNO rally scheduled for 1 November to show support for Dr Mahathir's leadership. A half-million Malays were expected to converge on the 40,000-seat Merdeka Stadium, located in a Chinese-populated area of Kuala Lumpur. This was an explosive situation, as the top police and army officers stated publicly in asking for the rally to be cancelled. Eventually Dr Mahathir called it off, but since this could be interpreted by Malays as a sign of weakness, he also ordered the arrests under the Internal Security Act (which allows preventive detention) of over a hundred persons (Mauzy 1988: 219). Many had been involved with the Chinese schools issue, but many others – critics of Dr Mahathir – had not been. A significantly higher number of non-Malays were arrested, whereas in the past ethnic numbers had usually been equally apportioned. Also, the three most independent-minded newspapers were closed down. Malaysians breathed a sigh of relief and, ironically, Dr Mahathir was praised by many for acting decisively to defuse dangerous ethnic tensions.

In February 1988, a High Court judge stunned Malaysia with an oral opinion that since illegal branches had participated in the UMNO elections, in accordance with the law under the Societies Act, UMNO itself was an illegal organisation. In the subsequent scramble to register a new party using 'UMNO' in the name, the prime minister had the advantage of inside information (from the Registrar of Societies) and was able to register his party as UMNO Baru (New UMNO). The 'Baru' was quickly dropped, and Dr Mahathir now had an UMNO without any internal opposition and with new rules completely consolidating control of the party at the top (*Far Eastern Economic Review*, 14 April 1988: 22–31; 28 April 1988: 40). There remained two outstanding issues: the legal dispute over who should get 'old' UMNO's vast assets, and a court appeal by the excluded group to re-legalise the old UMNO. If the old UMNO were to be re-legalised, Dr Mahathir would find himself heading a splinter party without any assets.

In early May 1988, the Lord President set a June date for hearing the UMNO appeal in the Supreme Court – and ordered it heard by a full bench (all nine judges), thus nullifying the government's ability to manipulate the assignment of judges. Shortly thereafter, the Lord President was suspended for 'gross misbehaviour and misconduct' and a tribunal to hear grounds for his dismissal was ordered. The charges stemmed from a March letter the Lord President had sent to the king expressing dismay over Dr Mahathir's relentless attacks against the judiciary, which in some minor ways breached protocol.[3]

The tribunal was set up by the prime minister's department and put under the presidency of the Deputy Lord President, who stood to gain promotion by the Lord President's dismissal. When the tribunal was about to submit its report, the Supreme Court met in a special session on 2 July and handed down a restraining order on the tribunal. Four days later the five Supreme Court judges involved were also suspended.

With six of the nine original judges thus suspended, the reconstituted Supreme Court set aside the restraining order, and the Lord President was dismissed. A few days later the Supreme Court rejected the UMNO appeal. This travesty of constitutionality, of the executive trampling the judiciary, coupled with a constitutional amendment earlier in the year to exclude the supervisory powers of the courts to review executive decisions, meant that the judiciary could no longer be used, literally, as the court of last resort. 'Rule by law' (meaning executive acts passed by a rubber-stamp parliament) had replaced the rule of law in Malaysia.

Not only has the judiciary lost its independence and the executive become completely dominant, but the citizens of Malaysia have progressively lost individual rights commonly found in democracies, and the protection originally afforded them in the constitution. The Sedition Act, Internal Security Act, Police Act, Official Secrets Act, Legal Profession Act, Universities and University Colleges Act, and Printing Presses and Publication Act have all been amended recently to silence critics and to demolish sources of power that in the past have served as mild, but salutary, checks on a powerful executive.

All of this has implications for ethnic relations and the prospects for consociationalism in Malaysia. As it becomes clear that the predominantly Malay executive can change the laws of the land at will, the whole basis of ethnic trust unavoidably shifts away from reliance on the system and institutions, towards mere hope that Malay political elites will take non-Malay interests into account. To the Malays there is a perception that there are no limits or boundaries to what the government can do to further Malay interests. The non-Malays, on the other hand, are on the defensive. Malay attacks on their vital interests have such low political costs that their protection cannot be guaranteed.

When the 1990 termination date for the NEP approached, various ethnic and sub-ethnic groups began to voice concerns and issue contradictory demands about what sort of socio-economic policy should follow. The government had already proclaimed that restructuring quotas had not been met and that, therefore, preferential policies would need to be continued, but had not announced any policy guidelines. Given the history of a consensus achieved in the National Consultative Council in 1969 that legitimised the NEP, it was obvious that an opportunity existed to recapture the faded spirit of ethnic accommodation through the formation of a similarly representative group to work out a post-1990 socio-economic policy to replace the NEP.

Ultimately, a 150-member National Economic Consultative

Council (NECC) was formed in December 1988 with some fanfare, and charged with the task of reaching consensus, behind closed doors, on recommendations for a policy to supersede the NEP. The NECC was widely representative of a broad cross-section of society in its composition, including most political parties (both government and opposition), trade unions and associations, ethnic minorities, economists, academics and intellectuals, and former government officials. Because the NECC bore some resemblance to the earlier (1969) National Consultative Council, some believed that the NECC had its antecedents in the NCC (or perhaps the even earlier (1949) Communities Liaison Committee) (Milne and Mauzy 1980: 89–92; von Vorys 1975: 96–104). There was one critical difference between the NECC and the NCC (and CLC), however: no one in government sat on the NECC, whereas the NCC included all the top decision-makers (and the CLC comprised the most influential ethnic leaders in the country at that time).

Dr Mahathir promised to accept NECC recommendations if consensus could be reached, saying that, 'The government promises to implement the policy decided by the Council as the basis for the national economic policy after 1990' (*Straits Times* (Singapore), 20 December 1980). Unfortunately, he had only reluctantly agreed to the formation of the NECC, and from the beginning he issued public statements that impugned the credibility and legitimacy of the Council. In December 1988, just after the NECC was announced, he told an audience in Singapore that he was going to allow everyone to participate, including those with radical views, and he suspected that they would not be able to 'achieve anything' because they would 'fight each other' and in the end the government would have to do the job for them (*Aliran Monthly*, 1989, vol. 9, no. 4, p.10).

The existence of the NECC raised the expectations of some of the non-Malays and also those *Bumiputra* who were not Malays (mostly from Sabah and Sarawak) who had complained about the 'Malayness' of the NEP benefits (indeed, the joke was that the NEP had changed the meaning of '*Bumiputra*' to 'UMNO-putra'). Other non-Malays greeted the formation of the NECC with cynicism, believing that Dr Mahathir had set it up to channel and control debate, and, more importantly, to silence critics by including them on the Council and then placing the Council's proceedings, debates, documents and submissions under the restrictions of the Official Secrets Act (OSA). Some hardline Malays appeared to oppose the establishment of the NECC, insisting that there should be no compromise on the principles of the NEP, and at the same time setting forth extreme positions, arguing that preferences should be bestowed permanently on the basis of 'indigenous rights'. Other, moderate, Malays, mainly from the western-educated urban middle-class group, welcomed the opportunity to review the performance of the NEP objectively and to propose remedies for overcoming some of the perceived failures or shortcomings (e.g., the dependency syndrome, subsidy mentality and 'rentier' behaviour of Malays).

The NECC laboured at its task long after its original target for completing its final report by the end of 1989, and along the way some groups and individuals dropped out over various disagreements and disenchantments. It came very close to achieving a consensus in August 1990 with recommendations contained in a draft report. However, belatedly, someone in the Cabinet or the EPU apparently took a close look at the report and concluded that the UMNO members of the Steering Committee had conceded too much and that these views did not reflect UMNO's true position. Therefore, the UMNO Malay members at the plenary session, ignoring procedural rules, simply stated that the report was unacceptable and must be changed, or the government would ignore its recommendations. The list of objections was longer than the original draft report.[4] At this point, with morale in the NECC very low, Dr Mahathir delivered his Harvard Club speech in which he stated that since the NECC could not achieve a consensus, the government was not bound by its recommendations.[5] This speech led to more withdrawals from the Council.

Amazingly, in the end, the NECC did achieve a consensus and issued a 444-page report in February 1991, after twenty-five months of debate and struggle (*Laporan Majlis Perundingan Ekonomi Negara*, 1991). The report was clearly the product of delicately crafted compromises. For example, the MCA representatives had insisted on the condition that restructuring would continue for a period of no more than ten years, after which discussions on the possibility of terminating preferences would be held. The UMNO representatives preferred having no fixed deadline or timetable; however, they agreed to 'review' the programme after ten years. And the non-Malays won an important concession: the recommendation that an independent monitoring commission be established to oversee implementation. For the Malays, the report provided legitimacy to the use of preferential policies by securing the agreement of the non-Malays for continued economic restructuring. Altogether, the report represented a 'package deal' that could be likened to a new social contract.

This report – in Bahasa Malaysia only – was not made public until after the government's *Second Outline Perspective Plan 1991–2000* (OPP2) and *Sixth Malaysia Plan 1991–1995* (SMP) had been approved by Parliament in June and July 1991, respectively.[6] In the foreword to the OPP2 by the prime minister, the contribution of the NECC was tersely acknowledged (OPP2, p.vii). No other mention is made of the NECC in the OPP2 or SMP. Unfortunately, the government did not treat the NECC report as a 'package deal', but accepted recommendations selectively. A number of NECC recommendations can be found (sometimes slightly amended) in the OPP2, but there is no mention at all of a monitoring agency or anything similar.

The OPP2 is a ten-year programme encompassing the New Development Policy (NDP). The NDP retains many of the basic goals and strategies, as well as character, of the NEP, but adds some new emphases and variations. National unity based on the *Rukunegara* is once again stated as the overriding objective. For the Malays, national unity is regarded as synonymous with the protection of Malay political dominance and the correction of ethnic economic imbalances. For the non-Malays, it is preferable to tie preferential policies to the goal of national unity, and related notions of justice and fairness, so that serious objections can be argued with 'national unity' as the key *raison d'être* rather than ethnic self-interest.

Once again growth is deemed to be a necessary condition for restructuring under the NDP so that, theoretically, there will be redistribution of the increments of an expanding economy and no ethnic community will be unduly deprived. The system of quotas, licences, contracts and other special assistance to *Bumiputras* will continue until there is economic parity with the non-*Bumiputras*. However, the under-representation of the non-Malays in certain areas is acknowledged and an inducement is offered: 'The non-*Bumiputra* expectation of greater access to public sector employment, educational opportunities and participation in land schemes will be considered together with the progress made by the *Bumiputra* in the private sector' (meaning the small- and medium-sized private businesses which remain the last stronghold of the Chinese).[7] While the NDP commitment to ethnic preferences is strong and undiluted, the percentage targets and the timetable are more vague. The focus has shifted: 'There will be more emphasis on the capabilities of the *Bumiputra* to manage, operate and own businesses rather than on achieving specific numerical targets of equity owner-ship' (OPP2, pp.4, 107). The vagueness of percentage goals and deadlines in the NDP is a disappointment to some hardline UMNO Malays and is regarded as a positive step by many non-Malays. To other less trustful non-Malays, however, the vague-ness of the targets and timetable seem to present the danger of open-ended restructuring. The NDP reveals that some minimal elite bargaining remains, but is it anything more than tokenism? Milton Esman sums up the Chinese predicament:

> For even if, at some cost and inconvenience to them, the NEP's *economic* restructuring goals should be fulfilled, where would this leave the Chinese? No responsible Malay political figure has ever even intimated that once the NEP succeeds, the government would proceed to eliminate the identification of race with *political* function. Thus the Chinese can expect to remain less than first-class citizens, free to vote and to hold office, but under clearly restrictive conditions. They are excluded by formal quotas and by informal practice from all but a handful of senior posts in the security forces, the civil bureaucracies, and the public corporations. They cannot aspire to senior political positions in the Federal or, with the single exception of Penang, in State governments. They continue to be reminded that the country belongs to the bumiputra (Malays) whose 'special position' is entrenched in the Constitution. Symbolically, they are less than first-class; politically they feel marginal, often powerless. While moder-ate, pragmatic Malay governments continue to take their interests into account, they have no veto over government policies that vitally affect them and there are no guarantees for the future. This is not a pattern of national unity that is reassuring to Chinese.
>
> (Esman 1991: 735)

TRENDS: ETHNIC POLARISATION AND FRUSTRATION BUT NOT DESPERATION

There are two noticeable trends in Malaysia, and both have implications for ethnic relations: declining democracy and declining consociationalism.

First, the decline of democratic practices can be seen in the process of deinstitutionalisation that is taking place in Malaysia. The converse, the process of institutionalisation, involves not just the creation of protected institutions which acquire value and respect over time, such as the constitution, laws and courts, the legislature, political parties and elections, and the civil service, but also accepted procedures for resolving disputes which seem to represent a moral consensus and perceived mutual interest. All of this implies legitimacy, trust, and a degree of predictability. Deinstitutionalisation – leading to weak institutionalisation – refers to the tearing down of these institutions and procedures, resulting in perverted constitutions, the absence or inadequacy of the rule of law, and a prevalence of private interests which dominate public responsibility. The hallmark of weak institutionalisation is the inability to curb the excesses of personal rule.

The expansion of the power of the executive under Dr Mahathir has been directly at the expense of democratic constraints and practices. Dr Mahathir, who understands power very well and who is a master of political intrigue, does not seem to understand constitutionalism or the basic principles of democracy. He regularly defines democracy publicly as simple majority rule, and parliamentary democracy as simply unhindered rule by the leader of the party which commands a majority in the house. He seems to view parliament (as controlled by the leader) as sovereign, not the constitution. He does not appear to appreciate the fact that a vital component of democratic practice is the protection of the rights and interests of minorities. Most of those minority interests that have survived to date have been in the form of pragmatic concessions without guarantees or legal force, and, although some rights are protected in the constitution, they can be altered on the whim of the prime minister, since he commands a rubber-stamp parliament (an important exception is that citizenship rights have been entrenched in the constitution. An amendment to these would need, in addition to the consent of two-thirds of both houses of parliament, the consent of the Council of Rulers).

Under the most generous interpretation, Malaysia would no longer qualify as a 'consociational democracy' under Lijphart's definition (Lijphart 1977a: 4, 48, 105, 153). The question arises as to whether a state can be consociational without being democratic?[8] Lijphart views the two as parts of a single concept related to democratic theory, and probably believes that the separation of the elements undermines the integrity of the concept (as well as opening it to accusations of being a formula for repressive elite rule). There may be some practical, as opposed to strictly analytical, link between consociation and democracy in terms of providing legitimacy for the political elites, providing the citizens the security offered by adherence to the rule of law, and also through the open articulation of interests providing the government feedback on the condition of non-elite support. But the two can be analytically separated. Consociationalism can be described strictly as a formula for the management of political conflict in divided societies.

The second trend is that the practice of genuine consociationalism in Malaysia is declining, although the veneer of elite accommodation remains. The main prerequisites for consociationalism are met, at least formally. The government consists of a multi-ethnic coalition and there is a facade of power-sharing. In fact, some compromises over some issues are made with the non-Malays, and some of the top non-Malay elite benefit by standing in safe Malay-majority electoral seats in elections (whereas they would risk defeat in non-Malay-majority seats).

The reality, however, reveals declining consociation. The non-Malays no longer have full access to information, data and statistics compiled by the government. A recent, clear example of this was during the late 1980s when the MCA campaigned for, but was unable to obtain, disaggregated data from the government on the percentage of *Bumiputras* in the civil service to support its claim of a heavy preponderance of Malays (termed 'over-restructuring').[9] Further, since important decisions are not taken at Cabinet meetings, but rather only sometimes conveyed in them, the non-Malays are not consulted much any more and they have little influence except over a narrow range of cultural issues.[10] They have been reduced to defensive positions, trying to protect socio-cultural institutions, such as vernacular primary schools, the Lion Dance at Chinese New Year celebrations, and the preservation of Chinese burial grounds, while finding themselves unable to fend off or even debate important perceived threats, such as the demand by religious Malays for the replacement of civil law with Islamic law, and the use of *Jawi* (Arabic script) for written Bahasa Malaysia.

The non-Malay position is something akin to the 'liberal's dilemma' – every time they test the boundaries and push for more influence (or even to regain previously held influence), they are rebuffed and end up worse off. The most recent example of this was in 1988 when the MCA openly debated leaving the *Barisan Nasional* coalition and aligning itself with Tengku Razaleigh's rival *Semangat '46* Malay party composed of former UMNO members. *Gerakan* was also restless and was perhaps quietly contemplating a switch, as was the ruling party in the state of Sabah, *Parti Bersatu Sabah* (PBS), a multi-ethnic but primarily *Bumiputra* party labelled by UMNO as a 'Christian' party. In the event, the MCA and *Gerakan* stayed in the coalition, but the PBS switched to the Razaleigh side, thus incurring the considerable and ongoing wrath of Dr Mahathir. According to one MCA insider, the MCA was completely unsuccessful in gaining any concessions from the prime minister, who appeared to care little whether these component parties remained or left, even given the threat of genuine competition from a rival coalition as a result of the UMNO split. Apparently, Dr Mahathir said that UMNO preferred to share power with the non-Malays, but it was not a necessity.[11] They were told they could take it or leave it as far as policies and their participation in the coalition were concerned. So, the key non-Malay party in the government coalition found to its discomfort that its influence and value were such that not even a bit of political blackmail at a critical juncture could return any dividends.

Taking some liberties with Lijphart's model, I have labelled this situation 'coercive consociationalism'. This is consociationalism on Malay terms. The groups are unequal and the bargaining is one-sided; its value is strictly in the fact that it is better to have some accommodation than none at all. It could be argued that this is not consociation at all and certainly not consociational democracy; that it more properly describes something that could be labelled 'hegemonic group pragmatic paternalism'.

However, there is something at work that is more than just pragmatic paternalism and meaningless accommodative practices. First, it is important that there remains a mass perception, albeit eroding, that ethnic bargains are an integral part of how the system works. Second, the non-Malays can influence some policies that adversely affect their socio-cultural interests, and they can affect some economic and political decisions at the margins. Third, on occasion the non-Malays have been able to impress upon the ruling Malays that certain policy decisions might incur high political costs (this is probably what has protected Chinese primary education to date). In other words, being 'nearly powerless' but in the government, with channels of communication available, and with some prospect of compromise or concession as a possible outcome, and capable of causing political instability and disruption if pushed too far is different, and somewhat better, than being completely 'powerless' and dependent upon handouts from a government to whose decisions they were contributing no formal visible inputs. All this having been said, the consociational element in Malaysia has been sadly eroded. It is now so reduced that any further weakening would make the concept of consociationalism applicable only to the past.

Finally, many of the non-Malays in Malaysia today are frustrated and fearful as regards government and the future. The question arises: given the collapse of most consociational practices and the perception in Malaysia of growing ethnic polarisation, why hasn't there been ethnic violence, such as has occurred in Lebanon and Sri Lanka? There are a number of reasons. Memories and reminders about the armed might of the Malays and the coercive capacity of the state is one, especially since most non-Malays do not feel they have their backs to the wall. Another is the possibility of emigration for the better-off non-Malays (an option a number have exercised). The Malays, for their part, are more secure about their political dominance now, they are upwardly mobile and have high economic expectations, and, as one Malay editor noted, they are less likely to riot when it might be their own home, car or business that is torched (although many Malays remain susceptible to calls to mobilise to protect race, religion and land).

However, the overwhelming explanation offered by Malaysians[12] for why there has been no outbreak of violence is that Malaysia is a resource-rich country that is prospering (although historically it is a boom-and-bust type of economy), and the non-Malays have found that they can still make money so long as there is political stability and discriminatory policies are not measurably increased. It is quite likely that strong economic growth is the most important variable in explaining the absence of ethnic violence in Malaysia. If so, in this era where multi-ethnic states around the world are increasingly experiencing turmoil, Malaysia is particularly fortunate in its endowments. It is prospering despite some earlier expensive misplaced economic priorities, growing official corruption, the drag of preferential ethnic policies, and despite declining democratic rights and practices and the existence of a situation where coercive con-sociationalism can be seen as a virtue because it is better than the alternatives.

NOTES

1 On the NEP, see Milne (1976) and (1986).
2 Interview with a Malay economist and member of the National Economic Consultative Council in Kuala Lumpur in October 1990.
3 See Tun Salleh Abas (1989).
4 Information on the proceedings of the NECC has been derived from a number of interviews in Malaysia in 1990 with members of the NECC.
5 *New Straits Times*, 23 August 1990. The newspaper ran a bold headline that read: 'NECC Proposals Are Not Binding'.
6 See Government of Malaysia (1991a, b).
7 OPP2, p. 16. In the *Straits Times* (Weekly Overseas Edition), 19 October 1991, Malaysian officials noted that the Malaysian civil service would take in over 20,000 non-*Bumiputra* in the next ten years, to help to reflect the ethnic composition in Malaysia better. This would be a very small percentage.
8 Hans Daalder, 'The Consociational Democracy Theme', *World Politics*, 1974, vol. XXVI, no. 4, p. 167.
9 OPP2, p. 49, Table 2-7 on ethnic employment. In the table, 'government and other services' is lumped together with finance, and wholesale and retail trade.
10 Important decisions are taken by the prime minister, sometimes in consultation with members of his small inner Cabinet, normally following meetings of the UMNO Supreme Council. Quite often the first that the non-UMNO ministers hear about these decisions is when they are told about them in Cabinet.
11 Interview with an MCA official in 1990.
12 Every non-Malay (and many Malays) interviewed between October

and December 1990 cited the continued possibilities of making money as the chief reason why there has been no ethnic violence in Malaysia, despite more polarisation, less accommodation and more repression.

Chapter 6

Containment or regulation?

The British approach to ethnic conflict in Northern Ireland

Brendan O'Duffy

INTRODUCTION

It is widely agreed that the Northern Ireland conflict centres on conflicting national identities. Most Protestants desire to maintain their membership within the United Kingdom. Most Catholics wish, if only eventually, for a united Ireland. But why is this conflict so intractable? As I shall argue, the British government's overriding emphasis upon containing the conflict through security initiatives is a primary obstacle to the achievement of lasting regulatory mechanisms because they entrench rather than marginalise proponents of violence.

Not that conflict regulation is an easy task. Northern Ireland offers a paradigmatic example of a territory where the conditions for successful conflict regulation are lacking (Lijphart 1975: 99–101; O'Leary 1989: 572–9). Multiple parallel cleavages exist along the dimensions of ethnicity, religion and, to a lesser degree, socio-economic status. Potential cross-cutting cleavages such as language, class or a shared Ulster nationalism are subsumed by the overriding importance of conflicting national aspirations. These multiple parallel cleavages present significant obstacles to conflict regulation by limiting the room for compromise by leaders of the two primary communal blocs. This chapter assesses whether or not the British initiatives in Northern Ireland have been successful in improving the conditions which facilitate regulation and makes suggestions as to strategies which could be more effective in achieving that goal. But first, it is necessary to outline the factors which contribute to the intractability of the conflict.

THE HISTORICAL DIMENSION

According to Arend Lijphart, an important factor in facilitating conflict regulation is a past history of accommodation among or between parties to a given conflict (Lijphart 1977a). A history of accommodation can be facilitated where the parties to a conflict have a common enemy. Far from having a common enemy, the two communities in Northern Ireland have seen each other as the enemy for over 300 years, with the notable exception of the United Irish rebellion of 1798. Over this time attempts at reconciliation sponsored by the British or Irish governments have been interpreted as threats to the interests of one side or the other. The primary historic causes of the conflict in Northern Ireland have been classified as state- and nation-building failures on the part of British and Irish governments (Lustick 1985; O'Leary and Arthur 1990: 1–48). The history of state- and nation-building failures in Northern Ireland contributes to the current conflict by producing a multitude of precedent-setting events which constrain elites and activists into sustaining conflictual behaviour. For Protestant loyalists, numerous historical examples of compromises by past leaders are invoked in order to prevent contemporary leaders from compromising on the status of Northern Ireland within the United Kingdom. Describing someone as a 'Lundy' is a direct reference to Robert Lundy who surrendered the town of Londonderry to the forces of the Catholic King James II in 1689 (Foster 1988: 146–7). Similarly, for nationalist extremists a 'Redmondite' refers to John Redmond, the leader of the Nationalist Party who accepted the compromise which eventually led to the secession of Northern Ireland from the Irish Free State in 1921 (Lyons 1971, 1973: 307). This legacy is invoked in order to remind Catholic nationalists of the dangers of compromise on the national question (Adams 1986).

The historical legacy of the conflict also leads to a perpetuation of distinct and opposing cultures of violence within the two communities. When cultural identity is based on a legacy of conflict then at least one important condition for conflict regulation is absent. In Northern Ireland, Protestant triumphalism and Catholic republican nationalism are the primary foci of cultural identity for large portions of each community, providing a steady pool of potential recruits for paramilitary organisations as well as larger pools of tacit support for the activities of those organisations (Fraser 1973; Miller 1978). Opposing cultures of violence are enhanced by the geographic distribution of Protestants and Catholics (see *Northern Ireland Census, 1991*, 1992). The Provisional Irish Republican Army (PIRA) is well established in the Catholic strongholds of Derry/Londonderry, south Armagh and west Belfast. Loyalist paramilitaries are organised less formally but they are generally based within either the Ulster Defence Association (UDA) or the Ulster Volunteer Force (UVF). Both loyalist organisations prosper in the predominantly Protestant eastern county of Antrim (including Belfast) as well as north Armagh.

THE RELIGIOUS DIMENSION

There remains a lively debate about the role of religion as a cause of, or sustaining factor in, the conflict (for a general discussion see Jenkins 1986; Whyte 1990: 26–51). On the one hand are authors who view the conflict primarily as a religious war, as a relic of the Reformation/Counter-reformation struggle (Hickey 1984; Bruce 1986). These authors emphasise the exceptional religiosity of both Catholics and Protestants in Northern Ireland compared to most western states, the fear among Protestants of the effects of joining a state dominated by Catholic doctrine on issues such as abortion rights, contraception and divorce and the importance of religious institutions as umbrella organisations for numerous ancillary organisations (e.g. the Ulster Unionist Party (UUP) and the Orange Order; the Democratic Unionist Party (DUP) and the Free Presbyterian Church. On the other hand are those authors who dismiss religion as a mere badge of identity distinguishing natives and settlers (MacDonald 1986), as a tool used by capitalists to deflect attention from the exploitation of workers (Farrell 1976: 81; Bew, Gibbon and Patterson 1979: 221) or as a tool used by extremists to mobilise support to achieve political aims (Mooney and Pollak 1986: 258–60). The compromise position argues that religion is important in so far as it perpetuates several important secular dimensions of the conflict: endogamous marriage practices, denominational schooling and the legal status of divorce. For the purposes of this essay it is sufficient to cite the effect of religion as reinforcing and sustaining the ethnic cleavage rather than as a focus of the conflict itself.

THE ECONOMIC DIMENSION

Economic factors contribute to the conflict primarily in two ways. First, significant socio-economic inequality between Catholics and Protestants fuels Catholic grievances against both Protestants and the British state. As a result of systematic and non-systematic discrimination, Catholics are under-represented in higher management positions, professional and other skilled labour positions (Aunger 1975: 4; Smith and Chambers 1991: 164–6). Catholic males are approximately 2.5 times more likely to be unemployed than Protestant males and the gap does not appear to be closing despite the establishment of the Fair Employment Agency in 1976. While the debate about the causes of inequality between Catholics and Protestants continues (Whyte 1990: 61–4), there is widespread agreement that the gap exists and, more importantly, that Catholics perceive the cause of inequality to be systematic discrimination on the part of Protestants. Second, Northern Ireland's status as a highly dependent, peripheral region within the British economy has led to an economic malaise which exacerbates the conflict. Economic dependence hardens unionists' beliefs in the necessity of maintaining the union with Britain. A key indicator of the effects of dependency is that between 1951 and 1983 the percentage of the workforce employed in manufacturing declined from 41 per cent to 22 per cent while the proportion employed in the public sector increased from 16 per cent to 38 per cent in the same period (Canning, Moore and Rhodes 1987: 223). Priming the public sector as a short-term strategy for reducing unemployment could lead to long-term benefits if it was applied to much-needed sectors such as housing, communications and transportation. But approximately £600 million out of the £1.4 billion annual subvention is spent on the Protestant-dominated security apparatus. As a result, a cynical form of logic suggests that a large section of the public sector workforce has a corporate interest in maintaining the present level of conflict in order to maintain its livelihood. A less cynical interpretation suggests that continued financing of unproductive sectors will sustain the current level of dependency and preclude compromise on the part of unionists.

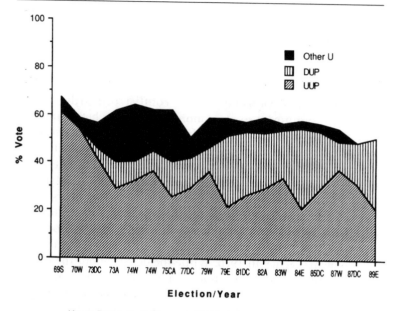

Key to Elections: S=Stormont; W=Westminster; DC=District Council;
A=Assembly; CA=Constitutional Assembly; E=European Parliament.
Source: Flackes and Elliott, 1989; O'Leary, 1990.

Figure 6.1 Distribution of votes within the Unionist bloc, 1969–89

THE POLITICAL DIMENSION

According to conventional conflict analysis, a key factor in the
achievement of conflict regulation is the political elites' willingness and ability to engage in accommodative behaviour (Nordlinger 1972: 43, 74). Willingness and ability in turn are determined largely by the structure of political alignments in the
contending blocs. The following conditions are important: (1)
elite autonomy and control over a well-organised constituency;
(2) intra-segmental stability, i.e., a lack of competition for votes
within each communal segment; (3) a history of elite compromise, usually facilitated by the existence of a common enemy
or threat shared by the communities in conflict.

As explained above, the third condition clearly does not exist
in Northern Ireland. The second condition is clearly more
important in Northern Ireland than the first because the
mutually exclusive national aspirations of the two communal

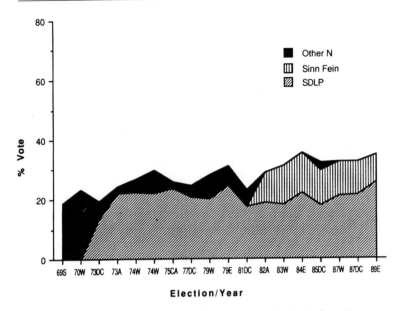

Key to Elections: S=Stormont; W=Westminster; DC=District Council;
A=Assembly; CA=Constitutional Assembly; E=European Parliament.
Source: Flackes and Elliott, 1989; O'Leary, 1990.

Figure 6.2 Distribution of votes within the Nationalist bloc, 1969–89

blocs have led to the formation of a dual-party system (Mitchell
1991: 77–82). Intra-segmental fragmentation within a dual-party
system restricts the ability of elites to achieve sufficient autonomy
and control within the respective constituencies even if elite
predominance exists. Thus Ian Paisley, easily the most char-
ismatic figure in Ulster politics, does not have sufficient autonomy and control within the DUP to offer significant compromise
on the national question without fearing a revolt from hardline
loyalists. Because the intra-segmental fragmentation of the communal blocs is of particular importance in this case, I will focus
upon its development and effects upon conflict regulation
strategies in the rest of this section.

The main political blocs, the nationalist and unionist, are each
internally fragmented into moderate and extremist sub-blocs (see
Figures 6.1 and 6.2). As a result, political elites are discouraged, if
not actively prohibited, from offering significant compromises
on the key issue of the conflict – national aspiration – for fear

that the extremists within their respective blocs will take advantage of any 'surrender' on issues perceived to threaten each side's position on the national question.

The fragmentation of the nationalist bloc was facilitated by the futility of constitutional representation of its minority interests under the Stormont regime (1920–72). During this time the unionist bloc was able to maintain hegemonic control over both local and provincial government through the (often abused) plurality system of representation (O'Leary and McGarry 1992: chs 3 and 4). As a result of its inability to challenge unionist hegemony through constitutional politics, moderate nationalism never completely eclipsed the physical-force tradition within the nationalist bloc. This allowed the Irish Republican Army (IRA) to retain a certain degree of legitimacy and cohesion despite military failures such as the border campaign conducted between 1956 and 1962. The potential political strength of PIRA was not realised until 1981 when, prompted by a wave of Catholic revulsion over the government's handling of the republican prisoners' hunger-strikes, its political wing, Sinn Fein, began contesting elections. Since this, Sinn Fein has garnered at least 30 per cent of the nationalist vote and has represented a significant threat to the main nationalist party, the Social Democratic and Labour Party (SDLP).

The fragmentation of the unionist bloc occurred when hegemonic control began to break down in the early 1960s (Farrell 1976: 227–56; Buckland 1981: 106–10; O'Leary and McGarry 1992: ch. 4). Following the decline of traditional industries and simultaneous increase in the size of the British welfare state, pressure from Britain to reform the economic and political structures in Northern Ireland became more acute. At the same time, the failure of violent nationalism to achieve a united Ireland created new movements within the nationalist community. These 'revisionist' groups challenged Protestant hegemony on issues of *British* rather than Irish citizenship – housing allocation, work-place discrimination, electoral representation – which could not be suppressed as forms of nationalist rebellion. Following the civil rights movement, the strengthened constitutional nationalist movement began to demand that any future structure of government in Northern Ireland should contain an 'Irish dimension' or role for the Irish Republic as a safeguard for nationalist interests. The combined internal and external pressures for reform caused the unionist bloc to split between moderates willing to accept reform in order to retain power, and extremists fearful that any reforms would facilitate a united Ireland.

The fragmentation of the two political blocs continues, allowing extremists on each side actively to pursue strategies meant to derail constitutional initiatives towards conflict regulation. The strength of extremist elements lies in their ability to combine militant tactics with constitutional political pressure. The symbiotic relationship between extremist proponents of violence and extremist constitutional parties has an explicit and an implicit dimension. First, as discussed above, the legitimacy of the extremist blocs negatively affects the constitutional moderates by constraining their ability to offer compromises for fear of being outflanked by the extremists. Second, the strength of the extremist blocs also affects positively the moderates by their ability to threaten to use violence if constitutional initiatives fail. The symbiotic relationship is equally strong in the nationalist bloc – between the PIRA–Sinn Fein coalition and the SDLP – and the unionist bloc – between Protestant militants and extremist tendencies within the UUP and especially in the DUP (Nelson 1984: 55–7; Weitzer 1987: 293). Moreover, the link between physical-force and constitutional movements does not have to be explicit to be real. Both the unionist and nationalist moderate sub-blocs benefit from the threat posed by their respective physical-force proponents. The knowledge that violence will increase if constitutional initiatives fail gives each moderate bloc a certain amount of increased bargaining power, even if they are loathe to admit it.

For unionists, the knowledge that the SDLP and Sinn Fein both support a united Ireland is sufficient evidence that the two parties are fundamentally united. For nationalists, the co-ordinated activity of loyalist paramilitary groups and constitutional unionist parties in opposition to the Sunningdale initiative and the Anglo-Irish Agreement provide ample proof that loyalist militants and unionist 'moderates' are fundamentally united when the status quo is threatened. Loyalist militants and unionist moderates also project a unified stance on the necessity of militarily defeating PIRA, leading nationalists to perceive unionist politicians' calls for further draconian security measures and the increasing revelation of collusion between security forces and loyalist paramilitary groups as less than purely coincidental.

THE SECURITY DIMENSION

An important aspect of Britain's role as an arbiter in the conflict has been the attempt to develop a security apparatus which achieves the correct level of repression necessary to marginalise the proponents of violence within the nationalist and unionist blocs. The combination of historical, political and economic factors outlined above makes the goal of marginalising the extremists very difficult. Nevertheless, pressure to address the violent manifestations of the conflict has led to an over-emphasis upon security as the primary means of conflict regulation. Some believe, for example, that the British government signed the Anglo-Irish Agreement for the security benefits which would result from co-operation with the Irish government (Wilson 1989: 194). However, the security initiative has failed to marginalise proponents of violence. Sinn Fein, the political wing of PIRA, consistently receives 30 per cent of the nationalist vote (10 per cent of the total Northern Ireland vote) in district council and Westminster elections, a clear mandate for the use of violence to achieve a united Ireland from a significant minority of the nationalist community. Loyalist paramilitary groups continue to be active and, though they rarely contest elections, are clearly tolerated if not actively supported by a significant proportion of the unionist community. While it is clear that the level of violence has receded from the high point of the early 1970s, most believe the paramilitary groups remain capable of atrocities on the same or an even greater scale.

Far from marginalising the proponents of violence, security policy in Northern Ireland has strengthened the physical-force tradition through a mixture of incompetence and ignorance of the nature of the symbiotic relationship between constitutional means and violence as tactics of social and political movements. The over-emphasis upon violence as a cause of conflict rather than as *both* a cause *and* effect of the conflict has led to security arrangements which are both counter-productive in their own right and a hindrance to efforts to achieve compromise among political elites. The failure of various security initiatives to complement consociational initiatives will be illustrated below but first it is necessary to outline the evolution of security policy.

The first significant security initiative following the deployment of British troops in 1969 was the imposition of curfews in the Falls Road area of west Belfast in July 1970, accompanied by house-to-house searches for arms. The curfew and searches alienated the nationalist community but the internment of suspected terrorists from 9 August 1971 infuriated them. Internment was introduced under pressure from unionist leaders. The attempt to round up PIRA's leadership failed because of inadequate military intelligence and the operation was preceded by 'practice' rounds which allowed most of PIRA's leadership to avoid the sweep. By March 1972, 900 people were in detention, most of them the wrong people and nearly all Catholic (Buckland 1981: 149–50; Bishop and Mallie 1987: 144–7). The debacle of internment undermined the British government's credibility as a neutral arbiter and led directly to PIRA's most successful recruitment drive (Buckland 1981: 162). In interviews, many contemporary IRA members claim that the alienation caused by internment was the singular most important 'life-event' motivating them to join the movement (White 1989: 1289–94). Violence escalated sharply following internment (see Figure 6.3). A total of 467 people were killed in 1972, the worst year of the current conflict. Following three particularly gruesome atrocities in the first three months of 1972 – including 'Bloody Sunday' (30 January 1972) – the British government prorogued the Stormont parliament and took direct control of the government of Northern Ireland in March 1972.

The escalation of violence led to the passage of two acts of legislation which remain the foundations of the legal component of the security apparatus: the Emergency Provisions Act (EPA-1973) and the Prevention of Terrorism Act (PTA-1974).[1] The current version of the EPA proscribes terrorist organisations and declares membership in such organisations to be a criminal offence, allows security forces to make arrests based upon a 'reasonable suspicion' of terrorist activity and in conjunction with legislation in the Republic, makes provision for suspected terrorists to be tried on whichever side of the border they are apprehended. Most controversially, the EPA provides for suspected terrorists to be tried by a single judge in juryless 'Diplock' courts.[2] The PTA was passed following the wave of

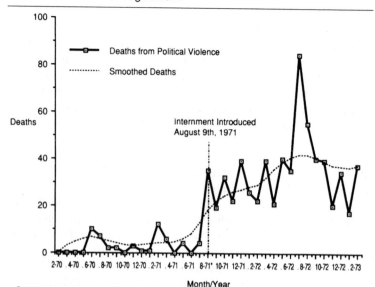

Source: calculated from RUC data.
Note 1: 34 of 35 deaths in August, 1971, occurred on or after August 9th.
Note 2: The data were smoothed using the technique known as 'Hanning' as described in Hartwig and Dearing, 1979:36–39.

Figure 6.3 Monthly deaths from political violence, February 1970 to February 1973

PIRA bombings in Britain, including the infamous Birmingham pub bombings of November 1974. In all, forty-two people were killed by PIRA in Britain during 1974 – the wave of revulsion undoubtedly influenced both the severity of the Bill and the ease with which it was passed. Under the PTA, suspected terrorists can be detained for an initial period of forty-eight hours without being formally charged. The detention period can be extended to a total of seven days with the permission of the Northern Ireland Secretary. Recent amendments to the PTA have given the security forces the power to seize the assets of front organisations which are a principal source of funds for paramilitary organisations and allow the British government to ban suspected terrorists from the UK. This has created a form of internal exile which is indicative of both the government's qualified recognition of Ulster's place in Britain as well as its policy of quarantining the security situation. Separate orders have been issued by the Home Secretary which prohibit the direct broadcast of the statements of suspected members of terrorist organisations and which constrain an individual's right to silence when questioned (McCrudden 1989: 339-41).

By removing suspected terrorists from normal judicial procedures and by widening the counter-insurgency capabilities of the security forces, the British government has implicitly recognised the political legitimacy of both nationalist and loyalist paramilitary groups. Explicit recognition of PIRA's political nature was given in 1972 when William Whitelaw conceded political status to republican prisoners, negotiated a cease fire with PIRA and conducted negotiations with its leadership. In 1975 another ceasefire was negotiated and PIRA was allowed to establish incident centres in nationalist areas. Loyalist paramilitary groups responded to the government's recognition of PIRA's political aims with a sharp increase in sectarian attacks. PIRA's response and the renewed escalation of violence throughout 1975 and 1976 convinced the government that negotiating with terrorists was futile. Starting in 1976 the government attempted to delegitimate PIRA's political movement by 'criminalising' its activity, removing PIRA prisoners' special category status (Boyle and Hadden 1985: 65-67).

Criminalisation was part of a larger strategy intended to 'normalise' public administration and politics in order to reduce expectations from grand political initiatives. An important feature was the 'Ulsterisation' of the security apparatus which gave the RUC and UDR the majority of the security burden. The proportion of locally recruited security forces increased from 45 per cent in 1970 to 51 per cent in 1977 and reached 58 per cent by 1989 (IIP 1989: 316). As a result, the proportion of security-force deaths suffered by 'Ulsterised' forces increased from 36 per cent between 1971 and 1975 to 67 per cent from 1976 to 1990 (calculated from the RUC, 1990). This attempt to contain the violence within Ulster thereby increased the sectarian nature of the internal conflict by pitting local, mainly Protestant, security forces against Catholic republicans.

Far from marginalising the republican movement, the combined effect of criminalisation and Ulsterisation has been to strengthen it in three ways. First, the improvement in the quality of local security intelligence and powers forced PIRA to create a more covert cell-structure which allows it to survive and maintain its effectiveness with less overt support from the nationalist community (Clutterbuck 1981: 141). Second, a knock-on effect of PIRA's reorganisation was the adoption by the security forces of illegal and quasi-legal operational procedures which add to the alienation of the nationalist community from the security forces. The legacy of complaints from the nationalist community against the security forces includes the undeclared use of SAS operatives in shoot-to-kill operations in Northern Ireland (and most spectacularly in Gibraltar in 1988); collusion between members of the UDR, the RUC and loyalist paramilitary groups; forceful interrogation methods; and the use of 'supergrass' methods to induce suspected terrorists to inform on co-operatives. As a result of these and other factors the level of violence has been reduced to what some in the British administration would consider 'acceptable levels' but at the cost of sustaining the long-term capabilities of both nationalist and loyalist militant groups. As Figure 6.4 shows, republican paramilitaries continue to cause considerable loss of life and, while the proportion of deaths caused by loyalist paramilitaries has been significantly reduced, the recent reorganisation and reactivation of loyalist death squads since the failure of the Brooke talks indicate that both sides are prepared to sustain their violent campaigns.

Third, criminalisation allowed the republican movement to develop its political machinery in reaction to community support for the prisoners' campaign against the elimination of political category status. The campaign evolved from a blanket protest in 1976 to a 'dirty' protest in 1978 to the hunger-strikes of 1980–1. PIRA was persuaded to limit its campaign of violence and concentrate on developing political support for the prisoners' movement (Beresford 1987: 93–8; O'Malley 1990: 211–14). Westminster's refusal to bend to the pressure of the protest was critical in extending support for the hunger-strikers well beyond the traditional basis of republicanism, resulting in the election of Bobby Sands to a seat at Westminster and the election of two hunger-strikers to seats in Dail Eireann in 1981.

Security policy during the period of direct rule has been dictated by three main considerations: reducing violence to levels deemed 'acceptable' for Britain's international reputation; appeasing unionists' demands for sufficient force to be applied to defeat PIRA; and marginalising the paramilitaries in order to elevate the constitutional parties to positions where compromise

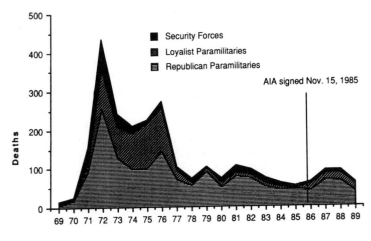

Key: Republican Paramilitaries include: PIRA, OIRA, INLA, IPLO;
Loyalist Paramilitaries include: UDA and UFF, UVF and PAF,
Red Hand Commandos and 'non-specific loyalists';
Security Forces include: British Army, RUC and UDR.
Source: IIP, Agenda Database

Figure 6.4 Deaths by agency responsible, 1969–89

can be achieved. While the level of violence has been reduced
significantly, unionist hopes that PIRA could be defeated have
not been realised. The latter's persistent strength allows unionists to deflect attention from their intransigence on constitutional
questions to matters of security.

THE DYNAMICS OF CONFLICT REGULATION

A successful conflict regulation strategy must be based upon the
primary dimensions of the conflict as outlined above. In order to
bolster moderates and allow them to compromise on the national
question, their extremist competitors within the respective blocs
must be marginalised. This requires a delicate balance between
effective and impartial security measures and a recognition of the
interests which motivate extremists. Recognising the importance
of social support networks in allowing militant groups to sustain
a paramilitary campaign, the grievances of the supporting
communities must be eliminated as much as possible. Most
importantly, the separate strands of a conflict-regulation strategy

must be complementary, recognising the symbiotic relationship between constitutional and militant groups aligned on the same basic objective. At first glance, British conflict-regulation initiatives appear to have followed the basic three-track strategy of political, security and socio-economic initiatives. On closer examination, however, the separate initiatives have either been failures in their own right, or have been hopelessly mismatched with one of the other dimensions. In the following discussion I will use three conflict-regulation initiatives to illustrate how the lack of co-ordination between security policy and constitutional initiatives has failed to achieve significant progress towards an internal consociational agreement.

Since 1969 the British government has concentrated on security and political initiatives to promote a resolution of the conflict. Social and economic dimensions have received less attention and continue to present considerable obstacles to conflict regulation by sustaining grievances which in turn contribute to a sustained polarisation of the two communal blocs. Some of the primary grievances of the civil-rights era have been addressed: housing allocation has been centralised under the Northern Ireland Housing Executive and the gerrymandering of election wards has been eliminated. Other grievances remain despite – or because of – partial reforms: discrimination and employment differentials have remained at much the same level throughout the conflict. The free-market principles of Thatcherism have exacerbated the already declining economic performance of the region. Overall unemployment doubled from 10 to over 20 per cent during Thatcher's reign and, if not for the significant rise in public-sector employment, would be considerably higher. This lack of attention to important underlying dimensions of the conflict reveals a British priority of containment rather than regulation, not to mention resolution, of the conflict.

The first political initiative, negotiated at Sunningdale in December 1973, established the creation of a power-sharing executive composed of unionists, nationalists and confessional neutrals in rough proportion to their relative electoral strengths. A Council of Ireland was to be established providing for regular ministerial meetings between members of the executive and the government of the Republic on issues such as cross-border security and economic co-operation. The intention of the initiative was to establish a power-sharing structure which would allow moderates to regain elite predominance within their respective blocs. Reaction to it was determined by 'rational' self-interests of nationalist and unionist elites. The SDLP participated because it offered their leaders a degree of power considerably greater than anything that had been available under the Stormont regime. The SDLP were given four of the eleven seats within the executive, including the position of deputy chief executive. Faulkner's Official Unionist Party (OUP) participated because Faulkner was made chief executive and his party was given six of the eleven executive seats. The Alliance Party was given one seat on the executive to match its electoral support.

The extremists on both sides rejected the initiative for obvious reasons. Sinn Fein would not accept anything short of a guaranteed commitment to a British withdrawal, while the extremists within the unionist blocs led by Bill Craig and Ian Paisley rejected both the principle of power-sharing as well as any Irish dimension. The opponents of the Sunningdale agreement formed an organisation called the United Ulster Unionist Council (UUUC) which successfully mobilised key labour unions and loyalist paramilitary groups, leading to a massive strike by the Ulster Workers' Council (UWC) which brought down the executive in May 1974 (Fisk 1975).

The Sunningdale initiative broke down over two primary issues: the refusal of many unionists to accept a power-sharing structure and nationalists' insistence on an Irish dimension. The escalation of communal violence following the security policy of internment was primarily responsible for the ascendant position of the extremists within each communal bloc which forced 'moderate' leaders to insist on maintaining mutually exclusive positions.

The refusal of the British government to either negotiate or use force against the UUUC and the UWC is regarded by some as a lost opportunity to undermine intransigent unionism (Fisk 1975). It is attributed to the overriding concern of British leaders to quarantine the Northern Ireland problem rather than bite the bullet of directly challenging Protestant hegemony (Buckland 1981: 172). However, such an interpretation ignores two key points. First, the power-sharing executive was effectively defeated before the strike commenced. The Sunningdale 'agreement' disguised the amount of disagreement which existed between the SDLP and OUP over the meaning and extent of the Council of

Ireland. The SDLP had to sell it to the nationalist community as a significant step towards a united Ireland while Faulkner had to sell it to unionists as a repudiation of Ireland's irredentist claims. These incompatible interpretations provided a fragile base for the power-sharing coalition. Second, assuming that the British government could have broken the UWC strike underemphasises the degree of Protestant popular opposition to power-sharing with an Irish dimension. The military force required to destroy the Protestant coalition may well have provoked a civil war.

Harold Wilson's refusal to negotiate with the UUUC was probably the more realistic 'lost opportunity'. By doing so, he could have forced the anti-power-sharing unionists to defend their intransigent position. Westminster could have attempted to fragment the anti-Faulkner coalition by offering limited concessions such as a second chamber within the assembly with limited veto-power over executive decrees. Instead, Wilson was determined not to legitimate the use of unconstitutional means to reach a negotiating position – a decision which served only to reveal the inconsistency of Britain's role as arbiter since in 1972 it had allowed PIRA to bomb its way to the negotiating table after helping to bring down the Stormont government.

Wilson's inconsistency reveals the lack of co-ordination between political initiatives and the security dimension. Internment set off a cycle of escalation which placed PIRA in a position to force the SDLP into a non-negotiable position on the Irish dimension. The ascendance of PIRA also legitimated the extremist loyalist reaction which was vital for the organisation of the UWC strike which brought down the executive. The result of the security fiasco of internment precluded the emergence of constitutional initiatives because the likelihood of elites achieving intra-bloc predominance during a period of intra-bloc fragmentation was extremely small.

A second example of uncoordinated initiatives was the process known as 'Rolling Devolution' initiated by Northern Ireland Secretary James Prior in 1982. By this time the PIRA hunger-strikes had resulted in ten deaths and a wave of domestic and international support for the republican movement. The Thatcher government refused to back down from its policy of criminalising terrorism and the familiar pattern of republican ascendancy and loyalist reaction followed. Despite the atmosphere of polarisation, Prior attempted to regain the consti-

tutional initiative by offering a plan whereby devolved government would be offered on an incremental basis as agreement
evolved between the nationalist and unionist blocs. A 70 per cent
majority (55 seats) was required within the seventy-eight-member
assembly to agree on a system of devolved government. Unionists
participated despite objections to the power-sharing element
enforced by the 70 per cent rule, but happy with the exclusion of
a guaranteed Irish dimension. However, the strength of Sinn
Fein prevented the SDLP from participating in an initiative
which did not include an Irish dimension. Instead, both the
SDLP and Sinn Fein contested the elections to the assembly on
abstentionism tickets, the SDLP objecting to the absence of an
Irish dimension and Sinn Fein refusing to recognise the constitutional validity of devolved rule from Britain but eager to
establish its political strength in the nationalist community in
the wake of the hunger strikes. Despite the nationalist boycott the
new assembly was formed and continued to meet until June
1986.[3] In the absence of nationalist participation its role was
reduced to that of a unionist advisory commission, scrutinising
draft legislation and publishing reports on devolution which
were interesting but not constructive in terms of progress towards
a constitutional settlement (Flackes and Elliott 1989: 367–70).

The British government's insistence on attempting to regain
the constitutional initiative during a period of republican
ascendancy reveals a lack of understanding of the symbiotic
relationship which prevents moderates within the SDLP from
offering compromises acceptable to unionists. Of course other
factors besides the continued vitality of PIRA prevented unionists from accepting power-sharing or a significant Irish
dimension. Given the irredentist claims of the Irish Republic,
embedded in Articles 2 and 3 of the Irish Constitution, unionists
are unwilling to allow any role to the Dublin government.

The two constitutional initiatives just described were exercises
in 'agreeing to disagree'. Two obstacles consistently undermined
any hopes of achieving a voluntary consociational settlement: the
Irish dimension and unionists' refusal to accept any form of
power-sharing with nationalists. Underlying these intransigent
positions are opposing backbones of militant threat which have
been entrenched with significant help from failed security
initiatives and insufficient social and economic reforms. Two
initiatives were undertaken in the early 1980s to attempt to

overcome the ostensible obstacles. Starting with the Haughey-Thatcher summit of December 1980, the two governments attempted to bypass unionist intransigence in particular by negotiating among themselves. The British–Irish Intergovernmental Council was created in 1981 with the intention of establishing formal relations at the ministerial, official and parliamentary levels. The council was a clear indication of London's recognition that a limited Irish dimension was necessary to assuage the nationalist minority into compromising on the national question.

It was also clear that a primary motivation for the Anglo-Irish initiative was the security benefits which would flow from cooperation between the two governments. The ability of PIRA activists to find safe haven in the Republic has been a constant obstacle to effective security along the border and it was hoped that pressure could be brought to bear on the Republic to change their restrictive extradition laws.

The second initiative was the New Ireland Forum in early 1983. The forum consisted of four of the five primary nationalist parties on the island: the SDLP, Fianna Fail, Fine Gael and the Irish Labour Party – excluding Sinn Fein. It was an attempt to create a united constitutional–nationalist position to stem the growth of Sinn Fein following the hunger-strikes. The forum's report expressed Fianna Fail's and the SDLP's aspiration for an eventual unitary state as its optimum solution but also reflected Fine Gael's and the ILP's recognition of the requirement of unionist consent to unity and included compromise scenarios based on joint British–Irish 'condominium' rule over Northern Ireland as well as a federal united Ireland. Sinn Fein rejected the consent proposal as a sell-out to traditional nationalist aspirations, unionists rejected the proposal as an example of continued Irish irredentism. Prior and Thatcher both rejected the proposals, the latter issuing her famous 'out, out, out!' response to each of the three proposals. Despite the frosty reaction within Northern Ireland and Britain, the forum's recognition of the necessity of unity by consent was hailed as a significant nationalist compromise by the influential Irish-American lobby, as well as the British Labour Party. The report's influence can be judged by the almost identical wording of the clause on unity by consent which was eventually included as Article 1 of the Anglo-Irish Agreement.

The British–Irish Intergovernmental Council and the New Ireland Forum signified a transition from voluntary to coercive political initiatives aimed at achieving a consociational structure (O'Leary 1989). The culmination of the new process was the Anglo-Irish Agreement (AIA) which was signed by the British and Irish prime ministers (Thatcher and Fitzgerald) on 15 November 1985. In order to appease unionists the agreement reiterated the commitment of the British government to maintain the link with Northern Ireland until a majority wished it to change. In order to appease nationalists the agreement legally established a strong Irish dimension through the establishment of an intergovernmental conference, which would meet regularly to discuss issues of concern to the nationalist minority community: security practices, the legal system, economic equality and human rights. A permanent secretariat based at Maryfield was established to service the conference. Moderate nationalists welcomed the clearly established Irish dimension while Sinn Fein labelled it a sell-out, arguing that it guaranteed the Protestant majority's ability to veto any proposal for a united Ireland for the foreseeable future.

Despite the renewed guarantee of Northern Ireland's status within the UK and the prospects of co-operation on security issues between the two governments, unionist reaction was uniformly hostile. They were correct in arguing that the Irish dimension had been imposed on them, as it was signed without their consent. Huge protests were organised against the agreement and the Northern Ireland Assembly was commandeered by unionists into a vehicle for denouncing the agreement, resulting in the abandonment of the Assembly by the Alliance Party and its eventual dissolution by London in June 1986. Republican militants were similarly hostile to the agreement due to its guarantee of the unionist veto over a united Ireland.

By attempting to coerce unionists into a form of power-sharing agreement while continuing to deny the political legitimacy of the republican movement, the AIA ensures the continuing entrenchment rather than the marginalisation of extremists. The overriding emphasis on the security dimension undermines progress towards an internal settlement by pandering to the opportunist political ambitions of unionist elites and by continuing to alienate a significant proportion of the nationalist community. The unionist bloc remains steadfastly united in its opposition to the agreement and all negotiations since its signing have been prefaced by a unionist insistence that the agreement be replaced. 'Talks about talks' initiated by Northern Ireland Secretary Tom King in 1987 and 1988 reached an impasse over the continued functioning of the AIA's secretariat. Most recently, the 'Brooke talks' – the first negotiations involving all of the major constitutional parties except Sinn Fein – broke down over the unionists' insistence that the scheduled inter-governmental conference be postponed. The DUP's Ian Paisley accused the British and Irish governments of forcing unionists to 'surrender' to the planned meeting of the inter-governmental conference (*Irish Times*, 26 June 1991). The proponents of violence reacted to the failed constitutional initiative by commencing a cycle of sectarian violence which was meant to re-establish the credentials of each group as defenders of the interests of their respective communities.

CONCLUSION

The overemphasis upon security policy at the expense of substantial social and economic reforms has not been successful in promoting conditions for consociationalism. The proponents of violence have been entrenched rather than marginalised and unionist intransigence on the issue of power-sharing has been facilitated by the emphasis upon the security threat. An alternative conflict regulation strategy based on the failures of past initiatives suggests that the significant bases of support for nationalist and unionist paramilitary groups should be recognised and exploited. First, reforms aimed at the underlying causes of support for paramilitary groups should be implemented, including: a bill of rights which protects against abuses by the security forces, the replacement of Diplock courts with three-judge courts, increased powers for the Independent Commission for Police Complaints, an industrial development programme aimed at creating long-term employment targeted at particularly deprived areas and actively monitored by a Fair Employment Commission with stronger enforcement powers. In return for the appeasement of nationalist grievances it would be necessary for the Irish Republic to repudiate its claims over the territory of Northern Ireland as stated in Articles 2 and 3 of its Constitution.

Second, if the reforms just mentioned are shown to be successful in reducing support for paramilitary violence, both Sinn Fein and the UDA should be unconditionally accepted into any *constitutional* negotiations. In order to convince the supporters of PIRA and the UDA that their immediate goals are both unjust and unworkable, the leaders of both movements should be forced to defend their positions in any constitutional initiatives which are brought forward. The encouragement of Sinn Fein as a legitimate political party could widen the already apparent internal split within the republican movement. The hardline proponents of violence will respond with flails of violence, but if real reforms are passed then the nationalist community will eventually repress the extremists. There is precedence for this scenario within the nationalist community. Following the failed border campaign from 1956 to 1962 it rejected the physical-force tradition in favour of the constitutional civil rights movement. More recently, the rise in support of Sinn Fein following the hunger-strikes acted as a serious impediment to PIRA's campaign of violence (Guelke 1986: 111).

The primary obstacle to an explicit recognition of the republican movement's political legitimacy is the threatened loyalist backlash. However, the suggestions made in this scenario would not necessarily provoke a violent backlash because they do not promote a united Ireland. In fact, a bill of rights was proposed by the UDA in 1988 and therefore should not in itself provoke a violent reaction from that group of loyalist extremists. The most recent mobilisation of loyalist extremists is further evidence that loyalists will respond with violence to any increase in the institutionalised Irish dimension. In order to counterbalance this trend, it is necessary to trade internal reforms for a withdrawal of Irish claims and thereby remove the uncertainty which fuels the cycle of violence. In the meantime, it is clear that unionist politicians will not presently agree to any negotiations involving Sinn Fein. However, if reforms are successful then a significant reduction in PIRA violence resulting from pressure within the nationalist community would undermine the unionists' ability to rationalise intransigence based on the security threat. Loyalist militancy during periods of low levels of republican violence has not been sufficiently threatening to undermine the reform process. The failed loyalist strike in 1977 and the failure of the predicted loyalist backlash following the signing of the

Anglo-Irish Agreement suggest that reducing republican violence through reform rather than repression holds the key to a consociational future for Northern Ireland.

NOTES

1 Both the EPA and the PTA are regularly reviewed and modified, the EPA was reviewed by Lord Gardiner in 1975 and by Sir George Baker in 1984, while the PTA was reviewed by Lord Shackelton in 1978, Lord Jellicoe in 1983 and Lord Colville in 1987. Lord Gardiner recommended the suspension of internment, the introduction of Diplock courts, the abolition of special-category status for terrorist offenders and the establishment of a bill of rights for Northern Ireland. The bill of rights was rejected in favour of the establishment of the Standing Advisory Commission on Human Rights (SACHR) which has considerably less enforcement power than a bill of rights (for a general discussion of security legislation see Hogan and Walker 1989; McCrudden 1989).

2 Diplock courts are named after Lord Diplock whose report in 1972 recommended the use of single-judge trials for terrorist offences because the potential intimidation of jurors and witnesses made trial by peers impossible in Northern Ireland.

Between 1974 and 1986 the acquittal rate of those who pleaded not guilty in Diplock courts was 33 per cent compared to 55 per cent in Crown Court cases.

3 The Official Unionist Party boycotted the first stage of the assembly from November 1982 until May 1984 due to a disagreement over the nomination of chairmanships and over security policy (Flackes and Elliott 1989: 369).

Chapter 7

Burundi in comparative perspective

Dimensions of ethnic strife

René Lemarchand

INTRODUCTION

In April and May 1972 the tiny central African republic of Burundi experienced bloodshed of a magnitude unprecedented in the country's history: an estimated 100,000 Hutu were rounded up and killed by government troops (of Tutsi origins) in one of the most appalling examples of human rights violations recorded in independent Africa.[1] The genocidal scale of the 1972 killings makes Burundi one of the continent's grimmest laboratories for the study of ethnic violence. This is not to imply that the country did not experience more common forms of violence, ranging from urban rioting to army coups and ethnic insurgencies; only in Burundi, however, does the definition of genocide contained in the United Nations Convention on the Prevention and Punishment of the Crime of Genocide (1948) – 'acts committed with intent to destroy, in whole or in part, a national, ethnical, racial or religious group' (art. 2) – find a more tragically accurate illustration.[2] As much as the extent of the carnage, the element of intent is what differentiates the Burundi killings from most other instances of ethnic violence.

Ironically, because of its long pedigree as an archaic kingdom, few other polities in the continent seemed better equipped to cope with the crises of legitimacy and identity that have beset other African states. There is nothing artificial about the country's boundaries; indeed its existence as a national entity precedes by centuries that of many East European states, including Yugoslavia or the Soviet Union. Nor were its political institutions imported from abroad. For as far back as can be remembered the kingship served as a prime focus of popular loyalties, and its legitimacy as an institution was never seriously questioned.[3]

On the other hand – and this is where the case of Burundi again differs from that of most other African states – the vertical structuring of ethnic differentiation (of which more in a moment) carried within itself the seeds of massive bloodshed. Although power traditionally gravitated in the hands of princely chiefs, the Tutsi minority stood as socially and culturally distinct from the subordinate Hutu majority. A potentially devastating asymmetry of group claims was thus inscribed in the traditional social structure; at the heart of the convulsions that followed independence lay a form of ethnic exclusivism that denied the Hutu majority the right to become full participants in the emergent political system. The singularity of Burundi thus stems from the ambiguous coalescence within its traditional political system of forces that made for both conflict and cohesion, with the former eventually asserting itself as the dominant force.

HISTORICAL BACKDROP

A country of almost Lilliputian dimensions (27,834 sq. km) and high population density (160 per sq. km) Burundi is also one of the poorest in Africa. Though now a republic, its boundaries remained virtually unchanged since its emergence as an archaic kingdom in the eighteenth century. Like Rwanda, its neighbour to the north, Burundi was once part of the German colony of East Africa, later to become a League of Nations Mandate and a United Nations Trust Territory under Belgian administration. Until its accession to independence in 1962 much of Burundi politics revolved around a thinly-veiled struggle for power between two princely factions, the Bezi and the Batare, the former identified with the ruling dynasty and the latter with rival claimants to the throne. Playing off one group of princes (ganwa) against the other became a standard feature of Belgian colonial policies, with the Batare faction eventually emerging as the residency's favourite partner against the Bezi. Thus as independence finally came into view, in the late 1950s, the stage was set for an increasingly polarised pattern of competition between the Parti Démocratie Chrétien (PDC) and the Parti de l'Unité et du Progrès National (Uprona), associated, respectively, with Batare and Bezi politicians.

The legislative elections of 1961, a year before indepedence resulted in a landslide victory for the Uprona and the appointment of its recognised leader, Prince Rwagasore, as prime minister designate. As the oldest son of King (Mwami) Mwambutsa, and a figure of immense popularity among both Hutu and Tutsi, Rwagasore stood as the embodiment of nationalist aspirations and the strongest supporter of the monarchy. His assassination on 13 October 1961 by a Greek gunman in the pay of the PDC opposition ushered in a crisis of legitimacy from which the country has yet to recover. His death created a political void which no other leader has been able to fill, thus setting the stage for endless conflict and increasingly violent claims and counter-claims by Hutu and Tutsi.

The assertion of Tutsi political hegemony is all the more surprising when one considers: (a) that they represent only 15 per cent of a total population of approximately 5 million, and the Hutu 84 per cent; (b) that their sense of unity is at best precarious given the regional and sub-ethnic divisions that have consistently pitted one group (Tutsi-Hima) against another (Tutsi-Banyaruguru); and (c) that, unlike what happened in Rwanda, the pre-colonial history of Burundi offers little evidence of ancestral hatreds between Hutu and Tutsi, both having lived peacefully side by side for centuries in the interstices of princely rivalries.

The Hutu-Tutsi conflict is a recent phenomenon, rooted in part in the process of social change introduced by the colonial state, in part in the rapid mobilisation of ethnic identities under the pressure of electoral competition. Perhaps no other factor has played a more decisive role in hardening the lines of ethnic cleavage than the psychological impact of the Rwanda revolution on the collective consciousness of both Hutu and Tutsi. While the proclamation of a Hutu republic in Rwanda served as a powerful source of political inspiration for many Hutu politicians, for most Tutsi the Rwanda model evoked a nightmarish vision of Hutu domination, to be avoided at all costs. What made it possible for the Tutsi minority to reverse the Rwanda scenario, and eventually emerge as the politically dominant minority, was a combination of extraordinary luck and ruthlessness.

The turning point came on 18 October 1965, when a group of Hutu gendarmerie and army officers unsuccessfully tried to overthrow the monarchy, yet came close enough to realising their objective to cause the panic-stricken Mwambutsa to flee the country. In the wake of the aborted coup the purge of some thirty-four Hutu officers – accompanied by the execution of scores of Hutu gendarmes and politicians, and hundreds of innocent civilians – was the first in a series of steps intended to give Tutsi elements control over the army, and ultimately over the institutions of the state. The second came in July 1966 with the appointment of the chief of staff of the armed forces, Colonel Michel Micombero, as prime minister. A Tutsi-Hima from Bururi province, Micombero had played a key role in organising anti-Hutu pogroms in the countryside. With Micombero at the helm ethno-regional ties became increasingly important as a source of solidarity within the ruling Tutsi stratum. Finally, with the formal overthrow of the monarchy in November 1966 – less than two months after the official transfer of the Crown from Mwambutsa to his younger son, Prince Charles Ndizeye – and the formal proclamation of the First Republic, the last obstacle in the path of Tutsi hegemony was removed (Lemarchand 1970: ch. 12).

Burundi's post-independence history is almost a parable on how traditional monarchies, in trying to contain the pressures of mobilised ethnicity, end up as casualties of their own efforts at centralisation. Here Huntington's paradigm of the 'king's dilemma' immediately comes to mind (Huntington 1968: 177). The rapid polarisation of ethnic identities in the years following independence made it imperative for the king to concentrate all powers around the throne; but by doing so he created the very conditions that led to the demise of the monarchy at the hands of the army. The initial challenge to the Crown in 1965 came from Hutu elements within the army and the gendarmerie. In trying to seize power from the king they took a gamble and lost; subsequent purges of disloyal (i.e. Hutu) elements left the Tutsi largely in control of the armed forces, and when, in 1966, another trial of strength opposed the predominantly Tutsi army to the Crown, the stage was set for the proclamation of the First Republic.

From then on Burundi politics have tended to revolve around factional struggles within the ruling Tutsi minority, unfolding against a background of repeated threats of Hutu insurrection, as happened in 1972 and 1988.[4] The bloodbaths of 1972 and 1988 were critical watersheds in the history of the Hutu–Tutsi conflict.

Besides crystallising the collective self-awareness of the Hutu people as a martyred community, they show how little weight is attached to moral or rational considerations when the stakes of conflict are suddenly reduced to the imperative of ethnic survival.

THE ROOTS OF CONFLICT

The roots of the Hutu–Tutsi conflict do not lie in the precolonial past (though claims that it does, on the part of some Hutu intellectuals, have contributed significantly to its persistence); as already noted, they lie in the bitter power struggle unleashed by the introduction of electoral processes in the years following independence. That the traditional society contained within itself a rich potential for conflict is undeniable: given the relative size of ethnic segments it is easy to see why majority rule should raise fears of permanent Hutu domination among Tutsi, and why, by denying them their fair share of political power, the Tutsi should have created a sense of outrage among the Hutu. Significant though these considerations are to an understanding of contemporary Burundi politics, they fail to address the crux of the Hutu–Tutsi problem. Rather than to look for a sudden resurgence of 'deep-seated' traditional enmities, a more fruitful approach is to focus on the changes in Hutu–Tutsi relations introduced through processes of political modernisation.

The impact of the colonial state

A major point of entry into the genesis of the Hutu–Tutsi conflict lies in the impact of Belgian policies on the redistribution of power and privilege between the two groups. The critical point to note is the extent to which Belgian administrators have tended to read into the traditional social structure of Burundi a replica of the Rwanda situation, where Hutu–Tutsi relations were characterised by a much more rigid pattern of stratification. Although the principle of *ganwa* rule (for which there was no equivalent in Rwanda) was never questioned, what ceased to be recognised were traditional Hutu claims to power within the limits allowed by the monarchy. By withdrawing recognition from those Hutu chiefs and court officials who held office by consent of the Crown, the colonial state significantly altered existing patterns of political recruitment (to the advantage of

Tutsi and *ganwa* elements); by imposing upon the peasant masses a wide range of obligations (ranging from taxes and corvée labour to porterage and compulsory crop cultivation) it added immeasurably to their traditional burdens; and by the selective allocation of educational opportunities to Tutsi and *ganwa* elements it further reduced the life chances of the Hutu as a group. The net result has been to set the stage for a pattern of restratification in which class cleavages tended increasingly to coincide with ethnic identities (Gahama 1983).

The demonstration effect of the Rwanda revolution

Just as colonial Rwanda provided the trusteeship authorities with a model of sorts for administering Burundi, the revolution in Rwanda (1959–62) also provided the nascent Hutu elites with the model polity they sought to emulate. Few other events have had a more decisive psychological impact on the rise of Hutu aspirations; from then on Rwanda entered the consciousness of many Hutu politicians as a crucially important point of reference for pressing their claims to recognition – and the Tutsi consciousness as the premonition of a nightmare to be avoided at all cost. With tens of thousands of Tutsi refugees from Rwanda entering the country – each with tales of horror on their lips – few were the Tutsi of Burundi who did not see the handwriting on the wall. In short, the Rwanda revolution carried a powerful demonstration effect on both Hutu and Tutsi, causing a rapid and irreversible hardening of ethnic solidarities.

The political mobilisation of ethnic segments

That the revolution in Rwanda happened to coincide with a major struggle for the leadership of the Uprona greatly magnified the psychological impact of the party crisis. The struggle for power between Paul Mirerekano (a Hutu) and André Muhirwa (a *ganwa* with strong pro-Tutsi sympathies) was widely perceived as a Hutu–Tutsi contest. The intra-party struggle thus quickly spilled over into the urban arena of the capital city, pitting Hutu trade unionists and politicians against young Tutsi militants for the most part affiliated with the Uprona youth wing. The feedback effect of urban rioting (the so-called Kamenge incidents, January 1962) was immediately felt within the rank and file of the party as well as within the govnerment and the National Assembly, thus bringing the machinery of the state to a near standstill. The Kamenge riots gave a decisive impetus to a process of ethnic mobilisation which gradually spread from the capital city to other localities. Until 1965, when the abortive Hutu-led coup set in motion a severe repression of Hutu 'suspects' in the Muramvya and Gitega provinces, ethnic mobilisation remained an urban phenomenon; after 1965, however, politicised ethnicity became the dominant characteristic of Hutu–Tutsi relations in the countryside. The polarisation of ethnic feelings did not just happen; it came about as the result of a deliberate, organised and sustained effort on the part of ethnic entrepreneurs to mobilise a substantial ethnic following.

Political exclusion

At the heart of anti-Tutsi violence lies the more or less systematic exclusion of Hutu elements from all positions of political responsibility in the party, the government, the civil service and the army. Denial of effective political participation in this case is all the more bitterly resented in view of the fact that Hutu account for approximately 85 per cent of the total population. There is more to Hutu attitudes and behaviour than just political frustration. Widespread moral indignation is indeed a critical element in the background of Hutu violence – a sentiment traceable to the decision of the Court (presumably acting under the pressure of Tutsi elements) to ignore the results of the 1965 elections which gave the Hutu full control of the National Assembly. This is where the appointment of Leopold Biha (a *ganwa*) as prime minister may well be regarded as the 'critical point' in the evolution of the Hutu–Tutsi conflict, as it robbed the Hutu of the fruits of their electoral victory and made a mockery of the electoral process. Hutu violence is hardly a matter of 'pent-up frustration'; its motivating force lies in the pervasive sense of moral indignation felt by many Hutu in the face of what they perceive to be an intolerable denial of their legitimate political rights. Not only is recourse to violence viewed by many

Hutu as the only available alternative to the perpetuation of Tutsi hegemony; more to the point is that it is seen as a morally and politically justifiable alternative.

The interlocking of reciprocal acts of violence

What might be referred to as *l'engrenage de la violence* draws attention to the 'infernal machine' phenomenon brought to light by the reciprocation of acts of violence. Anti-Hutu violence inevitably led to anti-Tutsi retribution: the 1965 'purge' of Hutu suspects in time led to the Hutu insurrection of 1972, which in turn triggered the 1972 genocide; likewise the sudden upsurge of anti-Tutsi violence in 1988 in turn brought forth a massive reprisal against Hutu elements. A kind of uneven *lex talionis* came to preside over the unfolding of acts of violence, whereby every challenge was met by a retribution in kind; yet each time repressive violence came into play, as in 1965, 1972 and 1988, the severity of the response clearly exceeded the nature of the challenge.

The redefinition of ethnic selves

To the rapid sharpening of ethnic polarities arising from the interlocking of reciprocal violence must be added the sense of martyrdom felt by the Hutu as a group. Their collective self-image is that of a victimised community, against whom deliberate atrocities have repeatedly been committed. Revenge rather than conciliation thus marks the attitude of a great many Hutu. Among Tutsi elements, on the other hand, fears of a possible retribution on a comparable scale are omnipresent. Anticipation of a Tutsi genocide certainly played a decisive role in the 'pre-emptive strikes' against Hutu elements in 1972 and 1988. Tutsi apprehensions of a wholesale extermination by Hutu are indeed central to an understanding of the horrendous scale of the repressive measures triggered by the 1972 and 1988 uprisings. The exigencies of self-preservation for many Tutsi make it imperative not only to retain control over the instruments of force but to use force whenever confronted with threats to their own survival as a minority.

THE STRUCTURING OF HUTU–TUTSI DIFFERENTIATION

As the foregoing plainly suggests, nothing is more detrimental to an understanding of ethnic conflict in Burundi than to fall back on the 'tribal' stereotype, where the tall Tutsi are seen as trying to reassert their traditional claims to supremacy over the smaller Hutu.[5] Ethnicity can be viewed from two different, though by no means mutually exclusive, perspectives. If the term is meant to refer to the political mobilisation of cultural identities under the pressure of electoral competition for the spoils of power, ethnicity is a relatively recent phenomenon; on the other hand, as a form of cultural self-awareness the phenomenon has been a long-standing feature of the social landscape. In the first instance ethnicity is largely a subjective phenomenon; in the other it is an objective correlate of cultural differentiation.

How, then, does cultural differentiation in Burundi differ from that of other African states? The answer lies in the structuring of group differentiation. The basic distinction here is between horizontal and vertical patterns of ethnic stratification. Almost everywhere in Africa the former predominates: the juxtaposition of discrete ethnic entities (misleadingly designated as 'tribes' in journalistic parlance) within the same territorial arena makes for 'unconnected co-existences', to use Max Weber's formulation; each group differs from the other in terms of language, religious beliefs, mode of social organisation and political institutions. Not so in Burundi. Here the vertical patterning of group solidarities implies a hierarchy of rank and privilege, but little in the way of objective cultural differentiation. Thus the concept of 'tribe' is singularly inappropriate to describe Hutu and Tutsi, given the fact that they share the same language (Kirundi), the same type of social organisation, often the same life-styles, and lived peacefully with each other for centuries while sharing the same collective commitment to monarchical symbols of legitimacy.

Looked at from the perspective of the traditional society, on the basis of what criteria could one group be differentiated from the other? Certainly not in terms of access to power: the real power-holders were the princes of the blood (ganwa), whose identity was perceived as ethnically distinct from that of Hutu and Tutsi. They differed from each other, first, in terms of numbers, the Hutu representing approximately 85 per cent of a total population estimated at 2.5 million at the turn of the century, and the Tutsi 14 per cent. Second, in terms of their participation in the economic life of the country, the Tutsi being essentially pastoralists and the Hutu agriculturalists. Third, and most importantly, as a group the Hutu occupied a somewhat subordinate social position in relation to Tutsi elements in the traditional pecking order. Finally, physical differences are not inevitably irrelevant in distinguishing Hutu from Tutsi, with the latter sometimes approximating the usual stereotype of the 'tall, nilotic cattle herder'.

Yet each of the foregoing characterisations immediately calls for the strongest qualifications: (a) although there is no gainsaying that *ganwa* elements stood as a ruling elite, chiefly and other authoritative positions were occasionally held by both Hutu and Tutsi; (b) even though the Tutsi are unquestionably a minority and the Hutu a majority, a considerable margin of error must be allowed in population statistics dating back to the 1930s; (c) the distinction between Tutsi pastoralists and Hutu agriculturalists was by no means as rigid as some might imagine, and has now become largely irrelevant; (d) the traditional society allowed for considerable upward mobility (partly through clientage relations, partly through selective appointments to positions of authority), thereby mitigating traditional status differences between Hutu and Tutsi; to this must be added that such differences were often blurred in practice through kinship affiliations (as between 'good', 'not so good' and 'bad' families); (e) as for the somatic differences between Hutu and Tutsi, the least that can be said is that they are notoriously unreliable for identifying members of each ethnic community.

The point of all this is that Burundi society offers enough evidence to sustain both the *primordialist and instrumentalist* interpretations of ethnic conflict: the first concentrates on objective cultural differences between groups; the second views ethnicity as a social construct whose 'reality' is inseparable from the political context in which it is fashioned, or indeed 'invented'. In the latter sense ethnicity is, in essence, a political resource that lends itself to all kinds of political manipulation, irrespective of how much 'objective' reality attaches to cultural particularisms.[6]

The significance of the distinction is far from academic. By recasting each interpretation in the form of a legitimising myth, and discarding the other, each group ends up with a radically different explanation of the roots of ethnic conflict. Some Hutu politicians use – and abuse – the primordialist argument to point to irreconcilable differences between Hutu and Tutsi. Some of these differences, we are told, are rooted in the 'feudal' oppression their kinsmen endured at the hands of Tutsi invaders; others are made manifest by the ruses employed by the Tutsi – ranging from gifts of cattle to gifts of 'beautiful women' – to impose their hegemony on the unsuspecting Hutu.[7] Once carried to the point of caricature the primordialist argument becomes a potent ideological weapon for mobilising the Hutu masses against the Tutsi minority. For the Tutsi, on the other hand, objective differences between Hutu and Tutsi simply do not exist. To the extent that conflict did indeed develop between them, it is in part a reflection of the 'divide and rule' policies of the colonial state, in part the result of the machinations of self-serving politicians who take their marching orders from foreign powers (notably Rwanda and Belgium). Here the aim is to deny altogether the existence of separate identities and instead emphasise the unity of the Burundi people.[8] The implication is clear: 'We are all Burundi'; if only Hutu ethnicity had not been manipulated by the Belgians there would be no conflict between Hutu and Tutsi; that Tutsi elements happen to control the state, the army and the economy is immaterial, and anyone objecting to this state of affairs is victim of a 'false consciousness'.

Thus out of two perfectly plausible and complementary lines of reasoning have emerged two radically different and incompatible 'mythologies' which, to this day, leave little room for compromise in so far as they have acquired the force of dogma among some groups on both sides of the ethnic fault line. Moreover, to the 'objective' referents of ethnic identity noted earlier has been added a class dimension. Although the Tutsi as a group could hardly be described as a dominant class in the Marxist sense, there is little question that much of the country's wealth does tend to gravitate in Tutsi hands. This is where the present situation differs in a fundamental way from what could be observed in pre-colonial times: besides their monopoly of force, Tutsi elements also control a significant share of the country's economy. How to operate a redistribution of both power and wealth is not the least of the problems confronting the regime of President Buyoya.

LEVELS AND VARIETIES OF ETHNIC STRIFE

If the 1972 genocide is unquestionably the most consequential, both in terms of the number of lives lost and of its long-term political consequences, it has been preceded – and followed – by several other types of confrontation. A complex chain of causality links one act of violence to the next, in the manner of a Greek tragedy, as if the ultimate retribution (in this case the 1972 genocide) was inscribed in the initial crime (Prince Rwagasore's assassination in 1961).

Political assassination

On 13 October 1961, less than a year before independence, the prime minister designate and eldest son of Mwami (King) Mwambutsa, Prince Louis Rwagasore, fell under the bullets of a Greek gunman in the pay of a rival princely faction (Batare). Although motivated by princely antagonisms and not by ethnic hatred, the death of Rwagasore deprived the country of a leader of enormous prestige, whose claims to authority were uncontested by either Hutu or Tutsi. The same cannot be said of Pierre Ngendadumwe, a leader of Hutu origins. At the time of his assassination by a Tutsi refugee from Rwanda, on 18 January 1965, he held the post of prime minister, and was therefore viewed with extreme suspicion by Tutsi elements. His death had an immediate impact on the heightening of ethnic tensions, which the Mwami tried to defuse by calling for legislative elections; these, however, only served to fan the fires of politicised ethnicity.

Urban rioting

Long before Ngendadumwe's assassination, but not unrelated to his elimination, one of the suburbs of Bujumbura became the scene of violent ethnic rioting, involving young Tutsi militants and Hutu trade unionists. The former were affiliated to the youth wing of the ruling party, the Union pour le Progrès National (Uprona), which drew its members from both Hutu and Tutsi;

the latter were members of the Syndicats Chrétiens, a trade union known for its pro-Hutu leanings and friendly connection with its Belgian counterpart. In the course of the riots four Hutu were clubbed to death, including the president of the trade union and the national secretary of a small Hutu party, the Parti du Peuple (PP).

Army coups and counter-coups

No other event has had a more decisive impact on the rise of Tutsi hegemony than the abortive, Hutu-instigated, coup of 19 October 1965. By then the palace had emerged as the principal fulcrum of power, and was seen by many Hutu elements as the key obstacle in the way of their political aspirations. Although the attempted coup failed to overthrow the monarchy, the whiff of grapeshot caused the Mwami to seek permanent refuge in Geneva, thus leaving the throne vacant. Extensive purges of Hutu elements from the army and the gendarmerie thoroughly altered the ethnic profile of the military, now firmly under Tutsi control. Soon thereafter hundreds of Hutu elites suspected of 'subversive' designs were rounded up and shot by government troops. Violence eventually spread to the Muramvya and Gitega provinces, where thousands more, mostly Hutu, lost their lives. Meanwhile, as the Mwami appeared unwilling to return to Bujumbura, his son, Charles Ndizeye, was consecrated Mwami under the dynastic name of Ntare III. The stage was set for another trial of strength between the Crown and the army, culminating in November 1966 with the peaceful overthrow of the monarchy and the proclamation of the First Republic (1966–76). From then on, coup-making became essentially an intra-Tutsi affair, reflecting growing ethno-regional tensions and disagreements among different factions of the army. Thus on 1 November 1976 a group of Tutsi officers peacefully overthrew the Micombero regime and proclaimed the Second Republic (1976–87); much the same scenario presided over the demise of the Second Republic when, on 3 September 1987, another faction seized power from President Jean-Baptiste Bagaza and proclaimed the Third Republic. While setting in motion a circulation of Tutsi elites within the armed forces, the 1966 and 1976 coups did little to alter the institutional parameters of Tutsi supremacy; hence the 1972 Hutu insurrection, and the appalling repression inflicted upon the insurgents.

Ethnic insurrections

Anti-regime violence erupted on a major scale in 1972 and 1988. Both insurrections were instigated by middle-class Hutu elements with strong roots in the countryside, the first centring in the southern provinces of Nyanza-Lac and Rumonge, the second in the north, in the communes of Ntega and Marangara; although both were quickly nipped in the bud, and followed by extraordinarily brutal repressions, the 1972 insurgency was by far the more costly in terms of human lives lost. Between 1,000 and 2,000 Tutsi elements were killed by the insurgents before the army could restore 'peace and order'. What happened in 1972 was a concerted, though poorly co-ordinated, attempt to seize power by force and proclaim a Hutu republic. The 1988 insurgency, on the other hand, was more in the nature of a spontaneous outburst of ethnic rage, ignited by repeated provocations and taunts on the part of local Tutsi authorities, and propelled by a '*grande peur*' phenomenon rooted in a diffuse fear of a wholesale slaughter of Hutu populations, as happened in 1972 in the wake of the first insurrection.

Genocidal violence

The worst atrocities were committed in the course of repressive operations designed to 'neutralise' future threats of Hutu insurrection. On three occasions, in 1965, 1972 and 1988, Hutu-instigated violence brought forth heavy retributions, but only in 1972 did the Tutsi-led repression reach genocidal proportions. The slaughter of some 100,000 Hutu in the wake of the 1972 insurrection was conducted with the intent to destroy all Hutu elites and potential elites, including schoolchildren. Because of the scale of the killings, and the element of intent that led to the carnage, its genocidal character is hardly in doubt. As such it differs in a fundamental sense from previous instances of violence, as well as from the 1988 massacre. In terms of the number of victims – estimated at anywhere from 15,000 to 30,000 – the 1988 repression is only slightly less horrendous than the 1972 genocide, and some may even argue that it deserves to be described in much the same terms. What needs to be stressed is that anti-Hutu violence in this case was essentially restricted to the communes of Ntega and Maranda (in contrast with the 1972 genocide which took its toll in virtually every locality throughout the country), and that the fury of the army is better seen as just that – an act of vengeful anger – rather than as a systematic and deliberate attempt to physically eliminate a specific segment of the Hutu population.

THE ANATOMY OF VIOLENCE: TARGETS, INTENSITY, LOCUS AND PARTICIPANTS

Variations over time in the scope and character of ethnic violence can best be grasped by looking at the phenomenon in terms of its targets, intensity, geographical location, and who were the main participants. Taking the events of 1965, 1972 and 1988 as our main points of reference, and beginning with Hutu-instigated violence, the following pattern comes into view: (a) there has been a substantial widening in the range of targeted groups between 1965 and 1972: the main target in 1965 were the king and his courtiers and the Tutsi soldiers in charge of the security of the palace; the 1972 insurrection, on the other hand, was directed at all Tutsi elites, and those Hutu elements who refused to join the rebellion; in 1988 Hutu violence took the form of a localised outburst of fear and anger directed at all Tutsi civilians indiscriminately; (b) Hutu-instigated violence reached its highest level of intensity in 1972, when an estimated 1,000 to 2,000 Tutsi and scores of Hutu lost their lives at the hands of the insurgents; in 1988 as many as 300 to 500 Tutsi civilians were massacred; (c) until 1965 Hutu violence was exclusively urban, and limited to the capital city; by 1972 its social bases were both urban and rural, with the rural dimension becoming even more pronounced (though limited to specific localities) in 1988; (d) predictably, the social bases of violence expanded significantly over the years: in 1965 the key participants were a handful of gendarmerie and army officers; in 1972 they were essentially middle-class elements (schoolteachers, petty traders and civil servants), to which must be added an undetermined number of former Zairian 'rebels'; in 1988 the main perpetrators of anti-Tutsi violence were Hutu peasants, most of them panic-stricken at the thought that another 1972-style bloodbath was in the offing.

Anti-Hutu violence reflects a corresponding widening of the scope of targeted groups, culminating in 1972 with the physical elimination of some 100,000 Hutu civilians; the social profile of the participants, however, remained basically unchanged. While there can be little doubt that government troops were responsible for most of the killings, in many instances (most notably in 1965 and 1972) they were assisted by elements of the Uprona youth wings (Jeunesses Rwagasore). For the sake of clarity the key variables involved in anti-Tutsi and anti-Hutu violence are summarised in Table 7.1.

PROSPECTS FOR ACCOMMODATION

Measured by the scope of political and constitutional reforms introduced in the wake of the 1988 massacre, there can be no doubt that Burundi is going through a major transition – if not yet to a pluralist democracy, at least to political liberalisation.

The record speaks for itself: for the first time in 23 years the country has been given a government consisting of an equal number of Hutu and Tutsi, headed by a Hutu prime minister; a Charter of National Unity has been adopted which formally proclaims the advent of a new era, dedicated to the construction of a society free of prejudice and discrimination; a new constitution, overwhelmingly approved by way of referendum, now sets specific limitations on the powers of the executive, stipulates the conditions of multiparty democracy, and enshrines the sanctity of basic human rights.

Like much else in Burundi, the emergent polity is by no means free of ambiguity. While 'national unity' is officially proclaimed as the fundamental precondition of democracy – meaning, in the words of the Charter of National Unity, that 'one's identity as a Burundi must hold primacy over ethnic, regional and clanic labels' – ethnic parity, in the form of equal representation of Hutu and Tutsi, is the rule for political recruitment to ministerial and other positions. At the time of this writing (1993) half of the 24 ministries are headed by Hutu and the other half by Tutsi; the 80-member central committee of the Uprona party consists of an equal proportion of Hutu and Tutsi; the same is true of the 16 provincial governors. Ethnic parity also served as the guiding principle for the appointment of the Commission on National Unity and the Constitutional Commission. Ironically, while

Table 7.1 Dimensions of ethnic violence

Variable	1965	1972	1988
1. Anti-Tutsi violence			
Target	King and courtiers and Tutsi officers	Tutsi elites and middle-classes	Tutsi civilians
Intensity	10–15 killed	12,000 killed	3,500 killed
Locus	Bujumbura	Nyanza-Lac and Rumonge	Ntega/ Marangara
Participants	Hutu gendarmerie	Hutu middle class (schoolteachers and petty traders) and Zairian 'rebels'	Hutu peasants/ communal and councillors
2. Anti-Hutu violence			
Target	Hutu army and gendarmerie officers and politicians	All Hutu elites, including school-children	Hutu civilians indiscrimin-ately
Intensity	12,000 killed, scores injured	Anywhere from 100,000 to 200,000	Anywhere from 15,000 to 30,000
Locus	Bujumbura, Muramvya Gitega	Throughout the country	Ntega and Marangara
Participants	Tutsi troops and Jeunesse groups	Tutsi troops, party militants and Jeunesses assisted by Rwanda refugees of Tutsi origins	Tutsi troops

Note: Omitted from this table are the Kamenge riots (1961) and the 1969 'purge' of Hutu elements from the army and the government following rumours of an impending Hutu-instigated coup.

urging his people to slough off their ethnic identities, no one is more acutely sensitive to the exigencies of ethnic arithmetic than President Buyoya himself.

What appears to be emerging is a limited form of consociational participation based on the belated (and reluctant) recognition that ethnic identity matters. The essential characteristic of consociational rule, according to its leading theoretician, 'is not so much any particular institutional arrangement as overarching co-operation at the elite level in a culturally fragmented system'

(Lijphart 1971: 10; see also Lijphart 1977b). It is in this general sense that recent political reforms in Burundi might be said to reflect a consociational or power-sharing approach to ethnic conflict.

Whether existing power-sharing arrangements can offer a meaningful guarantee of peaceful ethnic coexistence is an entirely different matter. As Arend Lijphart and others have argued, power-sharing works best where ethnic segments are roughly of comparable size, and where more than two protagonists face each other across the ethnic fault-line. Neither condition obtains in Burundi. Futhermore, at least three other factors come to mind which throw further doubts on the viability of the Burundi version of consociationalism: the depth of socio-economic inequalities between Hutu and Tutsi; the absence of geographical homogeneity in the distribution of ethnic aggregates, which rules out federalism as a means of promoting group autonomy; and the extent to which recourse to violence has become institutionalised into an almost routine-like mode of behaviour, making compromise and accommodation all the more difficult.

Although reliable statistical data on the distribution of income between Hutu and Tutsi is nowhere to be found, even the most casual visitor to Bujumbura cannot fail to notice the overwhelming preponderance of Tutsi elements in clerical, managerial and other relatively lucrative jobs. The explanation is not hard to find: after the 1972 bloodbath and for the next decade the only qualified applicants to positions of responsibility in the private and public sectors were drawn from the Tutsi stratum; meanwhile, much of the wealth previously owned by the victims of the massacre, including the refugees, passed into Tutsi hands. Subsequent restrictions on the admission of Hutu children to secondary schools meant that by 1988 only a tiny fraction of the Hutu population had the requisite skills for employment in the modern sectors of the economy. This is not meant to argue that poverty is unknown among Tutsi, or that among Tutsi ethno-regional identities make no difference. What is reasonably clear, however, is that no power-sharing arrangement can survive the strains and stresses generated by such profound socio-economic inequalities.

Equally plain is that the merits of federalism as a strategy for conciliation are largely irrelevant to the Burundi situation. Devolution of power to federal units, it has been argued, 'can support the maintenance of democracy by making hegemony more difficult to achieve' Horowitz (1991: 217). In theory the argument carries conviction, but where none of the federal units are ethnically homogenous – as would certainly be the case if such a system were applied to Burundi – one wonders how devolution could effectively mitigate conflict.

Again, much of the give-and-take and bargaining implicit in the concept of power-sharing is heavily mortgaged by the legacy of violence inherited by the Buyoya regime. Where the use of force recurs with such frequency and on such a scale that it threatens to become the 'normal' procedure for resolving ethnic conflict, it makes little sense to involve precolonial traditions of compromise and accommodation. A new tradition has taken root which makes recourse to violence the norm, and compromise the exception.

Given the difficulties involved in making room for a genuine consociational space, one can better understand why 'control' should have emerged as the central characteristic of the regime. Although the state is not reducible to any single set of institutions, the army and the ruling party (Uprona) play a critical role in ensuring its stability – the first through its monopoly of force, the second as a powerful instrument of political mobilisation. Both are therefore central to an understanding of control as a complementary feature of power-sharing, or, as Lustick would put it, 'as a model for the explanation of stability in deeply divided societies' (Lustick 1979: 330).

Entirely under the command of Tutsi officers, most of them from Bururi, and with only a tiny fraction of Hutu among the troops, the army is the linchpin of the regime. For years the army was expected to act as the custodian of Tutsi ethnocracy. Whether it now visualises its role differently is an open question. But for most politically conscious Hutu the issue is irrelevant. Their main source of anxiety is that the army remains entirely under Tutsi control, and that it continues to exercise undue pressure in civilian affairs. There appears to be no easy way out of the dilemma confronting the Buyoya regime: because the army is solidly Tutsi in composition its future role has become a profoundly divisive – and potentially explosive – issue between Hutu and Tutsi; precisely for this reason, however, the prospects for a significant alteration of its ethnic profile are extremely remote.

While the army holds a monopoly of force, the Uprona, on the other hand, serves as the organisational weapon through which the regime seeks to mobilise the masses, Hutu and Tutsi alike, on behalf of its unitarian ideology. Control here stems from several sources: from the enormous patronage resources made available by the state; from the party's privileged access to the media; and from the sustained efforts made by the regime to bring Hutu elements into the directing organs of the party, in hopes that they will serve as a magnet for attracting a solid phalanx of Hutu supporters in the countryside. Besides distributing rewards to the faithful and penalties to the recalcitrants, the party sets normative standards for members and non-members alike. Ideology, guided participation and co-optation thus interact in mutually reinforcing ways to legitimize – and conceal – the still politically dominant position of the Tutsi minority.

Insofar as the 'control' aspects of the present system clearly outweigh its 'power-sharing' characteristics, it confirms Lustick's observation that students of consociationalism have tended to ignore the 'antidemocratic, manipulative nature of consociational techniques'. But if the end result falls short of accepted democratic standards, consociational or otherwise, a convincing argument can be made that such a system, for all its obvious shortcomings, is none the less preferable to the ruthlessly oppressive form of ethnic hegemony that prevailed under the First and Second Republics, or, for that matter, to the renewed outbursts of violence and inverted forms of oppression that would likely accompany the institutionalisation of Hutu rule. However much one might object to the constitutional restrictions placed on the organisation of political parties along ethnic lines, this is a relatively small price to pay when one considers the alternatives.

NOTES

1 This chapter is a revised version of a paper presented at a workshop on ethnic conflict and development sponsored by the United Nations Research Institute for Social Development (UNRISD), Dubrovnik, 3–6 June 1991. The comments of the participants on an earlier version are gratefully acknowledged, as well as the support of the conference organisers, Dharam Ghai and Rodolfo Stavenhagen.
2 For an outstanding treatment of historical and contemporary cases of genocide, see Chalk and Jonassohn (1990).

3 For a more detailed discussion of the traditional dimensions of Burundi politics, see Lemarchand (1970).

4 On the 1988 killings, see Watson (1989); on the 1972 genocide, see Lemarchand (1973).

5 For an excellent illustration of such a stereotype, see Perlez (1988).

6 On the 'primordialist' vs 'instrumentalist' distinction, see Horowitz (1985), especially chapter 1.

7 For specific examples, see Ntibazonkiza (1991).

8 This is the essence of the argument set forth in the report issued by the National Commission on National Unity in the wake of the 1988 carnage; see *Rapport de la Commission Nationale Chargée d'Etudier la Question de l'Unité Nationale*, Bujumbura, April 1989, especially pp. 37–87.

Chapter 8

The rise and fall of Yugoslavia

George Schöpflin

States require cohesive ideas and identities to legitimate themselves. In most cases in Europe states are based on a single dominant ethnic group, a *Staatsvolk*, which frames the purposiveness of political institutions. Yugoslavia (born 1918, died 1991) is significant because no one single ethnic group was in a position to act as the *Staatsvolk*. It also experienced no durable and convincing construction of a state based on ethnic consensus, through authentic federation or consociation, admittedly a difficult undertaking. The principal national communities never sought genuinely to understand the other's perspectives, interests or aspirations. The consequences were predictable. Under the impact of incipient democratisation the previous system of control collapsed. There had developed some interests in the perpetuation of Yugoslavia but they were too weak to withstand ethno-national movements that sought self-determination through separate statehood.

THE FIRST STATE AND NATION-BUILDING FAILURE: INTER-WAR YUGOSLAVIA

There were two significant attempts at state-building around the concept of Yugoslavia. The first, inter-war Yugoslavia, rested on two not wholly mutually supportive pillars, language and monarchy. As elsewhere in Central and Eastern Europe nineteenth-century nationalists had equated language, nation and state, but what they declared an identity was in fact an arduous programme. The linguistic strategy of the newly created Yugoslavia was a muddled form of elite accommodation, interwined with elements of hegemonic control (to use McGarry and O'Leary's category). Many in the Serbian elite never really understood the need for accommodation especially as the nineteenth-century Serbian tradition of conquest and expansion dominated the new state. The suspension of the fragile semi-democratic institutions established in 1918, the creation of a royal dictatorship in 1929, and the slide into full hegemonic control proved an easy step for much of the Serbian elite. This outcome, however, was to have fatal long-run consequences, because it ethnicised the state in the eyes of non-Serbs and eroded whatever loyalty they had to Yugoslavia. The monarchy, far from legitimating the state, came to be perceived as alien and oppressive by non-Serbs; separate ethnic discourses came to the centre of politics and talked past each other in the forums of the South Slavs.

Building a Yugoslav nation would always have been problematic given that it was by no means self-evident that language in the region meant what the protagonists of linguistic nationalism in the west suggested. In central and eastern Europe, with the exception of Polish, no language enjoyed an unbroken history as a medium of high cultural and political communication. While many had some medieval or early modern existence as the language of a court or literature, they had generally fallen into desuetude; and existed only as dialects spoken by peasants. The construction of a national language as a cultural medium required an act of will, undertaken by intellectuals entering the political scene and securing for themselves a solid status and base for power. The definition and codification of these old–new languages – Serbian, Croatian and Slovene – were acts of rational (re)construction, laden with hidden and not so hidden political agendas. Nationalists claimed that all they were doing was reviving long-suppressed languages, and thereby providing opportunities for the spirit of the people to find expression. However, the way in which a language was defined had definite implications for the size and population of the nation and state being called into existence.

In the South Slav lands language-definition was acutely complex. Philologically, the entire Slavonic-speaking Balkans was a single linguistic region. Slavonic dialects shaded off into one another, and by linguistic criteria no fundamental distinction could be made between the dialects that became Slovene, Serbian, Croatian, Macedonian and Bulgarian. When nationalist intellectuals began their homogenising linguistic endeavours, therefore, their decisions were to have far-reaching results (Banac 1984). Macedonian did not become an issue until after the Second World War, but the activists of the Slovene and Bulgarian proto-nations opted early on for dialectal variants that were recognisably different from their neighbours. The 'Serbian' and 'Croatian' languages bedevilled relations between these ethnic communities virtually from the outset, even though a group of Croatian intellectuals in the nineteenth century decided to opt for the particular dialect of Croatian (*stokavski*) that was closest to Serbian, believing that in consequence, the groups would come to constitute a single nation and thereby eventually find statehood together.

This 'Illyrian idea' attracted considerable support from Croats, who found the thought of Serbian backing against Vienna and Budapest rather congenial. A minority of Croats, however, argued that the Croatian nation was separate and different from the Serbs. This division of opinion was never fully settled, but during and immediately after the First World War, the great majority of the Croatian elite opted for Illyrianism and Yugoslavia, although Stjepan Radic, the future leader of the Peasant Party, rejected this project from the outset (Dragnitch 1983). The Croatian elite had constructed a precarious national identity which overemphasised language and understated the significance of history and religion (Roman Catholicism).

The Serbs likewise came to accept the Yugoslav idea, but with a different history. Under Ottoman rule, the Serbian patriarchate at Pec had been the only Serbian political institution and thus the identification between Serbianism and Orthodoxy had grown very strong over the centuries. Linguistically virtually all Serbs spoke the same stokavian dialect, but politically could be divided into two broad groups, the Serbs of Serbia proper and the Serbs of Austria–Hungary. The former lived in the Kingdom of Serbia, which had carved out its independence from the ailing Ottoman empire in the nineteenth century and had added new territories, inhabited mostly by Eastern Orthodox Slavophones, who were easily integrated into the Serbian national ideal. The Serbs outside Serbia, the *precani*, in the Vojvodina, Bosnia and Croatia, shared the language and religion of the Serbs, but their political culture was determined by different considerations – relations with Vienna, Budapest and Croats. They identified themselves as Serbs by language, religion and history – sharing the memory of the glorious defeat at Kosovo (which had ended the medieval Serbian state) commemorated in their great cycle of oral ballads. All Serbs were reluctant to accept that other South Slavs, speaking the same language as themselves, could have a substantially different culture. They tended to see the Croats as Catholicised Serbs, who would return to Serbdom once demonstrated the error of their ways. They also expressed reservations about Illyrianism, which they regarded as an attempt by the Croats to denationalise the Serbs. The strongest current among the Serbs, as represented by the cultural innovator, Vuk Stefanovic Karadzic, was that all speakers of the stokavian dialect were Serbs. There thus arose two diametrically opposed conceptions of the South Slav nation – the Croats' Illyrianism, which sought to include all the South Slavs while recognising some of the differences among them, and the Serbian version, which was purely linguistic and ignored cultural, religious and historical factors.

By the mid-nineteenth century, the Serbian kingdom was influenced in the direction of expanding its power over all speakers of stokavian, whom it regarded as Serbs: and this unification of Serbs would have to take place under the monarchy, the only possible counterweight to Austria. The Serbs of Croatia were both subjects and objects of this ambition. They looked back on a tradition of separateness defined by the military frontier (Rothenburg 1966), under the jurisdiction of Vienna, and had an identity of their own. The rise of Croatian nationalism disturbed them, and they tended to look simultaneously towards Serbia, Vienna and Budapest as possible guardians, especially in the last years of the nineteenth century, when the Hungarian government heavily relied on them. However, in the early years of the twentieth century, the project of Croatian and Serbian co-operation against Budapest was born. Eventually it culminated in the war-time Corfu Declaration, laying the foundations for a South Slav state, based on agreement involving the leaders of the three main protagonists – the Croats, the Serbs of Croatia and the Serbian leadership. The new state came into being on 1 December 1918 based on the principles of one language, giving rise to one nation, and the Serbian monarchy which was now elevated to an all-South Slav kingdom.

The state was initially called the Kingdom of Serbs, Croats and

Table 8.1 Major ethnic groups in Yugoslavia 1921–81 (in millions)

	1921[a]	1961[b]	1981[c]
Serbs	4.66	7.80	8.14
Croats	2.86	4.29	4.43
Slovenes	1.02	1.56	1.75
Muslims	0.73	0.98	2.00
Macedonians	0.59	1.05	1.34
Montenegrins	–	0.51	0.58
Albanians	0.44	0.91	1.73
Hungarians	0.47	0.50	0.43
Yugoslavia	12.01	18.56	22.42

Sources:
[a] Banac's calculations (Banac 1984: 58).
[b] Shoup (1968) citing *Statisticki godisnjak SFRJ 1964*, p. 268.
[c] Ramet (1984), citing *Statisticki kalendar Jugoslavije 1982*, p. 21.

Slovenes, but it was a state of convenience, based on serious mutual misperceptions on the part of both Serbs and Croats, exacerbated by differences of style and aspirations derived from different historical experiences. The Serbs insisted on establishing Yugoslavia as a unitary state. They were able to write this into the Vidovdan Constitution (not least because Radic insisted on boycotting the constitutive assembly). Vidovdan, St Vitus's Day, 28 June, was the day on which the Battle of Kosovo was fought: its significance as a symbol of national affirmation for the Serbs was enormous, but its adoption as a Yugoslav symbol was an ominous indication of how the Serbian elite viewed the new order. Unitarism had been the key Serbian experience, so their hostility to federal ideas was unsurprising. However, the Croats' political experience had been precisely the opposite: continuous argument with Vienna and Budapest from a recognised position of a separate co-existence within a partially decentralised empire.

The new ruling elite was dominated by Serbs and Yugoslav-inclined Croats (as well as Slovenes) and it was decided early on that these two ethnic groups were in fact one nation and that they spoke one language, Serbo-Croat. The 1921 census did not ask questions about national allegiance and returned Serbo-Croat speakers as a single category (though according to Banac's calculations Serbs constituted about 39 per cent of the population in 1921, see Table 8.1).

The monarchy was, as agreed, the Serbian monarchy writ large, but King Alexander had no real understanding of the need to appear in a different light to his Croat subjects. He shared the view of the Serbian elite that Croats were essentially Serbs, and when they behaved in an unexpected, non-Serbian fashion, ill-will, deviancy or disloyalty must be responsible. This attitude was underpinned by the Serbs' historical baggage: the idea that the new state must be strong, unitary, centred on Belgrade and run by Serbs. There was no suggestion of ethnic proportionality, power-sharing or any redefinition of the state ideology in a way that would satisfy the Croats.

Pro-Yugoslav Croats accepted the system with reservations, not least because parts of Croatia, notably the littoral, were under threat from Italy and the Serbian connection provided a vital defence. Not that the Croats were without baggage of their own. Their political experience in their struggle against Vienna and Budapest had been legalistic and argumentative. They were used to petitions, pleas, counter-pleas and the like, which left the Serbian elite, to whom this was alien, perplexed and impatient. The relationship between the prime minister, Nikola Pasic and the leader of the largest Croatian party, the Peasant Party, Stjepan Radic, was one of mutual incomprehension. The Serbs thought the Croats could never be satisfied with what was on offer, while the Croats felt cheated that Yugoslavia did not mean liberation but a new semi-colonial dependency, made all the worse by the fact that the Serbs operated with very different ground rules from those that they had learned in Budapest. Nor were matters helped by the king, who intervened indirectly in politics whenever he thought royal or Serbian interests were affected. Finally, the Serbs of Croatia were initially euphoric about the new state, but gradually concluded that the new dispensation did not bring them as much as they had hoped.

Matters were resolved in a highly negative way with the murder of Radic in 1928 on the floor of the Yugoslav parliament (he died two months later), shot by a deputy who insisted that he could no longer tolerate the way in which Radic insulted the honour of the Serbian nation (Dragnitch 1983). Using Radic's murder as the pretext Alexander suspended parliament and instituted a royal dictatorship from which the Croats felt themselves excluded. The Croats eventually enacted their revenge. In 1934, two Croatian gunmen murdered Alexander in Marseilles, where he had just arrived on an official visit (and shot the French foreign minister for good measure too).

The agreement of 1939, known as the Sporazum, came too late to reconcile Serbs and Croats, and when Germany invaded Yugoslavia in 1941, their responses were very different. The former resisted, the latter used the opportunity to establish a state of their own.

WAR-TIME COLLAPSE, FRAGMENTATION AND GENOCIDE

The collapse of Yugoslavia was followed by four years of war. The war years were extraordinarily cruel (Djilas 1977). The pent-up frustrations and passions of the interwar years, the sense of humiliation felt by the Croats and the sense of betrayal felt by the Serbs, were released amidst the collapse of state power. Three main currents emerged. The new rulers of the Croatian state (known by its initials, NDH – *Nezavisla Drzavna Hrvatska* or Independent State of Croatia) embarked on a policy of constructing an ethnically pure Croatia by genocide and many thousands of Serbs were massacred. The Serbs in Serbia rallied behind the monarchy, as represented by the Cetniks, while those in Croatia joined the communist-led Partisans.

Both Serbs and Croats underwent the experience of genocide, in 1941 and 1945 respectively. These events structured their attitudes to the past and the present, building in fear and intransigence in equal measure into their political cultures. Trust towards the other is non-existent. This is not to imply any kind of moral equivalence between the two genocides, only to explain the utter intransigence of both communities. The fact that the 1941 massacre was committed by a regime long since vanquished or that the 1945 killings were the work of the Partisans remains irrelevant. All Croats are tainted in the eyes of the Serbs as legatees of the Ustasa state and all Serbs are guilty as the beneficiaries of Titoism. The Croatian contribution to the Partisans is perceived as having been ignored in the calculus of death, while for the Serbs the summary identification of all Serbs from Croatia as 'communist' ignores the reality that not all of them were supporters of Tito and, indeed, that some of them suffered discrimination, whether as non-communists or as pro-

Soviet Cominformists. Perceived genocide and similar experience of perceived collective destruction leaves deep scars and makes the communities affected ultra-sensitive towards anything, real or symbolic, that appears to threaten their collective existence.

This phenomenon was particularly acute in Croatia, where a clear ethnic pattern was established under the post-war communist veil. The Serbs who joined the Partisans to escape the Ustasa massacres automatically emerged as the winners in the post-war order and were highly influential in the Croatian party and the instruments of coercion. These institutions guaranteed that the Serbs of Croatia would never again by menaced by fascist genocide.

As the war unfolded, the Partisans offered the clearest and most attractive programme and were successful in creating a three-fold legitimating myth: that they were the only truly committed force dedicated to fighting the foreign occupation forces; the true representatives of inter-ethnic reconciliation; and the most effective champion of the radical peasant masses, who had been largely excluded from the inter-war regime (Bicanic 1935). Neither the Croatian nationalists nor the Cetniks were able to match this dynamism and persuasiveness and the partisans emerged from the Second World War as two-fold victors. They expelled all the foreign occupation forces and they defeated their enemies in a civil war. In 1945, they were definitely the masters.

THE NEW SYSTEM OF CONTROL: COMMUNISM AND THE YUGOSLAV NATION

The post-war order was consciously built on the proposition that the pre-war system had failed, that a revolution had taken place and that the new communist ideology was the wave of the future. The self-confidence and the energy of the new rulers were unquestionably bolstered by their unshakeable belief in communist ideology and practice, viz. that class was invariably more significant than nation and, say, a Serbian worker could by definition not have different interests from a Croatian worker. Where a different national interest was perceived, this false consciousness could be corrected by agitation and propaganda, by resocialising the population and by ridding society of its reactionary elements. Nationhood was a bourgeois device aimed at dividing the proletariat and at preventing it from recognising its true interest, viz. proletarian internationalism.

The enormous prestige of the communist leader, Josip Broz Tito, who was of mixed Croatian–Slovenian descent but always regarded himself as a Yugoslav, helped the consolidation of communist rule. To the Tito factor should be added the prestige derived from victory in the two-fold war and the associated prestige of the Soviet Union (in a population which had been sympathetic to Pan-Slavism and tended to regard the Soviet Union as the revitalised Slav power).

The communists established a nominally federal system that remained under the very tight control of the Communist Party. The underlying idea was that communist ideology would serve as the unifying formula to hold the different nations together and that Leninist organisation would provide the cement. Consequently the reduction of ethnicity to its cultural aspects was intended to be a first step in the direction of a political order in which ethnicity would eventually disappear.

The 1946 constitution was the outcome of this thinking. It made low-level provision for cultural rights, established a federation on the Soviet model and sought to ensure the cohesiveness of the system through the political monopoly of the party. In relation to the pre-war arrangement, it did set up the new federal republics with new frontiers. Serbia was divided three ways. Serbia proper was the largest segment and was populated overwhelmingly by Serbs, except for the Sandzak of Novi Pazar, where there was a local majority of Serbo-Croat-speaking Muslims. Kosovo had a sizeable Albanian population, which was still restive after the 1944 uprising, which had been put down by the communists. The Vojvodina was very mixed, with an absolute majority of Serbs, with a somewhat different tradition from those of Serbia proper, plus Hungarians, Croats, Slovaks, Ruthenes, Romanians. The Germans were expelled and their places were taken by Serbian and Montenegrin settlers from the impoverished regions of the south. In addition, the eastern half of Srem (Srijem), to which Croatia had a claim, was added to the Vojvodina. The Croats thus held only Western Srijem (Srem) and otherwise returned to the old Austro-Hungarian frontier, especially with Bosnia-Hercegovina, where there was no frontier change to speak of; in addition, the coastal area of Gulf of Kotor, the population of which is party Croatian, was given to Montenegro. The German-inhabited areas in Slavonia were settled in part by Serbs from the mountainous areas, including those from

Bosnia. Only in Istria did the Croats probably get the better part of the bargain, where they gained some territory that could just as easily have been claimed by Slovenia. The Croats did appear to have had a major gain when the plans to carve out an autonomous Serbian region in the Krajina were shelved – despite the fact that the Serbs had to make this concession in the Kosovo and Vojvodina. In the long term, however, this arrangement gave the Serbs of Croatia a preponderant role in Croatia itself, which caused considerable resentment.

From the outside, then, communist Yugoslavia resembled a state based on elite accommodation with elements of coercive consociationalism built into the system (see Table 8.2). The mix also included a degree of territorial rearrangement and linguistic realism. The federal system was to make provision for the former and the recognition of Macedonia, indeed its active promotion, corrected a major anomaly. At the same time, the new structures, although facades, offered important symbolic satisfaction to the various different ethnic groups who made up the newly constituted state – even though both Serbs and Croats sustained losses too (severe repression of culture and history in Croatia, and a redivision of Serbia into three units).

However, the real weakness of the system was that it swept the ethnic issue under the carpet. Ethnicity was not so much dealt with as declared non-existent. Titoist Yugoslavia, having for all practical purposes declared the issue solved (at any rate at the rhetorical level), found it hard to confront the issued when it re-emerged on the political stage in the 1960s. The automatic response was repression.

In 1948, the new Yugoslavia faced its first major test. Stalin launched a political assault on the Yugoslav communists, whom he regarded as far too independent, and expected that they would crumple. They did not do so; on the contrary they were able to mobilise support from virtually all elements in the country very largely on the tacit argument that Yugoslavs had not fought for their independence in order to see themselves subordinated to the Soviet Union. This was effective, but it undermined internationalism, especially as it involved communist Yugoslavia in a conflict with the fountainhead of internationalism, the Soviet Union. This conflict represented the first shift in Yugoslavia's ideology in the direction of relying on a form of civic or state nationalism, in preference to immersion in a proletarian super-

Table 8.2 Methods of ethnic control: applying McGarry and O'Leary's 'Grand Categories' to Yugoslavia

Type	Description	Consequences
Genocide	Serbs of Croatia massacred by Croatian state 1941. Croats by communists, but perceived as Serbian revenge	Deep-seated mutual distrust, giving rise to intransigence. No basis for negotiation, let alone compromise
Mass-population transfers	Germans expelled after 1945, their lands taken largely by Serbian and Montenegrin settlers. 'Ethnic cleansing' in Croatia and Bosnia 1991–	Changes in the demographic balance in Slavonia, Vojvodina refugees, famine
Hegemonic control	Inter-war years: Serbian monarchical domination Communist control: 1945–90; practised behind a psuedo-federal facade.	Croatian ultra-nationalism Perceived as communist control in Serbia, elsewhere perceived as Serbian control likely to provoke Albanian reaction
Self-determination	Serbian control in Kosovo and Vojvodina, 1987– Denied under the communists.	Ethnic pressure focused on existing institutions, leading to ethnicisation of party.
	Seized by secessionists in 1990–1	Disintegration of state and protracted wars outside of Slovenia
Assimilation/integration	'Yugoslavism' propagated as a national identity	Acceptable to those in mixed marriages, and to party members, but not to others
Cantonisation	Not attempted, although unsuccessfully proposed for Bosnia in 1991	
Federalism	Initially a facade, but gradually federal organisations assumed a real and ethnic content	Republicanisation, eventually facilitating secession
Arbitration	To an extent Tito played this role, but it was personal to him, and he used it coercively	With Tito's death there was no alternative and his successors were left to face ethnic problems with weakening control mechanisms
Consociationalism	Elite consultation through the party was tantamount to psuedo-consociationalism, and the effective vetoes enjoyed by the republics in the 1980s also looked consociational	Consociational arrangements were never formalised, and with the demise of the party there were no institutional mechanisms to establish democratic consociationalism

state. Emerging successfully from the confrontation, Tito and his lieutenants realised that they would need to transform their own legitimating ideology and, as much by good luck as by conscious planning, they hit upon the idea of a national communism not dependent on the Soviet Union, something that was an epoch-making innovation at the time. It boosted their legitimacy, especially when it was buttressed by self-management at home and non-alignment abroad.

However, as long as tight political control by the party – renamed the League of Yugoslav Communists in 1952 as an (almost entirely) symbolic move away from Leninist democratic centralism – was in place, ethno-national identities could not find any space for political expression. Indeed, in the immediate aftermath of the war-time killings, the strict policy of the party in clamping down very hard on anything that might remotely threaten its monopoly attracted a certain amount of approbation when it affected nationhood. The proposition that Serbian, Croatian, Slovenian and other identities should fade away, except perhaps as cultural relics, received a measure of popular approval (Shoup 1968).

One move by the party, however, was to have far-reaching and ultimately fatal results, a classic illustration of the law of unintended consequences. This was the creation of a federal system. Initially, these newly established republics were no more than facades. Real power lay with Tito, his close associates and the party. Gradually the republics acquired identities of their own and came to see themselves as real loci of power. In the early years it did not matter. There were no significant differences between, say, Slovenes and Serbs and anything that arose could be settled by Tito. But by the 1960s, this arrangement would no longer operate quite as smoothly as it had before. The origins of the 1960s' crisis was a seizing-up of both the political and the economic machinery.

In a sense, the communist rulers of Yugoslavia were the victims of their own success. They had stabilised the country, created a system which had more than a degree of legitimacy, as well as international recognition, and they were well on the way to industrialising parts of Yugoslavia, in particular the northern republics of Croatia and Slovenia. A threshold had been reached in politics, economics and in society which would require a redistribution of power; how much, in what way and by what criteria then became a matter for debate. This debate was to give rise to the first really serious internal crisis of the post-war era, the Croatian crisis of 1971 (Rusinow 1977).

CRISIS, CONSERVATISM, ETHNICITY AND REFORM

The crisis of the 1960s, which was to culminate in the events of 1971, was extraordinarily complex and involved democratic, Marxist, socialist, national, managerial and market ideas. Its centre was the question of what kind of a state Yugoslavia was to be. No attempt will be made to disentangle any of this complexity here, nor any assessment of the crisis, only an examination of the way it impacted on ethnicity.

All the participants in the political debates of the 1960s, despite their subsequent rhetoric, started from the assumption that Yugoslavia would remain in being as a state and that it would continue to be ruled by a self-managing Marxist ideology. The difficulty was that both these notions could be open to a variety of interpretations.

By the early 1960s, the Croatian communist leadership, supported by the Slovenes, but also by the liberal Serbian intellectuals, had begun to challenge the centralising, hard-hat and conservative Partisan generation. A wide variety of interests were hidden behind the facade of communism and by reference to the Partisan struggle, and the Partisans could hardly be accused of possessing a very high level of political sophistication. They had come from the villages to sweep away the old, corrupt, exploitative order, found a seemingly perfect recipe in communism, a tailor-made leader in Tito, but carried with them all the baggage of the simple messianistic world of the epic struggle against the enemy. They were quite unfit to rule an increasingly complex society but were not about to yield power to those who were.

The pre-eminence of this elite was strengthened by another factor that was almost unique to Yugoslavia in Eastern European communism. Not only was the *ancien régime* discredited, but its representatives had very largely disappeared. They had died during the war or had gone into emigration, with the result that the new elite had a fairly free hand in determining the patterns and codes of elite behaviour, which they took overwhelmingly from their radical peasant beliefs and from communism. Neither predisposed them to patience, subtlety and compromise. Yet if this elite firmly believed that it was creating a new, anti-national communist identity, in reality matters were more complex. Whatever people's ostensible motives might have been, those affected by communist policies did not automatically abandon their ethnic identities and a Serbian official continued to be perceived as a Serb, however much he might protest that he was acting out of communist conviction.

The conservative Partisan elite simply ignored Croatian resentment at the idea that Croats could not even be trusted to build communism on their own, but had to do it under Serbian tutelage: that the majority of communists in Croatia were Croats did not disturb this picture. Nor was Croatian commitment to communism helped by the widely propagated thesis about the 'Ustasa nature' of the Croatian nation. Any expression of Croatian identity could be and was branded and delegitimated in this way, regardless of its content.

While in Croatia the Serbian minority's economic interests had merged with the structures of Communist Party power, in Yugoslavia at large, two larger coalitions of interests had come into being by the 1960s, both of which had an ethnic, as well as a non-ethnic, base. At this time the economy was beginning to slow down as extensive resources were exhausted. The political factories – enterprises subsidised for political purposes, mainly in the underdeveloped southern republics – were proving uneconomic and the shift of excess rural population to towns was producing unemployment or under-employment. It was clear that this system could not be sustained for long without dire consequences, and in 1965 the reformers succeeded in pushing through a major economic reform; they were opposed by the conservatives, who recognised that their economic resources and sources of power and patronage would be threatened if the reform was successful.

The reformers were mostly concentrated in Croatia and Slovenia, though they also had some strength in Serbia, whereas the conservatives were in the other, less developed republics. Hence the republican structures, which Tito and Kardelj, the Yugoslav party's long-serving ideologist, had intended to be nothing more than administrative agencies, were increasingly acquiring real political content and given that the republics did have an ultimate ethnic base, the arrival of the ethnic issue on the agenda

Table 8.3 Major ethno-national groups in Serbia (including Kosovo and Vojvodina) 1991 (in millions)

Serbs	6.43
Albanians	1.69
Hungarians	0.35
Croats	0.10
Muslims	0.24
'Yugoslavs'	0.32

Serbs make up 65 per cent of the total population.
Source: *Tanjug*, 20 December 1991.

could not be long delayed. When it occurred, it showed that attempts to eviscerate the ethnic elements of nationhood and to overlay them with an all-embracing Yugoslav identity had failed.

Yugoslavism deserves a short discussion. It was launched by Kardelj, who acted as a kind of ideological tailor for the Yugoslav party throughout his long career – if the party needed a new ideology, he would run it up; if it wanted it shortened or a tuck taken in or a turn-up removed, he would invariably oblige. In the 1950s, the need was for a justification of federal domination and Yugoslavism met the bill. It had several aspects – history, language, class, in all of which a single Yugoslav variant was distilled and then declared to have been the authentic version and imposed on the population (Shoup 1968). While the attempt to construct a 'Yugoslav' identity through the rewriting of history and the merging of the Serbian and Croatian languages were largely a failure, it did work in one respect – the creation of a category of Yugoslav identity within the country allowed individuals to opt out of rooted ethno-national identities. This proved to be an option of lasting value for a statistically significant number of people, even in Serbia (see Table 8.3). Various individuals, who found it difficult to classify themselves as, say, Serbian or Croatian, could escape from what they regarded as an ethnic constraint and avoid self-definition by calling themselves 'Yugoslav, nationally undetermined'.

Those in mixed marriages and their children used this option voluntarily, but it was also subject to abuse. Conscripts, those living in ethnically mixed areas who might be afraid to give their identity openly to enumerators (e.g. a sizeable number of Hungarians), could be put under pressure to declare themselves Yugoslavs. Professional soldiers, high party and state officials

Table 8.4 National composition of cadres in federal institutions and organisations 1969 (percentages)

	Sb	Cr	Sv	Mc	Mg	O[a]
Leading cadres	32	15	9	7	9	28
Professional staff	73	7	3	3	9	5
Technical assistants	78	7	3	2	5	5

[a] 'O' includes 'other' 'undecided' and 'unknown'.
Source: Burg (1983: 113), citing Milan Matic, *Republicki i nacionalni sastav kadrova u organima Federacije*, p. 73.

(see Table 8.4) did so probably out of conviction. It is, however, another question as to whether the category was recognised as authentic by all those professing an ethnically undetermined nationality. Certainly, once the civil war had begun in 1991, Serbs refused to take Tito's 'Yugoslav' identity seriously and insisted that he had been a Croat; Tito himself had always stressed that he was a 'Yugoslav' and pedagogically refused to refer to his Croatian birth, even to the extent of veiling his participation in the First World War in the Austro-Hungarian army in the campaign against Serbia. Nevertheless, the category had some validity. In the 1970s and early 1980s, younger urban Yugoslavs recounted to me with some pride that Yugoslavia was a melting pot and that a new identity was definitely emerging. Yet despite some fifteen years of socialisation, this endeavour failed, partly because of its inherent implausibility, partly because of the memories it raised of the inter-war period and partly also because of the crass way in which it was enforced. Evidence of the repercussions became apparent in the late 1960s.

The reformers discovered that despite having the best of the intellectual argument, they could not easily overcome conservative forces – even though they had a windfall advantage when Alexander Rankovic, the conservative federal Minister of Interior,was found to have bugged Tito's residence and was subsequently sacked. Their ethnic and political base was in the southern republics, fearful of the winds of market competition; in the armed forces, the JNA, fearful of republican power; in the veterans' organisations, fearful of losing their privileges; and in the instruments of coercion, fearful of coming under direct political control. The result was stalemate, neither side was strong enough to defeat the other. In 1969 the Croatian leadership sought to break the log-jam by using popular support, which automatically meant reference to ethnic aspirations. They moved in the first instance against their local conservatives (the Zanko affair), many of whom were ethnic Serbs; so the affair was automatically interpreted by the local Serbs as an initiative directed against them.

What permitted the reformist–conservative conflict in the 1960s was that for the time being Tito was neutral (Pavlowitch 1988). This neutrality removed a vital curb on the Croatian leadership, which by 1970 was openly encouraging the population in its attempt to garner power. Croatian opinion, long suppressed, immediately began to push for a restoration of its national world, especially in the symbolic realm, much to the alarm of the local Serbian minority. This development could then be used by the conservatives to delegitimate the Croatian strategy in communist terms. In effect, there was a conflict of codes, with the ethno-national discourse perpetually denied legitimacy by those who controlled power and thus the language of public discourse in Yugoslavia. In a sense this was understandable. The moment that a communist ruler permits the use of nationalist language, his own credibility as a communist will be undermined, given the theoretical incompatibility between nationalism (basing its ultimate rationale on culture) and communism (on class) (Gellner 1990; Szporluk 1990).

The Croatian nationalists who challenged the party leadership did so on a variety of grounds. What threatened most disruption was the question of language. Philologically there is nothing to differentiate Serbian from Croatian, and this fact was given a programmatic quality by the Novi Sad agreement of 1954, signed by Serbian and Croatian intellectuals at the height of the campaign in support of Yugoslavism. This proposed that there was one Serbo-Croat language which existed in two variants, each of full validity. But when Croatian intellectuals began to inspect the dictionary of the language published in Belgrade, they discovered that words in the Croatian variant were frequently described as 'dialect', so much so that some of them denounced the agreement and began work on the development of a fully-fledged Croatian literary language. An orthographical dictionary of Croatian was subsequently suppressed. The attempt to differentiate Croatian identity linguistically was a clear indication that self-definition by language retained its force as an expression of identity in Central and Eastern Europe, however artificial such initiatives might initially be. In the case of Croatian, the newly revived medium took root (Franolic 1984).

The Zagreb party leadership discovered they were fighting on two fronts: on the defensive against the conservatives, warding off charges of nationalism in a system that regarded – and had to regard – nationalism as a most serious deviation; and on the other hand knowing that however far they might go in placing themselves at the head of a national–patriotic movement, they could never be fully accepted as the authentic agents of nationhood, but were perceived as a means to an end. They were always vulnerable to being outbid by those who were genuinely nationalist, were not concerned with heeding the limits required of those who sought to enfold their national appeal in pseudo-Marxist language, and could appeal directly to national aspirations. An outbreak of fully fledged Croatian nationalism finally convinced Tito to throw his weight behind the conservatives and purge the Croatian leadership at the end of 1971, threatening them with military intervention. Tito then went on to eliminate 'the rotten liberals' from other republican leaderships in an attempt to return to authentic Marxism. This heralded a renewed Marxist attempt to control the ethno-national issue (Burg 1983).

THE 1974 CONSTITUTION AND REPUBLICANISATION AFTER TITO

This chapter has concentrated on the Serbian–Croatian conflict as the core of the national question in Yugoslavia, but it is appropriate at this point to expand the perspective and to look at the issues raised in the context of other national groups as well, because they tended to gain increasing saliency in the 1970s, particularly as a result of the 1974 constitution (another of Kardelj's excursions into the intellectual rag-trade). The new experiment sought to re-establish the central party as the dominant factor in politics, but it recognised that genuine forces were released in the 1960s which would require some satisfying. These forces would as far as possible be restricted to the republican level and even within the republics, self-management would be upgraded through greater power being given to the communes (*opstina*) and the enterprises, in the hope that they would emerge as the true foci of power, loyalty and identity, thereby transcending ethnicity. The external limits of the system would be safeguarded by the armed forces, now formally declared the guardians of *bratstvo i jedinstvo* (brotherhood and unity) the code words for the integrity of the state against nationalist challenges. This political order was fleshed out by a revitalisation of the secret police, the reintroduction of nebulous 'moral-political fitness' criteria for various appointments, the re-ideologisation of education, and symbolic campaigns to re-enact unity (e.g. in the numberless films churned out in the 1970s to celebrate the Partisan victory which reinforced the message of unity in arms under communist and thus anti-nationalist leadership). Trials of those accused of nationalism were particularly tough in Croatia, with long prison terms of four years or more being the norm. This was the time when Franjo Tudjman served his first prison sentence; he served a second one in 1982–4.

The crucial unintended consequence of the 1974 constitution was republicanisation, a process whereby the republics increasingly became the true centres of power at the expense of the centre, something they were able to do through the introduction of the republican veto in federal affairs. By the 1980s Yugoslavia consisted of eight separate sub-polities (the six republics and the two provinces). The republican parties never lost control of their own *nomenklaturas*, but they were able to deflect some of the initiatives of the centre and increasingly they had to legitimate themselves through a mixture of self-managing ideology and the republican interest. This latter was a curious hybrid of regionalism and ethnicity, inevitably so given the original ethno-cultural content with which the republics had been endowed, so that ethnicity, which had seemingly been buried by the 1971 intervention, returned by the back door.

By the 1970s, the great innovation of Titoism, the creation of new nations as a means of resolving ethnic competition, i.e. by removing the object of such contests from the political scene through promoting the inhabitants of particular areas into nationhood, had begun to assume a reality and acquire authentic support from those affected. These facts did not emerge immediately after Tito's death in 1980. For a while the post-Tito leadership attempted to rule as if Tito were still alive. Various symbolic re-enactments of his personal authority were tried and criticism of the late president was prohibited. Decisions were made collectively and consensually – republicanisation meant the republican veto. But it was evident that this system could not work without Tito's authority, as the republican interests were growing, without there being any effective countervailing force. It was now difficult to avoid the conclusion that the institutional arrangement left behind by Tito was deficient not only in that it required a semi-monarchical figure like himself to make it work, but also that the absence of either an effective all-Yugoslav identity and an all-Yugoslav interest made the problem of constructing a new political formula insurmountable.

The process of decay was accelerated by a number of contingent factors. Yugoslavia's economic situation deteriorated steadily, as it was running out of extensive resources and the system proved weak in generating new ones; foreign loans kept the economy ticking over, but only at the cost of mounting indebtedness. Then, the party's legitimating myths were beginning to wear out. Whereas in the 1960s, the Titoist package of self-management, foreign policy success through non-alignment attracted a measure of support, this was less and less the case by the 1980s. It was much the same with the myth of the partisan struggle; to a generation born after 1945, what happened during the war had little relevance. And the key proposition, that the communists were the most effective in resolving the national question, was similarly under threat from republicanisation (Ramet 1984).

Still, some of the successes of the Titoist solution continued to hold. Macedonia was one instance. Before the war, the Slavophones of the Vardar valley were described as Southern Serbs and the area was run as a *de facto* colony by the Belgrade authorities. In the terms of the language they spoke, these Slavophones could opt to become either Serbs or Bulgarians or Macedonians, and being Orthodox Christians religion was not an impediment. During the war, Macedonia was annexed by Bulgaria, and the Partisans, in order to mobilise support, promised the Macedonians that they would receive recognition as an independent nation in their own right. This move gave the Macedonians a vested interest in both Yugoslavia and in the communist variant of Yugoslavia that Tito established. Hence communism operated hand-in-glove with nationalism in Macedonia. Communist support for the declaration of autocephaly by the Macedonian Orthodox bishops (autocephaly has universally been seen as a

Table 8.5 Major ethno-national groups in Bosnia-Hercegovina (in millions)

	1961	1971	1981	1991
Serbs	1.41	1.39	1.32	1.37
Muslims	0.84	1.48	1.63	1.90
Croats	0.71	0.77	0.76	0.75

Based on Ramet (1984) and Andrejevich (1991).

mark of independent nationhood in the Orthodox world) was a good case in point. Macedonian intellectuals busied themselves with creating a new language different from both Serbian and Bulgarian and constructing a history and literature, again with considerable success, so much so that towards the end of communism, Macedonia was a stable factor in the Yugoslav equation, because their overriding interest was in using the Yugoslav state framework as a protection against Bulgaria, which did not even recognise its autonomous existence.

The evolution of Muslim nationhood was a parallel and in some ways even paradoxical device used by the communists. Muslims of Serbo-Croat mother-tongue, i.e. speaking the stokavian dialect, and living in Bosnia-Hercegovina, had a weak national consciousness before the war and they tended to gravitate towards whoever was in power (before 1918, they were one of the bastions of loyalty towards Vienna). In the early years of Titoism, the communists did not really know what to do with the Muslims; in the 1953 census, the only category they could use was 'Yugoslav', but by the 1960s, the category 'Muslim' was introduced, and, as a result, many of those who had previously defined themselves as Serbs now declared themselves Muslim; some remained Croat. The net result was that in the 1971 census, they were returned as the largest ethnic group in the republic for the first time, at the expense of the Serbs, who took this shift rather badly (see Table 8.5).

On the other hand, the establishment of the Muslim national category did achieve a long-term aim. It resolved the national allegiance of this group by giving it a separate identity and thereby ended the simple competition between Serbs and Croats, both of whom had entertained hopes that the Muslims would join them. During the war-time Croatian state, which included

Bosnia, they were defined as 'Croats of the Islamic faith'. Both Serbs and Croats entertained the belief that at the end of a day, the Muslims would opt to join them. Had they been successful they could have claimed the whole of Bosnia-Hercegovina on ethnic grounds at the expense of the other rival: but this ambition was no longer feasible.

Yet at the same time the notion of creating a nation on the basis of religious adherence, especially when it was promoted by communists, was astonishingly contradictory. It cut across the formal consistency of Titoism and weakened the legitimating power of its ideology, while it simultaneously moved ethnic criteria to the foreground of the public stage. This contradictory posture applied to Macedonian nationalism as well. Some people in Serbia, Slovenia or Croatia asked themselves why it was permissible for Muslims and Macedonians to promote their ethno-national identities, but it was a major political deviation when they did so.

Something similar applied to Kosovo, though with important variations. By the 1980s, the Albanians in the province had come close to achieving parity with the other nations of the country. This political shift automatically raised major and intractable issues, notably it questioned the tacit South Slav nature of the state. The world 'Yugoslavia' means 'land of the South Slavs' and although under Titoism a Slav identity was never an overt symbol in the legitimation of the state, it undoubtedly existed at the affective level. Besides, Albanian assertiveness provoked serious questions about the very deep-seated emotional significance of the province in the Serbian view of the world, as the cradle of Serbian civilisation. Matters were exacerbated by the near-colonial regime run by Rankovic and the secret police in Kosovo between 1944 and 1966, which created far-reaching resentment among the Albanians. The disproportionately high Albanian birth-rate – the highest in Europe in the 1970s and 1980s – pushed the Kosovo Serbs into a demographic minority, to the extent that many of them concluded that they had no future in the province and emigrated. Finally, the reforms of the post-1966 period, like the establishment of an Albanian-language university in Pristina, permitted the Albanian intellectuals to begin mobilisation and to organise the population into a Yugoslav–Albanian national consciousness. In reality, there could be no long-term place for such an identity in a Titoist or a Slavonic order.

THE SERBIAN RESPONSE TO THE FAILURE OF YUGOSLAVISM

The foregoing processes had a major unintended consequence – the rise of a Serbian separatist nationalism. The Serbs had seen themselves as the strongest pro-Yugoslav element in the country, but by the 1970s a group of Serbian intellectuals was beginning to question the value of this status. They argued that the Serbs had always made the greatest sacrifices for Yugoslavia, but had gained little from it; that as a nation they had sustained defeat after defeat (in Croatia, in Bosnia-Hercegovina and in Kosovo); and, perhaps, that they might now reappraise their support for Yugoslavia, certainly as constituted at the time. This line of thinking was associated with the writer Dobrica Cosic and it found expression in the Memorandum of the Serbian Academy of Sciences in 1985 (Cviic 1991), which subsequently came to be perceived as having prepared the ground for Milosevic's strategy in the late 1980s. Serbian separatism was relatively uninfluential until Milosevic took power in an internal party coup in 1987. Until then, it had had to complete with the remnants of Titoism, which enjoyed support in the federal administration (obviously, this justified its continued power) and armed forces (likewise); and also with a relatively well-established liberal reformist current, which despite the defeats of 1972 (the purge of Nikezic) still claimed the loyalty of a significant section of Serbian intellectuals.

One of the particular tragedies of the Serbian experience of Titoism was that it came to be identified with the territorial dismemberment of Serbia. A lingering sense that Yugoslavia was, after all, a kind of Serbia writ large, a poor alternative to Greater Serbia incorporating all the Serbian-inhabited areas, never fully disappeared and was exacerbated by the sense of humiliation that Kosovo and Vojvodina had also been detached from the Serbian heartland, and that, in turn, was linked to a sense of defeat in the Second World War. As long as the Titoist order held, this sense of loss was not articulated, but with the decline of Yugoslav legitimation it came to be expressed ever more clearly. For all practical purposes, the Serbs were suffering a 'loss of empire' trauma at a time when the other national groups in the country regarded them with distaste on account of their 'unitarism' and 'hegemonism'. And this affective current among the Serbs was easily transformed into a political resource by those challenging the established order. The outcome was that when nationhood returned to the political agenda, many Serbs perceived it in strongly territorial terms.

The Yugoslav state was perceived as only semi-legitimate at best by the different ethno-national groups. For the Serbs, Yugoslavia was meant to be a compensation for the loss of the Greater Serbian dream, but many Serbs regarded Yugoslavia as a dubious construct, superimposed on the Serbian nation, while for the non-Serbs, the Yugoslav state was increasingly an ethnicised entity serving Serbian interest: the symbolic 'proof' being the federal capital in Belgrade. Once the Serbs recommenced defining their identity in territorial terms, there was virtually nowhere else for them to go but to define their aims as Greater Serbian.

The year 1987 marked the death-knell of post-war Yugoslavia. It marked the moment when the republicanisation process of 1974 culminated in an unbridgeable split on the future of the civic aspects of Yugoslav politics (as distinct from the ethnic ones) and implied that it would be increasingly difficult to maintain the state as a single polity. As already argued, republicanisation was initially kept in check by the federal party, the armed forces and to some extent the federal government; until Tito's death in 1980, his towering personality was more than enough to resolve conflicts, mainly by simple intervention. What he said went. Unfortunately no one could succeed him, despite somewhat pallid attempts by the federal defence minister, Nikola Ljubicic and the secretary of the party, Stane Dolanc, to don Tito's mantle.

In reality, there was stand-off between the centre and the republics. The republican leaderships increasingly referred to their tacit ethnic base as a source of power. Nevertheless, until 1987 the system was still broadly similar throughout the country, inasmuch as republican parties (Leagues of Communists) exercised a leading role and eliminated challenges to their monopoly. The results were at times highly contradictory. Central legislation was frequently ignored by the republics, even when they had actually agreed to it (e.g. with the stabilisation plan of 1983) and as the 1980s wore on, there were growing divergences in how the different republic parties interpreted their leading role. Some were neo-Stalinist (e.g. Bosnia-Hercegovina), others were very relaxed (e.g. Slovenia). It was clear even at the time that this state of affairs was so unstable as to be untenable. In fact, it was the Slovene party which broke ranks and gradually permitted a shift towards one-party pluralism.

SLOVENIA MOVES TOWARDS DEMOCRACY

Although the Slovene changes were argued in non-ethnic terms, it was understood in Ljubljana that Slovenia was in a position to determine its own fate and that this would be done regardless of the interests and opinions of other Yugoslavs. I received this message very clearly during a visit to Ljubljana in 1987. It was not clear whether those involved fully recognised that a move in this direction would mean accepting an ethno-national foundation for the new Slovenian order. One-party pluralism, as it turned out, was only an instrument of transition towards pluralism proper, and in a short period of time the Slovenes were pressing for a far-reaching autonomy with an increasingly explicit ethnic message. A part of this message, however, was non-ethnic – it implied that Slovenia was committed to establishing a democratic order and that they felt that this could not be done within a Yugoslav framework.

The proposition was never spelled out, but it was unmistakable from the way in which the Slovenes approached the problem, in that they rapidly gave up any idea of transforming the rest of Yugoslavia, which would probably have been beyond their abilities in any case. Hence the Slovenes' democratisation project carried within it the hidden message that as far as Ljubljana was concerned, the communist legitimation of Yugoslavia was finished and that at that point the sole alternative legitimation was national independence, coupled with statehood. The Slovenes did not, of course, shift in this direction overnight, but their attempts to maintain a single Yugoslav state declined in enthusiasm as each of their initiatives met with a rebuff from Belgrade, both on nationalistic and on neo-Titoist grounds. The confederation plan of October 1990 was the last gasp of Yugoslavism.

From the Serbian vantage point, the situation appeared to be quite different. Just as in Slovenia, the Titoist system was widely perceived to be, if not exactly bankrupt, certainly eroding in its capacity to command loyalty and support, but the sources of this process of erosion were different. The catalyst was Kosovo, where demonstrations by the Albanians in 1981 were followed by a rising outmigration of local Serbs. This outmigration produced a deep shock in Serbia, something that was enhanced by the result of the 1981 census, which returned an Albanian population in Kosovo of around 90 per cent.

The reaction was an outraged Serbian opinion, which could not bring itself to accept that ethnically they had lost the game and that the most sacred of Serbian lands was now in no way culturally Serbian. The visceral, racist anti-Albanian response of the Serbs – strengthened as it was by the religious cleavage, as the Kosovo Albanians are largely Muslim – not only had its historical roots, with Muslim Albanians substituting for Muslim Turks in this mythologically suffused mind-set, but it was spread by the Serbian media, which used the Kosovo issue to claim autonomy from political control.

The simultaneous challenge of a sense of national injury and the threat to communist power was exacerbated by the growing economic crisis, to which the Serbian leadership had no answer. It rejected proposals for moves towards democratisation, like the redistribution of power and the introduction of market conditions, as this would have undermined its power and privileges, as well as resulting in the probable collapse of many enterprises. In the event, Milosevic captured the leadership of the Serbian party and rapidly moved to consolidate his position by repeated reference to Serbian nationalism and the grievances of the Serbian nation. His liberal opponents were vanquished and the Titoists saw their opportunity to salvage their power by joining him. A new neo-Titoist-cum-Serbian nationalist political formula was well on the way to being born.

Milosevic had Yugoslavia-wide ambitions. He rejected the democratising programme of the Slovenes and insisted that only through recentralisation could the economic crisis be resolved. None of the other republics was prepared to accede to this, especially as they increasingly understood it to be a revived Greater Serbia programme, although it was argued in terms of both Titoism and pan-Serbianism. Fears of the latter were enhanced by the way in which Milosevic dealt with Kosovo and

Vojvodina, both technically provinces within Serbia but *de facto* enjoying the powers of a republic. In 1988-9, Milosevic put an end to this status. His supporters chased away the Vojvodina leadership (a coalition of hardliners and neo-Titoists who were united in seeking to maintain an authoritarian regime in Novi Sad) in the 'yoghurt revolution', so-called because the Vojvodina apparatchiks fled when they were pelted with yoghurt cartons by an angry crowd. Montenegro was an analogous case; it was a full republic, not a province of Serbia and its inhabitants have always considered themselves Serbs, though a minority of Montenegrins have sought to develop a separate Montenegrin consciousness. The ousting of the Montenegro leadership began at more or less the same time and Kosovo followed soon after, both processes being completed by the spring of 1989. Thus Milosevic effectively controlled the whole of Serbia and Montenegro as well, which put him in a strong position to dominate both federal state and party organisations.

MILOSEVIC AND THE OTHER REPUBLICS

This assault on Tito's legacy appalled the other republics, but they ultimately found themselves powerless to stop it. Milosevic successfully exploited the ambiguity of the situation, in which he could use party and state structures to promote Serbian national-ism. There was no answer to this, because the legitimating force of Titoism was largely exhausted and the only alternative was nationhood and democracy, the Slovenian road, but communists leaders lacked the ability and the plausibility to adopt this model. For all practical purposes, by 1989-90, the future of Yugoslavia as a single state had a major question mark over it. If Yugoslavia could not be held together as a communist state, was there an alternative? It was evident that Milosevic's Greater Serbian variant was unacceptable to the rest of the country and that the communists from the other republican leaderships would have to be replaced before an answer was available.

The answer was given in 1990. In essence, parallel to and to an extent influenced by the collapse of communism elsewhere in Central and Eastern Europe, the Yugoslav communists were eliminated from power in republic after republic as free elections were held. Democracy represented the death-knell for Yugoslavia because it implied consensus and there appeared to be no way to bring the Serbs to accept a compromise. Elections were held in Slovenia and Croatia in the spring of 1990, in Bosnia-Hercegovina and Macedonia in the autumn; in all cases the communists lost and ceded power to various nationalists, who proclaimed themselves democrats as well. In Serbia, Milosevic was well entrenched and was able to control the electoral process in December 1990.

It should be noted that in both Croatia and Serbia the electoral system influenced the ethnic composition of the new legislatures. The voting was a 'first past the post', two-ballot system; this allowed large parties to maximise their votes and produced the results that in Croatia, Tudjman's Croatian Democratic Alliance (HDZ) won 205 out of 356 seats (57 per cent) with only 41 per cent of the popular vote. Nor did it help matters that the Serbian minority divided its vote between the reform communists and the overtly Serbian parties. In the Serbian elections, after two rounds Milosevic's reform communists ended up with only 48 per cent of the vote, but this brought them 194 out of 250 seats (77.6 per cent); the voting was marred by various irregularities and a boycott by the Albanians, which obviously boosted Milosevic's total.

The previously mentioned confederal plan was put forward jointly by the Slovenian and Croatian leaderships in October 1990. It constituted the only attempt to transform the country on the basis of democracy. The plan proposed that the six republics become independent states in alliance, with some common institutions and all decisions to be taken unanimously. It was not taken very seriously by Milosevic and, conceivably, the authors of the plan knew this too, so that it was put forward more as an alibi than anything else. From that time on, the disintegration of Yugoslavia was no longer a question of if but of when.

In looking back on the process, it is striking that the key role in pushing for greater devolution leading to disintegration was played not by the Croats but by the Slovenes. Throughout 1988–9 there was a shrill dispute between Belgrade and Ljubljana, which confirmed the Slovenes in their belief that there was little to be gained from persevering with Yugoslavia. They concluded that the Serbs in general and Milosevic in particular were incapable of compromise and step by step the conviction grew that they would be better off outside the Yugoslav framework. There was, indeed, a certain correlation between the growth of democracy and the turning away from Yugoslavia, above all because both the old and new leaderships found it more congenial to rule by consent, enjoying a popularity denied to communists and this experience ineluctably pushed them to rely on their ethno-national base. As Slovenian nationhood was thrust further into the centre of the political stage, the Slovenes too found it more difficult to compromise or at least found fewer reasons why they should look for some kind of an agreement involving give and take. True, at no point was Milosevic ready to give; this made matters much easier for the Slovenes. Ironically, by contributing to raising the temperature the Slovenes ended by making matters much worse for the Croats. Slovenia could always be detached from Yugoslavia with comparative ease, as it enjoyed relative prosperity and good connections with the West, not to mention the fact that there was no minorities question to complicate relations, but for Croatia, the Yugoslav connection was far more intricate.

CROATIA AND THE ARMED FORCES

Two other factors require discussion – the fate of Croatia and the role of the last Titoist institution, the armed forces. During the period when the polemics and tension between Serbs and Slovenes were mounting, Croatia remained quiet, indeed it was almost a bastion of Yugoslavist loyalty. It took till the end of 1989 for the Croatian party to conclude that free elections, on a multi-party basis, could not be put off any longer. There were several reasons for this caution. It was far harder for the Croats to envisage full independence than for the Slovenes, given that there were Croatian minorities in Bosnia-Hercegovina and the Vojvodina; then, the Croatian leadership was full of trepidation at any move liable to lead towards democracy, because it understood that this would revive the issue of nationhood, something which had caused the crisis of 1971; finally, the Croatian communist leadership must have realised that in the event of any real move towards independence, the whole question of the Serbs of Croatia would leap back to the agenda with a vengeance.

This difficulty did not trouble their successors, who in the first flush of victory in April–May 1990 behaved with complete tactlessness and incompetence towards the local Serbs. Indeed, they adopted policies virtually calculated to mobilise Serbian opinion against Zagreb. They quickly adopted the symbols of the war-time independent state, on the proposition that these had always been the Croatian symbols, and ignored the Serbs' susceptibilities. More seriously perhaps when they began to purge the *nomenklatura*, the Serbs went first and, in some cases, Croatian members of the *nomenklatura* remained. In general, they did very little to reassure the local Serbs that Croatia would be a democratic state in which there would be enough space for Serbs to live as they wanted, with their own ethno-national agendas and symbols, like the Cyrillic alphabet.

Possibly the greatest error of all was that Tudjman made no attempt worthy of the name to build up a moderate Serbian leadership in Croatia, with which he could do a deal. On the contrary, it was as if he was doing everything to polarise the situation. When the Serbs presented their demands, these were dismissed and they were told that as only cultural rights were on offer, there could be no question of any territorial autonomy. And to rub it in, Croatian policemen were sent to the heavily Serbian-inhabited areas like the Krajina. In a very short period of time, moderate Serbs were marginalised and the hardliners from the rural areas seized the leadership. They were much less sophisticated and were not inclined to listen to argument about compromise. Indeed, in their world view, their worst fears were confirmed – for them it was a return to 1941 and soon the air was full of cries of 'the struggle against the fascist Croats'.

From this state of affairs it was a very short step to the *ad hoc* alliance with the armed forces, which turned out to be the fuse that eventually set off the fighting in the summer of 1991. The armed forces for their part viewed the disintegration of the country with dismay. They saw clearly that without a Yugoslavia, they would have no role and their power and privileges would be transformed into an insubstantial pageant. From an early date in 1990, the armed forces intervened in Croatia ostensibly and to some extent genuinely to protect the Serbian minority – it was a good case of a political actor looking for a role and finding it regardless of the consequences.

The attitude of the JNA was a mixture of military profession-alism, Titoism and, given that around two-thirds of the officers' corps was made up of Serbs and Montenegrins, with many of the

Serbs from the minorities outside Serbia, pro-Serbian sympathies. The armed forces, therefore, took the Slovenian and Croatian
declarations of independence in June 1991 as acts of treason and
decided to put an end to it by direct intervention. In other words,
they insisted that the protection of *bratstvo i jedinstvo*, with
which Tito had charged them so long before, was still their valid
role, utterly regardless of the very different circumstances in the
early 1990s.

This explains the initial intervention in Slovenia, which
turned out very badly through military incompetence, and the
subsequent intervention in Croatia, which seemed to have a
much more definite purpose. In reality there were at least three
such objectives – the restoration of Yugoslavia in the Titoist
mould; the protection of the Serbian minority; and support for
Milosevic's strategy of creating a Greater Serbia out of the
Serbian-inhabited areas of Croatia, Bosnia-Hercegovina, plus
Montenegro, Vojvodina and Kosovo. The armed forces vacillated
around these three, something which helped to explain the
hesitation and inconsistency with which it pursued the war.
Without a clear political direction – and there was no government behind the armed forces to provide this – and without a
political purposiveness of its own, the JNA's involvement
seemed senseless. It was almost as if it fought simply to demonstrate its own existence. *Bellum gero ergo sum.*

Towards the end of Yugoslavia Milosevic too found himself in
the position of having to run ever faster in order to remain in the
same place. His particular genius in 1987 and after was to offer
promise after promise of 'salvation' to Serbian opinion, which he
never had to keep, but to achieve this, he had to keep raising the
stakes. It began with Kosovo, continued with Montenegro and
Vojvodina, and then oscillated between a Serbian-dominated
Yugoslavia and Greater Serbia. To achieve his aims, he was
perfectly prepared to use the JNA in Croatia, while fully
understanding that their interests were only temporarily
coincidental. The motives of the armed forces were vague and
uncertain; Milosevic was protecting his own power and power
base. His legitimating ideology could not be anything other than
a Serbian one, and beyond a certain point Serbian opinion would
not support his project of a Greater Serbian Yugoslavia, hence
his shifting between the two.

CONCLUSION

This chapter is being written before the final consequences of the collapse of Yugoslavia are fully known: though war, ethnic cleansing, and territorial adjustments and multiple further secessions from the debris can be confidently predicted. Yugoslavia has been the site of every kind of ethnic conflict regulation identified by the editors, and the same fate may well befall many of its successor states. The solution to this Balkan question may well prove to be 'balkanisation'.

The chances of converting Titoist Yugoslavia into a democratic Yugoslavia were never very good. The failure of the two previous attempts to hold the country together – linguistic-monarchical and communist – meant that the conditions imposed by the various actors would be severe, almost certainly too severe. The necessary agreement on the benefits of keeping a Yugoslav state in being was absent and communism collapsed too suddenly, at different rates of speed in the different republics, for the various republican elites to find common ground. Then again, the democratic traditions in the different republics varied widely, with the Western aspirations of the Slovenes being in stark contrast to the volatility and political inexperience of the Serbs. The chance factor was also relevant – neither Milosevic nor Tudjman was fitted for the role of holding a complex state together at a time when it was riven by the deepest tensions and contradictions; Milan Kucan, the communist-turned-democratic president of Slovenia was. And the one institution with a genuinely all-Yugoslav purposiveness, the JNA, had no interest in democracy. Keeping Yugoslavia together was always going to be a very difficult operation; a democratic Yugoslavia would always have been nearly impossible. And the nearly impossible was not on offer when it was needed.

Chapter 9

Spain

Peripheral nationalism and state response[1]

Michael Keating

INTRODUCTION

It is a premise of this chapter that neither 'national' nor 'ethnic' identity is a natural or inherent characteristic of human communities. Rather, they are constructed in specific places in a process of historical development according to the needs of leading political forces (Breuilly 1985; Gurritxaga 1988; Keating 1988). This is not to say that national or ethnic identity can be created at will. There need to be tangible makers of community identity which can be pressed to the service of the national project. These may be linguistic, racial, geographical, institutional, economic or social. There is also usually a common history, though this itself is frequently a fabrication. It is less a history, indeed, which is needed for the nationalist project than a set of myths, beliefs about a people whose force and significance is largely independent of their truth or falsehood. Given that linguistic, racial, geographical, and historical differences abound in the modern world, though, the question remains as to why these are pressed into the service of nationalist, separatist or 'ethnic' politics at some times and places and not at others. Further questions arise as to the content of nationalist or ethnic politics and its project in relation to the state; and about the management of the issue by the state itself.

Spain provides an interesting case to explore these processes since it has seen a partially successful project for the formation of a nation-state, in competition both with separatist movements and with regionalist groups seeking a form of state in which their distinct needs would be accommodated. The term nation itself is deeply ambiguous. *Nación* can refer either to the Spanish nation or to the 'historic nations' of Catalonia, the Basque Country and Galicia, within it. The term *nacionalidad* is even vaguer, referring often to the three historic nationalities within the Spanish *nación* but not infrequently stretched to include regionalist movements in Valencia, Andalusia and elsewhere. *Regionalismo*, for its part, can be used both for the historic nationalities and for other parts of Spain; the constitution speaks of the *nacionalidades* and *regiones* of Spain. The limits of the historic nationalities are unclear and the markers of nationality are a complex web of linguistic, institutional and historical factors which vary from one case to another. In this respect, pre-modern Spain was much like the rest of Europe. It is in the modern era that Spain stands out, as different conceptions of nationality have competed in a struggle which is only now being resolved.

THE BUILDING OF THE SPANISH STATE

Spanish unity came about through a mixture of conquest and dynastic expansion and the extension of the national territory immediately preceded the creation of the empire. The political core of the state was the kingdom of Castile, expanding in the Middle Ages to conquer the Moorish territories of the south in a process later glorified as the *Reconquista*. Dynastic marriages united the kingdoms of Leon, Navarre, Aragon and Portugal to Castile by the end of the fifteenth century but not in a unitary state. Instead, the territories of the Spanish crown retained a variety of feudal privileges and institutions. Castile was a unitary monarchical state, with a weak Cortes (parliament) and a uniform tax system but in their other territories the powers of the monarchs were severely circumscribed. In Navarre and the Basque provinces, ancient *fueros* provided for separate customs duties and the payment of a lump sum of taxation by the provinces to the Crown, each province being free to determine how this should be raised (Vasquez 1981). The kingdom of Aragon was itself a confederation of four territories, Aragon, Catalonia, Valencia and the Balearic islands, each with its own parliamentary institutions, laws and taxes, the best developed of which was the Generalitat of Catalonia.

The non-Castilian territories were not obliged to raise taxes except for their own administration and defence. On the other hand, the new possessions in America were attached to the

Crown of Castile, and Castilians had an effective monopoly on their colonisation. This gave an advantage to Castile over the previously successful Mediterranean trading economy of Catalonia, though in the long run the effects were disastrous. The structure was further complicated by the accession of Charles V to the Holy Roman Empire, creating a multinational European empire within which was a multinational Spain, its component units themselves internally divided. With Spanish kings looking outwards, there was little incentive to nation-building at home (Linz 1973). Four languages remained: Castilian, Catalan, Gallego-Portuguese and Basque.

There were attempts by the monarchy to create a unitary state on the lines of Bourbon France. In 1635, with French troops threatening the frontier, the government demanded a financial contribution from the non-Castilian territories. Navarre and Aragon paid up but Portugal and Catalonia rose in revolt. Portugal's rebellion succeeded but Catalonia was forced back into Spain, apart from its northern province of Roussillon, which was incorporated into France. In the war of Spanish succession, support for the losing Carlos by the Aragonese territories sealed the fate of their representative institutions and in 1714 the victorious Bourbon Philip V set about creating a unitary state. Foral rights and the local *diputaciones* were suppressed in Aragon, Valencia and the Balearic islands, together with the Cortes and Generalitat of Catalonia. Local customs duties were abolished, municipal privileges suppressed, the four Catalan universities replaced with a new one, the laws unified and administrative units created which ignored traditional boundaries. Posts in the Aragonese territories were opened up to Castilians and the American trade to Catalans and others. In the Basque provinces and Navarre, which had supported the winning side, the old foral regime was left intact for another century.

This *Nueva Planta* programme was a step forward in nation-building but did not destroy territorial politics. Historians generally agree that union helped the economic take-off of Catalonia. Destruction of archaic local and municipal privileges aided trade while the mercantilist policies gave the nascent Catalan industries advantages in Castilian markets and, with the abolition of the colonial monopoly of Seville and Cadiz, those of America. The economic core of Spain began to shift decisively to the periphery. Yet the political core remained in Madrid and the abolition of the Generalitat would present a potent symbol to future nationalists.

THE FAILURE OF NATION-BUILDING

The nationality question in Spain, however, is the product of the age of nationalism in the nineteenth century. It was then that the failure to establish a modern state or to reverse Spain's secular decline as a world power provided the opportunity for rival national identities to emerge in the periphery. Spain's failure as a state must be seen against the background of military, political and economic decline from world power to poor periphery of Western Europe. Its culminating point was 1898, with the humiliating defeat by the United States and the loss of its last colonies. Internally, Spain was deeply divided. Monarchists fought with republicans. The Church and its supporters fought with liberal anti-clericals. Authoritarians fought with democrats. By the late nineteenth century, these divisions had been overlaid with a bitter class warfare. A retarded industrialisation produced a capitalist bourgeoisie tied to protectionism and a militant working class in which anarchist ideas made great headway. There was the territorial division. All these overlapped in complex ways to prevent the emergence of a stable politics.

Territorial identity was sustained in Spain by a number of factors. In Catalonia, Galicia and the Basque Country separate languages survived in daily use, though the official state language and the language of education was Castilian. Industrial development further differentiated the regions, being largely confined in the nineteenth century to Catalonia and the Basque Country. Spain did not therefore correspond to the core-periphery model of national development. While political power remained at the centre, the economic weight of the country from the nineteenth century shifted back to the periphery. Industrial development both marked these regions off from the rest of Spain and posed a threat to the traditional society and way of life through immigration of labour and the growth of material and secular values. Institutional bearers of identity included the surviving *fueros* and the memory of self-government. Both the *fueros* and memories of Catalonia's golden age as a medieval trading nation served as the basis for myths of national identity.

The forging of these elements into coherent national or 'ethnic' identities, however, was the work of political movements in the specific circumstances of Spain's entry into the world of nineteenth-century nation-states. In particular, peripheral nationalism was the result of the failure of the Spanish state to accommodate the demands of territorial elites or give them a place in the new state order.

Radically different conceptions of a modern Spanish state competed through the turbulent years of the nineteenth and early twentieth centuries, marked by periodic revolutions, military *pronunciamentos*, republics, reactionary monarchy and class conflict. In favour of a centralised state were the Bourbon monarchy and their right-wing followers up to Franco. These aimed for a unified, Castilian-speaking, authoritarian Catholic state. While the base of this position was in the traditional land-owning, aristocratic and military elites, elements of the capitalist bourgeoisie would sometimes buy into it for its promise of social order, repression of working-class demands and protectionism. A liberal republican element was inspired by the Jacobinism and the French revolution. These aimed for a democratic, secular, unitary state with a popular and exclusive Spanish national identity, committed to modernisation and development. Among the *regeneracionista* generation after the defeat of 1898, was a commitment to a modernised, European Spain and a presumption in favour of a unitary, uniform state, shedding the 'archaic' peripheral languages and culture. Also in favour of centralisation were elements of the emerging socialist movement. This was partly on grounds of working-class unity but also because of the weakness of the socialist party PSOE in Catalonia and among the indigenous working class in the Basque Country, won over to anarchism or nationalism. At the same time, like other European socialist parties, the PSOE had a decentralist element in its philosophy and throughout its history has displayed a profound ambiguity on the national question (Keating 1991).

Decentralisation and regionalism were also supported from a variety of political perspectives. Carlism, a movement in favour of the dynasty defeated in 1714, was strong in the rural areas of the Basque Country, Navarre and Catalonia. Bearing a strong resemblance to British Jacobitism and some of the provincial monarchist movements in nineteenth-century France, Carlism was anti-modernising, committed to traditionalism, Catholicism and the restoration of traditional privileges and autonomous institutions in the periphery. It thus opposed both monarchical centralism and liberal, secular republicanism. Also favouring regionalism were other traditional elements in Catalonia and the Basque Country, seeing modernisation and industrialisation as a threat to traditional values and the language and drawing on the romantic revival which from the mid-nineteenth century throughout Europe discovered or re-invented lost cultures. From the late nineteenth century, they were joined by sections of the Catalan bourgeoisie, a modernising force frustrated by their inability to advance their agenda of modernisation within the Spanish state and who developed an increasingly autonomist discourse. As regional identity was strengthened in the early twentieth century, with the continued failure of the Spanish state, the socialist left too found it necessary to adopt a regionalist language in order to penetrate Basque and Catalan society, though trying to reconcile this with a strategy for Spain as a whole. The anarchist movement, strong among the Catalan working class, rejected any form of politics, Spanish or regionalist, though by the early twentieth century the immigrant workers in the Basque Country had been largely won away from anarchism by the PSOE.

A third discourse was represented by federalist republicanism which had some influence in the late nineteenth century. Federalists were committed to a modernised, democratic and decentralised federation of the Iberian peninsula. Although such a formula might have accommodated the special demands of the peripheral regions, the failure of the brief First Republic discredited the idea and thereafter Catalan and Basque demands were couched in particularist terms. Federalism never completely died out. In 1918 the socialist party PSOE adopted a resolution (never repealed but long ignored) in favour of a federal republic and federalist ideas have informed the recent debate about the future of regional autonomy.

THE EMERGENCE OF PERIPHERAL NATIONALISM

Organised political nationalism in the Spanish periphery was the product of the late nineteenth century, starting in Catalonia and the Basque Country. Catalan nationalism developed from the ambiguous position of the local industrial bourgeoisie. In the

Spanish context an advanced and modernising force, they sought influence within the state and an end to the dominance of the land-owning, aristocratic, monarchical elite in Madrid. Yet in the European context, they were uncompetitive, requiring a protected Spanish market for their goods. Rejecting the Spanish state, they still called on it to suppress their own working class in the industrial turbulence of the early twentieth century. Committed to modern industrial values, they were still inspired by a traditional Catholic social ethos. Drawing heavily on the Romantic movement for an emotive element to their nationalism, they also emphasised the defence of language. This provided for an inter-class appeal as well as status differentiation, since Catalan has always been regarded locally as of higher status than the Castilian spoken by lower-class immigrants.

In 1892, the *Lliga Catalana* was formed to demand self-government and wider use of the Catalan language. In 1901 this gave way to the *Lliga Regionalista* which, with the aim of establishing a 'great Catalonia within a great Spain', broke the pattern of centralist, clientelist politics (*caciquismo*) at local and national elections in Catalonia, establishing a pattern of separate Catalan parties which has persisted since. At the 1907 elections, the alliance *Solidaridad Catalana* won forty-one of Catalonia's forty-four seats, with the ambivalent aims of gaining a degree of self-government while seeking the 'catalanisation of Spain' (Oltra *et al.* 1981). Conservative nationalism's fatal mistake was to collaborate with the dictatorship of Primo de Rivera (1923–31) in the hope that he would grant them autonomy while keeping the working class in order. They were to be disappointed since Primo, true to the right-wing *españolista* tradition, would make no compromises with Catalan nationalism.

There were also radical–democratic, republican and leftist varieties of Catalanism, appealing to the lower middle classes, artisans and sections of the proletariat not won over to anarchism. The left–regionalist position was filled by a succession of groups breaking away from the *Lliga* or PSOE until the Primo dictatorship. On the fall of the dictatorship in 1931, the *Esquerra Republicana de Catalunya* (ERC) was formed as a left-of-centre movement calling for Catalan self-government in a federal Spain. With the discrediting of the *Lliga*, the ERC was to dominate politics in Catalonia up to the civil war.

The turbulent events of the 1920s and 1930s pushed Catalanism further than it might otherwise have gone. The Primo dictatorship, with its suppression of regional identities, not only disillusioned the Barcelona bourgeoisie. By providing the left and the regionalists with a common enemy, it served to unite them. An invasion of Catalonia from France established Macia, founder of the ERC, as a popular hero (GEC 1976). Tactical considerations pushed the Catalan cause still further in the confused political manoeuvring of the Second Republic.

Basque nationalism was a very different phenomenon. Basque traditional privileges, the *fueros*, had been gradually reduced during the nineteenth century. In 1839 their free-trade privileges were abolished, with the application of Spanish tariffs at the ports and the removal of the customs barriers between Spain and the Basque provinces. In 1876, there were further changes which left intact only the *concierto economico*, whereby the three Basque provinces and Navarre raise taxes locally and pass on a negotiated amount to the Spanish treasury. These changes stimulated a rapid industrial expansion with a Basque capitalist class, unlike their Catalan counterparts, highly integrated into the Spanish political and economic system. Basque nationalism was a reaction to this, drawing its support from the most traditionalist sectors of society and strongly imbued with Catholicism and the Carlist legacy. Arana, founder of the Basque Nationalist Party, preached an uncompromising racial exclusiveness appealing to those marginalised by industrial society and threatened by the immigration of non-Basques. Its support was greatest among peasants, fishermen and artisans, with some appeal to the urban lower middle classes (Gispert and Prats 1978). Basque nationalism never established the ideological hegemony of Catalanism, gaining around one-third of the vote at elections before the civil war. Language was a key element in the Basque movement but one which limited its appeal to the proletariat, many of whom were immigrants from other regions. Unlike Catalan, Basque is a difficult, non-Latin language, making assimilation problematic. The absence of a written literature or vernacular cultural revival limited the mobilising appeal of nationalism among the middle classes.

For its Catholicism, its racial exclusiveness and its social conservatism, Basque nationalism was regarded with hostility by progressive and left-wing forces in Spain. For its separatism it was detested by the Spanish nationalist right and the military.

Unlike Catalanism, it contained no prospect for Spain as a whole. Only the advent of the Second Republic produced a tactical accommodation between republicans and Basque nationalists.

Galicia is the third region generally considered as a historic nationality. Yet, despite the existence of a distinct language and culture, there was no significant regionalist movement before the Second Republic. Galicia was a poor country of small farmers without political consciousness and a ruling elite integrated into the institutions of the Spanish state, notably the army and the court. Political representation took the form of client relationships based on the local *caciques*. Despite some stirrings from the turn of the century, it was not until the Second Republic in the 1930s that a Galician autonomist movement emerged, in imitation of Catalonia.

The Second Republic, 1932–9, had the task of accommodating Catalan and Basque demands while preserving the unity of the state. An agreement of sorts had been reached among republican forces in the Pact of San Sebastian, which included a recognition of Catalan and Galician demands and, more ambiguously, those of the Basques (Hernández 1980). On the fall of the monarchy, republican leaders had declared a Catalan republic as part of a non-existent Iberian federation and had to be persuaded to abandon this in favour of a legislated solution. The Basque Country presented more severe problems since republican forces were weak there and Basque nationalism dominated by clerical conservatives. When these proposed special links between the Basque Country and the Holy See, republicans in Madrid (and many socialists in the Basque Country) feared a 'Vatican Gibraltar' (Granja 1981). Eventually, the formula of the *Estado Integral* (loosely based on the Weimar Republic) was concocted to describe a new state which was neither unitary nor federal. From unitary theory, the *Estado Integral* took the sovereignty of the Spanish people as a whole and the need for autonomy statutes to be passed by the national parliament. From federalist and contractual theory, it took the principle of the framing of autonomy statutes in the regions themselves, their negotiation with the centre and approval in a local referendum. The autonomy provisions were of general application, and, except in the case of the Basque statute excluded reference to the *fueros*, traditional rights immune to state power and entrenching territorial and social interests (Clavero 1981). Yet in practice it was intended to limit autonomy to the historic nations of Catalonia, the Basque Country and Galicia. Regions could gain a statute of autonomy only if a majority of the town councils requested it, two-thirds of the entire regional electorate approved it in a referendum and the national Cortes accepted it. Certain matters were reserved to the exclusive competence of the centre; in others the state would legislate but regions could execute; all other matters could be devolved to regions by their individual statutes of autonomy (Olábarri 1981). A Catalan statute, approved by Madrid and by local referendum, went into operation in 1932 and the Generalitat was restored. In the Basque Country, the clerical issue slowed progress and autonomy was conceded only at the onset of the civil war, a move which committed the Basques to the republican side – and to Franco's vengeance. By this time, the expectations raised by the republic, the leftist opposition to the government elected in 1934 and the disintegration of central authority, had spawned regionalist demands not only in Galicia where an autonomy statute was conceded in 1936 but in Andalusia, Aragon, Mallorca, Valencia and Asturias (Gispert and Prats 1978). These tended to be left wing and republican, confirming the identification of regional autonomy with the left.

It is impossible to say how the autonomy provisions would have operated in peacetime for the whole process was caught up in the strife and political disintegration which led up to the civil war. The return of the right in the elections of 1934 halted the autonomy process and a conflict over land reform led to the suspension of the Generalitat (Clavero 1981) and pushed the Catalan left towards separatism. The restoration of the Generalitat by the Popular Front government in 1936 was rapidly followed by the Franco rebellion. Under war-time conditions, Catalonia effectively functioned independently, at least until the republican government itself moved to Barcelona. In the Basque Country, autonomy was rapidly conceded to ensure Basque support for the republic.

Franco's victory closed this phase of Spanish regionalism with the triumph of the most intransigent, *españolista*, militarist elements. In the Francoist 'crusade', regionalism ranked alongside communism and atheism as the deadly enemies of Spain and all traces of regional identity were wiped out.

Regionalist leaders like Companys, president of the Generalitat and the veteran Andalusian Blas Infante, were executed, and speaking Basque or Catalan in public became a crime. Such was the Francoist paranoia about regionalism that no attempt was made to gain regime collaborators among the Basque- or Catalan-speaking communities, despite the presence, especially in the former, of rightist, clericalist elements. Franco's persecution certainly crushed the Basque and Catalan movements but, in so doing, reinforced anti-regime solidarity in those regions and ensured that any return to democracy would need a regional dimension.

NATIONALISM UNDER FRANCO

Nationalism in Catalonia and the Basque Country is thus a product of the age of European nationalism in the late nineteenth century and a consequence of the failure of Spanish nation-building. This allowed the elements of cultural identity, institutional survival and political exclusion to be forged into an alternative conception of nationality. The Spanish state was further delegitimised by Franco's identification of Spain and the Spanish nation with the most reactionary centralist tendencies. Yet the repression of the Franco years did have its effect. Peripheral languages were banned and children educated in Castilian alone. Large-scale immigration continued, this time bringing Castilian speakers from the south into both Catalonia and the Basque Country. Thirty-seven per cent of the population of both Catalonia and the Basque Country by the late 1970s were born elsewhere in Spain (Hernández and Mercadé 1986; Linz 1986). Sections of the upper industrial bourgeoisie in both Catalonia and the Basque Country collaborated with the regime in return for protection and suppression of the working class. So the survival of peripheral national identity could not be taken for granted. It was necessary to reconstruct the alternative sense of national identity in the periphery, on the basis of a broad popular opposition to the regime, encompassing the petit bourgeoisie and the working class. After a period of quiescence in which formal leadership of the peripheral nationalist movements remained in the hands of exiles, internal activity resumed in the 1960s.

The first stirrings in Catalonia were cultural, in defence of a language still used regularly by some 60 per cent of the population (Vallverdú 1980). By the late 1960s, the language revival had joined with the youth culture and the spirit of protest in the universities linked to the international new left. Religion provided another element. The abbey of Montserrat, traditional centre of Catalanism, became a centre of opposition to Francoism and, with the liberalisation of the Church after the second Vatican Council, progressive Catholics began to attack the links between the Church and the regime and to address themselves to current social and economic problems. Despite the regime's political prejudices, the economy of Catalonia made great strides forward during the years of expansion (Trias 1972), retaining first place among Spanish regions, but there was resentment about subsidising the rest of Spain and thus sustaining an alien regime. While the large industrialists were integrated into the regime, benefiting from the policies of protection and subsidy, among the professional middle classes there was considerable contempt for the Madrid machine and little inclination to credit it with Catalonia's advance.

The revival of political activity dates from the early 1960s and cannot be separated from the figure of Jordi Pujol. Son of an upper-middle-class Barcelona family, a devout Catholic and conservative, Pujol was obsessed with the idea of creating a modern Catalonia. Characteristic of the conservative Catalan nationalist tradition, he combines mystic and spiritual elements and strong religious convictions with a concern with the here and now, the necessity to *fer pais*, that is, to make a modern Catalonia (Pujol 1976; 1980). In the absence of political structures, this would involve culture and economics, with politics coming later. In 1959, he founded the Banca Catalana (Baiges *et al.* 1985), which was to become the centre of a vast financial and political movement. His reputation established by a jail sentence, Pujol used the resources of the bank as well as his own to help not only Catalan businesses but a range of cultural and political activities (Baiges *et al.* 1985).

The left was more ambiguous about Catalanism. From the late 1940s, the Catalan Communists – the PSUC – following the lead of the Spanish communists, downplayed the issue and presented the workers' struggle as a Spanish-wide one. In 1952, Joan Gomorera, leader of the PSUC, was expelled from the Communist Party, despite his impeccable Stalinist credentials, for

Catalan nationalist deviation (Oltra *et al.* 1981). The Socialist PSOE, concerned with its position among the non-Catalan immigrant workers, also downplayed the issue. By the late 1960s, though, the success of the new Catalan movements and the ideological rethinking prompted by the emergence of third world national liberation movements had caused the left to change their line again. In 1965, PSUC resumed its support for Catalan autonomy, while PSOE gave more circumspect support.

A feature of the later years of the Franco dictatorship is the emergence within it of a modernised civil society, the product of education, economic growth and the opening to Europe (Pérez 1987). In Catalonia, this social modernisation took on a specifically Catalan colour and the demand for autonomy was a central part of the emerging democratic consensus. In 1969 a broad front, the *Coordinadora de Forces Politiques*, was formed, and in 1971 an *Assemblea de Catalunya* demanded liberty, amnesty and a statute of autonomy.

In the Basque Country, repression and immigration combined to reduce the proportion of people speaking the language to a third by 1981 (Llera 1986). The 1960s, however, saw a cultural revival. A network of voluntary schools, the *ikastolas* grew up and by the 1970s were enrolling some 50,000 pupils (Torrealday 1980). In the Basque context, such cultural activity was in itself political, bringing new recruits into the democratic resistance and the cause of Basque autonomy.

The impact of economic change was complex, producing some contradictory trends (Roiz 1984). Rapid industrial expansion in the 1950s and 1960s was accompanied by an increase of the urban population from 47 per cent in 1960 to 78 per cent in 1980 and large-scale immigration. Given the difficulties in learning the language, this created a greater division among natives and immigrants than in Catalonia. Only about a third of the population, strongly concentrated in agriculture and in the province of Guipuzcoa, spoke the language in the late 1970s (Llera 1986), though there was some evidence that younger immigrants, in contrast to their elders, were becoming bilingual (Torrealday 1980). By the end of the Franco era, though, there were signs of obsolescence in Basque heavy industry and unemployment levels soared, particularly among youth.

The Basque movement was divided and ineffective after the civil war, especially following the failure of a series of strikes in the late 1940s and early 1950s. The Basque Nationalist Party (PNV) continued its line of conservative nationalism but, dropping the exclusive and racist themes of Arana, joined the European Christian Democrat movement. From the 1960s, a militant offshoot, ETA, began a campaign of violence in pursuit of an independent and united Basque Country, sparking off a cycle of attacks and repression which marked the final years of the Franco regime. In 1974, ETA split into two and in 1976 the *politico-militar* wing renounced violence. The remaining elements carried on their campaign, adapting their ideology to a left-wing 'national liberation' line based on third world models. Nationalism did not, however, gain the hegemonic position which it held in Catalonia. The socialist party, PSOE, strongest among the non-Basque immigrant workers, was suspicious of nationalism and gave only lukewarm support to autonomy.

Galicia, as before, lagged in terms of political nationalism, despite having a strong sense of regional identity (Jiménez Blanco *et al.* 1977) and a language spoken by around 95 per cent of the population, 14 per cent of whom were monolingual (Gonzalez 1980). Gallego remained an oral language, used in the home and the farm but, despite an impressive literary/ intellectual tradition, popular levels of literacy were low since the extension of education had taken place in Castilian. Galicia's elites were well incorporated into the regime of Franco, himself a Galician and in the rural areas political activity was limited to client networks.

THE TRANSITION TO DEMOCRACY

The transition from Franco's dictatorship in the 1970s was managed by a series of 'pacts', elite accommodations among the major political formations (Pérez 1987). The dominant parties, the centrist UCD of prime minister Adolfo Suarez and the socialist PSOE, recognised the need to make concessions to Catalan and Basque nationalism but, as in the Second Republic, hoped to limit autonomy to those two regions and prevent a federalisation of the state. In contrast to the approach in other European countries where regional devolution has been introduced, the initiative for autonomy was to come from the regions themselves, with the statutes being framed locally and negotiated with the central government. Pre-autonomous assemblies could be established by the members of the national parliament in a region. At the same time, the state parties insisted that the state was not negotiating association agreements with sovereign regions. Rather, autonomy was to be conceded as a gift of the sovereign Spanish state. It was this claim to sovereignty which led the Basque Nationalist Party to recommend abstention in the 1978 constitutional referendum with the result that only 31 per cent of the Basque electorate (though a large majority of those voting) endorsed it. This was to cause major problems of legitimacy later on.

The autonomy process can be divided into three phases: an initial phase of concession which accelerated so fast as to threaten to reduce the central state to a residual; a phase of retreat represented by the 1982 LOAPA law and the early years of the Socialist government; and a phase of accommodation from the mid-1980s to the present.

The new regional regime in Spain bears much resemblance to the early *Estado Integral* as a compromise between federalism and mere regional devolution. The 1978 constitution declares the existence of a plurinational state in a rather confusing manner in Article 2:

> The constitution is founded on the indissoluble unity of the Spanish nation, common and indivisible motherland of all Spaniards, and recognises and guarantees the right to autonomy of all the nationalities and regions which comprise it and the solidarity among them all.

Three routes to autonomy were provided (Esteban 1982), with the undeclared object of confining full autonomy to the three historic regions with a capacity to threaten the stability of the state. In those regions where autonomy had been voted by referendum under the Second Republic (i.e. Catalonia, the Basque Country and Galicia), a statute drawn up by the pre-autonomous assembly and agreed by the parliament in Madrid could be adopted by referendum by a simple majority of those voting in each province. For other regions aspiring to full autonomy, there was a two-stage procedure. Autonomy proposals had to be initiated by a vote of three-quarters of the town councils and an absolute majority of the electors in each province of the region in a referendum. The statute then had to be negotiated and voted by an absolute majority of all the deputies and senators of the region and agreed with the constitutional committee of the Madrid parliament. The text then had to be submitted to a further referendum where it required a simple majority of those voting in each province. Finally, it had to be ratified by an absolute majority of the members of both houses of parliament. Other regions would have to make do with a lesser degree of autonomy, though after five years they could apply for full autonomy.

An autonomy statute for Catalonia was negotiated quite rapidly and duly adopted by referendum. The Basque Country proved more difficult because of the question of the historic *fueros* and the claim to Navarre. In the event, while the *fueros* were not accepted as the basis of the new statute, which came as a gift of the Spanish state, much of their substance was incorporated, notably the *concierto economico* which allows the Basque government to collect most taxes and hand over an agreed sum to Madrid. Navarre was eventually excluded at the insistence of its own representatives. The Basque statute was approved by a bare majority of the electorate in the face of heavy abstention by immigrant workers and by die-hard separatist supporters of ETA. An autonomy statute for Galicia was approved without great excitement. Thereafter, the autonomy process snowballed to the consternation of the central authorities, with proposals from regions throughout Spain. In Andalusia, a proposal to take the difficult clause 151 route to full autonomy was launched and, despite massive obstruction by the UCD government in Madrid and the state-owned media, passed the 50 per cent threshold in every province but one.

The threat of a generalised move to autonomy, with its federalist implications and a weakening of the central state, was enough to push the state-wide parties into a further pact. The attempted military coup of February 1981 reminded politicians of the army's historic image as guardian of a united Spain and provided a further incentive to stabilise the process. PSOE and the UCD, the two main state parties, agreed that Andalusia could proceed with clause 151 but that no other region should be allowed to do so. At the same time, measures were brought forward to harmonise the various types of autonomy, notably the *Ley Orgánica para la Armonización del Proceso Autonómico* (LOAPA). This provoked an appeal to the constitutional court by Basque and Catalan nationalists, who insisted that their autonomy statutes derived from their intrinsic national rights. The court's ruling supported the government's contention that the constitution provides equal rights for all Spaniards and the equality of all groups, but added that this did not entail institutional uniformity. All that was required was that all the autonomous communities were subordinate to the constitution and that their statutes should not enshrine social or economic privileges. Several of LOAPA's key provisions were therefore struck down in 1983 (Tribunal Constitucional 1985). This left matters very unclear. The court's decision would appear to reject the principle of self-determination or of entrenched foral privileges, but in practice to leave considerable scope for political accommodation. The latest phase in the autonomy process has involved just this.

THE POLITICS OF AUTONOMY

In the decade following the establishment of regional governments, public attitudes have become more favourable to regional autonomy, with less than 20 per cent wanting a return to the unitary state; this contasts with over 40 per cent support for centralisation in 1976 (Montero and Torcal 1990). Of more interest for our purposes is the extent to which regional autonomy has succeeded in accommodating Catalonia and the Basque Country into a stable constitutional order. There are two dimensions of integration involved here: the integration of the populations of the two communities into democratic regional politics; and the integration of the regions themselves into Spain.

In Catalonia, the autonomous government has been dominated by Jordi Pujol's CIU, with its combination of assertive nationalism and centre-right Christian Democratic politics. Pujol's success is based on beating the nationalist drum and constant demands for more powers, combined with something of a personality cult. Yet, while CIU wins majorities in the autonomous parliament, it is the socialist PSOE which dominates national elections in Catalonia. As these have a higher turnout, it appears that the difference is made up of immigrant workers who are less inclined to vote in the autonomous elections. Yet the extent of polarisation should not be exaggerated. The normalisation policy for Catalan has made it the normal language of administration and education, though anyone has the right to conduct official or private business in either Catalan or Castilian. A knowledge of both is required for school graduation. While there have been some conflicts over this, they are modest in comparison with those in other countries, and the children of immigrants are being assimilated into the culture. By 1986, 90 per cent of the population could understand Catalan, up ten points in five years. Just 30 per cent could write it but this figure rose to two-thirds among school students (Riquer 1989). Generous subsidies ensure a large availability of literature, television and radio in Catalan, much of it translated or dubbed. Local governments use Catalan as their normal language of work. There has been little immigration into Catalonia in the 1980s, though there are concentrations of Andalusians in large public housing schemes outside Barcelona who have yet to be assimilated. While some language enthusiasts demand a monolingual policy and restraints on the use of Castillian (e.g. Segarra 1990), there is virtually no support for this in a public opinion which remains committed to bilingualism. National identity in Catalonia has also been secularised and broadened. While the number describing themselves as exclusively Catalan has remained around 10 per cent since the 1970s, there has been a substantial increase in those subscribing to a dual Spanish–Catalan identity and a growing tendency to see Catalan identity in terms of residence and voluntary choice rather than race, birth or language (Montero and Torcal 1990).

Separatism has never been a powerful force in Catalonia. An extremist group, *Terra Lliure*, never of great importance, has abandoned its policy of armed struggle. More significantly, the historic ERC (*Esquerra Republicana de Catalunya*) adopted a policy of independence for the 1992 Catalan elections but gained just 10 per cent of the vote. Yet mainstream nationalists have an ambivalent attitude to the state, insisting on their right to national self-determination. After a resolution to this effect was passed in the Catalan parliament in 1990, Pujol had to assure everyone that this did not entail separatism. The difference with the nineteenth century is that this is now invariably placed in a European context. The slogan *Catalunya, Un País d'Europa* both appropriates the European symbol of generations of Spanish modernisers and provides the context for a more autonomous Catalonia. It also marks a break from the earlier nationalist strategy of protectionism within a Spanish market. While the European theme is quite deafening, however, there is little detail on just how Catalonia might fit into the emerging European order; rather an opportunistic search for possibilities.

The 1980s saw a constant recourse to the constitutional court by the Catalan government and the PSOE government in power in Madrid since 1982 but this has now given way to partisan dealing. PSOE's Catalan affiliate is aware of the need to emphasise Catalan themes. For its part, CIU, having failed in the 1986 elections to lead a restructuring of the Spanish centre-right (the old theme of Catalanising Spain known on this occasion and the *operación Roca*, after Pujol's deputy), has turned to deals with the dominant PSOE. By 1992 preparations were in hand for CIU support for the minority PSOE government expected after the next national elections. In the Basque Country, conservative nationalism has been the strongest force in both regional and national elections. PSOE, drawing its support from the non-Basque immigrant workers, is the second force. Around a fifth of the electorate support Herri Batasuna, the political wing of ETA. Establishing a stable regime in the Basque Country has proved extremely difficult. The Basque Nationalist Party (PNV), having recommended abstention in the Spanish constitutional referendum, helped delegitimise the new state. The assumption that the new regime was merely Francoism with a new face was reinforced by the presence of the Spanish national police and civil guard, long distrusted in the Basque Country. ETA refused to abandon its armed campaign and the transition to democracy was marked by a sharp increase in terrorist attacks. The Basque autonomous government under its first leader Garaicoetxea pursued a policy of confrontation with Madrid which did little to undermine the ETA campaign. By the mid-1980s, continued terrorism provoked a political crisis in the Basque Country, a split in the PNV and a political vacuum. After some manoeuvring, a coalition government emerged in 1986 of PSOE and the moderate wing of the PNV, allowing a broad front against ETA and co-operation with the PSOE government in Madrid. This elite accommodation was extended in 1988 with a pact by all parties in the Basque parliament with the exception of Herri Batasuna, condemning terrorism. Although the socialist-nationalist coalition was replaced in 1990 by a coalition of the various non-ETA nationalist groups, the consociational approach and isolation of ETA–Herri Batasuna continued.

As in Catalonia, a secularised regional identity appears to be growing, emphasising residence and choice rather than race and language. An exclusive regional identity is claimed by some 30 per cent, more than any other region. Yet the number claiming a dual identity has shown a marked increase (Montero and Torcal 1990). Support for independence is around 20 per cent, with a large majority favouring the existing degree of autonomy. Some 80 per cent of the population condemn ETA violence without reservation. The participation of PSOE in the regional government (1986–90) led it to emphasise Basque themes more strongly, helping to integrate the immigrant workers into the regional community. By the same token, the coalition and pact-making forced the constitutional Basque nationalists to accept the Spanish state. The language issue can be contained as a political issue, given that its use is accepted by all parties while general linguistic reconversion is seen as impractical. Bilingualism is therefore a consensus solution. There remains the intransigent minority represented by ETA and Herri Batasuna. This minority rejects the state, and insists on the unity of all the Basque territories (including the French Basque Country and Navarre), on separatism and that the national mission legitimises violence even in opposition to the expressed wishes of the peoples of the lands concerned. In the autonomous elections of 1990, Herri Batasuna retained 18 per cent of the vote, against 28 per cent for the conservative nationalists (PNV), 11 and 8 per cent, respectively, for breakaway nationalists (EA and EE) and 19 per cent for the socialists (Pallarés 1991a).

As in Catalonia, Europe provides a context for the assertion of an outward-looking Basque nationalism as an alternative to separatist exclusiveness. The PNV, which was converted to Europe through its participation in the Christian Democrat international, has adopted a symbol of thirteen stars, representing the existing EC twelve and the Basque Country, though the strategic aim is really a Europe of the regions, with forty or fifty components. In the short term, it serves to give Basque nationalism an outward-looking and modernist image in contrast with the Arana tradition.

In Galicia, autonomy continues to cause little excitement. Although Gallego and dual identification is strong, it is not politically mobilised or correlated with voting behaviour (Pallarés 1991b). Participation in elections is low. The Spanish conservative Popular Party has taken over many of the clientelist networks of the Franco era to establish a *caciquismo* which inhibits political mobilisation. In the 1980s, however, there was some advance by socialist and some nationalist forces to provide an element of real political competition and a brief coalition government (1987–9) before the Popular Party re-established its majority (Pallarés 1991b). Linguistic normalisation has involved extending to official use and education a language already known and used in the oral mode by the vast majority of the population.

CONCLUSION

The nationalities question no longer threatens to tear Spain apart. The context for its success in accommodating its territorial minorities is the experience, for the first time in its history, of a stable constitutional democracy. As part of the demographic experience, the *Estado de las Autonomías* is settling down to something like a federal system, though this was not the original intention. Democratic values are widely diffused through the society, and the legitimacy of the state is accepted both by the conservative right and military and by most of the regional nationalists of the periphery. With neither state nor minority nationalism making exclusive claims, dual identities are more acceptable. The widespread acceptance of European integration as a necessary element in Spanish modernisation and democratic consolidation adds another identity and provides an outlet for peripheral nationalist sentiment. The question of self-determination, whether autonomy is a gift of the Spanish state or an inherent right of the historic nationalities, does resurface periodically but does not challenge the legitimacy of the constitutional order. The exception is in the Basque Country where 15 to 20 per cent nurse separatist sentiments to the point of supporting the violence of ETA. Terrorism has become one of the most serious challenges to the Spanish state, despite the rallying of the constitutional parties and their at last drawing the line between democratic nationalism and separatist violence.

The party system has yet to adapt to a stable territorial division of power. Since the early 1980s, Spain has had a dominant centre-left party, PSOE and a fragmented centre and right. PSOE is the only truly national party, yet continues to find difficulty reconciling its centralist tendencies with the need to establish itself in the periphery. On the centre-right, Christian Democratic forces are strongest precisely in Catalonia and the Basque Country but for historic reasons have failed to establish themselves in Spanish politics more generally. Instead, the Spanish rights is represented by the historically centralist Popular Party which hardly features in Catalonia and the Basque Country. The result is an imbalance in the party system which has allowed conservative nationalists in Catalonia and (until the grand coalition) the Basque Country, to play constantly against the centre. PSOE and the other Spanish parties are accused of being *sucursalistas* (branch plants) unresponsive to particular needs.

This might be a destabilising force but for the recourse to pact-making among the dominant formations. Such a corporatist or consociational style of policy-making has been very important in Spain since the death of Franco. It explains the success in reconciling powerful nationalist sentiments with the construction of a stable national regime. Now that democracy is established, the tendency may be less healthy. The developing alliance between the PSOE in Madrid and CIU in Catalonia is an attempt to secure the two hegemonic parties at the two levels. Similar developments are in train between the PSOE and the Basque PNV. Combined with the continued weakness of civil society and participative life in Spain and the weakness of the Spanish conservative right, this carries a danger of depoliticising territorial politics, of excluding genuine political exchange as influence is carved up. Only when there is competition at central and regional level, with alternation of government, will the *Estado de las Autonomías* be fully mature.

NOTE

1 The research on which this chapter is based was supported by the Leverhulme Trust and the Social Sciences and Humanities Research Council of Canada. I am grateful to Antonio-Carlos-Pereira-Menaut for comments on it.

Chapter 10

South Africa: the opening of the apartheid mind[1]

Heribert Adam and Kogila Moodley

INTRODUCTION

A surprising 68.7 per cent of South Africa's 15 per cent whites supported a negotiated abolition of their minority rule in a referendum on 17 March 1992. Such rational foresight in a seemingly irrational racial conflict has been universally hailed as unprecedented in the annals of politics. The same cabinet ministers and Afrikaner National Party that presided over the implementation of apartheid in defiance of the world a few years ago, now act as democratic reformers with a two-thirds support of their constituency.

Faced with the choice of a beleaguered siege economy, the ruling group opted for a sharing of political power with its main opposition, the ANC. In the process it redefined its boundaries from an exclusive racial group to an inclusive ideological party that in future may even count on substantial support of like-minded black conservatives. Thereby the dwindling white minority did not set itself up as a resented target (as whites did with guaranteed racial group representation in Zimbabwe) but as a potentially even more powerful and legitimate force in a broad coalition government of national unity. Whites, therefore, did not vote 'to transfer power' to blacks, as the media reported, but only to democratise a system in which they will remain major stakeholders.

With the ANC strong only in symbolic support – but weak in its bureaucratic resources, military capacity and economic control – substantial real power will still remain in the hands of the present establishment, Mandela as president notwithstanding. For a long time, the South African civil service and the army, let alone the economy, will have to rely on white skills, capital and goodwill, regardless of the government in power. Unlike Gorbachev, de Klerk will not be swept aside by the liberalisation that he unleashed. De Klerk differs from Gorbachev in that he: (1) presides over a reasonably functioning, albeit depressed, but potentially buoyant industrial economy; (2) is not confronted by powerful secessionist forces, except a weakened right wing; and (3) has a democratic mandate from his constituency for the reform policy.

The apparent political miracle of a privileged minority voluntarily agreeing to give up exclusive political representation started much earlier than the March 1992 referendum or even the rise to power of de Klerk and the release of Mandela two years earlier. Apartheid – the gigantic Verwoerdian dream of social engineering – had increasingly proven a dismal failure despite all the zealous efforts of its advocates in power. Its rising internal and external costs, both real and symbolic, led to halting, ambivalent moves to reform since the late 1970s under the hardline Prime Minister Vorster. His successor, P. W. Botha, essentially continued the reluctant liberalisation without being able to break with the racial paradigm and blind anti-communism. It was the end of the cold war that made negotiations and compromise between impeccable ideological foes possible and imperative for both sides. Unlike the Middle East or Northern Ireland, no religious values impede bargaining over power and privilege in South Africa by pragmatic elites who are no longer constrained by dogma to adjust to new realities.[2]

One of the more striking aspects of South African society is that the abolition of formal apartheid and its replacement by informal stratification passed almost as a non-event. Many apartheid laws had already been largely ignored and remained unenforced. The reality of integration in some city housing, in English-language universities and private schools, but above all at the work-place, rendered the laws obsolete, long before they were formally abolished. No influx control measures, for example, could stem the flow of rural migrants into the cities in search of jobs and better living conditions. Repealing contrary laws simply verified social trends that had outpaced ossified regulations. Therefore, little or nothing changed under non-apartheid conditions.

In the absence of formal political power of the disenfranchised, the dominant minority remained unthreatened. Many whites now wondered why they had not supported the policy change earlier, since the immediate benefits outweighed the potential dangers. On the basis of non-apartheid, South Africans were admitted to places hitherto closed to them: from participation in the Olympic movement to freer travel and landing rights for South African Airways, whites were rehabilitated out of a deeply resented outcast status. The secret to the growing white approval rate of de Klerk lies in the realisation that the dominant minority could not continue to dominate without costs attached. Normalcy for whites returned despite the lasting abnormality from the legacies of apartheid. Few ruling groups in history have ever wriggled themselves out of a deadly predicament more elegantly. On top of it, the world praised and rewarded the change for what should have been normal policies and inter-group relations in the first place.

Nationalists made it repeatedly clear that negotiations would not be about surrender but power-sharing. In February 1990, with the mandate for negotiations just received four months earlier, the government could now move boldly without jeopardising seats. In any case, since another election under the tricameral constitution was quietly being ruled out, the government could stake its long-term chances on the success of negotiations.

Without considering here the complex, multi-faceted causes for the shift in strategy, the self-explanation is interesting. The National Party mouthpiece, *Die Burger* (5 February 1990), invoked historical character traits – 'the Afrikaner's desire for freedom' – as lying 'at the root' of this switch: 'The knowledge that their own desire for freedom may not involve the permanent subservience of others compels the continent's first freedom fighters now – only 80 years after Union – to take the lead in the quest for the joint freedom of all in the country.' There was no perception of defeat, or coercion by outside pressure, or admission that the new policy had to be adopted in order to regain entry into the world economy. On the contrary, supreme self-confidence reigned among Afrikaner policy-planners who congratulated themselves for grasping a unique opportunity to exploit the end of the cold war. Sanctions were hardly mentioned as the decisive trigger for the change. This view points to the increased self-confidence after the scare in mid-1989 when the country's reserves apparently were down to three days of obligations. 'What was crucial in the Cabinet's calculation was not the threat of sanctions but the government's belief that the economy would beat them and would survive risky political experiments which the unbanning of the ANC undoubtedly is.'[3]

The dramatic change, presented at the same time as a moral shift and verified by the long-stalled Namibian independence, caught the opposition and the international anti-apartheid forces by surprise. Normally well-informed analysts totally misjudged the dynamics of white politics and the determination of de Klerk to introduce a universal franchise, which increasingly gained the support of the white electorate.

THE PERCEPTION OF CONFLICT

In an intriguing comparative analysis Donald Horowitz detects in South Africa a unique feature: not only a conflict between divided segments as in other plural societies, but 'a conflict over the nature of the conflict' – what he calls a 'metaconflict' (Horowitz 1991). Horowitz overemphasises the cleavages in South African society. In reality there are only three irreconcilable positions on the present conflict. First, the extreme right-wing position of secession in a racial white homeland. While the disruptive power of armed ideologues must not be underestimated, the secessionist project has little chance of gaining establishment support, because it runs counter to business interests in an integrated economy. Since South African business, including Afrikaner capital, needs, on the one hand, to be part of the global economy and, on the other, is dependent on the willing co-operation of black labour, it would also be hostile to a military takeover. This distinguishes South Africa from Latin American regimes. Second, the Africanist/socialist position of no negotiation until the regime is defeated and ready to transfer power. This would be a threat only if current negotiations were to fail. Third, the emerging National Party–ANC alliance, which is more solid than Horowitz realises. The ANC leadership, including its South African Communist Party members, have moved close to a social-democratic economic compromise.

The simultaneous opening of state-controlled television to a more objective and freer reporting benefited the 'New Nats' in several ways. It demonstrated to their constituency the power of organised black opposition by having whites exposed to normal politics. Showing blacks not only in the traditional service roles or as destructive rioters but acting as citizens with reasonable leaders acclimatised a sceptical master-race to the necessity of negotiations as equals. Furthermore, the publicity given to black demands as well as to extremist right-wing rejection of these demands allowed the government to position itself in the centre as the reasonable middle ground, holding the country together. Conservative Party leader Treurnicht's ranting against the white sellout not only confirmed the new-found impartiality and objectivity of the broadcast service but also helped convince the huge black audience that the negotiation project was not a new neo-apartheid trick to perpetuate white rule in disguise.

Stephen Cohen has theorised the process of any conflict resolution as a cumulative ladder of four stages: (1) the begrudging acceptance of the adversary as an unavoidable fact; (2) mutual recognition of each other in a legal context; (3) interaction with the other as fully equal in status; and (4) partnership in a common post-conflict environment in which defined roles are shared (Cohen 1991). In 1992, South Africa has moved into the third phase with a likely 'semi-permanent, interim' coalition constituting the fourth phase. Both antagonists see themselves no longer as victims but, in Cohen's phrase, as 'creators of new realities'. A cluster of fearful attitudes has shifted to a syndrome of hope among those participating in negotiations. If those clinging to the status quo can have their fear/hate cluster reduced as well by the process, they may wish to join at a later stage, rather than being marginalised, as the wavering Conservative and PAC/AZAPO elements indicate.

The historic compromise increasingly takes on more concrete features. Economically, the ANC is likely to settle for black board representation, progressive taxation, equalisation payments, equity ownership and joint ventures rather than nationalisation. It is only worth capturing the 'commanding heights of the economy' if the heights have not been flattened by further economic decline. Anything more than a social democratic compromise towards drastic redistribution would flounder on the current power of the establishment to withhold the economic benefits from socialist political victors. All evidence points to the gradual embourgeoisement of the black middle-strata. The ANC leadership acts as their reluctant, posturing, but ultimately complying representative, because the spoils of entry into hitherto closed realms are real. The strong left within the South African opposition will try to block such neo-colonial accommodation, but fail to prevent it. It will split from the old Congress alliance and form the new opposition.

Theorising this new alignment has to come to grips with the now self-evident fact that some of the former victims of racial discrimination increasingly join the realms of power in perpetuating class domination. In this sense, South Africa has become normalised like other Western societies where exploitation is colour-blind. Instead of waiting for racial capitalism to change into non-racial socialism, a new multi-racial nomenclature will likely share relative privilege at the expense of an increasingly marginalised underclass. This has been referred to as the 50 per cent solution in South Africa, since the other half of the population is short-changed in political representation and influence. The National Party constitutional proposal, for example, envisages a double vote for people owning or renting property. In the ANC executive and voting constituency, migrant workers and unemployed are equally under-represented.

In short, South Africa is heading towards a corporatist state where business, state bureaucrats and unionised labour in the form of the ANC/SACP/COSATU alliance agree among themselves about the basics of an unwritten contract at the expense of the unorganised and weaker sections of the population. Electorally that may well be expressed in the substitution for elections of a series of appropriately worded and pre-tested referenda. This legitimises the stake of the major players without risking unpredictable outcomes that could lead to a declaration of civil war by the losing side.

The ANC has been far more open to compromise than its detractors had ever expected. While reaffirming that the political party with the most votes should form the government, Mandela assured his Stellenbosch audience, in Afrikaans, that all principles, democratic or otherwise, can be bent. 'Having regard to our background it may not be enough to work purely on one-person, one-vote because every national group would like to see that the people of their flesh and blood are in the government' (*Sunday Tribune*, 19 May 1991).

This principle dovetails with the National Party notion of mandatory, constitutionally entrenched participation of minority parties at all levels of political decision-making, including a statutory, collective presidency. This does not amount to majority rule in the traditional sense, but represents a notion of democracy that rests on a wider, compulsory participation by major interest groups. Whether it will paralyse decision-making and thereby preserve the status quo, remains to be seen. Undoubtedly, a power-sharing arrangement, and not rule by the majority party alone, will be the only achievable outcome at present, short of civil war. It is this context that the theorists of the ANC as an exclusive 'government-in-waiting' overlook. The ANC could only become the sole government if it were able to defeat the opponent. Pretoria is under little pressure to surrender. Neither has the ANC the intention any longer to declare war, and, by its own admission, the capacity to inflict defeat.

As Guillermo O'Donnell has pointed out, corporatism is not a static concept but changes from country to country (O'Donnell 1988). The semi-fascist corporatism in Latin America differs vastly from a 'corporatist' social-democratic accord in many Western European states. The role of the state in particular depends on the country's historical experience. The eurocentric bias by many Western scholars often overlooks these particularities outside the Western horizon. South Africa's main interest groups may well negotiate such a unique 'democratic corporatism' in both the economic and political realms. Indeed, as Denis Beckett (*Frontline*, May 1991) has editorialised: the country has no successful models to follow, 'only failures to avoid'. South Africa needs to pioneer a course of its own. Most indicators show that South Africa's historic compromise is proceeding remarkably well in both the economic and political arenas. Fond of quaint British analogies, a South African free-market advocate concluded that 'the space between Mr Ramaphosa's views and those of Finance Minister Barend du Plessis, it seemed to me, was less than the space between Neil Kinnock and Margaret Thatcher' (Owen 1991). In August 1990, the Minister of Constitutional Development, Gerrit Viljoen, even declared the government as part of the traditional opposition: 'But the government is no longer an apartheid regime, it is part of the anti-apartheid movement' (*Monitor*, August 1990, p. 31). Indeed, the new flexibility of Pretoria has deprived the ANC of its reliance on the intransigence of the opponent to mobilise against.

One of the crucial watersheds towards a corporate state was

established by COSATU's 1990 decision to join the National Manpower Commission. This participation, although later temporarily suspended, resulted from the successful negotiations of unions with employers and manpower officials over the controversial Labour Relations Act. The accord reached, and subsequently enshrined in law, provided a model of a social-democratic compromise. Since the state and employers need unions for ensuring stability, the union threat of withdrawal from the National Manpower Commission acts as a powerful bargaining tool against unilateral dictates by state bureaucrats in drafting labour laws. To be sure, there are great obstacles to be overcome and lessons to be learned on both sides.

For example, the ANC/COSATU opposition has challenged with increasing success the government's right to decide economic policy unilaterally. The two-day national strike over the introduction of a new value-added tax in November 1991 was called not because the unions disagreed with the tax in principle but because they had no say in introducing it. The mass actions were aimed at further undermining the legitimacy of the government by proving that it can no longer rule alone, based on a white vote only. Since Pretoria itself admitted that its apartheid constitution is wrong and needs to be renegotiated, it has also contributed to its own caretaker status. South African business is learning the corporate contract mentality the hard way. Nonetheless, it is reluctantly embracing necessity. The more sophisticated companies also discover new allies. The ANC/SACP alliance is willing to contribute its share to the compromise.

How much the ANC/SACP alliance wishes to achieve an accord and marginalise opposing groups outside its own disciplining structure was demonstrated in what the *South African Labor Bulletin* (November 1990) labelled 'the most high-profile dispute of the year'. In a bitter strike of workers against their union's policy of centralised bargaining at the Mercedes plant in Port Elizabeth in 1990, the ANC, SACP and NUMSA lined up with management in opposition to the strikers' demand for factory-based bargaining. The Mercedes labour aristocracy was rejected as 'industrial tribalism', with a grateful company rewarding the assistance of the 'socialist' mediators. Mercedes is now engaged in abolishing 'racial Fordism' in order to involve its workers in more autonomous decision-making on the factory floor as well as in the boardroom.

In early 1991 Thabo Mbeki indicated virtual consensus on the future constitution between the two adversaries: 'Now that we have arrived at more or less common positions on the basic constitutional issues, there is no reason why the process should take a long time' (Mbeki 1991: 62). On the devolution of power, the ANC and the government agree but differ only on whether the local/regional units should have authority in their own right or whether the federal rights be delegated by the central government. There is consensus on a justiciable bill of rights, a two-chamber parliament and a constitutional court and, most importantly, on the voting system.

ANC constitutional experts have increasingly embraced proportional representation. Thus, Kader Asmal, like Mandela, argues that 'there must be recognition that the cultural, social and economic diversity of South Africa requires the adoption of an electoral system at all levels which will enable sectoral groups and political tendencies to be adequately represented in decision-making' (Asmal 1991). A member of the Constitutional Committee of the ANC, Asmal praises the 'virtues of proportional representation' with the additional advantage that 'gerrymandering' will be prevented by voting according to party lists. 'The winner-takes-all majoritarian electoral system may have served its purpose in ensuring stability among the whites, but it is a form of stability which a democratic South Africa must reconsider.'

The newly-found preference of the ANC leadership for proportional voting, however, stems not only from concern for minority representation, but for leadership control over the process. Unlike the constituency-based Westminster system where candidates are selected by and accountable to the local electorate, proportional representation minimises grassroots control over candidates in favour of the party leadership that largely decides who is placed on the nation-wide list and in which ranking. It was this enhanced central control that made proportional representation attractive for the constitutional planners of the ANC/ SACP.

In reviewing the origins of apartheid legislation, Hermann Giliomee has astutely isolated two inextricably interlinked motivations: 'Without a privileged position the Afrikaners could not survive as a separate people; without safeguarding the racial separateness of the people, a privileged position could not be maintained' (Giliomee 1991). The ANC opposition needs neither separateness nor privilege. Free of the insecurities of a small disadvantaged people, the majority does not have to mobilise on exclusivist nationalist grounds but can trust democratic equality to have its interests secured.

The striking feature of South African negotiation is the absence of outside intervention, facilitation, mediation or arbitration by consensus of the adversaries. Compared with the decolonisation of Namibia or Zimbabwe, South Africa poses the problem of being a sovereign state. Neither Namibia (before 1990) nor Rhodesia were ever sovereign, internationally recognised states, but were legally colonies under the authority of Britain in the case of Rhodesia, and the UN and South Africa in the case of pre-independence Namibia. Once internal agreement had been reached under the tutelage of the metropolitan power, the foreign legal authority ceased its role by recognising the newly sovereign state.

In the South African case, on the other hand, the only legal body that can enact a new constitution is the present parliament. If there is to be legal continuity rather than interference by a non-legal third party, the present regime would have to legalise its own transformation. This is clearly recognised by the government agenda which sees precisely such a process unfolding.

The opposition, however, argues quite understandably that the government cannot be player and referee simultaneously. It therefore proposes a mutually agreed interim government and an elected constituent assembly that could transform itself into the first parliament once a constitution has been agreed upon. Pretoria, on the other hand, rejects elections before negotiations. From this perspective correctly, general elections before a new constitution has been agreed upon would amount to surrender, an abdication of power rather than negotiation about a new order. Pretoria also insists that lawful government and administration of the country must not be jeopardised during the period of constitution-making.

In adopting these legalistic positions, the government constantly confuses sovereignty with legitimacy. Sovereignty Pretoria possesses, legitimacy it widely lacks. It also falsely equates liberalisation with democratisation. Since de Klerk's rise to power, the South African state has clearly liberalised itself but at the beginning of 1992 still has to institutionalise meaningful democratic participation for all citizens. Liberalisation extends rights and opens up new political space. It reduces the costs and risks of individual expression. Democratisation aims at equality of citizens and an improvement of life-chances for everyone. It is the latter aspects that will prove the sticky parts – not the transitional arrangement and constitutional accords themselves.

There are two dangers that an interim government of national unity has to avoid: (1) it can easily trigger more violence from the right wing and plunge the country into a real civil war if the interim government is perceived as a surrender in these circles. Therefore, constitutional continuity and the legitimacy of any transitional arrangement among the majority of whites would seem an important consideration. Holding a last racial referendum among whites about a new non-racial constitution, as de Klerk had repeatedly promised, seemed the most feasible way to impede right-wing rebellion. An ANC veto of such a referendum risked substituting for the lesser evil of a one-time racial concession the real possibility of mass violence with private armies pitted against each other. The danger also points to the need for a constitutional accord to precede an interim government rather than emerge from it in dragged-out negotiations.

(2) For the ANC, the danger of an interim government lies in assuming responsibility without having power. While there would be a measure of control over the security forces in particular, it is doubtful that this newly acquired limited power would be sufficient to stop all the atrocities that would now be committed in the name of the ANC as well. The ANC would carry the burden of a declining economy, but would also be constrained to implement radical restructuring. Disappointed expectations and disillusionment with the ANC are likely to flow from a situation of responsibility without power.

Some more astute ANC leaders view with alarm the perception of being co-opted and wisely maintain a distance between themselves and Pretoria. How the inevitable ANC participation in government is to be reconciled with its aura of militancy remains to be seen. Nevertheless, when the ANC sets deadlines and declares, 'our patience with this regime is running out', everyone knows that the tough talk merely camouflages the even deeper involvement of the two antagonists with each other.

For example, in April 1991 the ANC issued an ill-considered ultimatum to the government to meet certain demands (sacking of two ministers), or it would withdraw from negotiations. Since Pretoria could not afford to be seen to heed ultimatums, and the ANC could not afford to pull out, the ultimatum necessarily backfired on the ANC which was locally and internationally criticised for a serious error of judgement. If the ANC were to use the threat again when it really became necessary, it would have lost its credibility. The ANC public relations exercise together with a serious concern for the escalating violence revealed the advantage of the government in having a relatively supportive constituency since it shed its right wing, while the ANC constantly has to reconcile conflicting demands from its heterogeneous support base. At this stage, the negotiating leadership must retain the radical wing in its ranks and does this mainly through strident posturing.

White South Africa has so far failed to recognise the need for symbolic victories on the part of the ANC. The more the ANC is drawn into constitutional politics, the more it loses its moral status as the movement of liberation. Vulnerable as a fallible political actor among a more powerful establishment, it must show its supporters either that it can deliver on their inflated expectations or that nothing has changed in the intransigence of the adversary, and, therefore, it cannot be blamed. Both choices, however, are detrimental to the need for compromise in negotiation politics. The less leverage the ANC can exercise within the narrow constraints of constitutional negotiations, the more the emphasis shifts to socio-economic issues. Against the establishment's attempt to restructure the economy through pre-emptive privatisation and constitutional guarantees, stands the ANC's need to guard against disappointing the economic expectations of its constituency.

Therefore, the rise or fall of the future South African democracy depends on an upturn in the economy. Only an expanding economy allows both antagonists to satisfy their supporters, and thereby eases the necessary compromises. The less economic leverage exists, the more the ANC will fall back on street mobilisations to guard its flanks and the more the establishment will view the necessary long-term redistribution as a zero-sum loss strategy. It would want to sabotage such attempts with all its leverage, including refusals to reinvest in South Africa. The ANC in turn loses its incentives for entering negotiations if they produce neither economic gains nor symbolic political victories. Yet the ultimate paradox remains that an economic recovery depends on a creditable political settlement. Therefore, negotiations cannot wait for an economic turnaround when conditions are more conducive for a democratic compromise.

It is sometimes uncritically assumed that if 'negotiations stall or break off, then South Africa could find itself back on the path to insurrection . . .' (Price 1990). Yet with the disappearance of the Soviet Union, the major outside sponsor of the previous insurrectionist strategy would have to be replaced. While Libya, China or smaller Stalinist relics like Cuba or North Korea could presumably step in, renewed exile or repression for South African activists is not an inviting prospect. The current ANC leadership at least would rather bend over to reach a compromise than repeat a failed historical experience. For the Afrikaner nationalists, too, there is no option of going back to the repressive era, because they are too weak and divided. A renewed consensus on racial repression is simply inconceivable. It would also be suicidal for the minority.

ASSESSING THE PESSIMISTIC SCENARIO: LEBANON OR PERU?

Against the optimistic scenario of a social-democratic compact with renewed high economic growth stand many well-documented pessimistic predictions of likely social disintegration. Authors in this school do not doubt the goodwill of the leadership on all sides to reach an accord quickly, but question their ability to enforce it against overwhelming objective odds. In addition, some distrust the democratic motives of the major parties who are said to be interested in a non-racial oligarchy at best. Editors like Ken Owen dwell on the theme of Africa reverting to the bush in the 'heart of darkness', while Barber (*Cape Times*, 24 April 1990) warns of the white establishment 'sliding into functional cahoots with the ANC and its totalitarian project'. The National Party is inclined to adopt this route, it is argued, because it strives for external recognition and that can only be won with ANC connivance. Both the National Party and ANC want order above the law. A future division of control with the National Party holding the right wing in check, and the ANC disciplining the townships under an authoritarian leadership, is thought to be looming. Negotiations would mainly be about zones of influence and hegemony. The National Party must only ensure that the relinquished share of power does not threaten its own privileges. In Barber's nightmare: 'A one-party state condoned by a specially protected white nomenclature.' If rightwing anxiety about 'a sellout to blacks' represents one side of white consciousness, the vision of an authoritarian unholy alliance constitutes the liberal other side of the same coin. Both sides deplore the moral decay of the ruling group. In Barber's phrase: 'The establishment lacks either the guts or the basic humanity.' The scenarios waver between de Klerk as the South African Gorbachev who loses control over the process he initiated, or de Klerk and Mandela as joint dictators.

In this vein, academics Pierre du Toit and Willie Esterhuyse argue that both the National Party and the ANC employ hegemonic models of bargaining (Toit and Esterhuyse 1990). In this view, democratic, inclusive rhetoric only masks the desire for total control. Negotiations aim at co-optation or defeat of the adversary by other means, as well as exclusion of those on the right or left who reject the new alignment. We do not share this despairing assessment.

There is little evidence at present that both antagonists would abandon a negotiated contest, although they both lack a democratic tradition and have illiberal hardliners in their midst. Even on the assumption that the pessimists are correct and the 'regime models' of both camps – 'technocratic liberation' versus 'people's power' – allow at best a non-racial oligarchy, the question remains whether the objective constellation of power would not constrain the anti-democratic interests. South African social forces are so diverse and multi-faceted that political legitimacy and economic stability simply cannot be reached by a new coercive alignment, even if it comprises a numerical majority. The resulting unrest and instability would defeat the main purpose of the new pact. Sooner or later a more inclusive and pluralist order would have to establish wider legitimacy of a polity in which all disruptive forces are accommodated.

Much more serious economic trends, however, may jeopardise the democratic recovery of South Africa and lead to social disintegration beyond the control of politicians. It has become a well-worn cliché to stress that South Africa sits on a time-bomb of economic frustrations. Only 125 of the estimated 1,000 people who come on to the job market daily can be accommodated in the formal economy. The capacity of the South African economy to absorb new job seekers declined from 73.6 per cent of the new entrants in 1970 to 12.5 per cent in 1989. The time-bomb analogy, however, falsely suggests an impending explosion. The real consequences of the rejected underclass lie in the more invisible slow societal disintegration, as indicated in rising crime rates, political violence, family dissolution and a breakdown of the social fabric and value system under the weight of general misery. An ANC government is likely to suffer the consequences of its advocacy of sanctions and ungovernability even more than the sheltered white sector which has many more options.

A comparison with Lebanon during its fifteen-year-long civil war (1975–90), masterfully analysed in an 800-page comprehensive survey by Theo Hanf, illustrates the unique South African dilemmas (Hanf 1990). For South Africans, an understanding of the Lebanese example is both encouraging and frightening. Lebanon was primarily destroyed by outside forces: the Palestinians, the Israelis, the Syrians, the Iraqis and even the Americans, all tried to impose their solution at one time or another on a weak central state. Unlike Lebanon, South Africa is relatively free from direct outside interference and sponsorship of competing factions. What has kept Lebanon together, on the other hand, is the persistence, throughout the war, of a surprising popular consensus on the unity of the nation, despite the progressive disintegration of the institutions of the state. 'It is not fanatical masses that prevent a new consensus,' Theo Hanf concludes, 'but short-sighted and power-hungry elites.' In South Africa, the opposite holds true. Compromising leaders on all sides are constrained by militant and alienated constituencies.

Hanf demonstrates perceptively that Lebanese society disintegrated at the top while life below continued with remarkable normality. The civilian population on all sides of the barricades suffered from intermittent shellings and devastating car bombs, but they were not massively debilitated. People across the communal divisions hated and feared the disruptions of routine – as they demonstrated in several mass protests – but kept up a remarkable pretence of normality. Despair expressed itself mainly through emigration.

Everyday life on the ground in South Africa's black townships is qualitatively different. Although far more and more substantial weapons are available in Beirut than in Soweto or Khayelitsha, lives are much more at risk in South Africa than in Lebanon. Not only do crime and simmering political feuds make physical danger more pervasive, but the psychological impoverishment, the hopelessness and alienation seem almost worse. If the well-worn sociological concept of anomie can be applied anywhere, it is in Sebokeng or Edendale. With people dreading to sleep in their own homes for fear of unprovoked attacks, with passengers in commuter trains scrambling out of the windows at the cry 'the Zulus are coming', with groups of girls abducted from a Salvation Army home and raped, and with the annual murder rate in Cape Town climbing to sixty-five per 100,000, as compared to four in Toronto, South Africa would seem to represent the epitome of normlessness. Random violence is almost less bearable than more brutal but predictable atrocities.

In the matter of social decay and the life-chances of the majority, South Africa resembles the Soviet Union more than the Lebanon. The powerful Afrikaner institutions of the centre still hold the society together, but conceal the rot at the bottom. As in the repressive era of the Soviet Union, the South African state thinks that it can best combat crime through more police deterrence without seriously addressing the underlying causes of alienation. Unlike Lebanon, South Africa needs a 'recovery movement', a collective therapy and moral revival that cannot be decreed from above. In Lebanon, an accord by the feuding elites on foreign military presence was sufficient to end the strife. In South Africa, an agreement of this kind is crucial, but it will not remedy the underlying social decay. And even if more houses are built and jobs created in an expanding post-apartheid economy, that will not be enough without some sort of moral renewal.

In the absence of strong religious communities, this renewal can best be built around the notion of a non-racial democracy. Rather than stressing the need for unity or allowing the 'will of the people' - as if the people had only one will - the opposition movements should speak up more loudly for the idea of respect for political opponents. Intimidation of antagonists - and worse - has a long history on a continent where the practice of 'loyal opposition' hardly exists. Were the ANC to fragment into warring factions, there would be little hope for such fledgling notions as individual autonomy, freedom of choice and pluralistic empowerment.

A functioning democracy requires autonomous citizens, civic organisations and a host of disciplining grass-roots institutions, from apolitical sports clubs to dedicated parents and committed teachers. The democratic state cannot create the foundations of its survival: it can only facilitate their emergence. The greater the variety of the civil society, the better the chances for democracy. Dozens of earnest Afrikaner and ANC think-tanks must watch that they do not build their sophisticated accords on shifting sands. Neither side has sufficiently prepared its constituency for the remarkable speed of the accommodations which its leadership has been prepared to make. The militant rhetoric is meant to camouflage all this moderation, but raises expectations which may prove counter-productive when it comes to selling the inevitably disappointing compromise.

With a further decline of the South African economy, an impoverished township society could conceivably produce a Peruvian scenario. Here Sendero Luminoso (Shining Path, or known simply by the faithful as the Communist Party), under a shadowy leader Abimael Guzman, directs a violent campaign not only against the country's establishment but against foreign-aid workers, the clergy, and even the urban poor who engage in self-help relief efforts and co-operative industrial activity. The Maoist movement with about 5,000 guerrilla followers views any improvement in the lot of the poor as counter-productive to the revolution. Organised relief is not to be tolerated since it pacifies the masses. The brainwashing of Shining Path followers guarantees blind loyalty in an escalating war to overthrow capitalism and turn Peru into a peasant-worker state.

In both Peru and South Africa, an alienated and unemployed youth accounts for the appeal of radical movements. The difference in South Africa is that this frustration was successfully channelled into a national resistance organisation that could legitimately claim to have the support of the entire world. By actively championing the cause of the excluded, foreign governments have pre-empted the rise of ultra-radical, irrational protest. Foreign intervention has so far prevented the isolated irrational protest that characterises Peru.

Given the interpenetration of reformist and revolutionary political cultures in contemporary South Africa, it seems unlikely at present that the Peruvian scenario would repeat itself. However, with little improvement in the life-chances of half of the South African population aged under twenty, even an ANC government could not rest for good on its past record, particularly if the radical SACP ally were to lose its appeal.

When has a post-apartheid order been achieved? The move away from racial domination does not necessarily ensure the achievement of democracy. How the process of dismantling domination is conducted strongly influences its outcome: it can create a culture of violence or it can lay the moral foundation for the lasting consensus about legitimate rules. F. van Zyl Slabbert has frequently stressed that 'there is not an event that can be seized upon by the outside world to symbolize how and when South Africa moves from an apartheid to a post-apartheid era'. Even a constitutional settlement must not be confused with the end of the conflict.

THE WHITE RIGHT WING: THE OPTION OF SECESSION

Ideologically, the black and white ethnic fundamentalists mirror each other in their intransigence to compromise, their advocacy of confrontation and their single-mindedness. The difference lies in the relative strength and military capacity of each camp. While only a small portion of blacks currently support fundamentalist views, 40 to 50 per cent of the white electorate would vote for parties on the right of the ruling nationalists. Moreover, the white right wing is over-represented in the police and security establishment. This segment is well trained and armed. It is able to cause serious violence and disruptions of the ongoing accommodation as numerous bombings and shootings have proven. Individuals on the white right wing have also tended towards 'representative violence', the random targeting of outgroup members which has been rare among black political activists.

The white ultra-right, however, is unlikely to provoke a military takeover under present conditions. Even if such a seizure of power were to take place during a civil-war situation, the right wing alone could not govern the country. This distinguishes South Africa from Latin American states where military juntas could count on domestic financial endorsement and influential international support; in the South African case they could count on determined opposition. The hope of the ultra-right, despite its martial rhetoric, lies not in a take-over but in secession from an increasingly integrated, non-racial state.

A minority of conservatives are drawn to the vision of an independent Boerestaat for reasons of ideological commitment to Afrikaner self-determination while the majority of whites who have joined the right wing did so out of anxiety about an uncertain future. The economic recession has swelled this segment. The tangible rewards of a booming non-racial state, if only it could be allowed to boom, would substantially reduce this fear. It is generally recognised that the white right wing represents the downwardly mobile sections of the group: white mine workers, farmers deprived of previous state subsidies and the lower echelons of the Afrikaner civil service, who are very concerned about Africanisation. Although political attitudes and identities cannot in general be crudely reduced to material considerations, a strong correlation between socio-economic conditions and political outlook remains most striking in South Africa.

There are different versions of a white homeland on which their respective supporters cannot agree. It is this disagreement which not only has split the right wing but paralysed the concept politically. In the late 1970s, the son of Hendrik Verwoerd set up the 'Orange Werkers Unie' in search of a growth point for a white homeland. His choice of Morgenzon, a nondescript hamlet in the eastern Transvaal, proved unattractive to all but twenty families who moved and bought land in the town. These odd inhabitants, surrounded by 6,000 blacks, insist that they will not employ black labour and become dependent on 'outsiders'.

The Boerestaat Party of Robert van Tonder strives to revive the traditional Boerrepublics in the Transvaal and Orange Free State, but rejects the notion of a white homeland as racist. Just as Zionists asked for the ancient Jewish state to be reinstated without excluding all Arab inhabitants, according to van Tonder, so the Boerestaat will co-exist with a black majority in its midst. But by dividing these blacks into different nations, the Afrikaners will still be in the majority. According to Piet 'Skiet' Rudolph, the Free State, Transvaal and northern Natal are still part and parcel of the Boerevolk. He equates the Boere claim for land with the dispossessed black community's demands for land restitution. The Boere homelands then would form a loose federation for economic co-operation with the rest of South Africa.

Carel Boshoff, the head of the *Afrikanervolkswag,* presents the more sophisticated and pragmatic version of the nationalist territorial dream. He considers it unrealistic to move or dominate millions of people against their will. Instead, he looks for an area with low population density as well as great development potential, 'where a new settlement can be developed, and where new high technology can be placed, and where a country, a republic, a state can develop in time'. Boshoff's most recent map identifies an area along the Orange river in the north-eastern Cape and southern Namibia as the future Boerestaat.

The Conservative Party itself has also begun drawing up boundaries for a white state. It has informally dropped its former position that the whole of apartheid South Africa should be restored to white rule. For the Conservative Party, a minimal homeland would include the western Transvaal, including Pretoria, the Orange Free State Province and the Northern Cape Province. Since this conservative heartland is interspersed with 'black spots', influential white conservatives seek an alliance with the black conservative Mangope of the Bophutatswana Bantustan who is equally opposed to the ANC hegemony. This secessionist coalition in the name of national self-determination may well include Buthelezi's Kwa Zulu territory.

The Conservative Party is deeply split on whether such a plan should be negotiated with other parties and whether the conservatives should, therefore, participate in the ongoing all-party talks. The party is in danger of being marginalised by its boycott politics. Its hope to gain power through another white-only election is increasingly exposed as a fiction despite a string of victories in by-elections. In the meantime, the militarisation on its fringes continues.

The militants of neo-fascist groups, like the AWB, accuse the Conservative Party of 'giving our country away' for a parliamentary salary. The CP members of parliament rejected calls to resign and thereby force country-wide by-elections that would have demonstrated the decline of white support for the government. In Terre-Blanche's view this would be 'the last chance' before 'Tambo's communists start the black revolution'. Others in this group now openly declare: 'The time for voting politics is over – it is now time for bullet politics' (*Cape Times*, 1 March 1990). However, after first announcing a boycott of the 1992 referendum, all right-wing groups participated in the campaign and formed an alliance.

The Conservative Party deplores the violence associated with the AWB and likes to project an image of respectability. However, it also emphasises its ideological affinity. Despite the contempt that the leaders of each faction express for the other's style, the AWB can be considered the armed wing of the CP. What the one party tries to achieve through legal and institutional means, the other complements through extra-parliamentary threats and military mobilisation for the coming 'volks war'.

A future ANC/NP government clearly faces the prospects of either; (a) accommodating the right-wing separatists, at least symbolically in some more or less autonomous territory; (b) repressing a substantial section of a hostile population group and thereby becoming itself undemocratic; or (c) being destabilised by an uncooperative civil service and suffering sabotages in the strategically still crucial productive sectors in agriculture and mining. It would, therefore, seem wise to make all and any possible efforts to draw at least some sectors of conservatives into the ongoing negotiations, although the ANC will have great difficulty in ever accepting the legitimacy of secessionist claims.

In conclusion, the uniform demonisation of all political activity on the right of the National Party in the South African English-language press and foreign media needs to be corrected with a much more nuanced view of conservative motivations and behaviour. Not all right-wingers are the swastika-waving fascists who form what is really a vociferous minority among many more honourable ideologues and plainly fearful voters in feudal rural settings or declining mining towns. Neither South African liberals nor the ANC, let alone Western policy-makers, have yet engaged the right's anxiety-ridden ideologues, as unpalatable as this may be for anti-racist tastes.

As the moderate middle ground – the ANC and the National Party – explore their common interests and draw closer together, the extremes on the white right and black left step up their rhetoric or even their physical attacks. In his intriguing analysis Donald Horowitz views this dynamic of pressure from the flanks as the best guarantee for the fragile centre to hold. Yet the possibility of a growing right-wing renewing a civil war cannot be ruled out. They may not win a war, but they could certainly start one. In a less frightening but still alarming scenario, even if the ultra-conservatives are unsuccessful in preventing a settlement between the ANC and the NP, they can prolong the uncertainty and mutual recrimination. Already the government is using the symbolic existence of MK as an excuse that it cannot ban private armies and disarm the right wing. Thus the right wing can also succeed by causing friction at the centre and undermining successful negotiations, just as settlements have been prevented in Northern Ireland or presently in Israel.

In practical terms, the white right wing can only be controlled by the white centre, ultra-conservative Afrikaners by more reformist Afrikaners. If this is to be a relatively non-violent process, the centre's legitimacy is crucial for carrying the right wing along. As long as the transition is managed with white majority electoral support and constitutional legality is maintained, the right-wing insurrectionists place themselves outside the 'law and order' that they themselves fetishise. Therefore, the ANC has to allow the NP forces its posture of legal respectability, including a separate voters count in a universal franchise referendum rather than push the party into a perception of surrender. Indeed, as many commentators have pointed out, if an NP–ANC solution were to be foisted on a defiant white majority, the ground would have been laid for a costly long-term IRA-type destabilisation. The paradox of the South African power equation is that both sides can prevent the other from exercising power. Therefore, neither side can rule alone peacefully without taking the vital interests of the antagonists seriously. The alternative is violence without victory which only the most rigid ideologues prefer over accommodation. Similar considerations apply to a much maligned black antagonist of an NP–ANC alliance, the Inkatha Freedom Party of Chief M. G. Buthelezi.

CLIENTELISM AS SECESSIONISM

Leader–follower relationships among the majority of Zulu supporters of Inkatha are hardly based on ideological identifications but on reciprocal instrumental advantages and ethnic symbolic gratifications. Inkatha's poor and illiterate constituency depends on patronage, handed out by strong leaders and local power-brokers in return for loyalty, regardless of the leaders' ideological outlook or ethical behaviour. Past political powerlessness reinforced the importance of African auxiliaries to whom the impoverished could turn for protection and favours. When the South African state decentralised control by letting trusted African clients police themselves and administer their own poverty, their status and actual importance were further strengthened. Thus emerged a classical system of clientelism and patrimony. Clientelism flourishes in conditions of inequality, where marginalised groups depend on patronage networks for survival, or at least for small improvements. It is the exclusive control of scarce goods (permits, houses, civil service positions, etc.) that give patrons their power. This clientelism thrives with rightlessness.

Once equal citizenship, however, gives formal access to basic goods to all, and all are entitled to equal treatment, the monopoly of patrons has been undermined. Hence, democratic equality that allows claims to be made through formal channels pre-empts the dependence on informal patronage. If the police, for example, act impartially, there is no need to be protected by a warlord. If people acquire confidence in the law, they need not rely on vigilantes. If justice is done through impartial courts, it need not be sought through private vendettas.

However, as long as comrades attack the police as agents of a hostile system, the police will hardly act impartially. Inasmuch as town councillors are forcefully driven from office, they will seek protection from wherever they can find it. As long as 'collaborators' are stigmatized and their houses are destroyed in the name of the people's anger, it is highly unlikely that a coalition for reconstruction will emerge. Continued violent confrontation will be the outcome. Instead of denouncing the local notables as enemies to be replaced with their own, the civic organisation would be much wiser to engage and coopt them, if they are interested in accommodation. This applies both at the local and national level.

There are two common objections to such a policy of reconciliation with regard to Inkatha: (1) that the support of Inkatha is so low that the movement can be ignored, pre-empted or even eliminated; (2) that the price demanded for incorporation by Buthelezi is too high and, therefore, continued exclusion is preferable.

Against the first argument Lawrence Schlemmer has pointed out that conflict resolution has to take into account not only size and scope but also *intensity* of interests. 'The intensity of the IFP's [Inkatha Freedom Party's] interaction in the political process has clearly signalled the potential costs of excluding it, or reducing its leverage in negotiations' (Schlemmer 1991: 7–10). From a moral point, this position can be interpreted as yielding to violence. From a pragmatic perspective, however, there is little choice if greater damage is to be avoided. Weighing the costs of continued confrontation against the potential benefit of peaceful competition through compromise amounts to a political calculation that separates ideologues from pragmatists.

It remains to be seen whether equality before the law and new life-chances for the formerly disenfranchised will pre-empt clientelism and the quest for ethnic separateness. It may be easier to achieve with regard to Inkatha's constituency than with regard to the separatism of the white right wing. Observers remain sceptical, even with Inkatha. *Sunday Times* editor Ken Owen notes that a relatively autonomous Natal in a federal structure might be a co-operative partner in a greater South Africa, 'while a Kwazulu forcibly incorporated in a structure controlled by its bitterest enemies, might become as indigestible as the IRA in Britain, or the Turks in Cyprus, or the Basques' (*Sunday Times*, 8 September 1991). Buthelezi too has threatened that the civil wars in Angola and Mozambique could pale in comparison with the future destructive upheavals in South Africa. The ANC, on the other hand, is not inclined to heed such predictions and would rather risk a repetition of Biafra than compromise on the relative centralisation of political power or bend towards recognition of Zulu claims. This sets the new South Africa on a collision course not only with Inkatha but the Boerestaat advocates as well.

In order to avoid such possible civil-war scenarios, it may be worthwhile to consider a valuable suggestion by the American moral philosopher Allen Buchanan who has argued the moral right to secede by any group in any state. Such a right to secede could be constitutionally recognised and specified (referendum, qualified majority support, treatment of minorities). A constitutionally entrenched right to secede under regulated conditions and international arbitration would spare any country the civil disorder in the wake of a political divorce or the forceful retention of an unwilling partner. Buchanan, who considers even the discussion of the constitutional right to secede too divisive in the present South African climate, nonetheless concludes: 'If non-Zulus are unwilling to adopt constitutional measures that would add further power to the numerical superiority that Zulus already enjoy, the only possibility for a peaceful solution may be Zulu secession' (Buchanan 1991). However, Buchanan overlooks the fact that there would be strong opposition from a large section of the Zulu speakers themselves. This is one of the differences between the repressed independence movements in Eastern Europe and the apartheid-encouraged Bantustan sovereignties.

Although it has hardly been discussed in South Africa, it may be timely to consider a secession clause in the new South African constitution in the light of recent experiences in Eastern Europe. A serious discussion of the right to secede would also constitute the necessary incentive to bring the potential secessionist parties into the constitutional negotiations.

NOTES

1 There are a number of acronyms used in this chapter, which are as follows:

ANC	African National Congress
AWB	Afrikaner-Weerstandsbeweging
AZAPO	Azanian People's Organization
COSATU	Congress of South African Trade Unions
MK	Umkhonto We Sizwe
NUMSA	National Union of Metalworkers South Africa
PAC	Pan-Africanist Congress

2 This has been argued previously in Heribert Adam (1971) and Heribert Adam and Kogila Moodley (1986).
3 H. Giliomee, *Weekend Argus*, 24 February 1990.

Chapter 11

Balance and ethnic conflict in Fiji

Ralph R. Premdas

INTRODUCTION

Using the slogan, 'Fiji for Fijians', on 14 May 1987 the military justified the overthrow of the political order that brought stability for nearly two decades to Fiji's multi-ethnic society. Despite international pressure, the coup-makers oversaw the promulgation of a new constitution which assigned disproportionately higher representation to ethnic Fijians over other groups. Specifically, Fijians constituting about 46 per cent of the population were allocated thirty-seven (53.6 per cent) of the seats in the seventy-person House of Representatives.[1] Further, in all major areas such as taxation, civil service appointments, recognition of religion, Fijians were accorded preferential treatment. Only a Fijian can become prime minister or president. At least 50 per cent of all public-service posts must be allocated to Fijians. In a democratic world of individual human rights, these inegalitarian provisions are bound to supply the incendiary raw materials for both internally and externally-derived designs for destabilisation.

Yet Fijians, the indigenous peoples of these islands, overwhelmingly God-fearing Methodists, see nothing wrong with this system of government. They assert instead that it is intended to prevent their culture and community from being marginalised in the manner experienced by the Maoris in New Zealand, the Aborigines in Australia, and native peoples in North America. Fear of an ethnic seizure of power by the Fijian nationalists came in the wake of a breakdown of a formula for inter-ethnic accommodation.

This chapter provides an interpretation of the rise of ethnic dominance in Fiji. It begins by offering a descriptive overview of the making of Fiji's multi-ethnic state. This is followed by a discussion of the major issues which came to bedevil inter-ethnic relations in Fiji. The chapter concludes by looking at an attempt to form a government of national unity, its failure, and the military intervention.

THE ETHNIC GROUPS AND FOUNDING A MULTI-ETHNIC STATE

Fiji is an archipelago of some 844 islands lying at the centre of the South Pacific. It was colonised on 10 October 1874 when Chief Cakobau ceded Fiji to Britain. The Deed of Cession bound Britain to protect the Fijians from European commercial interests and to preserve the Fijian way of life. To halt the steady decline of Fijian customs, Sir Arthur Gordon, the first British governor of Fiji, initiated three policies that laid the cornerstone of communalism. First, all land which was not yet alienated to Europeans, consisting of nearly 90 per cent of the country, was to remain under Fijian ownership. This policy curtailed economic development of the islands because growth depended on the availability of Fijian land for commercial exploitation. Land, then, became an issue. The second policy was the importation of labour to substitute for Fijians. Protection of the Fijian way of life required not only that their land which was an integral part of the traditional culture be kept from alienation, but also that the people be free from the labour impositions of European plantations. Governor Gordon recommended the importation of Indian coolies from India as had been done successfully in British Guiana, Mauritius and Trinidad. From 1879, when the labour indentureship was inaugurated, to 1916, when it was terminated, about 60,537 Indians were introduced into Fiji.[2] About one-half returned to India, the rest remaining under a scheme that allowed them to become legal residents 'with privileges no whit inferior to those of any other class of Her Majesty's subjects resident in the colonies'.[3] The Indian population grew steadily so that by 1945 they outnumbered the Fijians for the first time. From the policy of labour immigration, then, a new community was settled in Fiji.

The final policy was the establishment of a separate native Fijian administration through which the British governed the

Fijians indirectly; the Fijian hierarchical political structure was recognised and Fijian chiefs continued to govern their own people. While this policy substantially preserved the traditional Fijian culture by virtually establishing a state within a state, it so protected the Fijian that he was almost wholly unprepared to compete effectively with the Europeans and Indians once his circle of interaction had enlarged beyond the village. The upshot was the institutionalisation of Fijian economic inferiority.

By 1990, some 40 per cent of the Fijians still subsisted mainly in villages. The typical Fijian worker in the modern economic sector tends to maintain intimate material connections with his or her village. The Fijian community continues to own about 83 per cent of the land which is held communally by over 7,000 *mataqali* patrilineal groups (Spate 1959). Fijians who no longer rely on their villages for their income are employed by the government as policemen, army officers, teachers, nurses, medical officers, office workers, and in a variety of other public-sector jobs. From the government services has sprung a well-to-do Fijian middle class. Many Fijians regard the government bureaucracy as their pre-eminent domain in much the same way as many Indians regard the commercial and sugar sectors. Fijian penetration of the business sector has been generally unsuccessful (Watters 1969; Hailey 1985).

Most Indian immigrants to Fiji came as indentured labourers. They came from many parts of India, from different language and religious groups, and overwhelmingly without their families. Indians who remained in Fiji leased or bought land on which they planted their own cane; by the end of the Second World War, they practically took over the entire sugar-growing business. Today, some 80 per cent of cane farmers are Indians. However, most of the lands are leased from Fijians rendering what would normally be a powerful political base into a tinder box of communal conflict. Sugar is the most significant crop in the economy providing more than half of Fiji's foreign reserves.

About 3 to 6 per cent of the Indians came as free settlers, mainly Gujaratis. They established businesses but were later joined by other Indians who left the sugar fields to start small stores and trade shops. In contemporary Fiji, most small and intermediate-size commercial operations are in Indian hands. Many Indians and Fijians have moved to urban areas such as Suva and Lautoka. As in the rural areas where Indians and Fijians live apart (Fijians live in small concentrated nucleated villages while Indian family units are dispersed on sprawling leased *mataqali* land), in the towns such as Suva similar voluntary ethnic residential segregation occurs thereby rendering city wards predominantly Fijian or Indian. Census reports revealed that in four-fifths of the enumerated areas on the two main islands, 70 per cent were either predominantly Indian or Fijian (Walsh 1970: 1–2). Cultural features also separate the two major communities. While English is the cross-communal language, Indians speak Hindustani among themselves and the Fijians their indigenous language. The radio stations carry separate programmes in Hindustani and Fijian and, until recently, the educational institutions were segregated. Finally, most voluntary social and economic organisations such as sports clubs and trade unions are predominantly uni-ethnic. Inter-marriage between Fijians and Indians is practically non-existent.

Europeans, although numerically insignificant, have dominated the direction of the colony. First, the traders and planters stamped a capitalist economy on Fiji. Second, missionaries converted the Fijians to Christianity. Finally, the Europeans, who at first served as instigators of Fijian inter-tribal conflict, won political domination of Fijian society through the Deed of Cession in 1874. The political imprint was a form of government which at independence in 1970 was a variant of the Westminster parliamentary model. The overall social impact has been the *de facto* establishment of English ways as the measure of excellence. The *lingua franca* is English. Consequently, Europeans are over-represented as managers, supervisors, professional and skilled workers generally (Norton 1978: ch. 1). Constituting less than 1 per cent of the population, they command high status. Nongovernment workers are employed in high executive positions in foreign multinational corporations. Big business remains in the hands of the Europeans and European-owned companies.

The remaining population categories are the Chinese, mixed races and other Pacific Islanders. The Chinese are mainly small businessmen and skilled professional workers. They, like the various mixed races of light pigmentation, enjoy a moderate socio-economic well-being and are among the most urbanised of Fiji's population. The other Pacific Islanders are mainly the Rotumans who belong to the adjacent island, Rotuma, which is part of Fiji's territory, and to Solomon Islanders and other nearby island groups who were originally recruited to serve on European plantations. These Pacific Islanders identify politically with indigenous Fijian interests.

A number of cross-cutting cleavages, a few mentioned above, has moderated the effects of the ethnic compartments in Fiji society. In the same areas of primordial segmentation, important instances of cross-cutting experiences co-exist (Premdas 1987a: 67–101). Specifically, in the language area, most Fijians and Indians speak English which is the language of communication between the two groups. Additionally, a number of Fijians speak Hindi and Indians speak Fijian, although this cross-linguistic competence is not very extensive. In the social sphere, all Fiji citizens share common educational facilities and teachers in primary, secondary and tertiary institutions. Separate language schools have only recently been abolished. In the areas of residence and occupation, especially in towns, many cross-cutting contacts are still enacted daily. In voluntary group life, however, trade unions are still preponderantly uni-ethnic in Fiji, including the two unions representing Fiji teachers. And most social and cultural associations remain primarily but not exclusively subscribed to by one ethnic group. Religion is a major divider with practically all Fijians adhering to Christianity while Indians overwhelmingly adhere to Hinduism or Islam. Language is also a divisive influence, for when in their own company, Fijians speak their own tongue. Cultural practices such as rituals and observances around religion, diet, marriage and family matters separate the two groups literally into worlds apart. Hence, racial, linguistic, religious and cultural cleavages fall one on top of the other in a pattern of coinciding reinforcements separating Indians and Fijians.

While major cleavages divide the ethnic groups into cultural compartments, each segment in turn is not monolithically unified. Internal divisions within the Fijian and Indian communities can assume salience in the right circumstances. Within the Indian group, there are Muslims and Hindus, with the former constituting about 15 per cent of the Indian population. A further division exists between North and South Indians as well as between separate sub-identities such as Punjabis and Gujaratis. The politics of this internal differentiation, especially prior to the military intervention in 1987, has seen certain Indian subgroups in whole or in part supporting the Fijian-dominated government.

Within the Fijian section, internal regional and linguistic divisions compounded by coinciding economic disparities split Fijian political solidarity. In part, these divisions have influenced the formation of the Fijian Nationalist Party and the Western United Front. All of this however does not constitute a powerful enough force to modify Fiji's deeply bifurcated society. The numbers are too marginal to restructure radically the watershed which separates ethnic sections.

TOWARDS AN EXPLANATION OF ETHNIC CONFLICT IN FIJI: THE CONCEPT OF BALANCE

Like Arend Lijphart, we do not accept the claim of plural-society theorists who argue that the condition of multi-ethnicity inevitably engenders ethnic domination by one of the segments in order to maintain order and stability (Lijphart 1977a: ch. 1; Premdas 1986: 107–38). Alternatives exist for peaceful inter-ethnic accommodation. In the concept 'balance' inheres an idea of a just apportionment of shares so that domination is averted and sharing is emphasised (Premdas 1980a: 189–201). It is the opposite of the concept of all-out competition in which a zero-sum struggle decides an absolute winner. We shall elaborate on this concept of balance using it as our critical concept to explain ethnic harmony and conflict in Fiji.

Not a written constitutional law prior to the military intervention in 1987, the idea of balance had been embedded in Fiji's multi-ethnic politics by practices whereby sectoral pre-eminence was distributed as follows: (1) the Fijians controlled the government, in particular, the prime minister's office. They also owned 83 per cent of all the land; (2) the Indians dominated the sugar industry and the intermediate-size businesses; and (3) the Europeans owned the very large businesses, such as banks, hotels, factories, etc. This distributive sectoral 'balance' was not a rigid formula for the sharing of power in all its details. Room existed for one ethnic group to penetrate and participate in another group's domain. For instance, the government had used subsidies to encourage the entry of Fijians into businesses, while the prime minister, a Fijian, deliberately appointed several Indians to his cabinet. Fijians leased their land to Indians and others. In the end, this limited 'mix' had moderated the sharp edges and virtual monopoly rights of the 'balancing' concept. At various times in recent Fiji history, the balance was in danger of being upset, leading to efforts to rectify the disequilibrium. For example, when Indian population growth had threatened to overwhelm the demographic balance, the government initiated two effective policies informally to offset it: (1) a vigorous birth-control and family-planning programme more oriented to the Indian than the Fijian population; and (2) a policy enabling Indians to emigrate from Fiji taking their property with them. We shall see how a perception that the balance was being nullified led to Fiji's military coup.

'Balance' assumes asymmetrical areas of dominance and sustains equality by requiring reciprocity. Such exchanges are, however, not imposed by sentiments of love for another community but are informed by self-interest. Each group needs the resources of the other group to survive and maintain its standard of living. Each group is its brother's keeper in a mundane, practical, self-interested sense. It is no more in the interest of the Fijians to deny Indians access to land than for Indians to stop paying taxes to the Fijian-dominated government. 'Balance' has been an evolving act constantly needing nurture by inter-communal consultation and co-operation. It is not a rigid or written agreement but a dynamic concept that requires revisions and adaptations to be made in contemplation of changes in society. However, 'balance' can only be a short-term solution for intercommunal conflict and sustenance revolves around amicable relations among inter-sectional elites. The balancing act is bound to face assault sooner or later by chauvinistic outbidders who, at a moment of opportunity, may want to instigate nationalist adherents not to accept part of the pie but to seize all of it. In such a situation 'balance' will be displaced by 'hegemony' and all the consequences this entails, or it could trigger civil strife and the destruction of the society. To upset the balance is to attempt to convert an unranked to a ranked system of ethnic relations.

In this part, using the concept of balance, we examine a number of issue areas in detail to see how the contest for resources and policy favours was conducted among the ethnic elements in Fiji. We shall see how ethnic identity originated in the colonial order and influenced the claims to niches of power and privilege, and how, in a circular dynamic of reinforcement, the struggle stimulated intensified competition and ethnic antagonism, justifying further assertions for a system of distribution sensitive to ethnic fears. Specifically, we look at the perennial problems of political representation, land, and the allocation of employment opportunities in the private and public sectors. To understand how ethnic claims to privileges and power were legitimated, it is crucial to look at the concept of 'balance'. In discussing 'balance' in relation to representation, land and employment, we shall see how Indians and Fijians enunciated their own ideas of balance to assert their claims and to prevent encroachment on their own territory. In effect, 'balance' is repeatedly invoked to justify an ethnic claim; its meaning, however, is often so manipulated that it serves to legitimate self-interest, and therefore requires adjudication. Until 1987, when the military intervention occurred, negotiations served to resolve rival claims so as to maintain the balance.

Representation and the problem of political paramountcy

Representation has been one of the persistent problems that have created tensions between Indians and Fijians. By a peculiar interpretation of the Deed of Cession (1874) under which Fiji became a British colony, Fijians have interpreted their position *vis-à-vis* other ethnic groups as one of 'paramountcy' (Hagen 1978: 2–18). No such term or its equivalent is in the document, but through periodic assertions of their political pre-eminence among the immigrant population, Fijians have maintained a claim to the right to govern Fiji regardless of their numbers. In particular, when Indians arrived in Fiji and demanded equal representation with Europeans in the colonial legislative councils, the assertion of Fijian 'paramount' rights emerged as a counter-claim to the threat of Indian dominance.

When an element of popular representation was first introduced in Fiji in 1904, the colonial council included six elected Europeans, two nominated Fijians, and ten European official members. In effect, the two nominated Fijians represented a white population of 2,440. The 22,000 Indians were completely without representation. The exclusion of the Indian sector, however, was only temporary. By 1916, when a new council was introduced, Indians were allocated one nominated representative after agitating for the franchise. The impetus for Indian representation came from recently arrived Indian immigrants, mainly Gujaratis, who emulated the nationalist struggle of the Indian Congress in India for equal rights. As British subjects, they demanded equal representation with the white sector of the population.

Indian demand for electoral equality was couched in terms of a 'common' roll (one man, one vote) as distinct from a 'communal roll' (sectional representation). Because the Fijians were governed under a separate native administration, the Indian demand for a common roll challenged European control of the colonial council and was interpreted as an attempt to introduce Indian political domination in Fiji. The equation of the demand for a common roll with the alleged desire of Indians to dominate politically the entire society has since become a pervasive theme in the communal politics of Fiji.

No significant alteration in the mode of representation was made until 1966 (Meller and Anthony 1967: 10–15). Prior to this date, in 1963, universal adult suffrage was introduced. In 1963 also, Fijians were first allowed to elect directly their representatives from among the Fijian people. Previously, Fijians were nominated to the council. In 1966, a new legislative council in which elected representatives constituted a majority was inaugurated and a ministerial member system under which elected members were given cabinet supervisory responsibilities came into effect. The 'wind of change' inspired by the post-Second World War anti-colonial movements in Africa and Asia had reached the Fiji islands. The wheels of political change were turning rapidly making their most significant impact in the transfer of the government to local leaders. A full-blown party system came into existence by 1966 consisting of two major parties, the National Federation Party (NFP), supported predominantly by Indians and the Alliance Party supported mainly by Fijians, Europeans, Chinese and others. What did not change under the new political order of 1966 was the communal system of representation.

Although the Fijians initially resisted independence, fearing Indian designs to dominate Fiji, they gradually came to accept it as inevitable. The results of the 1966 elections in particular heartened the Fijians since they gave the Fijian-dominated Alliance Party an overwhelming victory against the predominantly Indian

Table 11.1 Composition of the lower House of the National Parliament – Group as percentage of population

Roll	Communal	National	Total
Fijians–Indians (50.8%)	12	10	22 (42.3%)
Fijians and Pacific Islanders (45.7%)	12	10	22 (42.3%)
Europeans, Chinese, Mixed Races (3.5%)	3	5	8 (15.4%)
Total	27	25	52 (100%)

National Federation Party. Independence meant that the country required a new constitution and, in turn, this implied that the outstanding issues which separated Fijians and Indians had to be reconciled. Between August 1969 and March 1970, the representatives of the NFP and Alliance met to work out a constitutional solution for Fiji, and particularly to reconcile Indian claims for a common roll with the 'paramount' rights of the minority Fijians.

On the system of representation, the Alliance accepted the common roll as a long-term objective and acceded to the NFP demands that: (1) a Royal Commission be established sometime between the first and second elections after independence to re-examine the entire issue of common versus communal roll, and; (2) common roll elections be held for the municipalities of Suva and Lautoka. In the meantime, a system of communal and cross-communal voting was entrenched. The lower House in the proposed bicameral Parliament was to be composed as shown in Table 11.1.

Parity of representation was accorded the Fijians and Indian communities, while the European, part-European and Chinese sectors (referred to as 'General Electors'), although constituting only 3.5 per cent of the population continued to be over-represented with 15.4 per cent of the seats. On paramount rights for Fijians, the NFP conceded that additional 'weightage' should be allocated to Fijian interests. The device through which this was to be implemented was a second chamber, a Senate, in the national parliament. It was agreed that the Senate should be composed as shown in Table 11.2.

The power of the Senate resided not only in the representation

Table 11.2 Composition of the Senate of the National Parliament

Fijian Great Council of Chief's nominees	8
Prime Minister's nominees	7
Opposition leader's nominees	6
Council of Rotuma's nominees	1
Total	22

of superior numbers of Fijians, but in the amending procedure which entrenched Fijian interests by requiring consent of the Fiji Great Council of Chiefs on matters related to Fijian land and custom. This it did by requiring a two-thirds majority in each chamber for altering the constitution. Here, it must be noted that the Fijian Great Council of Chiefs has eight out of twenty-two seats, that is, more than a third of the seats capable of blocking any constitutional change without their consent.

Representation in the independence constitution was not permanently solved; the delegates from the Fijian and Indian sections deferred resolving the claims of 'common roll' versus 'communal roll' until after independence had been attained. In 1975, the Royal Commission was appointed. If its recommendations were accepted by the Fijian-dominated government, given the persistence of intransigent ethnic voting behaviour, the Indian communal party would probably have wrested power away from the incumbents. This would have upset the balance in the distribution of spheres of influences, in particular Fijian political control. The recommendations of the Royal Commission were therefore rejected outright by the ruling regime. But with the rejection, a shadow of illegitimacy descended on the government. To Indians, the Fijian prime minister had broken his word for fear of losing power. To Fijians, it was the right thing to do to maintain balance in the system. What was more salient, however, pertained to the future of inter-ethnic relations. The old problem of reconciling common roll with communal roll was once again on the political agenda. In the future general elections that were held, the problem of representation and other issues bedevilling the relations between Fijians and Indians would be vented openly.

Land

The land issue is perhaps the most significant triggering point of Fijian–Indian racial conflict. Fijians own most of the country's land under a system of traditional communal tenure that prohibits private individual alienation to non-Fijians. They equate ownership of land with their heritage and identity. In the modern cash economy dominated by Europeans and Indians, land constitutes the Fijians' most powerful pillar of political bargaining. Being mainly farmers, Indians view land as the indispensable means for their survival. Since they own very little of it, however, they require predictable access to land use since alternative avenues of employment are practically non-existent. The struggle, then, between Fijian owners and Indian lessees is cast in terms of vital needs generating unusual emotional intensity around the issue. There is also a public interest in land. If political stability and economic viability dictate that Fijian–Indian conflict over land be contained, then this compels the state to strike a balance on one hand between making land available to the tillers (Indians) and on the other assuring Fijians that their land will not be used by others to build an economic base against Fijian interests. Public policy must tread the narrowest of sensitive options, for communal passions become easily inflamed over land. The idea of 'balance' seemed to have guided the British administrators to frame its land policy so as to preserve a balance between the interests of the two communities.

Fiji has about 4,505,000 acres of land; at the time of cession, the Europeans had claimed about 1,000,000 acres. A land commission subsequently recognised their ownership of only 415,000 acres. Nevertheless, these tracts represent the best agricultural land in Fiji. Since 1874, apart from a brief period between 1905 and 1911 when an additional 100,000 acres of Fijian land were alienated, land policy has remained very tight. Essentially, the government intervened to terminate all private sales in an effort to preserve the Fijian way of life. Land ownership in Fiji is distributed as shown in Table 11.3 (Spate 1959).

The freezing of the tenure pattern has bequeathed a legacy of wide disparities in land ownership among the ethnic communities. Fijians constituting about 46 per cent of the population retained ownership over 83.8 per cent; less than 10 per cent of this is cultivable. Europeans constituting about 2 per cent of the

Table 11.3 Distribution of land ownership

	Estimated acres	% of total
Fijian communal land	3,714,990	82.16
Rotuman communal land	11,000	0.24
Freehold	368,000	8.15
Crown lands combined	377,420	9.45

population own in freehold 5.5 per cent of prime commercial land. Indians forming about 48 per cent of the population own 1.7 per cent. The overwhelming majority of Indians are tenants and sub-tenants who depend on Fijians for leased land. About 62 per cent of the leases issued by Fijians are held by Indians. Indians utilise the land mainly for sugar farming; about 80 per cent of the sugar farmers are Indians who continue to demand more land on ninety-nine-year leases. Interestingly, up to the First World War, Europeans were the most insistent on the release of more land for commercial development causing antagonistic relations with Fijians. Thereafter, with the termination of the Indian indentureship system and the adoption of Fiji as their home, the pressure for more land came from Indians. This latter fact has launched Fijians and Indians on a collision course that continues to the present.

Fijian fear of losing their land as well as their desire to retain land unencumbered by long leases for future use led to the enactment of the controversial land reserves policy in 1940. Called the Native Land Trust Ordinance, the legislation established the Native Land Trust Board (NLTB) to administer the leasing of Fijian land and to terminate leases where necessary so as to create 'reserves' for future Fijian use. The architect of this legislation, Ratu Sir Lala Sukuna, viewed the reserves policy as the embodiment of the Fijian vital interests. Indians did not share Ratu Sukuna's views of the NLTB and especially the land reserves policy. The selection of land for reserves has yet to come to a completion. For over three and a half decades, year after year, land leased to Indian families who had no other alternative source of income was taken out of cultivation and placed in reserves. Bitter Indian reaction stemmed from three consequences of the reserves policy. First, many farms which went into reserves were not cultivated; they soon reverted to bush. The Indian family which suddenly became landless was forced into an over-supplied pool of farm labourers available for hire. Second, because the length of leases under the new NLTB regulations was erratic with no guarantee of renewal, the insecurity of tenure provided little incentive for the Indian farmer to develop and care for the land. Third, as more land was placed in reserve, the country lost revenues from taxes, fewer people were employed, and more persons moved into already overcrowded urban areas in search of jobs.[4]

Fijians defend the land reserves policy saying that the availability of land would provide the incentive for them to cultivate the soil commercially. Because of long leases, many Fijians in a single lifetime may not have the opportunity to use their land. Further, they argue that the overwhelming majority of leases are renewed so that the commotion and criticisms over non-renewal are exaggerated and unfair.[5] Indians are not happy, especially with the first of these rebuttals, because Fijians already have more than an adequate supply of land much of which is not cultivated. Consequently, the reserves policy is seen as an expression of jealousy of Indian growing prosperity and fear that, in the long run, Indian economic power may be translated into political power.

Caught between the expansive needs of Indians for long-term secure leases and Fijian demands for more reserves, the British colonial administrators oversaw the passage of the Agricultural Landlord and Tenants' Ordinance (ALTO) in 1966, which required the NLTB to offer tenants an initial lease for ten years plus two similar ten-year periods if the land was not needed by Fijians. The legislation was a balancing compromise that temporarily stabilised Indian–Fijian relations over land. Fijian interests in land were safeguarded in the 1970 independence constitution which validated all Fijian land claims to 83 per cent of the country's land and entrenched Fijian land rights by requiring that two-thirds of the Fijian Council of Chiefs in the Senate support any alteration of the land-related aspects of the constitution. Indian access to land was further strengthened in 1976 by an amendment to ALTO giving leases for an initial period of twenty years instead of ten years, followed by a twenty-year extension.

As long as Fiji remains an agricultural country and land ownership and sugar cultivation are in the hands of the two separate and hostile ethnic elements, the land issue will persist as a fundamental feature in inter-ethnic relations. The intensity of sentiments derives from the fact that, 'land is seen as a scarce resource and competition for it is regarded in ethnic terms. The symbolic significance makes it more than just an ordinary issue' (Milne 1982: 65).

Employment: public bureaucracy and the private sector

Employment, especially in the public sector, has emerged as a vicious arena in which competitive claims for ethnic shares have attained a special intensity. While the two areas, representation and land, were bound by colonial precedent and yielded to formal compromises, jobs from the modern commercial sector and from the public bureaucracy, both spheres expanding significantly in the post-Second World War period, were left wide open for competition by the ethnic communities. In the absence of a formula, each group staked its own claims guided by its own interests.

The civil service, the professions and private business represent the modern monetary sectors in Fiji. It was from jobs in these activities that stable and high incomes were earned and access to modern urban-type services were acquired. The quest for these positions by Fijians and Indians acculturated to European ways and trained in skills, conferred dignity and status not only to the individual incumbents of these positions but also onto the respective communities. Hence, great symbolic gratification was attached to them as significant as the monetary rewards. Employment opportunities in the modern non-agricultural public and private sectors were, however, limited. It would be in this crucible of scarcity for a very highly prized value that government policy would play a pivotal part in determining the distribution of benefits.

The public service, including the education service, has become the largest single source of employment in Fiji. Until independence, the highest posts were occupied by European personnel. To gain access, the non-white population needed European education and training. English-language schools, however, were not set up until 1916. Indian and Fijian schools depended on their own communities for supplementary resources. Because of their lack of land and insecure leases,

Table 11.4 Examination pass rate by race (per cent)

	Fijians	Indians	Others
Secondary School Entrance Examination, 1967	39.7	61.9	67.6
Cambridge School Certificate Examination, 1967	44.8	65.4	67.2
New Zealand University Entrance Examination	25.0	30.0	44.7

Indians spent heavily on upgrading their schools. To them, education was the only alternative to land scarcity; it held the promise of employment in the emerging modern public and private sectors. Indian expenditures in education were reflected after the Second World War in their steady incremental displacement of many Europeans in positions that required skills. Fijian educational achievement was retarded by comparison. A government inquiry assigned the reasons as 'the geographical scatter of the Fijians, the isolation of the rural Fijian teacher from much intellectual stimulus, the shortage of Fijian primary school teachers, rural poverty, social distractions and other less tangible and psychological factors . . .' (Lal 1986: 18).

Fijian students suffered a greater rate of attrition also as they moved to senior grades in school; this was bound to reflect adversely in their effort to obtain post-secondary qualifications essential for high paying and senior echelon ranks. Table 11.4 demonstrates the disparate results in examinations between Fijian and Indian students pointing in part to the inferior emphasis that Fijians placed on education and the poor facilities at their schools (Vasil 1984: 194). It was almost inevitable, then, given the trend in Indian education, that most university positions would go to Indians. In 1968, out of 643 graduates with university degrees, 464 were Indians, seventy-seven Fijians, sixty-three Chinese and thirty-one others (Vasil 1984: 194). Indian employment in the professions underlined an emergent preponderance especially after many European expatriates left after independence.

As the state undertook an increasing number of development projects and more services were extended to citizens, the public bureaucracy expanded. In a scheme where merit determined

Table 11.5 Fijian armed forces

	Fijian	Indian	Others	Total
Regular force	372	5	19	396
Territorial force	502	29	32	563
Naval squadron	59	2	10	71
Total	933	36	61	1,030

appointments, the public service was swamped by educated Indian personnel. But the concept of balance entered into the picture. After independence, a Fijian-dominated government offset Indian preponderance in the private-business sector by higher Fijian employment in the public bureaucracy.

In the armed forces, Fijian lopsided representation has evoked vehement protests against the government which has been charged with obliquely guaranteeing Fijian paramountcy by the threat of an ethnic army (see Table 11.5) (Vasil 1984: 194). In the Ministry of Fijian Affairs and Rural Development, and in the Ministry of Fijian Affairs, Fijians overwhelmed. In the 1980s, Fijian preponderance in the public service had become very lopsided, especially at the senior echelon levels. This compelled the Indian opposition leader to accuse the government of implementing a policy designed to ensure that all strategic levels of government are staffed by Fijians in order to deliberately create an alienated out-group, namely, the Indians. This is reflected in all aspects of governmental work and activities, from its composition, its development strategies, appointments to boards, promotions in the civil service, and its Crown lands policy (Premdas 1980b: 10). For Fijians, however, public service employment is the primary access route to middle-class well-being and status. In their view, their excess numbers are balanced by Indian preponderance in the private sector. Fijians constitute only 2 per cent of the entrepreneurs in the country. Europeans control the large businesses while Indians predominate in middle-sized enterprises. Fijian under-representation in business is being remedied by a government policy of affirmative action through its Business Organisation and Management Unit (BOMAS) which trains Fijians in business practices and also through extending interest-free loans from the government's Development Bank.

The Fiji-dominated Alliance government had acted in one other major area to aid Fijians. Foreign aid for capital projects has been directed mostly to Fijian regions or to activities benefiting mainly Fijians. Examples include the pinewood industry and its predominantly Fijian-staffed Fiji Pine Commission, the tuna fisheries project and the sugar-cane seaquaqua scheme, on the island of Vanua Levu.

Balance and the problem of outbidders

In the three preceding areas of inter-ethnic contest – representation, land and jobs – a balance in tension has been maintained. Despite the fact that Fijians and Indians had retained pre-eminence in their respective areas, however, it is clear that a progressively significant tilting of policies was enacted to the advantage of the indigenous Fijian. For 'balance' to succeed as the means to regulate inter-ethnic relations, it is essential that elites in each section exercise restraint in maintaining the boundaries of the system. Without a formal adjudicator established to redress territorial intrusions, the delicate system of harmony depends on its own internal discipline on the one hand and on the absence of external destabilisers on the other. It is with the emergence and pressure of the latter factor, the external destabiliser in the form of an ethnic outbidder, that the Fijian system of balance became disrupted and succumbed to a system of ethnic dominance.

How this occurred in Fiji must be briefly recapitulated. The evidence indicates that even while a system of balance prevailed and successfully maintained order, it was under extremist assault by outbidders. For five years after the London constitutional conference in 1970, the Fijian prime minister Mara and the Indian opposition leader, Koya, consulted each other and co-operated in running the government. But communal peace in multi-ethnic societies is a fragile affair. Moderate party leaders who attempt to maintain inter-ethnic harmony by making concessions and compromises are always threatened by 'outbidders' who seek to assert chauvinistic claims to the entire national pie (Rabushka and Shepsle 1972: 82). In 1975, both Mara and Koya faced 'outbidders' who alleged a conspiracy between communal elites. Mara was challenged by Sakiasi Butadroka, a Fijian member of parliament, who claimed that the Alliance Party presided over a government that was inimical to indigenous Fijian interests (Premdas 1980c: 30–44). Koya confronted a challenge that he had 'sold out' Indian interests. Butadroka introduced a motion in parliament to expel all Indians from Fiji. Towards the end of 1975 and early 1976, the pressure against Mara and Koya drove them apart. The open public exchanges became acrimonious, torpedoing the cordial relations between the two leaders and launching a new era of inter-communal hostility that endangered the balance in inter-sectional harmony. Butadroka's attack on the system of balance was embodied in the motto 'Fiji for Fijians' of the new Fijian Nationalist Party that he formed (Premdas 1980c: 30–44). He obtained a minority of indigenous Fijian support, barely enough to cause a significant swing that could give the Indian-based party victory. The March–April 1977 elections in Fiji's history were momentous, for the Alliance lost the elections having obtained only twenty-four out of the fifty-two seats in the House of Representatives. The National Federation Party won twenty-six seats. The diversion of votes from the Alliance to the Nationalists led directly to Federation victory in at least six seats. The Nationalists justified their vote-splitting role among Fijians in terms of providing proof that Fijian rights were neither paramount nor protected.

The March–April elections traumatised the Fijian population, whose belief in the concept of 'balance' led them to conclude that the Indian victory violated the Fijian domain (Premdas 1980a). If the victory had been allowed to stand, then Indians would have had control over most of the economy, as well as the polity, upsetting radically the distribution of spheres of influence among the Fijians, Indians and Europeans. Because the Indian-based NFP obtained just half (twenty-six) of the fifty-two seats in the legislature and, most importantly, because they could not agree on a leader to succeed Ratu Mara, the Fijian governor-general invited Mara to form the next government. In the first meeting of the House, the minority Alliance government was toppled in a vote of no confidence, requiring new elections in September of the same year. If the March–April elections must be viewed as a dramatic upset of the 'balance', then the September elections should be seen as an attempt to restore it.

The September 1977 elections gave the Alliance an overwhelming victory. It obtained thirty-six seats, the NFP fifteen seats and an Independent one seat. The Alliance's victory was accountable in part to the self-decimating fractional infighting that attended the split of the NFP into two competing camps, and also because of the reduced strength of the Nationalists from 25 per cent of the Fijian communal votes in March–April to 17 per cent in September. During the election campaign, the Alliance government had jailed several of the Nationalists, including Butadroka, on a variety of charges (Premdas 1980c).

Ethnic conflict resolution in a government of national unity

For a few years after the restoration of the balance, internal inter-harmony prevailed in Fiji. Because of the vulnerability of the balancing idea to outbidders, there was even an attempt made in 1980 to formally weld the two ethnically-based parties into a government of national unity. The leaders of the two major ethnic communities agreed that communal conflict in Fiji was destabilising, divisive and destructive. The Fijian prime minister proposed a government of national unity; he proposed that institutionally it 'will be reflected in a Cabinet which draws upon the best talents in the country, having in mind simultaneously adequate representation of the various ethnic groups in Fiji' (Premdas 1980b: 15). It was argued that through Indian and Fijian leaders working together in a co-operative cabinet arrangement, a salutary example would be imparted to the entire population of a model of good inter-communal behaviour. On the question of ethnic proportional representation in the cabinet, Mara proposed that the Indian/Fijian ratio should be guided by two factors: (1) relative ethnic population size in the country, and (2) percentage control by the various parties in parliament and of the majority party as a result of the previous general election (the September 1977 elections). In the House of Representatives, at that time, the Alliance had thirty-six members while the Federation Party had fifteen. Whatever the final numbers of Indians and Fijians would have been under this formula, its anticipated consequences were 'to ensure adequate participation by all communities in the decision-making process' thereby nullifying 'a sense of alienation in any one or more ethnic groups through apparent or real exclusion' (Premdas 1980b: 16–17). Mr Reddy, the Indian leader, agreed that the solution to Fiji's communal politics resided in some form of joint government, but whether the form was 'consociationalism', 'coalition' or 'government of national unity', it had to be subordinate to the salient issue of honour or what he called 'any arrangement that is honourable' (Premdas 1980b: 16–17). The opposition leader said that a joint government could only be forged on the basis that permitted his party relatively equal leverage and representation with the Alliance Party. He called for discussions between the two parties to explore the subject further.

The timing of the Mara proposal coincided with the fact that the Alliance was at its most powerful parliamentary level in its history, while the Federation Party, plagued by internal dissension, was at its weakest. If Mara was negotiating from a position of strength, Reddy was from weakness. In the end, the vital interests of the Fijian party, namely the retention of power and the protection of Fijian interests, would be promoted; but those of the Indian party would still be locked up in a sphere of ambiguity. The leader of the opposition was put in a quandary. His party, weak both in parliamentary numbers and internal cohesion, was challenged to what seemed to be a higher purpose of preserving communal peace in Fiji. Not surprisingly, genuine fears were felt that a powerful Alliance would absorb the Federation Party, eliminating the latter's identity in a government of national unity. The timing of the Alliance proposals was ill-opportune for the Federation Party. Indeed, *time* was essential to Reddy's strategy in responding to Mara's proposals, so that he could: (1) sort out his party's internal difficulties, and (2) increase his party's parliamentary strength. The fulfilment of these conditions would give him the leverage to negotiate with the Alliance.

The opposition leader in the meanwhile dealt critically with various aspects of the Mara proposal. He also decided to raise some substantive issues on the problem of balance which would require urgent attention if a joint government should be agreed upon. He pointed to the Alliance government policies which had progressively tilted more benefits to Fijians causing Indian unhappiness in the country. He criticised specifically the Alliance policy of reverting Crown land to native reserves, drew attention to the alleged discriminatory hiring practices of the government in favour of Fijians and commented on the lack of consultation with the opposition on sensitive issues. 'Can you sow the seeds of strife and sue for peace? Is this how we build national unity?', Reddy asked (Premdas 1980b: 16–17). The response by Ratu Mara to the opposition leader's comments amounted to a withdrawal of his proposal. Mara blamed his action on the attitude of the Federation Party and the opposition leader. What started off as a promising arrangement for inter-ethnic accommodation suddenly was torpedoed.

Several factors further complicated the treatment that the unification proposals received. First, it was a publicly disclosed design; it was not adequately discussed in private by the two major communal leaders before it was tossed into the inevitable turmoil of communally-bound public discourse. Second, the proposals became the arena in which a contest for political upmanship transpired at two national conventions. Reddy had to show that he was capable of standing up to the Alliance while Mara, in response, had to show that he could put down the Federation Party. The main casualty was the proposals. Finally, the timing of the unification proposals was unsuitable, particularly to the opposition leader, who would have lost his party's leadership had he chosen to negotiate from a position of weakness. In Mara's unification proposal, the NFP would undoubtedly have had to settle for a very subordinate partnership role. Both the Alliance and the NFP had vital internal needs to protect; no serious negotiation was likely to overlook these. Consequently, the proposal fell victim to political exchanges informed by internal communal interests.

From balance to dominance

The collapse of negotiations for a government of national unity prefigured a period of inter-ethnic rivalry which saw the setting aside of ethnic balance for ethnic pre-eminence. In the 1982 elections, the Alliance Party was able to return to power. However, in the 1987 elections a fundamental change occurred leading directly to the first military intervention by the Fijian-dominated Royal Fijian Armed Forces.

The 1987 elections were different in some ways to previous elections in that the governing Fijian Alliance Party confronted a rejuvenated Indian-based Federation Party which joined forces with a newly-formed Labour Party to form a Labour–Federation Party. Space does not permit recounting how the latter group, which was led by an indigenous Fijian physician, successfully caused a small enough shift of Fijians away from the Alliance

Party to permit the Labour–Federation Party to eke out a narrow victory (Premdas 1987b). Suffice it to note that the new government, although led by a Fijian (Bavadra), was preponderantly supported by the Indians. To most Fijians, this spelled a vital blow to their view that they should have 'paramount' political power in Fiji. It radically upset the balance as they conceived it.

To the mass of native Fijians, there was initially a silent acceptance of the change of guard. The fact that a Fijian remained prime minister temporarily assuaged Fijian anxieties of the future of Fiji under an Indian-dominated government. However, the deliberate and systematic instigation of latent Fijian fears by a small contingent of disaffected Alliance leaders aroused Fijians to mass action. At meetings and demonstrations organised and led by Alliance parliamentarians and ex-cabinet ministers, Fijians were told that the Bavadra government was a front for Indian interests and that their immediate objective was to deprive Fijians of ownership and control of their land. Labelled the 'Taukei Movement', the meetings picked up momentum at first from small half-hearted gatherings, then included road blocks, fire-bombings (including that of the law offices of Jai Ram Reddy), and outright ethnic appeals to Fijians.[6]

It was in the shadow of the demonstrations and breakdown of order directly instigated by the 'Taukei Movement' that the military intervened. The coup-maker, Lieutenant-Colonel Rabuka, third-in-command of the Fijian Armed Forces, declared that the military assumed power to prevent racial conflagration and to pre-empt the government's call on the military to repress the Fijian people (Premdas 1989: 67–70). The military forces, from the beginning, were almost completely dominated by ethnic Fijians. When the coup took place, the 5 per cent contingent of Indians in the armed forces were placed under house arrest.

Whatever were the motivations, inspirations and surreptitious manoeuvrings involved in the making of the coup, the fact remained that Bavadra and the Labour coalition were unceremoniously evicted from office just thirty-three days after peacefully assuming power. The coup leader echoed the fears and demands of the Taukei demonstrators. The military junta proclaimed that 'Fiji was for Fijians', and that in their own land, Fijians would not be dominated by an alien race. It was proclaimed that only a Fijian-run government could protect Fijian interests. To this end, the military announced that the old constitution was abrogated and a new one would be prepared to guarantee Fijian political paramountcy in perpetuity. The new constitution of 1990 embodied these aspirations.

CONCLUSION

The ethno-genesis of sectional conflict can be traced to colonial practice of diverse labour importation for plantation needs. Under British administration, neither Fijians nor Indians predominated even though there was a claim by Fijians of 'paramountcy'. After the departure of the British, the two major ethnic groups reached an agreement in which they 'balanced' their rival claims in a system of territorial sharing of values. This worked to maintain inter-ethnic harmony and stability for nearly two decades. The constitutional formula for sharing was, however, tested severely by outbidders who precipitated the collapse of inter-ethnic elite accommodation leading to a system of ethnic dominance after the military coup of 1987. The Fiji case clearly shows that inter-ethnic agreement is very practicable but needs restraints on open competition zero-sum politics to ensure its stability and continuity. The new inegalitarian constitutional dispensation that came into being following the military coup has already inflicted heavy costs on Fiji's well-being, including the heavy loss of skilled personnel through mass migration; severe restrictions on human rights; and increased budgetary allocations to the military and coercive forces to secure the state from sabotage (Premdas 1991). The Fiji case therefore also illustrates the alternative to inter-ethnic accommodation in the loss of both democracy and stability.

NOTES

1 See Constitution of the Republic of Fiji (1990).
2 Ali (1973). See also Gillion (1962).
3 These words are from the colonial document known as 'The Salisbury Dispatch' and are often quoted by Indians to assert their rights in Fiji.
4 'Cane Farmers: Fiji's Unrewarded Peasants', *Unispac*, 1960, vol. 7, no. 5, pp. 1-2.
5 'NLTB Facts and Figures', *Vanua* (NLTB journal), March 1977, p. 1.
6 'Coup: Army Seizes Power', *Fiji Times*, 15 May 1987, p. 1; see also Robertson and Tamanisan (1981); Howard (1987).

Chapter 12

Belgium

The variability of ethnic relations

Maureen Covell

INTRODUCTION

Ethnic interaction in Belgium is usually analysed in terms of a language conflict between Dutch-speaking and French-speaking Belgians, or between 'Flemish' and 'Walloons'. However, this approach seriously underestimates the complexities of ethnic relations in that country, including the number of groups in place, the differences in their basis and organisation, and their relations with each other. It also underestimates the degree to which there have been changes in the nature of the groups over time, in their relationships with each other, and in the relationship between the groups and the state. This chapter examines the variability of ethnicity and ethnic relations in Belgium, and argues that explaining this variability requires context-specific rather than general theories.[1]

Belgium represents an interesting example of the various forms ethnicity, ethnic consciousness, and relations between ethnic groups themselves and between the groups and the state can take. First, the groups constituted by Dutch- and French-speaking Belgians are not precisely parallel to each other. Organised activity on the part of Dutch-speaking or Flemish Belgians has a history that goes back to the nineteenth century. Francophone consciousness is more recent and more diffuse. In particular, Francophones are divided between those living in Wallonia, and those living in Brussels, originally a city whose majority spoke Flemish, and still located within the boundaries of modern Flanders. In addition, the smaller numbers of Flemish living in Brussels do not always identify with the Flemish of Flanders (see Beaufays 1988; Claeys 1980).

There is also a small enclave of German-speaking Belgians on the country's eastern border, the result of post-First World War border changes (Brassinne and Kreins 1984). Most recently, Belgium has received large numbers of immigrants from southern European countries and from northern Africa (Roosens 1989). The results of the November 1991 elections suggest that attitudes to these immigrants, particularly those from the Islamic countries of northern Africa, will be an important factor in Belgian politics in the foreseeable future.

The chapter concentrates on relations between French- and Dutch-speaking Belgians since these relations have been the most important ones for Belgian politics throughout the country's history. First, it argues that ethnic identity is not a given but, rather, a potential identity that must be constructed and brought into prominence as a basis for political action. Not all members of the potential group prefer that identity to others or are willing to make it the basis of political action.

Second, the goals and strategy of the politically active segment of the group can be expected to vary over time in response to the political context, including the prevailing political discourse, and the structure of society and the state. Goals and strategy also depend on the political resources available to the group. It can be expected that the nature of what constitutes a political resource can change over time in a given system. For example, numbers are a more important resource under conditions of universal suffrage than under a restricted suffrage. Finally, and particularly relevant for this volume, it can be expected that there will be an interplay between group activities and public policy. As Rudolph and Thompson (1989) argue, state action is affected by the demands of ethnic groups, but it also affects both the goals and the strategies of the groups (also see Hooghe 1991).

The chapter will first outline the historical development of the relationship between the two language groups. The passage of the language laws of 1962–3 has been chosen as the turning point for the emergence of the quarrel in its modern form, since many of the points at issue were either exacerbated or created by those laws. It is also at this period that the Belgian political system as a whole entered a new phase of its development.

In the period before 1963, the Belgian political system was dominated by three 'political families' each headed by a corresponding political party: Social Christians, Liberals and

Socialists. These parties and their associated interest groups formed the 'pillars' of the Belgian political system. By the mid-1960s, however, the cement that held the pillars was beginning to weaken, and the increased vulnerability of the parties was an important factor in the growing impact of the language question (see Lorwin 1966; Huyse 1983; Van Den Bulck 1992).

BELGIUM

The territory that is now Belgium is crossed by the boundary between Germanic and Romance languages that runs through much of Western Europe. There are several theories about the reasons for the existence and persistence of this boundary, none of which has won general acceptance. However, it is important to note that within the territory that is now Belgium, there was not, until the constitutional revisions of 1970, a correspondence between political unit and language use. 'Flanders' and 'Wallonia' are, as I will argue later, modern creations (Murphy 1988; Zolberg 1974, 1978).

Most of what is now Belgium was ruled first as part of the Spanish and then as part of the Austrian empires (the principality of Liège, which at times was larger and at times smaller than the current province of Liège, had a separate existence until the French annexation of 1795). Studies of early language usage suggest that it was mixed, although towards the end of Austrian rule French came to predominate as the language of higher officials. The general population spoke a variety of dialects, Dutch- or German-based in the north, and Romance-based in the south.

It can be argued that language usage first became politically, if not socially, relevant with the French annexation. Certainly the first official state language policy dates from that time. The various provinces of what is now Belgium, including Liège, were incorporated into the French Empire as *departements* and subjected to an official assimilationist language policy that made French the language of public life, including education.

This policy was reversed after 1814, when what were known as the Belgian provinces (including Liège) were joined with the Netherlands in the United Kingdom of the Low Countries. The new government introduced Dutch as an official language in the provinces of East and West Flanders, Antwerp and Limbourg, and had plans to introduce the official use of Dutch in the Flemish portion of the province of Brabant. The resistance of the Francophone elite to this policy was one of the causes, although hardly the major reason, for the revolt of 1830 that led to the creation of an independent Belgium (Hasquin 1989).

The period of Dutch control was too brief to reverse the effects of the practice and policy of the previous rulers, with the result that the newly independent Belgium was ruled by what Zolberg has called a 'trans-ethnic' Francophone elite drawn from Flanders, Wallonia and Brussels. In other words, in addition to the geographical language boundary, there was a sociological boundary that was particularly important in Flanders. The existence of these two boundaries is important for the forms of action taken by both Flemish and Francophone groups (Zolberg 1974; Mabille 1989). An important symbol of this boundary was the capital city of Brussels, located in Flanders, but increasingly dominated by Francophones given its importance as an economic, cultural and political centre (Obler 1976; see also the series *Taal en Sociale Intergratie* published by the Vrije Universiteit Brussel with some articles in English).

Given the domination of public life by the Francophone elite, it was not surprising that although the Belgian constitution guaranteed liberty of language usage, the 1830 provisional government also took steps to solidify the use of French in public life. Citizens could use French, Flemish or German in their relations with the administration or in the courts (provided the judges and lawyers involved could understand the language), but the government did not undertake to provide services in all languages. In practice, the state functioned in French. The same was true of education. Although some primary schools in Flanders functioned in Flemish, at the secondary and post-secondary levels, institutions on both sides of the language border offered instruction in French only.

THE EARLY FLEMISH MOVEMENT

The early Flemish movements began almost with the creation of the Belgian state, and had as their first goal the introduction of the use of Dutch in public life in Flanders (Clough 1930). Later the goal of increasing the use of Dutch in the national government was added. In addition, early leaders of the movement had the objective of 'uplifting' the Flemish people. The strategies that followed included pressure on the government and on the developing political parties, and the creation of a network of Flemish organisations (Covell 1985; Hermans 1992).

Pressure on existing political parties became more important as the right to vote was extended, first at the municipal and provincial levels. This meant that the electorate in Flanders began to include members whose only language was Dutch. At the same time as the criteria for voting were relaxed, the spread of education and urbanisation and therefore of middle-class occupations meant that the number of people who fit into the new categories was increasing (Zolberg 1978).

The electoral pressures led to the passage of a series of language laws at the end of the nineteenth century. A law passed in 1873 introduced the use of Dutch in criminal proceedings in Flanders, an 1878 law provided for the use of Dutch in the administration in the region, and an 1883 law introduced the use of Dutch in the middle level of state education. At the national level, the 'Equality Law' of 1898 gave Dutch and French equal status as languages for parliamentary debates and for the publication of statutes.

It was the First World War that saw both a consolidation of a mass base for the Flemish movement and an enforced pause in its activities. During the war, the Frontist movement was created among Flemish infantrymen, who comprised the majority of the troops at the Front but whose officers were in large majority Francophone. The goals of the movement evolved from an emphasis on language use in the army, to demands for unilingualism and increased autonomy for Flanders itself. After the war, members of the movement formed a Flemish Nationalist Party that won 3.9 per cent of the national vote, or over 8 per cent of the Flemish vote in the election of 1919, and reached a high of 7.5 per cent of the national vote in 1939 (Witte and Craeybeakx 1987).

However, the 'divide and conquer' policy of the German occupation left sequels that hurt the efficacy of the movement in the immediate post-war period. The policy had included the conversion of the state university at Ghent into a Dutch-language institution, and the creation of a 'Council of Flanders' with some degree of formal autonomy. The post-war rejection of collaboration with the occupier and the criminal prosecution of some of the more prominent Flemish collaborators meant that the Flemish movement went into a period of retreat. However, the end of the war also saw the elimination of the plural vote, and by the mid-1920s the force of Flemish votes was being felt both through the Flemish National Party and within the traditional Catholic, Socialist and Liberal parties.

The result was another series of language laws that went a further distance to meeting Flemish demands, but that, with the compromises necessary to gain Francophone support, left enough demands unmet to guarantee the continuance of the movement. The most important of these laws was the 1932 law that eliminated bilingualism in Flanders, and created two unilingual regions, Flanders and Wallonia. In other words, Dutch was to be the only language in public life in the Flemish region. The capital, Brussels, was to be the only bilingual region of the country.

The law had two provisions that laid the basis for future conflicts. First, the border between the French- and Dutch-speaking regions of the country was not fixed, but was to be revised if the decennial census showed shifts in language usage. The law also provided that language minorities of sufficient size could enjoy 'facilities' in their language in education and in communication with the state. These provisions worked largely to the benefit of Francophones, since language shifts from Dutch to French were still occurring, and since the most important language minority was that constituted by Francophones living in the Flemish suburbs of Brussels.

Like the First World War, the Second World War deterred visible action on the part of the Flemish Movement, again partly as a result of divide and conquer tactics on the part of the occupying forces. However, the period after the war hardly represents a pause in the importance of the issue. The 1947 language census, the first since 1931, demonstrated a northward movement of the language border and the increased francisation of the area around Brussels. The results were considered so sensitive that they were not published until 1954. In another demonstration of the sensitivity of the issue, a commission to study relations between Flemish and Francophone was established in 1948 (although it did not make its report until 1958).

The immediate post-war period was also dominated by two

issues that appeared to cut across language divisions, but that in retrospect can be seen to have highlighted differences between the north and the south of the country. The first was the Royal Question, that is, the debate over the conduct of Leopold III during the war and the question of whether he should remain king. A plebiscite was held on the issue in 1950. A majority of over 57 per cent voted for his return, but the vote was sharply different in the different parts of the country. A majority of 72.2 per cent voted in favour of his return in Flanders, while majorities of 52 per cent in Brussels and 58 per cent in Wallonia voted against his return. In reaction to the results, these two regions broke into civil unrest and in the end were able to force Leopold's abdication.

The other issue that appeared to cut across language boundaries was the Schools War, a debate over state financing of church-run education. This conflict was precipitated when a Socialist–Liberal coalition government, succeeding a Social Christian government in 1954, began to reduce state subsidies to the church-run schools system. This time it was the Catholics, particularly in Flanders, where the church-run system was dominant, who organised public demonstrations. This disagreement was settled by the 1958 Schools Pact, which established criteria for the division of government expenditures on education and set up a commission to oversee the distribution of funds (Méan 1989).

In the short run, each of these quarrels strengthened the existing political parties, but they also showed the differences in political outlook in each part of the country. For Francophones, particularly those on the left, they raised the fear of being permanently outvoted by a conservative Flemish majority. For the Flemish, the issues demonstrated the ability of Francophones to overturn or threaten Flemish interests in spite of the Flemish majority in the country.

It was against the background of these divisions that mobilisation in favour of a new round of language laws began. The mobilisation itself was precipitated by the 1954 publication of the results of the 1947 language census and the prospect of the 1960 census. In 1954, the Flemish nationalist party, the Volksunie, made its first electoral appearance, and gained 3.9 per cent of the vote in Flanders. In 1956, the Vlaamse Volksbeweging was created to co-ordinate the efforts of the various Flemish organisations, and in 1958 the Vlaams Aktiecomite voor Brussel en de Taalgrens (Flemish Action Committee for Brussels and the Language Frontier) was established. In conjunction with the refusal of Flemish burgomasters to administer the bilingual census documents, the activities of this committee led to the suspension of the census and provided the impetus behind the drafting of the 1961–3 language laws (Curtis 1971).

THE EARLY WALLOON MOVEMENT

The Francophone/Walloon movements began later, and have been less organisationally rich than the Flemish movement. There are several reasons for this. First, the early activities of the Flemish movements were directed at winning concessions from the trans-ethnic Francophone elite of the country. Francophone opposition to these efforts took the form of resistance by the government and its agencies to the changes demanded. This state-based defence of the unitary organisation of the Belgian state continued to be a dominant strand of Francophone activity at least until the language laws of 1961–3. In the beginning, more specific defence of Walloon interests not only against Flemish interests but also against the centralised state was confused with this effort, and the confusion was even more so in the case of the defence of the interests of Brussels Francophones (Hasquin 1989; Jongen 1989).

The first organisational activity on the part of Walloons, as opposed to the folkloric defence of Walloon culture against homogenisation into a general Francophone Belgian culture, began with the activities of Walloon civil servants, particularly those stationed in Flanders. They were fearful that the proposed changes in language usage in Flanders would limit their career chances, as indeed they would. The first Walloon Congress, held in 1890, was held in Brussels, and Walloon organisations also existed in Flemish cities in this period.

The post-First World War language laws were resisted in the name of Francophones rather than Walloons, although Walloon insistence on unilingual rather than bilingual regions constituted a *de facto* support of the Flemish position, and demonstrated the complexity of the Francophone side of the situation. The real organised activity of the Walloon movement begins during the Second World War and in the post-war period, culminating with the Great Strike of the winter of 1961–2. Organised activity of Francophones in Brussels began only in 1964 in reaction to the marches on Brussels organised by VAK and to the passage of the language laws dealing with the status of the city.

During the Second World War, resistance networks based in Wallonia also debated the post-war shape to be given to the Belgian state. Many argued that a federal form of the state would be desirable, not just because of language divisions, but because they believed that the 'progressive' state they desired could not be achieved as long as Wallonia was tied to the more conservative Flemish region. In October 1945 a Walloon National Congress organised by the resistance movements, after passing a 'sentimental vote' in favour of union with France, passed a 'vote de raison' in favour of autonomy within the Belgian state.

It was, however, the Great Strike of 1960–1 that re-energised the movement, and broadened its base. The strike was organised in response to a financial austerity law put forth by the Social Christian/Liberal government of the day. The trade unions associated with the Socialist Party split along language lines, with the Walloon sections favouring the strike and the Flemish sections, in general, opposing it (the Brussels sections abstained). The strike was also opposed by the unions associated with the Social Christian Party, which were dominant in Flanders. As a result, the strike became a Walloon strike, with demands not only for economic change, but also for the reform of work and social organisation and for the reform of the Belgian state along federalist lines (Féaux 1963; Neuville and Yerna 1990; also see Quevit 1978, 1982).

After the failure of the strike, the leader, Renard, attempted to establish an organised Walloon movement, creating the Mouvement Populaire Wallon in March 1961. However, the Socialist Party leadership of the day treated the Walloon activities as intra-party dissidence, and declared membership in the MPW incompatible with membership in the party. As a result, the first movements to present candidates at elections were drawn from outside the party. Again, it was the language laws of 1961–3 that gave the Walloon parties their first important share of the vote, and radicalised Francophone opinion in the other parties.

THE BEGINNING OF THE MODERN PERIOD: THE LANGUAGE LAWS OF 1961-3

The language laws passed by the Belgian Parliament between 1961 and 1963 were, ironically, designed to contain the centrifugal forces created by the Flemish and Walloon movements and remove the conflict between Flemish and Francophone from Belgian political life. However, there were several characteristics of the content of these laws and the way in which they were passed that exacerbated relations between Francophone and Flemish and contributed to the current shape of the conflict.

The laws themselves left both sides dissatisfied and resentful of the compromises consented to. The laws left two major issues that were to poison Belgian political life for the next thirty years: the status of Brussels and the question of the Voeren/Fourons (both to be discussed below), and the fact that some of the provisions were passed by a legislature voting along language rather than party lines weakened the attachment of Francophones to the unitary state by demonstrating the consequences of their minority position.

The laws dealt with several issues. The first law fixed the language frontier permanently and eliminated the language census. This law can be considered to have created the problem of the Voeren/Fourons. These communes (since the 1977 fusion of the communes a single commune, Voer/Fouron) were located in the province of Liège, with a local dialect that was a mixture of Dutch and German. They had been administered as a bilingual area of the province, with some services in French and some in Dutch, and with educational services at the post-primary level largely in French (CRISP 1979).

The original government-proposed law transferred the territory to the Dutch-language region, but left it in the province of Liège, since the region was cut off from the nearest Dutch-speaking province, Limburg, by the Netherlands. However, in parliamentary commission, the Voeren/Fourons were transferred to Limburg, in return for a transfer of the communes of Commines-Mouscron, part of the French-speaking region, from the province of West Flanders to the province of Hainault.

Although the government originally opposed these transfers, in the end it was obliged to mobilise its parliamentary majority behind their passage, for fear that the whole set of laws would collapse. The transfers met with immediate resistance from much of the population of the Fourons, and, like the issue of the boundaries and internal political organisation of Brussels, left problems that were to sabotage many future negotiations and lead to the fall of more than one government (CRISP 1979; McRae 1986).

It was the provisions on Brussels, passed in 1963, that created the greatest conflict at this stage. The bilingual area of the capital was fixed at the existing nineteen communes, a long-time goal of the Flemish. Children were to be educated in the language of their parents, with an inspection mechanism to verify parental declarations. The internal administrations of the city's communes were to become bilingual, a measure that had obvious implications for hiring practices. All these measures aroused fierce resistance from Francophones. On the other hand, the maintenance of 'facilities' in French in six suburban communes of the capital represented a defeat for the Flemish and raised the possibility of further migration of Francophones into Flemish territory.

The other language laws left less in the way of subsequent problems. They dealt with language usage in the administration and established a Permanent Commission of Linguistic Control, and a post of vice-governor of the province of Brabant, each charged with overseeing the implementation of their provisions. They did arouse Francophone resistance as a sign of Flemish intentions to assert their majority status in the country (see Curtis 1971; Méan 1990).

MOVEMENT TO CONSTITUTIONAL REVISION

The conflict-generating results of the language laws were seen in the election of 1965. The Flemish nationalist party, the Volksunie, increased its vote to 11.6 per cent in Flanders, the new Walloon party, the Rassemblement Wallon, gained 3.3 per cent of the vote in Wallonia, while the Front Democratique Francophone, formed in reaction to the language laws, gained 10 per cent of the Brussels vote. These 'community parties' as they were known, continued to increase their vote. The Volksunie vote reached a high of 18.8 per cent of the vote in Flanders in 1971, the

Rassemblement Wallon reached a high of 21.2 per cent of the regional vote, also in 1971, and the FDF had a high of 39.6 per cent of the Brussels vote in 1974 (Mughan 1983).

The established parties of the system were thus under pressure from two directions. The electoral gains of the community parties threatened their electoral base and claims to government participation. To meet this threat, the members of the language wings of each of the traditional parties were under pressure to adopt some of the positions of the community parties. This created strains along the language divide in each of the parties. On the other hand, the leadership of the parties was also threatened from within, by a younger generation of politicians who were more attracted to the federalist idea than the older generation, and less inclined to accept the compromises necessary to keep the parties together as national institutions (Covell 1981). The result of these pressures was seen in the Louvain/Leuven crisis of 1968.

This crisis centred on the fate of the French section of the Catholic University of Leuven, located in the Dutch-speaking region of Belgium. With Brussels, this section and its attendant population was seen by the Flemish as another pole of 'Francisation' in Flanders, and the proximity of Leuven to the capital fed Flemish fears of a linkage between the two areas. The dispute over the fate of the French section of the university split the Social Christian Party (most of whose members were, of course, graduates of the university). The two language wings of the party first 'distanced' themselves from each other, and then split definitively. The French section was eventually moved to Wallonia, again over the protests of Francophone politicians.

The splitting of the Social Christian Party was followed over the next ten years by the division of the other major parties. The Liberals split in 1971, largely as a result of disputes over Brussels, where they were losing votes to the FDF, and the Socialists split in 1978 as a result of the collapse of the Egmont Pact. This division of Belgium's national parties has, as we shall see, played a part in the entrenchment of the dispute between Francophone and Flemish in the operations of the political system. The immediate result of the Louvain crisis, however, was to give the final impetus to a project of constitutional revision that had been under discussion at least since 1963.

CONSTITUTIONAL REVISION

The constitutional revision of 1970 opened a period in Belgian politics in which the form of the state was under constant question, and the topic of dividing the state a perennial subject of political debate, usually dominating politics to the exclusion of other questions. It was succeeded by two other revisions, in 1980–1 and 1988. Debates over the degree of decentralisation to be undertaken, and specific topics like the future of Brussels, were kept continually under discussion. Disagreements between Francophone and Flemish were further exacerbated since the opponents of decentralisation did not hesitate to use these issues to abort discussions that looked as if they might lead to a successful decentralisation, as happened, for example, with the 1977 Egmont Pact.

There are several reasons both for the delays in revising the constitution and for the persistence of the issue. The first reason for delay was a basic disagreement on whether or not the proposed decentralisation was desirable. Unitarists, who were found in both the Flemish and Francophone camps, came from several groups. Among the Flemish, there were those who argued that dividing the power of the Belgian state constituted an act that threw away decades of effort to assert the Flemish position as a majority in that state.

Political minorities in both language groups feared the consequences of trading a more equal balance of power at the national level for an unequal one at the regional level. Thus Francophone Social Christians, Flemish Socialists and Liberals from both language groups could be found opposing decentralisation projects. Politicians for whom economic issues were paramount also opposed decentralisation both on the grounds of inefficiency and on the grounds that it was folly to change from the well-known and respected 'brand name' of Belgium to the lesser-known names of 'Flanders' and 'Wallonia'. Taken together, these groups were strong enough to delay the process of decentralisation, and dilute the steps that were taken.

Another reason for the slowness of constitutional reform lay in a disagreement between Flemish and Francophone about the subject areas in which decentralisation should take place, and the units to which powers should be devolved. The Flemish desire for decentralisation came from their felt need to defend and strengthen the Dutch language. Therefore, they were interested in gaining autonomous powers in this area, and wanted those powers given to the two language communities.

In the early period, Francophones were largely interested in protecting themselves against the consequences of their minority position at the *national* level. They were not really interested in the devolution of language authority, although some, particularly in the Socialist Party, were interested in gaining powers in economic matters. Also, they wanted powers handed down to three 'regions': Flanders, Wallonia and Brussels. The Flemish were particularly opposed to granting Brussels the status of a third region on a par with the other two, since this would free the Francophone majority of the capital from central control, and would set up a balance of power in which two Francophone regions confronted one Flemish region.

As a result of these differences of opinion, and as a result of the continuing strength of unitarist forces, each constitutional revision was incomplete, leaving unfinished business to be pursued in subsequent negotiations. Moreover, until the 1988 negotiations, no solution was found for the problems of Brussels that would be acceptable to attentive publics, leaving this issue as a centre of the debates.

1970

The 1970 constitutional revision was the result of a long process of negotiations that had begun as early as the creation of the Harmel Centre in 1948. More specific negotiations had begun in 1963, and an all-party round table in 1968 had developed many of the specific proposals. The revisions dealing with the decentralisation of power settled the dispute between Flemish and Francophone over the number and type of units to receive the new powers by not settling it. Powers in language and cultural matters were to be devolved to the two language communities, while a corresponding set of articles provided for the devolution of powers in economic matters to the three regions. A lack of specificity in the economic powers to be handed over reflected a lack of agreement about the degree of decentralisation that was desirable, while a lack of specificity about the boundaries of the regions reflected a lack of agreement on Brussels.

At the national level, the Francophones received some of the guarantees they were seeking for protection against their minority status. A requirement that the cabinet include equal numbers of Francophone and Dutch-speaking ministers, with the possible exception of the prime minister, was entrenched in the constitution, as were requirements for special majorities in parliamentary votes on language and cultural matters. In addition, an 'alarm bell' procedure, which allowed a language group of parliamentarians that considered their interests to be endangered by proposed legislation to block, at least temporarily, that legislation, was established (Dunn 1974; Heisler 1974; Zolberg 1977).

THE EGMONT PACT

This pact was negotiated in May 1977 as part of the negotiations for the formation of a government following the elections of that year. It represented the first major agreement on institutional reform since the 1970 constitutional revisions, and the negotiations were notable in that they involved not only two 'traditional' parties, the Socialists and the Social Christians, but also included two 'community' parties, the Volksunie and the FDF (the RW had participated in a government from 1974 to the party's breakup in 1977, but this participation had not involved global negotiations for institutional reform).

The pact proposed a further devolution of powers to both communities and regions, and a solution to the problem of Brussels. The proposals for further devolution created opposition from unitarists, but it was the proposals on Brussels that created the most dramatic opposition and that, in the end, were the immediate cause of the collapse of the pact.

The proposals for devolution included a list of economic powers to be handed over to the regions, but the most innovative part was the creation of a category known as 'personnalisable matters'. These were defined as matters in which language formed an important part of the delivery of government services and included areas such as health care and many social services. These were to be handed over to the communities, as a counterpart for the increased powers to be handed over to the regions (Brassinne 1980).

The provisions on Brussels were complicated. The Francophones agreed to a permanent limit on the boundaries of the city, in return for an entrenchment of the facilities in the suburbs and their extension to other Flemish suburbs through a right of 'fictive residence' in a bilingual commune for Francophones residing in unilingual Flemish communes.

It was these provisions that aroused the opposition of the Flemish movement. An Anti-Egmont Committee was formed, and pressure was put on the Volksunie and, more crucially, on the Flemish Social Christians. In the end, this pressure led to the threat of revolts against the proposed legislation and to the fall of the government that was to put through this legislation.

1980

The collapse of the Egmont Pact led to an extended period of government instability as successive cabinets attempted to draft and pass the legislation necessary to incorporate the desired reforms. It was not until 1980, and at the cost of abandoning attempts to resolve the question of Brussels, that a further constitutional revision was completed.

This revision extended the economic powers of the regions and established their institutions. It also incorporated the 'personnalisable matters' in the powers of the communities. Independent executives for each of these units were gradually established, although their councils remained composed of members of the national parliament.

Dispute-settling mechanisms were also created. These included a Court of Arbitration to rule on disputes between the different levels of government, and a 'Concertation Committee' composed of members of the executives of the different units.

1988 REVISIONS

The revisions of 1988 were developed during the governmental negotiations that followed the collapse of the Social Christian/Liberal coalition over the status of Francophone officials in communes in the Dutch region, crystallised by the case of Jose Happart, burgomaster of the Voeren/Fourons (Mabille 1987). The revisions, the result of negotiations between Socialists and Social Christians from both sides of the language border, and the Volksunie, led to a transfer of powers and resources representing about 40 per cent of the national budget, and settled several outstanding questions (Delmartino 1988; Hooghe 1991; Sennelle 1989; for an account of the negotiations that led to the revisions, see De Ridder 1989).

Control over education was handed over to the communities, and the powers of the regions over economic matters were strengthened, moving to a system of the transfer of whole competences rather than the system of mixed authority that had characterised the 1980 revisions. In particular, the regions acquired control over areas of energy policy not included in the transfers of 1980, over employment policy and over infrastructure.

These transfers, particularly the transfer of education to the communities, had been resisted by the SP and the PSC. To reassure them, the principles of the Schools Pact were entrenched in the constitution, and the Court of Arbitration was given new powers to hear appeals against discrimination brought by individuals.

The financing of the new system had also been a source of controversy. The Flemish had insisted that each new unit finance its activities from its own resources, while Francophones had put forth the principle of national solidarity. The final agreement gave different financial bases to the communities and regions, and represents a compromise between the Flemish and Francophone points of view (Installé et al. 1989).

The communities still rely largely on grants from the central government and have limited ability to raise funds on their own. The regions are financed by returns from the income tax, and can add 'additional centimes' to the taxes. During a transitional period, to last until 1999, a grant from the central government, partially based on expenditure rather than tax returns, is also part of the revenue of the regions. The principle of 'reversible solidarity' allows for continued transfers of additional revenue to any region whose resources are less than the national average. At the moment, of course, this region is Wallonia (De Ridder 1989; Installé et al. 1989).

BRUSSELS

The 1988 agreements also attempted to achieve a permanent resolution of the issues connected with the status of Brussels and its suburbs. The Francophones accepted the entrenchment of the

official territory of the capital as the existing nineteen communes. In return, the Flemish accepted the entrenchment in
legislation that can only be overturned by a special majority in
each language group of the facilities in French in the six
peripheral communes in which the regime existed.

Brussels also *finally* received its regional institutions and
powers. Ironically, it is now the only region with a directly
elected council. The minority group in the council, for the
foreseeable future the Dutch-speakers, is guaranteed parity on the
five-member executive, with the exception of the president.
However, the national government still keeps a measure of
control over the activities of the region, since the Senate can, by a
double majority in each language group, overturn its legislation
in the areas of urban planning, transportation and public works.
How practicable this provision is remains to be seen (Loumaye
1989).

THE VOEREN/FOURONS

The question of the language knowledge to be required of
municipal officials had implications both for the peripheral
communes of Brussels and for the Voeren/Fourons. The legislation is complicated, and represents a compromise by which the
Francophones agreed to provisions that essentially barred
Happart from the possibility of holding office as the mayor of the
commune in return for flexibility on the question in general.
The legislation states that elected municipal officials such as
councillors will benefit from an 'irrefutable' presumption of
knowledge of the language of the region in which they are
elected. The exception to this is that burgomasters and presidents
of municipal social assistance centres can be removed if they do
not know the language of the region. The exception to this is
officials who held office from 1983-9, a condition that Happart
did not meet, but that several other office-holders from the
Brussels periphery did.

The compromise also contained provisions that allowed voters
in Voer/Fouron to vote in Liège province and voters in Com-
mines to vote in West Flanders in national and European
elections. The acceptance of these compromises, with their
'abandonment' of Happart, caused major disputes in the PSC
and especially in the PS, but the leadership of the parties was able

to contain the revolts, and in the PS even strengthen its position through demotions of the rebels (De Ridder 1989).

CONCLUSIONS

The 1988 agreements appeared to have settled several of the major issues of dispute between Flemish and Francophone. In the summer of 1989, the Brussels regional council was installed amid general expressions of satisfaction, and relations between the two communities appeared to be as calm as they had been in a generation. By the autumn of 1991, however, relations between Flemish and Francophone ministers were tense, and in October the government collapsed after a dispute over shipments of Walloon arms to the Middle East, a dispute that one observer characterised as the most vicious he had ever seen. Can it be concluded from this that the dispute between Francophone and Flemish in Belgium is beyond institutional resolution?

Before answering the question, it is necessary to limit statements about how serious the dispute is. First, it is incorrect to label the dispute as one between 'Flemish' and 'Francophone' in the sense that ordinary citizens from each language group are antagonised towards each other, or can even be readily mobilised on the issue. The dispute has been fought out in its most recent form almost entirely between elected and non-elected party officials, with some interventions from the media and from interest-group leaders.

The Volksunie did lose votes in the election that followed the 1991 collapse of the government, a loss that it interpreted as a consequence of the compromises it had made in 1988 and in government. However, all governing parties lost votes, and these votes went, not to new parties taking a harder line on community issues, but to what might loosely be termed anti-system parties of the left and right: the ecological parties and the anti-immigrant parties.

The question, then, is why has the question of Flemish–Francophone relations come to dominate politics at the national and official levels, and to have such a paralysing effect on the institutions of central government? Several reasons, some institutional and some political, can be suggested for this situation.

One major reason lies in the effects of previous disputes and their resolutions. By now, almost every major institution in Belgian society is either split into Flemish and Francophone versions or consists of a loose confederation of the two groups. This is true, most obviously, of the political parties, but it is also true of interest groups like trade unions and employers' associations. Most government departments are divided into Dutch-speaking and French-speaking sections (McRae 1986).

As a result, there is no pressure, and no arena, for arranging compromises except in the central institutions of government, and particularly in the cabinet. In the cabinet itself, the ministers sit, in part and 'with the possible exception of the prime minister', as representatives of their language group and are judged by their ability to defend the interests of their group and region. Small wonder, then, that the system works only by the use of non-routine negotiations and outside mediators.

This division of the system is reinforced by the fact that the communities and regions still do not have their own legislatures. Members of the national parliament are still also the legislators for their community and region and have to switch identities according to the day of the week. Again, this hardly contributes to the development of elites with a commitment to the development and defence of a national point of view.

Another reason for the continuance of conflict lies in the nature of the current political leadership of Belgium. Most of the current leaders of parties and other groups came to power in the atmosphere of, and often on the basis of, continuing quarrels between Flemish and Francophone. Van Den Bulck (1992) suggests that politicians acquire 'normal' conflict responses. It is probable that the viewpoints acquired over thirty years of political practice lead both Flemish and Francophone politicians to see most issues through 'community' eyes.

Finally, the evolution of the party system itself is also at the root of the continuing importance of the community dispute. With the loosening of the 'pillars' of Belgian society, and the declining importance of the basis of the parties, little remains to unify several of the parties in the system except their language basis. The decline of heavy industry has weakened the Socialist parties, and increasing secularisation has diminished the philosophical basis of the Social Christians. Casting conflicts with other bases in terms of a Flemish–Francophone confrontation reinforces the unity of the parties.

There are, however, factors that diminish the inevitability of confrontation. The first is the combined shifting of the powers of the Belgian state to the communities and regions and to the institutions of the European Community. As the powers of the state decrease, so does the importance of control over its policies. It is entirely possible that a new constitutional revision will shift further powers to the communities and regions, while the Treaty of Maastricht, if ratified, will shift major areas of policy to the European Community.

Second, and related, is a generational shift in attitudes. There are signs that for a younger generation 'Flanders', 'Wallonia' and 'Brussels' no longer have the emotional resonance they had for their elders. Other issues, including the economy, the environment, and the presence of immigrants from other countries, seem to have gained greater importance.

In other words, the variability of ethnic conflict also includes variability of intensity. In Belgium, this intensity has been high but it has also declined, and there are signs of the possibility of a new decline.

NOTE

1 There is an extensive literature on ethnic relations in Belgium. In general, I have tried to restrict my references to works in English and, to a lesser extent, French, although the literature in Dutch is also large and important. More complete bibliographies can be found in Hermans (1992), Hooghe (1991), McRae (1986), Murphy (1988), and Verdoodt (1983).

Bibliography

Abas, T. S. (1989) *May Day for Justice* (with K. Das), Kuala Lumpur: Magnus Books.

Adam, H. (1971) *Modernizing Racial Domination*, Berkeley: University of California Press.

Adam, H. and Moodley, K. (1986) *South Africa without Apartheid*, Berkeley: University of California Press.

Adams, G. (1986) *The Politics of Freedom*, Dingle: Brandon.

Addruse, R. A. (1990) *Conduct Unbecoming*, Kuala Lumpur: Walrus.

Akbar, M. T. (1985) *India: The Siege Within*, London: Penguin.

Ålands landsting (1988) *Åland in Brief*, Marie-Hamn: Ålands landskapysstrelse.

Alcock, A. (1970) *The History of the South Tyrol Question*, London: Michael Joseph.

Ali, A. (1973) 'The Indians of Fiji', *Economics and Political Weekly*, vol. 8, no. 36.

Amnesty International (1978) *Report of an Amnesty International Mission to Northern Ireland*, London: Amnesty International.

Anderson, B. (1983) *Imagined Communities: Reflections on the Origin and Spread of Nationalism*, London: Verso.

Andrejevich, M. (1991) 'The future of Bosnia-Hercegovina: a sovereign republic or cantonization', *Report on Eastern Europe*, RFE/RL Institute, vol. 2, no. 27 (5 July), 28–34.

Anon (1962) 'Cane farmers: Fiji's unrewarded peasants', *Unispac*, vol. 7, no. 5, 1–2.

Anon (1977) 'NLTB facts and figures', *Vanua* (NLTB journal), p. 1.

Arthur, P. (1990) 'Negotiating the Northern Ireland problem: track one or track two diplomacy?', *Government and Opposition*, vol. 25, no. 4.

Asmal, K. (1991) 'Constitutional issues for a free South Africa', *Transformation*, no. 13, Durban: University of Natal.

Aunger, E. A. (1975) 'Religion and occupational class in Northern Ireland', *Economic and Social Review*, vol. 7, no. 1.

Bahcheli, T. (1990) *Greek–Turkish Relations since 1955*, Boulder and London: Westview.

Baiges, F., Gonzalez, E. and Reixach, J. (1985) *Banca Catalana. Más que un banco, más que una crisis*, Barcelona: Plaza y Janes.

Banac, I. (1984) *The National Question in Yugoslavia: Origins, History, Politics*, Ithaca: Cornell University Press.

Barrier, N. G. and Dusenbery, V. A. (eds) (1989) *The Sikh Diaspora*, Delhi: Chanakya Publications.

Barry, B. (1991a) 'Political accommodation and consociational democracy', in *Democracy and Power: Essays in Political Theory 1*, Oxford: Oxford University Press, pp. 100–35.

—— (1991b) 'The consociational model and its dangers', in *Democracy and Power: Essays in Political Theory 1*, Oxford: Oxford University Press, pp. 136–55.

—— (1991c) 'Self-government revisited', in *Democracy and Power: Essays in Political Theory 1*, Oxford: Oxford University Press, pp. 165–86.

Beaufays, J. (1988) 'Belgium: a dualist political system?', *Publius*, vol. 18, no. 2.

Beran, H. (1984) 'A liberal theory of secession', *Political Studies*, vol. 32, no. 1.

—— (1987) *The Consent Theory of Political Obligation*, London: Croom Helm.

—— (1988) 'More theory of secession: reply to Birch', *Political Studies*, vol. 36, 316–23.

Beresford, D. (1987) *Ten Men Dead: The Story of the 1981 Irish Hunger Strike*, London: Grafton.

Bew, P. and Patterson, H. (1985) *The British State and the Ulster Crisis: From Wilson to Thatcher*, London: Verso.

Bew, P., Gibbon, P. and Patterson, H. (1979) *The State in Northern Ireland, 1921–1972: Political Forces and Social Classes*, Manchester: Manchester University Press.

Bhullar, J. S. *et al.* (1985) *The Betrayal of Sikhs*, Birmingham: ISYF.

Bicanic, R. (1935 [1981]) *How People Live: Life in the Passive Regions*, J. Halpern and E. Murray Despalatovic (eds), Research Report no. 21, Amherst MA: University of Massachusetts.

Bishop, P. and Mallie, E. (1987) *The Provisional IRA*, London: Heinemann.

Bolt, M. and Long, J. A. (1984) 'Tribal traditions and European-Western political ideologies: The dilemma of Canada's native Indian', *Canadian Journal of Political Science*, vol. 17, 537–53.

Botte, R. (1982) 'La guerre interne au Burundi', in J. Bazin and E. Terray (eds) *Guerres de lignages et guerres d'état en Afrique*, Paris: Editions des Archives Contemporaines.

Bowie, A. (1991) *Crossing the Industrial Divide*, New York: Columbia University Press.

Boyle, K. and Hadden, T. (1985) *Ireland: A Positive Proposal*, London: Penguin.

Brass, P. R. (1974) *Language, Religion and Politics in North India*, Cambridge: Cambridge University Press.

—— (1987) 'The Punjab crisis and the unity of India', in A. Kholi (ed.) *India's Democracy*, Princeton: Princeton University Press.

Brassinne, J. (1980) 'Les matières "culturelles" + les matières "personnalisables" = les matières communautaires?', CRISP, *Courrier Hebdomadaire*, no. 889.

Brassinne, J. and Kreins, Y. (1984) 'La réforme de l'état et la communauté germanophone', CRISP, *Courrier Hebdomadaire*, nos. 1028–9.

Breuilly, J. (1985) *Nationalism and the State*, 2nd edn, Manchester: Manchester University Press.

Bruce, S. (1986) *God Save Ulster! The Religion and Politics of Paisleyism*, Oxford: Clarendon.

Buchanan, A. (1991) *Secession: The Morality of Political Divorce from Fort Sumter to Lithuania and Quebec*, Oxford: Westview Press.

Buckland, P. (1981) *A History of Northern Ireland*, Dublin: Gill and Macmillan.

Burg, S. L. (1983) *Conflict and Cohesion in Socialist Yugoslavia: Political Decision-Making since 1966*, Princeton NJ: Princeton University Press.

Cairns, A. C. (1991) *Disruptions: Constitutional Struggles from the Charter to Meech Lake*, Toronto: McClelland & Stewart.

Canning, D., Moore, B. and Rhodes, J. (1987) 'Economic growth in Northern Ireland: problems and prospects', in P. Teague (ed.) *Beyond the Rhetoric: Politics, the Economy and Social Policy in Northern Ireland*, London: Lawrence & Wishart.

Cannon, G. E. (1982) 'Consociationalism vs. control: Canada as a case study', *Western Political Quarterly*, vol. 35, 50–64.

Capron, M. (1989) 'Cockerill Sambre, de la fusion à la "privatisation" ', CRISP, *Courrier Hebdomadaire*, nos 1253–4.

Centre de recherche et d'information socio-politiques (CRISP) (1979) *Courrier Hebdomadaire*, no. 859: 'Le problème des Fourons de 1962 à nos jours'.

—— (1988) *Courrier Hebdomadaire*, no. 1207: 'La révision de la constitution, juillet, 1988'.

Chalk, F. and Jonassohn, K. (1990) *The History and Sociology of Genocide: Analyses and Case Studies*, New Haven: Yale University Press.

Chretien, J. P., Guichaoua, A. and Le Jeune, G. (1989) *La crise d'août 1988 au Burundi*, Cahiers du Centre de Recherches Africaines, no. 6, Paris: Editions Karthala.

Claeys, P. H. (1980) 'Political pluralism and linguistic cleavage: the Belgian case', in S. Ehrlich and G. Wootton (eds) *Three Faces of Pluralism: Political, Ethnic and Religious*, Westmead: Gower.

Clavero, B. (1981) 'Los Fueros en la España contemporanea: de la reacción anti-liberal al federalismo vergonzante', *Revista de Estudios Políticos*, 20.

Clough, S. (1930) *A History of the Flemish Movement in Belgium: A Study in Nationalism*, New York: R. H. Smith.

Clutterbuck, R. (1981) 'Comments on Chapter 7', in D. Watt (ed.) *The*

Constitution of Northern Ireland: Problems and Prospects, London: Heinemann.

Cohen, S. P. (1991) 'Conflict resolution: principles in practice', Paper presented at the Institute for the Study and Resolution of Conflict, University of Port Elizabeth, 29 July.

Connor, W. (1972) 'Nation-building or nation-destroying?' *World Politics*, vol. 24, no. 3.

—— (1973) 'The politics of ethno-nationalism', *Journal of International Affairs*, vol. 27, no. 1, 1–21.

Constitution of the Republic of Fiji (1990) Suva: Government Printers.

Cook, R. (1966) *Canada and the French-Canadian Question*, Toronto: Macmillan.

Covell, M. (1981) 'Ethnic conflict and elite bargaining: the case of Belgium', *West European Politics*, vol. 4, no. 3.

—— (1985) 'Ethnic conflict, representation, and the state in Belgium', in P. Brass (ed.) *Ethnic Groups and the State*, London: Croom Helm.

—— (1986) 'Regionalization and economic crisis in Belgium: the variable origins of centrifugal and centripetal forces', *Canadian Journal of Political Science*, vol. 19, no. 2.

—— (1987) 'Federalization and federalism: Belgium and Canada', in H. Bakvis and W. Chandler (eds) *Federalism and the Role of the State*, Toronto: University of Toronto Press.

Craig, G. M. (ed.) (1963) *Lord Durham's Report*, Toronto: McClelland & Stewart.

Cros, M. F. (1991) 'Le Burundi en proie a la destabilisation', *La Libre Belgique*, 27 November.

Curtis, A. (1971) 'New perspectives on the history of the language problem in Belgium', unpublished PhD thesis, University of Oregon.

Cviic, C. (1991) *Remaking the Balkans*. London: Pinter for Royal Institute of International Affairs.

Daalder, H. (1974) 'The consociational democracy theme', *World Politics*, vol. 26, no. 4.

Darby, J. (1976) *Conflict in Northern Ireland: The Development of a Polarised Community*, Dublin: Gill and Macmillan.

—— (ed.) (1983) *Northern Ireland: Background to the Conflict*, Belfast: Appletree.

Darby, J., Dodge, N. and Hepburn, A. C. (eds) (1990) *Political Violence: Ireland in a Comparative Perspective*, Ottawa: Appletree.

Delmartino, F. (1988) 'Regionalisation in Belgium: evaluation of an ongoing crisis', *European Journal of Political Research*, vol. 16, no. 4.

De Ridder, H. (1989) *Sire, donnez-moi cent jours*, Louvain-la-Neuve: Duclot.

Djilas, A. (1991) *The Contested Country: Yugoslav Unity and the Communist Revolution 1919–1953*, Cambridge, MA: Harvard University Press.

Djilas, M. (1977) *Wartime*, London: Secker & Warburg.

Dragnitch, A. (1983) *The First Yugoslavia: Search for a Viable Political System*, Stanford: Hoover Institution Press.

Dunn, J. A. (1974) 'The revision of the constitution in Belgium: a study in the institutionalization of ethnic conflict', *Western Political Quarterly*, vol. 27, no. 1.

du Toit, P. and Esterhuyse, W. (eds) (1990) *The Mythmakers: The Elusive Bargain for South Africa's Future*, Johannesburg: Southern Books.

Erasmus, G. (1989) 'Twenty years of disappointed hopes', in B. Richardson (ed.) *Drumbeat: Anger and Renewal in Indian Country*, Toronto: Summerhill Press.

Esman, M. J. (ed.) (1977a) *Ethnic Conflict in the Western World*, Ithaca: Cornell University Press.

—— (1977b) 'Perspectives on ethnic conflict in industrial societies', in M. J. Esman (ed.) *Ethnic Conflict in the Western World*, Ithaca: Cornell University Press.

—— (1987) 'Ethnic politics and economic power', *Comparative Politics*, vol. 19, no. 4.

—— (1991) 'Book review', *Journal of Asian Studies*, vol. 50, no. 5, 735.

Esteban, J. de (1982) *Las Constituciones de España*, Madrid: Taurus.

Faaland, J. *et al.* (1990) *Growth and Ethnic Inequality*, Kuala Lumpur: Dewan Bahasa Dan Pustaka.

Farrell, M. (1976) *Northern Ireland: The Orange State*, London: Pluto.

Féaux, V. (1963) *Cinq semaines de lutte sociale: la grève de l'hiver 1960–61*, Brussels: Institut de Sociologie de l'Université Libre de Bruxelles.

Fisk, R. (1975) *The Point of No Return: The Strike which Broke the British in Ulster*, London: Deutsch.

Fitzmaurice, J. (1983) *The Politics of Belgium: Crisis and Compromise in a Plural Society*, London: C. Hurst.

Flackes, W. D. and Elliott, S. (1989) *Northern Ireland: A Political Directory 1968–88*, Belfast: Blackstaff.

Foster, R. F. (1988) *Modern Ireland 1600–1972*, London: Penguin.

Franolic, B. (1984) *An Historical Survey of Literary Croatian*, Paris: Nouvelles Editions Latines.

Fraser, M. (1973) *Children in Conflict*, London: Secker & Warburg.

Fraser, T. G. (1984) *Partition in Ireland, India and Palestine: Theory and Practice*, London: Macmillan.

Furnivall, J. S. (1948) *Colonial Policy and Practice*, Cambridge: Cambridge University Press.

Gahama, J. (1983) *Le Burundi sous administration Belge*, Paris: Editions Karthala.

GEC (1976) *Gran Enciclopedia Catalana*, Barcelona.

Gellner, E. (1983) *Nations and Nationalism*, Oxford: Basil Blackwell.

—— (1990) 'The *dramatis personae* of history', *East European Politics and Societies*, vol. 4, no. 1, 116–33.

Gibson, G. (1992) 'Self-government: isolating aboriginal people from the mainstream is a mistake', *Globe and Mail (Toronto)*, 1 June.

Giliomee, H. (1991) 'The leader and the citizenry', unpublished manuscript.

Gillion, K. L. (1962) *Fiji's Indian Migrants*, Melbourne: Oxford University Press.

Gispert, G. and Prats, J. (1978) *España: un estado plurinacional*, Barcelona: Blume.

Glazer, N. (1987) *Affirmative Discrimination: Ethnic Inequality and Public Policy*, Cambridge, MA: Harvard University Press.

Golubovic, Z. and Stojanovic, S. (1986) *The Crisis of the Yugoslav System*, no. 14 in the series 'Crises in Soviet-type systems', Cologne: Index e.V.

Gonzalez Pérez, G. (1980) 'Galzia: Lingua, Territoria e Migracións', in Centre Internacional per a les minories etniques i nacionals, *Nactionalia V. Quartes Jornadadas de Ciemen, Abadia de Cuisca, 16–23 d'agost 1979*, Publicacions de l'Abadia de Montserrat.

Government of India (1984) *White Paper on the Punjab Agitation*, New Delhi.

Government of Malaysia (1971) *Second Malaysia Plan 1971–1975*, Kuala Lumpur: Government Press.

—— (1973) *Mid-Term Review of the Second Malaysia Plan 1971–1975*, Kuala Lumpur: Government Press.

—— (1991a) *Sixth Malaysia Plan 1991–1995*, Kuala Lumpur: National Printing Department.

—— (1991b) *The Second Outline Perspective Plan 1991–2000*, Kuala Lumpur: National Printing Department.

Gow, J. (1991) *Legitimacy and the Military: The Yugoslav Crisis*, London: Pinter.

Granja, J. L. (1981) 'Autonomías regionales y fuerzas políticas en las Cortes constituyentes de 1931', *Sistema*, 40.

Guelke, A. (1986) 'Loyalist and republican perceptions of the Northern Ireland conflict: the UDA and the Provisional IRA', in P. Merkl (ed.) *Political Violence and Terror: Motifs and Motivations*, Berkeley: University of California Press.

Gurritxaga, A. (1988) 'Procucción de la Comunidad y Realidad Nacional', *Revista Internacional de Sociología*, vol. 46, no. 2, 263–87.

Hagen, S. (1978) 'Race, politics, and the coup in Fiji', *Bulletin of Concerned Asian Scholars*, vol. 19, no. 4.

Hailey, J. M. (1985) *Indigenous Business in Fiji*, Honolulu: East–West Centre.

Hanf, T. (1990) *Koexistenz im Krieg: Staatszerfall und Entstehung einer Nation im Libanon*, Munich: Nomos Verlag.

Hannum, H. (1990) *Autonomy, Sovereignty, and Self-Determination: The Accommodation of Conflicting Rights*, Pennsylvania: University of Pennsylvania Press.

Harff, B. (1992) 'Recognising genocides and politicides', in H. Fein (ed.) *Genocide Watch*, New Haven: Yale University Press, pp. 27–41.

Hartwig, F. (1979) *Exploratory Data Analysis* (with B. E. Dearing), Beverly Hills: Sage.

Hasquin, H. (1989) 'Les Wallons, la Belgique, et Bruxelles. Une histoire de frustrations', in M. Uyttendaele (ed.) *A l'enseigne de la Belgique nouvelle*, Brussels: Editions de l'Université Libre de Bruxelles.

Heisler, M. (ed.) (1974) 'Institutionalizing societal cleavages in a cooptive polity: the growing importance of the output side in

Belgium', in *Politics in Europe: Structures and Processes in some Postindustrial Democracies*, New York: McKay.

Hermans, T. (1992) *The Flemish Movement: A Documentary History*, London, Athlone Press.

Hernández, F. and Mercadé, F. (eds) (1986) 'Estructura social de Cataluña', in *Estructuras Sociales y Cuestión Nacional en España*, Barcelona: Ariel.

Hernández Lafuente, A. (1980) *Autonomía e Integración en la Segunda República*, Madrid: Encuentros.

Hickey, J. (1984) *Religion and the Northern Ireland Problem*, Dublin: Gill and Macmillan.

Hoffman, M. (1992) 'Third party mediation and conflict resolution in the post-cold war world', in J. Baylis and N. Rengger (eds) *Dilemmas in World Politics*, Oxford: Oxford University Press.

Hogan, G. and Walker, C. (1989) *Political Violence and the Law in Ireland*, Manchester: Manchester University Press.

Hooghe, L. (1991) *A Leap in the Dark: Nationalist Conflict and Federal Reform in Belgium*, Ithaca: Cornell University Western Studies Program, Occasional Paper no. 27.

Horowitz, D. (1985) *Ethnic Groups in Conflict*, Berkeley and Los Angeles: University of California Press.

—— (1989) 'Cause and consequence in public policy theory: ethnic policy and system transformation in Malaysia', *Policy Sciences*, vol. 22, nos 2-3.

—— (1991) *A Democratic South Africa? Constitutional Engineering in a Divided Society*, Berkeley and Los Angeles: University of California Press.

Howard, M. (1987) 'Is there still hope for Fiji?', *Australian Left Review*.

Huntington, S. (1968) *Political Order in Changing Societies*, New Haven: Yale University Press.

—— (1972) 'Foreword' to E.A. Nordlinger *Conflict Regulation in Divided Societies*, Cambridge, MA: Harvard University Centre for International Affairs.

Huyse, L. (1983) 'Pillarization reconsidered', *Acta Politica*, vol. 19, no. 1.

Installé, M., Peffer, M. and Savage, R. (1989) 'Le financement des communautés et des regions', CRISP, *Courrier Hebdomadaire*, nos 1240-1.

Irish Information Partnership (IIP) (1989) *Agenda Database*, London: IIP.

Jeffrey, R. (1986) *What's Happening to India?*, London: Macmillan.

Jenkins, R. (1986) 'Northern Ireland: in what sense "religions" in conflict?', in R. Jenkins, H. Donnan and G. McFarland (eds) *The Sectarian Divide in Northern Ireland Today*, Royal Anthropological Institute of Great Britain and Ireland, Occasional Paper no. 41, London: Royal Anthropological Institute of Great Britain and Ireland.

Jennings, I. (1956) *The Approach to Self-Government*, Cambridge: Cambridge University Press.

Jesudason, J. V. (1989) *Ethnicity and the Economy*, Singapore: Oxford University Press.

Jiménez Blanco, J., García Ferrando, M., López Aranguren, E. and Beltrán Villalva, M. (1977) *La Conciencia Regional en España*, Madrid: Centro de Intestigaciones Sociológicas.

Jonassohn, K. (1992) 'What is genocide?', in H. Fein (ed.) *Genocide Watch*, New Haven: Yale University Press, pp. 17–26.

Jongen, F. (1989) 'Communauté française et region wallone. Wallonie – Bruxelles même combat?' in M. Uttendaele (ed.), *A l'enseigne de la Belgique nouvelle*, Brussels: Editions de l'Université de Bruxelles: 95–103.

Kasfir, N. (1979) 'Explaining ethnic political participation', *World Politics*, vol. 30, no. 1.

Keating, M. (1988) *State and Regional Nationalism. Territorial Politics and the European State*, Brighton: Harvester-Wheatsheaf.

—— (1991) 'Do the workers really have no country? Socialism, regionalism and peripheral nationalism in Britain, France, Spain and Italy', in J. Coakley (ed.) *The Social Origins of Nationalist Movements*, London: Sage.

Khoshla, G. D. (1950) *Stern Reckoning: A Survey of Events Leading up to and Following the Partition of India*, New Delhi: Bhawnani.

Kuper, L. (1981) *Genocide: Its Political Use in the Twentieth Century*, New Haven: Yale University Press.

Kymlicka, W. (1991) *Liberalism, Community and Culture*, Oxford: Oxford University Press.

Kyriakides, S. (1968) *Cyprus: Constitutionalism and Crisis Government*, Philadelphia: University of Pennsylvania Press.

Lal, B. (1986) 'Fiji: politics since independence', in B. Lal (ed.) *Politics in Fiji*, London: Allen & Unwin.

Lawyers Committee for Human Rights (1990) *Malaysia: Assault on the Judiciary*, New York.

Leaf, M. J. (1985) 'The Punjab crisis', *Asia Survey*, vol. 25, no. 5.

Lemarchand, R. (1970) *Rwanda and Burundi*, London: Pall Mall Press.

—— (1973) *Selective Genocide in Burundi*, London: Minority Rights Groups.

Lemkin, R. (1944) *Axis Rule in Occupied Europe*, Washington DC: Carnegie Endowment for International Peace.

Leslie, P. M. (1988) *Ethnonationalism in a Federal State: The Case of Canada*, Kingston, Ontario: Queen's University Institute of Intergovernmental Relations.

Lijphart, A. (1968) *The Politics of Accommodation*, Berkeley and Los Angeles: University of California Press.

—— (1975) 'The Northern Ireland problem: cases, theories and solutions', *British Journal of Political Science*, vol. 5, 83–105.

—— (1977a) *Democracy in Plural Societies: A Comparative Exploration*, New Haven: Yale University Press.

—— (1977b) 'Majority rule vs. democracy in deeply divided societies', *Politikon*, vol. 4, no. 2.

—— (1979) 'Consociation and federation: conceptual and empirical links', *Canadian Journal of Political Science*, vol. 12, 499–515.

—— (ed.) (1981) *Conflict and Coexistence in Belgium: The Dynamics of* a *Culturally Divided Society*, Berkeley: Institute of International Studies.

—— (1984) *Democracies*, New Haven: Yale University Press.

—— (1985) *Power-Sharing in South Africa*, Berkeley: University of California Press.

—— (1989) 'The power-sharing approach', in J. V. Montville (ed.) *Conflict and Peacemaking in Multiethnic Societies*, Lexington, MA and Toronto: Lexington Books.

Linz, J. (1973) 'Early state building and late peripheral nationalism against the state: the case of Spain', in S. Eisenstadt and S. Rokkan (eds) *Building States and Nations*, Beverly Hills: Sage.

—— (1986) *Conflicto en Euskadi*, Madrid: Espasa-Calpe.

Llera, F. J. (1986) 'Procesos estructurales de la sociedad vasca', in F. Hernández and F. Mercadé, *Estructuras Sociales y Cuestión Nacional en España*, Barcelona: Ariel.

Long, J. A. (1990) 'Political revitalization in Canadian native indian societies', *Canadian Journal of Political Science*, vol. 23, no. 75, 1-73.

Lorwin, V. (1966) 'Belgium: religion, class, and language in national politics', in R. A. Dahl (ed.) *Political Opposition in Western Democracies*, New Haven: Yale University Press.

—— (1974) 'Belgium: conflict and compromise', in K. McRae (ed.) *Consociational Democracy: Political Accommodation in Segmented Societies*, Toronto: McClelland & Stewart.

Loumaye, S. (1989) 'Les nouvelles institutions de Bruxelles', CRISP, *Courrier Hebdomadaire*, nos 1232-3.

Lustick, I. (1979) 'Stability in deeply divided societies: consociationalism versus control', *World Politics*, vol. 31, 325-44.

—— (1985) *State-Building Failure in British Ireland and French Algeria*, Berkeley, Ca: Institute of International Studies.

—— (1987) 'Israeli state-building in the West Bank and Gaza Strip: theory and practice', *International Organization*, vol. 41, no. 1, 151-71.

Lyons, F. S. L. (1971) *Ireland since the Famine*, London: Fontana.

Mabille, X. (1979) 'Le système des partis dans la Belgique post-unitaire', CRISP, *Courrier Hebdomadaire*, no. 864.

—— (1981) 'Les facteurs d'instabilité gouvernementale (décembre 1978– avril 1981)', CRISP, *Courrier Hebdomadaire*, no. 916.

—— (1986) *Histoire politique de la Belgique. Facteurs et acteurs de changement*, Brussels: Centre de Recherche et d'Information Socio-Politiques.

—— (1987) 'La crise gouvernementale', CRISP, *Courrier Hebdomadaire*, no. 1176.

—— (1989) 'La faille du compromis', in M. Uyttendaele (ed.) *A l'enseigne de la Belgique nouvelle*, Brussels: Editions de l'Université Libre de Bruxelles.

McCarthy, J. (1989) *Turks and Armenians: A Manual on the Armenian Question*, Washington DC: Committee on Education, Assembly of Turkish–American Associations.

McCrudden, C. (1989) 'Northern Ireland and the British constitution', in

J. Jowell and D. Oliver (eds) *The Changing Constitution*, 2nd edn, Oxford: Clarendon Press.

MacDonald, M. (1986) *Children of Wrath: Political Violence in Northern Ireland*, Cambridge: Polity.

McGarry, J. (1990) 'A consociational settlement for Northern Ireland?', *Plural Societies*, vol. 20, no. 1, 1-21.

McGarry, J. and Noel, S. J. R. (1989) 'The prospects for consociational democracy in South Africa', *Journal of Commonwealth and Comparative Studies*, vol. 27, no. 1, 3-22.

McGarry, J. and O'Leary, B. (eds) (1990) *The Future of Northern Ireland*, Oxford: Oxford University Press.

—— (forthcoming) *Resolving Ethnic Conflict*, London: Macmillan.

McKinley, M. (1987) 'The Irish Republican Army and terror international: an inquiry into the material aspects of the first fifteen years', in P. Wilkinson and A. M. Stewart (eds) *Contemporary Research on Terrorism*, Aberdeen: Aberdeen University Press.

McNeill, W. (1986) *Polyethnicity and World History*, Toronto: Toronto University Press.

McRae, K. D. (ed.) (1974) *Consociational Democracy: Political Accommodation in Segmented Societies*, Toronto: McClelland & Stewart.

—— (1986) *Conflict and Compromise in Multilingual Societies: Belgium*, Waterloo: Wilfrid Laurier University Press.

—— (1989a) 'Theories of power-sharing and conflict management', in J. V. Montville (ed.) *Conflict and Peacemaking in Multiethnic Societies*, Lexington, MA and Toronto: Lexington Books.

—— (1989b) 'Canada: reflections on two conflicts', in J. V. Montville (ed.) *Conflict and Peacemaking in Multiethnic Societies*, Lexington, MA and Toronto: Lexington Books.

Malik, Y. and Vajpeyi, D. K. (1989) 'The rise of Hindu militancy: India's secular democracy at risk', *Asia Survey*, vol. 29, no. 3.

Mandell, B. (1992) 'The Cyprus conflict: explaining resistance to resolution', in N. Salem (ed.) *Cyprus: A Regional Conflict and its Resolution*, New York: St Martin's Press.

Markides, K. (1977) *The Rise and Fall of the Cyprus Republic*, New Haven: Yale University Press.

Mauzy, D. K. (1983) *Barisan Nasional: Coalition Government in Malaysia*, Kuala Lumpur and Singapore: Marican & Sons (Malaysia).

—— (1988) 'Malaysia in 1987: decline of "the Malay way" ', *Asian Survey*, vol. 26, no. 2.

Mayall, J. (1990) *Nationalism and International Society*, Cambridge: Cambridge University Press.

Mbeki, T. (1991) 'Interview', *The Watershed Years*, Cape Town: Leadership Publication, 1991, p. 62.

Mean, A. (1989) *La Belgique de Papa*, Brussells: Editions Politicshistoriques, La Libre Belgique.

—— (1990) *Comprendre la Belgique fédérale*, Brussels: Promo-livres, La Libre Belgique.

Means, G. P. (1972) ' "Special rights" as a strategy for development: the case of Malaysia', *Comparative Politics*, vol. 5, no. 1.

Mehmet, O. (1986) *Development in Malaysia*, London: Croom Helm.

Meller, N. and Anthony, J. (1967) *Fiji Goes to the Polls*, Honolulu: University of Hawaii Press.

Mercredi, O. (1990) 'Indian self-government and sovereignty in Canada', *Humanist in Canada*, Autumn, 3–6.

Merkl, P. (ed.) (1986) *Political Violence and Terror: Motifs and Motivations*, Berkeley: University of California Press.

Mill, J. S. (1988) *Utilitarianism. On Liberty and Considerations on Representative Government* (edited by H. B. Acton), London: Dent.

Miller, D. (1978) *Queen's Rebels. Ulster Loyalism in Historical Perspective*, Dublin: Gill and Macmillan.

Milne, D. (1989) *The Canadian Constitution: From Patriation to Meech Lake*, Toronto: Lorimer.

Milne, R. S. (1976) 'The politics of Malaysia's new economic policy', *Pacific Affairs*, vol. 49, no. 2, 235–62.

—— (1982) *Politics in Ethnically Bipolar States*, Vancouver: University of British Columbia Press.

—— (1986) 'Malaysia – Beyond the New Economic Policy', *Asian Survey*, vol. 26, no. 12, 1364–82.

Milne, R. S. and Mauzy, D. K. (1980) *Politics and Government in Malaysia*, Singapore and Vancouver: Times Books International and University of British Columbia Press.

—— (1986) *Malaysia: Tradition, Modernity and Islam*, Boulder and London: Westview Press.

Mitchell, P. (1991) 'Conflict regulation and party competition in Northern Ireland', *European Journal of Political Research*, vol. 20, 67–92.

Montero, J. R. and Torcal, M. (1990) 'Autonomías y comunidades autonómas en España: preferencias, dimensiones y orientaciones políticas', *Revista de Estudios Politicos*, 70.

Mooney, E. and Pollak, A. (1986) *Paisley*, Dublin: Poolbeg.

Mughan, A. (1979) 'Modernization and ethnic conflict in Belgium', *Political Studies*, vol. 27, no. 1.

—— (1983) 'Accommodation or defusion in the management of linguistic conflict in Belgium?', *Political Studies*, vol. 31, no. 3.

Murphy, A. B. (1988) *The Regional Dynamics of Language Differentiation in Belgium*, Chicago: University of Chicago, Geography Research Paper, no. 227.

National Commission on National Unity (1989) *Rapport de la Commission Nationale Chargée d'Etudier la Question de l'Unité Nationale*, Bujumbura.

Nelson, S. (1984) *Ulster's Uncertain Defenders*, Belfast: Appletree.

Neuville, J. and Yerna, J. (1990) *Le Choc de l'hiver 60–61: Les Greves contre la loi unique*, Brussels: Politique et Histoire.

Nielsen, F. (1980) 'The Flemish movement in Belgium after World War II: a dynamic analysis', *American Sociological Review*, vol. 45, no. 1.

Noel, S. J. R. (1971) 'Consociational democracy and Canadian federalism', *Canadian Journal of Political Science*, vol. 4, 15–18.

—— (1977) 'Political parties and elite accommodation: interpretations of

Canadian federalism', in J. P. Meekison (ed.) *Canadian Federalism: Myth or Reality?*, Toronto: Methuen, pp. 64–83.

—— (1990) *Patrons, Clients, Brokers: Ontario Society and Politics 1791–1896*, Toronto: University of Toronto Press.

Nordlinger, E. (1972) *Conflict Regulation in Divided Societies*, Cambridge, MA: Harvard University Centre for International Affairs.

Northern Ireland Census 1991 (1992) Belfast: HMSO.

Norton, R. (1978) *Race and Politics in Fiji*, Queensland: University of Queensland Press.

Ntibazonkiza, R. (1991) *Au royaume des seigneurs de la lance*, La Louvière [Belgium] : Centre d'Animation en Langues.

Nugent, N. (1990) *Rajiv Gandhi: A Son of a Dynasty*, London: BBC Publications.

Nusseibeh, S. (1990) 'A Palestinian view of the occupied territories', in H. Giliomee and J. Gagiano (eds) *The Elusive Search for Peace: South Africa, Israel and Northern Ireland*, Oxford: Oxford University Press, pp. 132–5.

Obler, J. (1976) 'Assimilation and the moderation of ethnic conflict in Brussels', in J. Obler and S. Clarke (eds) *Urban Ethnic Conflict: A Comparative Perspective*, Chapel Hill: University of North Carolina.

O'Donnell, G. (1988) *Bureaucratic Authoritarianism*, Berkeley: University of California Press.

Olábarri Gortazar, I. (1981) 'La cuestion regional en España, 1808–1939', in R. Acosta Es)aña (ed.) *La España de las Autonomías*, Tomo 1, Madrid: Espasa-Calpe.

O'Leary, B. (1987) 'The Anglo-Irish Agreement: Meanings, Explanations, Results and a Defence' in P. Teague (ed.) *Beyond the Rhetoric: Politics, the Economy and Social Policy in Northern Ireland*, London: Lawrence & Wishart.

—— (1989) 'The limits to coercive consociationalism in Northern Ireland', *Political Studies*, vol. 37, no. 4.

—— (1990) 'Party support in Northern Ireland, 1969–1989', in J. McGarry and B. O'Leary (eds) *The Future of Northern Ireland*, Oxford: Oxford University Press.

O'Leary, B. and Arthur, P. (1990) 'Introduction – Northern Ireland as a site of state- and nation-building failures', in J. McGarry and B. O'Leary (eds) *The Future of Northern Ireland*, Oxford: Oxford University Press, pp. 1–47.

O'Leary, B. and McGarry, J. (1993) *The Politics of Antagonism: Understanding Northern Ireland*, London: Athlone.

—— (forthcoming) *Explaining Northern Ireland*, London: Basil Blackwell.

Oltra, B., Mercade, F. and Hernández, F. (1981) *La Ideología Nacional Catalana*, Barcelona: Anagrama.

O'Malley, P. (1983) *The Uncivil Wars: Ireland Today*, Belfast: Blackstaff.

—— (1990) *Biting at the Grave. The Irish Hunger Strikes and the Politics of Despair*, Belfast: Blackstaff.

Owen, K. (1991) Editorial, *Sunday Times*, Johannesburg, no. 3.

Pakenham, T. (1969) *The Year of Liberty: The Story of the Great Irish Rebellion of 1798*, London: Panther.

Pallares, F. (1991a) 'Las elecciones autonomicas en el Pais Vasco', in Fundaci Carles Pi i Sunyer, *Informe Pi i Sunyer sobre las Comunidades Autónomas, 1990*, Barcelona: Civitas.

—— (1991b) 'Estado autonómico y sistema de partidos: una aproximación electoral', *Revista de Estudios Políticos*, vol. 71, pp. 281–323.

Pappalardo, A. (1981) 'The conditions for consociational democracy: a logical and empirical critique', *European Journal of Political Research*, vol. 9, 365–90.

Parti pour la Liberation du Peuple Hutu (Palipehutu) (1989) *Republique du Burundi: fondements de l'unité et du développement du Burundi*, Bujumbura.

Patrick, R. (1976) *Political Geography and the Cyprus Conflict*, Waterloo: Department of Geography Publications Series, no. 4.

Pavlowitch, S. K. (1988) *The Improbable Survivor: Yugoslavia and its Problems 1918–1988*, London: C. Hurst.

Pérez Diaz, V. (1987) *El retorno de la sociedad civil*, Madrid: Instituto de Estudios Económicos.

Perlez, J. (1988) 'The bloody hills of Burundi', *New York Times Magazine*, 6 November.

Pettigrew, J. (1975) *Robber Nobleman: A Study of the Political System of Sikh Jats*, London: Routledge & Kegan Paul.

—— (1991) 'Betrayal and nation-building among the Sikhs', *Journal of Commonwealth and Comparative Politics*, vol. 19, no. 1.

Phadnis, U. (1990) *Ethnicity and Nation-Building in South Asia*, New Delhi: Sage.

Premdas, R. (1980a) 'Elections in Fiji: restoration of the balance', *Journal of Pacific History*, vol. 14, no. 1, 189–201.

—— (1980b) 'Towards a government of national unity', *Pacific Perspective*, vol. 10, no. 2.

—— (1980c) 'Constitutional challenge: the rise of Fijian nationalism', *Pacific Perspective*, vol. 9, no. 2.

—— (1986) 'Ethnic conflict management: a government of national unity in Fiji', in B. Lal (ed.) *Politics in Fiji*, London: Allen & Unwin.

—— (1987a) 'Fiji', in J. Sigler (ed.) *International Handbook on Race and Ethnic Relations*, New York: Greenwood Press.

—— (1987b) *Fiji: Elections and Communal Conflict in the First Military Coup D'état*, Montreal: Monograph 50, Centre for Developing Area Studies, McGill University.

—— (1989) 'Fiji: the anatomy of a revolution', *Pacifica*, vol. 1, no. 1.

—— (1991) 'Fiji: ethnic conflict and indigenous rights in the new political order', *Asian Survey*.

Price, R. T. (1990) *The Apartheid State in Crisis*, New York: Oxford University Press.

Pujol, J. (1976) *Una política per Catalunya*, Barcelona: Nova Terra.

—— (1980) *Construir Catalunya*, 4th edn, Barcelona: Portie.

Quevit, M. (1978) *Les causes du declin Wallon*, Brussels: Editions Vie Ouvrière.

—— (1981) 'Economic competition, regional development and power in Belgium', in A. Kulinski (ed.) *Polarized Development and Regional Policies*, New York: Mouton.

—— (1982) *La Wallonie: l'indispensable autonomie*, Brussels: Entente.

Rabushka, A. and Shepsle, K. A. (1972) *Politics in Plural Societies: A Theory of Democratic Instability*, Columbus, Ohio: Charles E. Merrill Publishing Co.

Ralston, B. (1986) 'Reformism and sectarianism: the state of the union after civil rights', in P. Darby (ed.) *Northern Ireland: Background to the Conflict*, Belfast: Appletree.

Ramet, P. (1984) *Nationalism and Federalism in Yugoslavia, 1963–83*, Bloomington: Indiana University Press.

—— (ed.) (1985) *Yugoslavia in the 1980s*, Boulder, Co: Westview.

Reddaway, J. (1986) *Burdened with Cyprus: The British Connection*, London: Weidenfeld & Nicolson.

Riquer, B. de (1989) 'Cataluna', in J. P. Fusi (ed.) *España. Tomo 5. Autonomías*, Madrid: Espasa-Calpe.

Roberts, H. (1990) 'Sound stupidity: the British party system and the Northern Ireland question', in J. McGarry and B. O'Leary (eds) *The Future of Northern Ireland*, Oxford: Oxford University Press, pp. 100-36.

Roberts, W. R. (1973) *Tito, Mihajlovic and the Allies 1941-1945*, New Brunswick, NJ: Rutgers University Press.

Robertson, R. T. and Tamanisan, A. (1981) *Fiji: Shattered Crowns*, Canberra: Pluto Press.

Robinson, F. (1974) *Separatism among Indian Muslims: The Politics of the United Province Muslims, 1860-1923*, London: Cambridge University Press.

Roiz Celix, M. (1984) 'Los limites de la modernizacíon en la estructura social de Cataluña y Euskadi', *Revista Española de Investigaciones Sociológicas*, 25.

Roosens, E. E. (ed.) (1989) 'Ethnic minorities in Belgium: among potential equals', in *Creating Ethnicity: The Process of Ethnogenesis*, London: Sage.

Rothenburg, G. E. (1966) *The Military Border in Croatia: A Study of an Imperial Institution, 1740-1881*, Chicago: Chicago University Press.

Royal Ulster Constabulary (RUC) (1990) *Report of the Chief Constable*, Belfast: RUC.

Rudolph, J. R. and Thompson, R. J. (1989) *Ethnoterritorial Politics. Policy and the Western World*, Boulder: Rienner.

Rudolph, L. I. and Rudolph S. H. (1989) 'Cultural policy, the textbook controversy and Indian identity', in A. J. Wilson and D. Dalton (eds) *The States of South Asia: Problems of National Integration*, London: C. Hurst.

Rusinow, D. (1977) *The Yugoslav Experiment 1948-1977*, London: C. Hurst for the Royal Institute of International Affairs.

Saffran, W. (1991) 'Ethnicity and pluralism: comparative and theoretical perspectives', *Canadian Review of Studies in Nationalism*, vol. 18, nos 1-2.

Said, E. *(1988) 'Michael Walzer's Exodus and Revolution*: a Canaanite reading', in E. Said and C. Hitchens (eds) *Blaming the Victims: Spurious Scholarship and the Palestinian Question*, London: Verso, pp. 159-78.

Sanders, D. E. (1983) 'The Indian lobby', in K. Banting and R. Simeon (eds) *And No One Cheered: Federalism, Democracy and the Constitution Act*, Toronto: Methuen.

Schlemmer, L. (1991) 'Negotiation dilemmas', *Indicator South Africa*, vol. 8, no. 3, 7-10.

Scott, J. C. (1991) *Domination and the Arts of Resistance: Hidden Transcripts*, New Haven: Yale University Press.

Segarra, M. (1990) 'Autonomia política i conflicte lingüistic a Catalunya entre 1976 i 1987', in M. Pares i Maicas and G. Tremblay (eds) *Catalunya, Quebec. Automia i Mundialitzacio*, Barcelona: Generalitat de Catalunya.

Senelle, R. (1989) 'Constitutional reform in Belgium: from unitarism towards federalism', in M. Forsyth (ed.) *Federalism and Nationalism*, Leicester: Leicester University Press.

Shoup, P. (1968) *Communism and the Yugoslav National Question*, New York: Columbia University Press.

Siegfried, A. (1906) *The Race Question in Canada* (reprinted 1966), Toronto: McClelland & Stewart.

Singh, G. (1987) 'Understanding the "Punjab problem" ', *Asian Survey*, vol. 27, no. 12.

—— (1991) 'The Punjab problem in the 1990s: a post-1984 assessment', *Journal of Commonwealth and Comparative Politics*, vol. 29, no. 2.

—— (1992) 'Punjab elections 1992: a breakthrough or breakdown?', *Asian Survey*, November.

Smiley, D. V. (1977) 'French–English relations in Canada and consociational democracy', in M. J. Esman (ed.) *Ethnic Conflict in the Western World*, Ithaca and London: Cornell University Press.

Smith, D. and Chambers, G. (1991) *Inequality in Northern Ireland*, Oxford: Oxford University Press.

Smith, M. (1991) *Burma: Insurgency and the Politics of Ethnicity*, London: Zed Press.

Spate, O. H. K. (1959) *The Fijian People*, Council Paper 13, Suva.

Stein, M. (1968) 'Federal political systems and federal societies', *World Politics*, vol. 20, no. 4, 721-47.

Szporluk, R. (1990) 'In search of the drama of history or, national roads to modernity', *East European Politics and Societies*, vol. 4, no. 1, 134-59.

Taylor, D. and Yapp, X. (1979) *Political Identity in South Asia*, London: Curzon.

Ter Hoeven, P. J. A. (1978) 'The social bases of Flemish nationalism', *International Journal of the Sociology of Language*, vol. 15, 21-32.

Torrealday, J. M. (1980) 'Territorio, lengua y migraciones en Euskadi', in Centre Internacional per a les minories etniques i nacionals, *Nactionalia V. Quartes Jornadadas de Ciemen, Abadia de Cuisca, 16-23 d'agost 1979*, Publicacions de l'Abadia de Montserrat.

Trias Fargas, R. (1972) *Introducción a la economía de Cataluña*, Madrid: Alianza.

Tribunal Constitucional (1985) *Repertorio Aranzadi del Tribunal Constitucional*, Pamplona: Aranzadi.

Trudeau, P. E. (1989) 'Who speaks for Canada? Defining and sustaining a national vision', in M. D. Behiels (ed.) *The Meech Lake Primer: Conflicting Views of the 1982 Constitutional Accord*, Ottawa: University of Ottawa Press.

Underhill, F. H. (1964) *The Image of Confederation*, Toronto: CBC Publications.

Uyttendaele, M. (1989) *A l'enseigne de la Belgique nouvelle*, Brussels: Editions de l'Université Libre de Bruxelles.

Vallverdú, F. (1980) 'La Lengua Catalana', in Centre Internacional per a les minories etniques i nacionals, *Nacionalia V. Quartes Jornadadas de Ciemen, Abadia de Cuisca, 16–23 d'agost 1979*, Publicacions de l'Abadia de Montserrat.

Vanaik, A. (1990) *The Painful Transition: Bourgeois Democracy in India*, London: Verso.

Van Den Bulck, J. (1992) 'Pillars and politics: neo-corporatism and policy networks in Belgium', *West European Politics*, vol. 15, no. 2, 35–55.

Vasil, R. (1984) *Politics in Biracial Societies*, New Delhi: Vikas.

Vasquez de Prada, V. (1981) 'La epoca moderna: Los siglos XVI à XIX', in R. Acosta España (ed.) *La España de las Autonomías*, Tomo 1, Madrid: Espasa-Calpe.

Verdoodt, A. (1983) *Bibliographie sur le problème linguistique belge*, Laval, Quebec: International Centre for Research on Bilingualism.

Vile, M. (1982) 'Federation and confederation: the experience of the United States and the British Commonwealth', in D. Rea (ed.) *Political Co-operation in Divided Societies*, Dublin: Gill and Macmillan, pp. 216–28.

Von Vorys, K. (1975) *Democracy without Consensus*, Princeton: Princeton University Press.

Vrban, D. (1985) *Culture Change and Symbolic Legitimation: Functions and Traditional Meaning of Symbols in the Transformation of Yugoslav Ideology*, unpublished doctoral thesis submitted at the University of Bielefeld.

Walsh, A. C. (1970) 'Fiji's changing population', *Unispac*, vol. 8, no. 1, 1–2.

Watson, C. (1989) 'After the massacre', *Africa Report*, January–February pp. 51–5.

Watters, R. F. (1969) *Koro: Economic Development and Social Change in Fiji*, Oxford: Clarendon Press.

Weitzer, R. (1987) 'Contested order: the struggle over British security policy in Northern Ireland', *Comparative Politics*, vol. 19, no. 3 (April), 281–98.

White, R. (1989) 'From peaceful protest to guerilla war: micromobilization of the Provisional Irish Republican Army', *American Journal of Sociology*, vol. 94, no. 6 (May), 1277–1302.

Whyte, J. (1990) *Interpreting Northern Ireland*, Oxford: Oxford University Press.

Wilson, T. (1989) *Ulster: Conflict and Consent*, Oxford: Blackwell.

Witte, E. and Craeybeakx, J. (1987) *La Belgique Politique de 1830 a nos jours: les tensions d'une democratie bourgeois*, Bruxelles: Editions Labor.

Young, C. (1986) 'Cultural pluralism in the third world', in S. Olzak and J. Nagel (eds) *Competitive Ethnic Relations*, Boston: Academic Press.

Zolberg, A. (1974) 'The making of Flemings and Walloons: Belgium: 1830–1914', *Journal of Interdisciplinary History*, vol. 5, no. 2.

—— (1977) 'Splitting the difference: federalization without federalism in Belgium', in M. J. Esman (ed.) *Ethnic Conflict in the Western World*, Ithaca: Cornell University Press.

—— (1978) 'Belgium', in R. Grew (ed.) *Crises of Political Development in Europe and the United States*, Princeton: Princeton University Press.

Index

THE WORLD NEWS PRISM

Seventh Edition